QUEST FOR MEANING

Quest for Meaning

L. Francis Edmunds

CONTINUUM • NEW YORK

1997
The Continuum Publishing Company
370 Lexington Avenue
New York, NY 10017

Printed in the United States of America

Library of Congress Cataloging-in-Publication Data

Edmunds, L. Francis
    Quest for meaning / L. Francis Edmunds
        p.   cm.
    ISBN 0-8264-1070-7
    1. Anthroposophy.   I. Title.
BP595.E35   1997
299'.935--DC21   97-37892
                                                                      CIP

DEDICATION

To the wife I love, mother of
my children,
To England for whose destiny
I care,
To American friendship, true
in spirit,
And to mankind everywhere

Mr.X

About the Author

L. FRANCIS EDMUNDS was born on the March 30, 1902, in Russia. In his early youth he moved to England, where he later became a medical student at University College, London . At the age twenty-one he interrupted his studies and returned to Russia as part of a Quaker relief mission. Later he taught adolescents in Lebanon and then at the International School in Geneva. While taking courses at the Goetheanum in Dornach, Switzerland he met the first teachers of the Rudolf Steiner* School in London. Although he always intended to finish his medical training, the urgent need for teachers in that school decided his destiny for Steiner's educational impulse.

In the early Fifties he began his annual travels, first to America and then to the Southern Hemisphere, helping to found and develop Steiner Schools and other groups and centers based on Steiner's work. At the age of sixty and after years of preparation, Edmunds founded Emerson College in Sussex, England in the autumn of 1962. He called it a world center for Anthroposophic** adult education and research. With the help of his wife, Elizabeth, and other colleagues who joined the work, Edmunds designed the Foundation Year program, directed the Steiner Schools Teacher Training and helped further courses and trainings come into being. He wished the college to be an adult learning community rather than an academic institution — one strongly connected to the land, with both arts and crafts as well as scientific research. It soon became a place where the world began to meet — a world college meeting world needs, creating a global nexus of alumni who, with what

---

* Austrian scientist and philosopher (1861-1925)
** "Anthroposophy," lit. "wisdom of man," is the term used by Steiner for the approach to knowledge and personal development that he created.

they had found at Emerson College, could give new expression to their life's work on all the continents of the earth.

At the time of his death in November 1989, Francis Edmunds was still busy writing and rewriting the last chapter of this book, QUEST FOR MEANING — the fruit of over thirty years teaching science courses in Steiner Schools and later his Study of Man seminar at Emerson College. The book reflects his deep interest in science as a developmental stage in the evolution of human consciousness and moral discernment.

George Locher
Director of Education Studies
Emerson College

Acknowledgments

My FIRST MEETING with Francis Edmunds took place in the spring of 1970 in his office at Emerson College. The visit was occasioned by my interest in learning how he had established this adult education centre based on the philosophy of Rudolf Steiner. I wished to utilize his advice with a project I was attempting to establish in America. He became my mentor, providing me with the most sapient and completely objective counsel. I have always felt deep gratitude for his leadership and guidance during that time.

My last meeting with Mr. Edmunds was in August of 1989; we had tea in his home at Emerson College. He spoke enthusiastically of his work on the manuscript which he described as nearly finished. Months later when I learned of his death, I asked Elizebeth what was going to happen to the manuscript.

During the summer of 1993, John and Jane Stromberg and I made an alumni visit to Emerson College and spoke with Elizabeth at length about the project of preparing the manuscript for publication. And so we began the process.

I wish to thank Elizabeth Edmunds for entrusting us with this wonderful task and for guiding our course with such attentive care and love. I am pleased that the extended Edmunds family has expressed its satisfaction with this publication.

My sincerest thanks to John and Jane for being there to share concerns, decisions, and resolutions. And to John my special thanks for solving the 'Macintosh attacks' and teaching me the ins and outs of data transfers to Oregon.

To my cousin Taggart Deike, I wish to say thank you for sending me to my first meeting with Mr. Edmunds and also for guiding us to our publisher, Mr. Gene Gollogly, president of Continuum. I am delighted with the warm and enthusiastic support that Gene and the staff at Continuum have provided.

My special gratitude to Mr. Robert Youdelman for handling all the necessary contractural arrangements with such conscientious expertise.

I am so gratified that I have had this personal oppurtunity to work with Mr. Edmunds' words and thoughts. When he travelled and spoke throughout the world he was always an inspiring and vital teacher. To those who knew Mr. Edmunds, I hope his voice will resonate for you throughout this text. For those who are meeting here for the first time, may this introduction be a wonderful beginning for you.

Helen Lee Henderson
President
Chiron Productions, Ltd.

Contents

· 1 ·

A Call: Where Are We?

Modern science, dating from Copernicus and Galileo, is not five hundred years old. In this short time it has totally revolutionized humanity's thinking about man, the earth, and the universe. For a century or two it was the concern of a few but now it reaches into the whole of life. There are different religions and philosophical outlooks but there is only one universally accepted science. Men may differ in all other respects but agree in regard to science in the daily practice of life. Whether north, south, east, or west upon this globe, the same science is taught in every classroom, even at college level. Science has taken possession of us influencing our habits, the items we use, and even largely determining our personal tastes and choices. There is scarcely a person who is not in some degree a practicing scientist. It rules industry, medicine, agriculture, domestic arts, and has even become the main line of defense of governments. Architectural design and the houses we live in subscribe heavily to it. History, archaeology, even biography draw their tenets from it. Edmund Blunden, the poet, opened his study of Shelley with a review of his genetic ancestors, in quest of elements that were influential in shaping his characteristic genius.

Science has taken possession of the mind of man so completely that scarcely a week or a month goes by without some new achievement or discovery causing one to pause and wonder.

Science has spread much ill through the world. It has multiplied unnecessary wants, pandered to egotistical desires, loaded life with artificiality, prompted foolish ambitions, raised false hopes, made thinking arbitrary, and faith a superstition. It has also taught man to regard himself as the plaything, or even the dupe, of his subconscious. Science has robbed men of their status and their existence of its real meaning. It has led to the sacrifice of high motives for lesser gains. Mankind may live longer but time hangs heavier, lacking in a sense of real fulfillment. Life is more crowded than ever, yet feels empty.

Thus, it may be asked whether science has led to human advancement or decline. We certainly have much evidence of the latter, following on the disasters of two global wars; yet ambitions or fear of falling back drive men and governments onward. It has been said, *What shall it profit a man if he gain the whole world, and lose his own soul?** Today one may add, 'What shall it avail man if he conquers the whole of outer space and cannot compass the void within?'

The story of science is contradictory from the start. Its pioneers were people not only of exceptional ability but of admirable worth, dedicated to the disinterested pursuit of truth. Their sole aim was for the advancement of knowledge in service to life. Yet this same science, inspired though it was by selfless motives, has become the instrument for the callous disregard of man, beasts, plants, and the air we breathe. It has released untold greed for power, not only power over things but also over men. In unscrupulous hands the science of today presents the greatest menace the world has known. We live and labour in that shadow.

Through science humanity has gained vastly in its control of outer nature but has lost enormously in inner vision and moral certainty. Is it not drummed into us continually that our existence is of no significance within the world-existence that contains us? The disruptive effects of this concept are encountered daily in irresponsible living, moral weakening and growing destructiveness. The result is inner, as well as outer, pollution.

---

* EDITOR'S NOTE: Direct quotes and references to technial terms will be italicized in this text. Words and phrases referred to as such will be in single quotes. When the author intends special emphasis, in either his own text or quoted material, underscoring will be used. The author's preference for British spelling has been maintained.

The scientific impulse was to have brought man forward on the road to freedom. It was to have opened up a prospect of widespread unanimity and peace. With what zeal men fought to banish illiteracy in the world so that greater knowledge might create greater independence for all. Who could have foreseen that an age of enlightenment would unleash global wars of unprecedented might and horror and that, in addition to the millions cruelly sacrificed in actual warfare, other millions of men, women, and children would be deliberately submitted to unwarranted and ignominious death? Who were more shocked and humiliated than the scientists labouring for good when confronted with the perversion of their labours in Hiroshima, an event now inscribed for lasting shame in the history of mankind? Many vainly appealed to governments to abandon this research but fear and distrust were to prevail. Pressures bear down daily upon a world where complexities have grown so interlaced that a careless or thoughtless act in any one place could trigger off a global crisis of unthinkable dimensions. In addition to 'balance of rights' and 'balance of power' there now has been added 'balance of fear.' So-called 'peace' now has the character of 'suspended war.'

Amidst all this one hears the cry for freedom. There was a time of 'freeborn' men and slaves. Today we are all supposedly freeborn and yet, in a manner, we are all slaves. To be truly freeborn touches the mystery of the human spirit. To be freeborn in the spirit is to be the bearer of a higher devotion and love. Without the inborn freedom of the heart there is no freedom. For freedom means freedom from oneself and a heart for others. That is not easy to come by these days.

The need is for a science which makes a true distinction between the spirit in man and physical nature. Only such a science might open the way to a new-born inner freedom and set the world on a happier course. If today's view that men are 'things' in a world of 'things' prevails, all notions of genuine freedom must vanish from this earth.

So far, the science mankind has produced is undermining him mentally, morally and physically. Only a superb effort to engender a new source of moral energy from within can give humankind a new measure of itself. Only a new awakening of conscience and consciousness possible to humans alone, but only possible if they will it, can bring sanity and balance into a world situation which sadly lacks both.

A revolution in the mind brought forth the scientific adventure with all its great promise. Now the scientific world is calling for another revolution of the mind to open new perspectives and new hopes for the future. The whole of life calls for 'a new age' but this new age in turn calls for a new man and a new quality of consciousness. Before responding to this call, we must first take a serious reflective pause to examine clearly where we are and how we got there and then, and only then, consider what the next step might be.

· 2 ·

Warning Voices

We are living through a time of continual crisis. First World Wars I and II, then the Korean and Vietnam Wars, shook life to its foundations but, looking back, they all appear to have solved nothing. Is the present time really only an interim period before the next and greatest cataclysm of all? There have been warnings and not a few. One of the most trenchant is contained in Charles Lindbergh's short but vividly written book, ON FLIGHT AND LIFE (1948).*

> We are in the grip of a scientific materialism, caught in a vicious cycle where our security today seems to depend on regimentation and weapons which will ruin us tomorrow.
>
> . . . the intellectual achievements of great scientists are being perverted by the material exploitation of industry and war. . . . Hiroshima was as far from the pure scientists as the Inquisition was from the Sermon on the Mount.
>
> I have lived to experience the early results of scientific materialism . . . have watched pride of workmanship leave and human character decline as efficiency of production lines increased. . . . I have seen the science I worshipped and the aircraft I loved destroying the civilization I expected them to save. . . . In my memory the vision of my mail-plane boring northward over moonlit clouds is now mingling with the streaks of tracers, flaming comets of warplanes, and bombs falling irretrievably through air.

---

* EDITOR'S NOTE: See Select Bibliography for publishing information on works cited. Because of discrepancies in pagination of the many editions of some cited texts, page references have not been included. All succeeding references in a chapter are from the last source cited unless otherwise noted.

Our salvation, and our only salvation, lies in controlling the arm of western science by the mind of a western philosophy guided by the eternal truths of God.

These words were written with utmost sincerity by a man who had both dared and done courageous deeds. The appeal itself we cannot doubt, yet it raises a number of questions. What philosophy can reconcile the tenets of scientific materialism with *the eternal truths of God?* Is it not science which brought in its wake religious skepticism and agnosticism? And the moral deterioration described, is that not to be attributed to the same cause? The question still stands, why did science have to be materialistic? What made it so?

The pioneering scientists most certainly did not set out to promote materialism. They were devotedly religious men. The new investigation of nature's laws was to have brought human understanding closer to God. Faith confirmed by knowledge! That was to be the great adventure and what one might have expected; yet, as time went on, the reverse took place. Scientific materialism entered upon the scene with Copernicus and Galileo, took root in eighteenth-century rationalism, reached a climax in the nineteenth century and then swept over into the twentieth century. Here, however, we have entered an era of much earnest questioning.

Technology has made, and is making, incredible advances. The scientific age is still young but life grows more precarious with each and every advance. Two great dangers confront us. The more obvious one is the ever-present threat of annihilation, on a scale no one can know. The other danger — world dictatorship — has been prognosticated for a long time. The former means death to the body; the latter brings death to the soul through moral extinction.

The words of Moses from Christopher Fry's play THE FIRSTBORN gain in significance, for he says, *I followed a light into blindness.* And the leading character in John Osborne's play, THE ENTERTAINER, while addressing an imaginary audience, speaks of *the blindness behind the eyes.* Maybe these are prophetic hints of an awakening to a new kind of seeing. If they are, they come none too soon.

In 1900, Vladimir Solovyov, an outstanding Russian Christian philosopher, wrote a book entitled WAR AND CHRISTIANITY. The

extended title is: FROM THE RUSSIAN POINT OF VIEW; THREE
CONVERSATIONS. The book ends with one of the characters reading
a manuscript entitled, SHORT NARRATIVE ABOUT ANTICHRIST. The
narrative portrays a world which is reminiscent of the general
confusion of today. Suddenly, as though from nowhere, a brilliant
young man with all the answers appears upon the scene. By the
age of thirty his fame is widespread. His total success persuades
him that he must be the true Son of God, and that the historical
Christ was merely his forerunner. There comes a moment when
the young man undergoes an experience which can only be paralleled with that of the Baptism of Christ in the river Jordan.

> . . . *two piercing eyes approached closely to his face, and he felt as if a
> sharp, icy current was entering into him, filling all his being. Moreover,
> he felt a marvelous strength, daring, light and ecstasy.*
>> Vladimir Solovyov, WAR AND CHRISTIANITY

All were amazed at his inspired appearance. *With supernatural
swiftness . . . he wrote a paper, The Open Way to Peace and Prosperity,
which ran into countless editions.* In short, he became master of the
world, the greatest benefactor that ever was. He granted to each
according to his needs, but with one condition: that all submit to
his law in total obedience.

The tiny few who pierced through this mask were representatives
of the three leading churches, the Catholic, the Greek or Russian
Orthodox, and the Protestant. They saw *the signs of an absolutely
exceptional, intense self-love and conceit, with the absence of true simplicity, rectitude, and zeal.* In his moment of greatest pomp and glory
they denounced him for the antichrist that he was. This led to his
eventual downfall. The piece ends with the appearance of the
Christ in His Second Coming, perceived and acknowledged by the
Jews no less than by all the rest of the world. This vision of
Solovyov carries in it the inborn faith that the Russians have
always had in the destiny of their people.

Solovyov was a close friend and admirer of Dostoyevsky. We
need only think of Alyosha, the youngest of the three brothers
Karamazov, to recognize the germinal seed of a new kind of
Christianity born from within. This seed lived strongly in the
soul of Solovyov. He foresaw the approaching evil but he also
saw beyond it.

In the years after World War I, a book was published by the Irish poet, artist, and seer, A.E. (George William Russell) entitled THE INTERPRETERS.

A.E., from his home in Dublin, initiated a movement for the revival of Celtic culture with its ancient beauty and forgotten wisdom but he was not just a dreamer. During his time as Minister of Agriculture he proposed the introduction of regular civil conscription whereby the young would contribute two years of work to build up the economic life of their very poor country. This might have been beneficial but was never adopted.

THE INTERPRETERS depicts a world on the eve of a revolution two or three centuries hence, a world that has become one gigantic network of mechanistic transmissions and controls under a centralist world dictatorship. One by one the leaders of the revolt are seized and locked into a tower room overlooking Dublin city. They are the last defenders of freedom against the prevailing state of world dictatorship. Locked in with them by mistake is a representative of the state. The book unfolds as a symposium on the meaning of life. With the approach of dawn, the poet of the company withdraws into a corner and there composes a poem, MICHAEL. There the book ends.

Later in the century came Aldous Huxley's well know BRAVE NEW WORLD. Huxley, with his consummate descriptive powers, needed only to follow the trend of events to its inevitable conclusion. His later criticism of his own work was that events were moving much faster than he had imagined. It was sheer irony that led him to take the title of his book out of the very mouth of Miranda in a scene from Shakespeare's TEMPEST. . . .

Miranda beholds a company assembling that she had never seen before — she knew only her father Prospero and her lover Ferdinand — and is filled with wonder at the sight of these others. The audience knows them in their frailties and follies, even wickedness, but she, with the unspoiled purity of her vision, sees them not as they are but as they might be. Thus she exclaims:

> O, wonder!
> How many goodly creatures are there here!

How beauteous mankind is! O brave new world
That hath such people in't.

Is this Shakespeare's own redemptive vision for the future as he
prepares to leave his world of the theater? Huxley's BRAVE NEW
WORLD, in its irony, bespeaks of a world deprived of all hope.

George Orwell's 1984 and ANIMAL FARM are likewise despairing
calls to awaken. What was it that inspired C.S. Lewis to write THAT
HIDEOUS STRENGTH, so truly hideous and grimly fantastical? Yet the
objective is clear enough, a battle for moral freedom. With Lewis
the good prevails.

Who can say that a state of world domination by an unassailable
power of authority is inconceivable? One power in command of a
world police force and all the resources — legal, mental, biological
— which science could provide in order to mold the human framework to its pattern? Such instances on a lesser scale are near to hand.

In 1955 THE DIGNITY OF MAN, a posthumous work by Russell W.
Davenport, was published. None saw more clearly the gathering
threat to freedom and none pointed more earnestly than
Davenport to the need for a radical change of outlook, not only
politically but in the whole of life.

He saw the real menace contained in the communist ideology,
based as it is on a totally materialistic creed propounded by Marx
and Engels. They named it Dialectical Materialism.

> *It is not just a dry philosophical system stored away in dusty tomes, but*
> *a way of thinking which has enormous impact upon twentieth-century*
> *minds, and wields consequentially enormous power over their concepts*
> *and judgments.*
>
> *We see Dialectical Man as a kind of robot of state, a human being reduced*
> *to an animal status, an ant living in a highly disciplined anthill . . . if he*
> *comes to dominate the earth, our own ideas about man cannot survive*
>
> *. . . the ideas behind Dialectical Materialism . . . are not wholly confined*
> *to communism. They are, rather, endemic to the twentieth century.*
>
> *Dialectical Man, we must note, is an Idea that has not yet been realised*
> *. . . he is coming into being.*

Communist doctrine calls for the use of force . . . if force is used intelligently enough, and relentlessly enough, men will all be changed; they will become the conscious and loyal representatives of the Idea of Dialectical Man.

. . . to miscalculate this drive is to mistake the very nature of our enemy. . . . For our enemy is not any particular nation. It is not even any particular form of government. It is this Idea of Man.

. . . Dialectical Man was not even born in Russia. He has grown to power there, but he does not recognize a river or range of mountains as a boundary, he does not belong to the Kremlin but to humanity. His home is in the minds of men.

Military power as such cannot come to grips with Dialectical Man. Ideas can only be met and overcome by ideas. If then the Idea of Dialectical Man is to be overcome, another Idea of Man must arise capable of overcoming it.

Russell Davenport, THE DIGNITY OF MAN

For Davenport the real enemy is a frame of mind born of thinking, which reduces man to matter, the kind of thinking on which Marx and Engels built their philosophy.

The universe was created out of matter by the operation of the laws of matter; and these laws in turn led eventually to the creation of life, animals, and man. Everything can and must be accounted for in materialistic . . . natural terms.

Engels, THE DIALECTICS OF NATURE

If that be true, then the case for communism is stronger than the case for our way of life. Matter is not free in any meaningful sense of the word; the concept of man as a materially created being is, therefore, incapable of giving freedom any meaning. . . . [F]reedom is only an illusion, and communism spares man the dreadful and futile struggle for this illusion by defining freedom in terms of the very opposite of freedom . . . in terms of human conformance to the laws of matter, as these may be interpreted by the masters of society.

Davenport, DIGNITY OF MAN

It simply is not recognized that this doctrine of man and matter is as much in contradiction with *our way of life* as it is with Lindbergh's *eternal truths of God.* It is the doctrine taught everywhere. It did not originate in the Russian soul. Communism as a political system arising out of materialism was imported into Russia. Karl Marx wrote out of his CAPITAL in the British Museum.

It is the materialistic thinking of the West and the education arising from it that is the active promoter of communism.

The communist leaders were consistent in their philosophy. They
knew and acknowledged nothing else. They regarded their theories as foolproof. They relied on the fact that the West was as
steeped in materialism as they were. They were convinced, therefore, that in the end they must win. Moreover, ideas that were theoretical in the West became crusading creeds in the East. The
Russians, despite their imbibed materialism and atheism, remain
mystical zealots at heart. They have an inbred faith in the glorious
future of their land and those in power brook no contradiction of
this belief. They believed that out of Russia the salvation to the
whole world would evolve. In their own minds, they were the
faithful servants of pan-Communism.

Davenport quotes Lenin, but he could equally well be quoting
many ordinary textbooks of today.

> *Matter is that which, acting upon our sense organs, produces sensa-
> tions. . . . Matter, nature, being, the physical is primary and spirit, con-
> sciousness, sensations, the psychical is secondary.*

If this is to be the prevailing view for the next fifty, a hundred, two
hundred years, it can only lead to the undoing of everything that
has hitherto been held sacred to life.

> *Thus, the whole human struggle changes its meaning. The great ideals
> for which humility has suffered . . . the eight fold path of Buddha, the
> Christian vision of redemption, the Moslem communion with God . . .
> all these inspired revelations and ideals are just illusions on the surface
> of reality, eruptive phenomena, thrown up from the depth of matter.
> They have played an important role in the shaping of history, not
> because they were real, but because men erroneously believed them. The
> realities of history are quite different, in the Marxist view of things.*

Time is short, said Lindbergh. We must next explore how the dilemma in which humanity now finds itself first arose.

· 3 ·

Whither?

How and when did the present state of mind described as *the blindness behind the eyes* evolve? Today we observe a multiplicity of warring factions, each demanding the freedom of its choice. Concurrently, there is an overall dangerous trend moving towards centralist controls, where submission to authority becomes the dominating rule. Science, with its claims to objectivity, should have ushered in an era which offered maximum scope for individual initiatives and freedom for self-expression and self-determination. Instead humanity lives under varying degrees of un-freedom with growing uncertainty from one day to the next. This is the world dilemma. Our quest is to examine what has led mankind into this predicament and what might lead us out again.

At the outset of this inquiry let us consider the book, THE LIMITATIONS OF SCIENCE, by W. J. N. Sullivan (1886–1937), first published in 1933. Given the swift rate at which life has progressed, 1933 may seem a long time ago but the substance of this text is equally pertinent today. Sullivan does not set out to criticize. On the contrary, his starting point is his great enthusiasm for the potentials of the human mind.

> *The invention of the non-Euclidean geometries is one of the most remarkable feats in the intellectual history of man. For two thousand years Euclid's axioms had reigned unchallenged. That they were 'necessary truths,' true for angels as well as men, true for even God himself, was admitted by all the philosophers. Merely to wonder whether these truths could be transcended, merely to wonder whether there was a*

world of ideas outside them, was an effort of extraordinary daring. And to translate this skepticism into the creation of a new, coherent, and complete system of geometry, was a wonderful and exhilarating achievement of the free human mind. In this achievement the human intellect had reached a new level of abstraction; there was a veritable growth of consciousness. Of course, so stupendous an achievement was not at first understood. Even the mathematicians of the time thought that Lobachevesky and Bolyai were mad. And the great Gauss, who had in private reached similar conclusions to theirs, confessed that he had been afraid to publish his discovery. But gradually the new ideas were assimilated. Gradually the human imagination learned to expand to these concepts. A new mathematical era had dawned.

Sullivan, a penetrating thinker, also has a great appreciation of art and wrote an admirable thesis on Beethoven. The experience of *abstract thought,* as he calls it, brings with it an element of freedom. The perception of beauty brings 'living-ness' into consciousness; art leads to an enhancement of consciousness.

While rejoicing in this expansion of mind with its novel and extensive possibilities, Sullivan witnessed in everyday life much that was constricting and belittling. Instead of the expectant hopes of advancing tolerance and understanding amongst the peoples, he witnessed the shattering effect, both physically and morally, of World War I. Even beyond the horrors of war, the rise of communism, nazism, fascism, and lesser similar movements presaged fiercer struggles ahead. There was unrest in the East, instability in the West, troubles brewing in Africa to the South. There was much soul-searching, bitter questioning, and a sense of foreboding in the air. Atomic fission had not yet been released but during and following the war scientific research was promoted at a great pace, not only by private interests but by governments, with growing power to build or to destroy. Who would ultimately wield that power, and to what end? Of what real benefit was science to man?

Science itself was making the transition from the robust, if relatively materialistic, three-dimensional physics of Newton to the ephemeral, intangible, four-dimensional, and spectral physics of Einstein, which would be more shattering than had been imagined. What world was humanity actually in and to what future was this leading?

In his search for meaningful answers, Sullivan turned to the earlier cultures of Babylon and Egypt but it was Greece that provided
his illumination.

> *Thales of Miletus (c. 580 B.C.), we are told, set out to answer the ques-*
> *tion 'Of what and in what way is the world made?' Here we recognize*
> *the spirit, necessary to science though not peculiar to it, of disinterest-*
> *ed curiosity. The Greeks appear to have been the first people with whom*
> *this feeling became a passion. They wanted to know . . . for the sake of*
> *knowing. . . . It really şeems as if the human consciousness, with the rise*
> *of the ancient Greeks, took a genuine leap forward. An unexampled free-*
> *dom of the mind was born. This was a necessary condition for science to*
> *come into the world.*
>
> *In another respect, also, the Greeks were unique. They seem to have been*
> *the first people with a thorough grasp of mathematical reasoning. . . .*
> *Mathematical reasoning, the most powerful of man's intellectual*
> *instruments, was created.*
>
> *Overwhelmed by the almost magical power of this instrument, the*
> *Greeks thought that in mathematics they had discovered the key to all*
> *things. To the Pythagoreans, in particular, number was the principle of*
> *all things. Every thing, whether physical properties or moral qualities,*
> *was manifestation of number.*

For the Greeks, number had a very different connotation from
what it has come to have in more recent times. It was the qualities or the relationships in the strings of the lyre, in the propor-
tions of a temple, in the planetary modes (named after the planetary gods) that primarily interested them. The music of the
spheres of the Pythagorean school later captured the imagination
of Kepler. These higher aspects of number were already lost to
the Romans.

> *. . . under the Roman Empire, the spirit of disinterested curiosity, and*
> *man's delight in this new and wonderful mathematical faculty withers*
> *and dies. . . . The Romans were an essentially practical people, and they*
> *adopted the 'What is the use of it?' attitude to all abstract speculation.*

What is the nature of *abstract speculation?* For Sullivan, the abstract
was not a bloodless region remote from the real, but an inner realm
of enterprise and discovery. Roman genius rested upon outer
acquisition and conquest; at best it could only echo what was
inwardly living for the Greeks.

This abstract quality in thinking Sullivan recognized again in the philosophy of mediaeval times, in the great scholastics, though mathematics played no part in it.

> . . . some of the greatest abstract thinkers the world had ever produced appeared at this time. But they had an outlook on life which made science unnecessary. Science could tell them nothing that they wanted to know, and they had no curiosity about the sort of things science could tell them. The mediaevalist lived in an orderly universe. He knew the principles on which it was constructed, and he knew the meaning and purpose of everything in it. He knew the scheme of creation; he knew the end that every created thing was made to serve. He derived his information from two sources, reason and revelation. The highest discoveries of human reason were embodied in the works of Aristotle; the Scriptures contained divine revelations on matters not accessible to reason. By synthesizing these two kinds of information everything worth knowing could be learned. This synthesis was accomplished, magnificently, by St. Thomas Aquinas.

Sullivan then adds the highly significant words:

> It is only when faith in the all-pervading purposefulness of natural phenomena had faded that the scientific method of inquiry became important.

Sullivan assembles three qualities — two from the Greeks, *disinterested inquiry* and *mathematical reason*, and one from the mediaevalists, *the view of nature as a rational whole* — as having contributed directly to the forming of the scientific mind. For the mediaeval thinker the life of *reason* was a manifestation of the divine within the conscious mind of man. It is thus that the mind could aspire to grasp through reason the nature of the unity of plan which underlay the divine ordering of the world. Belief in *nature as a rational whole* took a very different form, as we shall see, in later times. A thinking divorced from spirit was not yet known. Yet Sullivan seems justified in regarding the idea of *the rational whole* as having contributed towards the shaping of the modern scientific outlook.

He describes Leonardo da Vinci *as a scientific genius of the first order* but one who unfortunately *never published his scientific research.* Copernicus, despite the revolution he brought about, did not *so completely manifest the scientific spirit as did Galileo.* Even Galileo was not yet *the perfect scientific man.* Of Kepler, Sullivan writes: *His three*

laws of planetary motion are not only of the first importance scientifical-
ly, they are also beautiful. It is in Newton that *the scientific outlook . . .*
reached full consciousness.

> *It would be fair to say that science, in the hands of Newton, has become*
> *a completely autonomous activity, for, although Newton had a philoso-*
> *phy and a religion, they did not play any part in his science.*

It is clear from this that Newton evolved a science which left him,
in his humanity, quite out of it. This came to be called 'objective
science' and it has continued in this character until today. Man has
arrived at a view of the world in which his own presence is not
essential. If man were wiped off the face of the earth, which today
is no longer improbable, nature, or what would be left of it, would
continue its own course quite unperturbed. This is *the blindness*
behind the eyes referred to earlier. Man has grown blind to himself;
therefore, as far as he is concerned, life is void of meaning. That is
the peril humanity is in.

It is the task of this book to trace the course of science by entering
into the lives of eminent scientists, to discover its bearing on man
himself. Our quest will be to search for a way from Blake's THE LITTLE
BOY LOST to his THE LITTLE BOY FOUND. To achieve this there must be
a radical change of outlook on all points. We have to advance from a
science of external nature to a science inclusive of man.

THE LITTLE BOY LOST

"Father! father! where are you going?
O do not walk so fast.
Speak, father, speak to your little boy,
Or else I shall be lost."

The night was dark, no father was there;
The child was wet with dew;
The mire was deep, & the child did weep,
And away the vapour flew.

William Blake, SONGS OF INNOCENCE

THE LITTLE BOY FOUND

The little boy lost in the lonely fen,
Led by the wander'ring light,
Began to cry; but God, ever nigh,
Appear'd like his father in white.

He kissed the child & by the hand led
And to his mother brought,
Who in sorrow pale, thro' the lonely dale,
Her little boy weeping sought.

Blake, SONGS OF INNOCENCE

· 4 ·

The Copernican Revolution

The modern age is often recognized as beginning with Copernicus (1473–1543); his seventy-year life span covered a period of remarkable developments. In the year that Columbus discovered America, Copernicus was nineteen and just entering college. His contemporaries included such outstanding and contrasting figures as Michaelangelo, Leonardo da Vinci, Raphael, Martin Luther, John Calvin, Savonarola, Machiavelli, and the Borgias. Yet his own life seemed to progress apparently undisturbed by all that surrounded him. Following three years at the University of Cracow he transferred to Bologna for further study in mathematics and astronomy. He became a monk but was never a recluse and later was a canon in the small cathedral town of Frauenburg. After a few years he departed to continue his studies in Padua where he acquired a Doctorate in Law. He returned to his position as canon in Frauenburg for the remainder of his life. Throughout those years he performed his daily round of duties and occupied himself with his astronomy. Apparently having no interest at all in astrology or anything mystical, he was purely an astronomer. Thus he lived as a pious, discreet, unassuming Christian priest of the old tradition along with his special interest in the stars.

He utilized the only extant astronomical system, established by Ptolemy in the second century A.D. According to this system the earth was the centre of the universe and everything else revolved around it. Copernicus had no reason to doubt this. His problem was a technical one. He found the calculations tediously long and wearisome. It caused him to wonder whether there might not have been someone since the time of Ptolemy with a different system; thus he began to read all he could in his quest for an alternative. In Cicero he found mention of a man named Nicetus who thought the earth moved, and there were references in Plutarch to others who agreed. This idea has since been traced back to Aristarchus in the third century B.C. In any case it did not originate with Copernicus. He merely borrowed it and applied it to his calculations. To his astonishment the calculations resolved more easily. The Ptolemaic system of calculations was not at fault but rather, in assuming that the earth moved instead of being immobile, his calculations were simplified, requiring only thirty-four epicycles in place of Ptolemy's eighty. It is difficult to imagine the effect this had on Copernicus. He accepted this greater simplicity as proof positive that it must stand nearer to the truth and therefore to God. But if this were true the world order as held by the Church from ancient times was reversed. He did not care to declare such a thought openly; yet if he did not was his inaction not tantamount to denying God? Clearly he had to exercise utmost caution in his presentation of the matter. In the end he did not actually dedicate his completed work, DE REVOLUTIONIBUS ORBIUM COELENTIUM, to the then-ruling Pope. The following excerpts are quoted from his dedicatory letter.

> When from this, therefore, I had conceived its possibility, I myself also began to meditate upon the mobility of the earth. And although the opinion seemed absurd, yet because I knew the liberty had been accorded to others before me of imagining whatsoever circles they pleased to explain the phenomena of the stars, I also thought I might readily be allowed to experiment whether, by supposing the earth had some motion, stronger demonstrations than those of the others could be found as to the revolution of the celestial sphere.
>
> John Langdon-Davies, MAN AND HIS UNIVERSE

So nothing more was suggested than an improbable surmise and a mere exercise out of harmless curiosity, with no hint at all of heresy. Copernicus then proceeds to come nearer to the heart of the matter.

> I found at length by much and long observation, that if the motion of the other planets were added to the rotation of the earth and calculated as for the revolution of that planet, not only the phenomena of the others followed from this, but also it so bound together the order and magnitude of all the planets and the spheres and the heaven itself, that in no single

*part could one thing be altered without confusion among the other parts
and in all the universe. Hence for this reason in the course of the work I
have followed this system.*

There was still nothing to suggest that he had adopted this system
as his personal belief. He had merely followed it out of curiosity or
general interest. Yet there came a point when he could not refrain
from breaking into a hymn of praise to the sun as the enthroned
centre of the heavens.

*There in the middle of all stands the sun. For who, in our most beauti-
ful Temple, could set this light in another or better place, than that from
which it can at once illuminate the whole? Not to speak of the fact that
not unwittingly do some call it the light of the world, others the soul,
still others the governor. Tresmegistus calls it the visible god; Sophocles'
Electra, the All-seer. And in fact does the sun; seated on his royal
throne, guide his family of planets as they circle round him.*

This still does not state outright that the earth, like the other planets, circles round the sun. Strangely enough Tycho Brahe, a
renowned astronomer and astrologer who lived somewhat later
(1546–1601), wished to preserve the dignity of the earth so he took
up the image of the 'family of the planets' circling round the sun.
But he evolved a system whereby the other planets circle the sun
and then, together with the sun as their centre, they circle round the
earth. Thus the earth remained central and at rest. It is extraordinary that using this system the calculations and predictions were
no less accurate and reliable than with the Ptolemaic or Copernican.
As regards calculation it seems all three systems serve equally well,
whether the earth is central and at rest or whether it moves.

To return to Copernicus' dedicatory letter . . . as though expecting
trouble he adds the words:

*If there be some babblers who, though ignorant of all mathematics, take
upon them to judge of these things, and dare to blame or cavil at my
work because of some passage of Scripture which they have wrested to
their own purpose, I regard them not, and will not scruple to hold their
judgment in contempt.*

The publication of the book was long delayed. When it was finally published a preface had been inserted by a concerned friend,
without Copernicus' knowledge. This preface emphasized that the
book was to be regarded only as a mathematical exercise and of no

greater significance. A copy reached Copernicus on his deathbed. The Pope was happy to have had the book dedicated to himself. Apart from arousing a bit of scoffing here and there, it lay neglected and forgotten. Even Martin Luther has been quoted as saying:

> . . . . *such are the times we live in: he who wants to be clever must invent something all his own, and what he makes up he naturally thinks is the best thing ever! This fool wants to turn the whole art of astronomy upside down! But as the Holy Scripture testifies, Joshua ordered the sun to stand still, and not the earth!*

But Galileo, faced with the same issue, pointed out how it was much easier to account for the Joshua miracle using the Copernican system instead of the Ptolemaic. How much easier it was merely to stop the earth than to upset the ordering of the entire heavens by stopping the sun! However, in defending the Copernican system Galileo succeeded only in having the book put on the Index where it stayed until 1835.

As for Copernicus himself, Sir Oliver Lodge states:

> . . . . *that Copernicus was a giant intellect or power . . . such as had lived in the past and were destined to live in the near future . . . I see no reason whatever to believe. He was just a quiet, earnest, patient and God-fearing man, a deep student, and unbiased thinker, although with no specially brilliant or striking gifts; yet to him it was given to effect such a revolution in the whole course of man's thoughts as is difficult to parallel.*
>
> Sir Oliver Lodge, PIONEERS OF SCIENCE

This is all the more remarkable because the Copernican calculations carried their own measure of inaccuracies and have never been shown to be an improvement on the Ptolemaic. The revolution lay not in the calculations but in the displacement of the earth from its central position in the heavens, a view held from ancient times and accepted by the Catholic Church. Martin Luther, the foremost rebel in rejecting the authority of the Church, obviously still concurred with the Ptolemaic theory.

To evaluate the significance of the Copernican revolution one needs to consider the greatest Christian document of the time, Dante's DIVINE COMEDY. Dante died in 1321, a little over a century before Copernicus's birth. The work portrays a journey through the realms of the dead, including hell, purgatory, and heaven. Its whole form is a Christian adaptation of the Ptolemaic system.

Hell is portrayed as a series of nine concentric spheres around the internal centre of the earth. With every descending sphere increasing in intensity of suffering, this realm is excluded from the open heavens above. Purgatory extends beyond the earth, representing the classical elements of earth, water, air, and fire as the four stages of purification in ascending towards the heavens. Heaven also ascends in stages according to the classic naming of the family of planets: Moon, Mercury, Venus, Sun, Mars, Jupiter, and Saturn. Beyond Saturn, the outermost planet, is the Zodiac, or the eighth heaven, which Dante enters by way of Gemini or the Heavenly Twins. There we meet the spirits of Peter, James, and John, immortalized as Faith, Hope, and Charity.

The ninth heaven is the Crystal Sphere where *our poet is permitted to behold the Divine Essence and then sees, in three Hierarchies, the nine choirs of Angels.* Beatrice, his beloved, comes to meet him and records the choirs in their descending order, three by three: Seraphim, Cherubim, Thrones *in whom the first trine ends*; Dominions, Virtues, and Powers; and then Princedoms, Archangels, and Angels. The order of naming is attributed in Christian tradition to Dionysus the Areopagite, *St. Paul's convert on Mars' Hill.* In Canto XXX of PARADISE Dante, led by Beatrice, ascends to the tenth and highest heaven, the Empyrean. There he beholds *the triumph of the Angels and the souls of the blessed.* In the closing Canto he is permitted to behold the Trinity.

It is amazing how, even in translation, the poetic diction rises from the fearsome imagery of hell below to ever growing subtlety, refinement, and sublimation at the end.

> *Here vigor failed the towering phantasy:*
> *But yet the will roll'd onward, like a wheel*
> *In even motion, by the Love compell'd*
> *That moves the sun in heaven and the stars.*
>
> Dante, DIVINE COMEDY

So ends this mightily mediaeval work, a vision of the universe in which the outwardly perceptible was a perfectly structured vessel for the life it held within. The earth was at the centre, the seat of human destiny to which Christ Himself descended to take the form of Man. This vision formed the heart and soul of the world in which Copernicus and his contemporaries lived. While he studied his calculations which followed the improbable idea that the earth was not the centre but moved. This vision of the universe was structured in its Christian form on the system of Ptolemy who had culled it from ancient traditions, which long preceded the Christian era. Ptolemy's mediaeval world would be blown away like chaff with the coming of Galileo, who brought an army of telescopic observations in defense of the Copernican system.

There is, however, something else of great importance to be attributed to Copernicus. He also provided a first step for wresting thinking free from its dependence on sense-perception. In daily life we see naively and think abstractly. We see the sun rise in the east and set in the west and our feelings follow the sun — that is how we live. But then we have learned to know that the sun neither rises nor sets — it is only the earth rotating on its axis — that is how we think. We watch the sun moving higher and higher towards the midsummer equinox and witness the growing abundance of life in the fields, in the thickening foliage, the soaring festival song of the birds and the wealth of colourful flowers. Our hearts rejoice in it all — that is how we live. We watch the sun begin to sink lower and lower towards the horizon through the declining days of autumn into winter. Deeply pondering moods take hold of our life of feeling — that too, is how we live. We celebrate the great festivals of the year, in particular the Christian festivals as they occur within the seasons. All this we live: it warms out hearts and nourishes our souls. But then we recall what we have learned of the earth careering along at nineteen miles a second on its orbital path around the sun with its axis at an angle of 23½ degrees and that is how we think. Life demands this of us. We learn to rely on the mind's eye, independent of what the senses naively tell us. This offers a ground for inner freedom. This, too, we owe to the deed of Copernicus, who arrested the sun that we see moving and set the earth moving in the mind's eye when to the senses it is still. In this respect we may regard Copernicus as a benefactor, a bringer of gifts on the road to freedom as well as an innovator. He has taught us to see with the mind's eye, independent of the senses.

· 5 ·

Galileo's Intervention

Galileo, like Shakespeare, was born in 1564. Two more contrasting geniuses can hardly be imagined. Shakespeare considered the life of the soul while Galileo contemplated outer phenomena. Both in their different ways were servants of freedom.

Galileo was not of a narrow nature. He loved music and was accomplished on the lute. He loved poetic diction and could recite much poetry. He delighted in colour and at one time wanted to be a painter. He was an enthusiastic gardener who took great pleasure in the flowers of his garden. He prided himself on his keen taste in foods and was an excellent cook.

His outstanding gift was in mathematics, above all its application to outer observations. His real endeavours focused here. At the age of seventeen his father entered him into the School of Medicine at Pisa. A year later, while attending mass in the cathedral, he noticed that when the verger lit the great central lamp he caused it to swing gently. This caught Galileo's attention and he applied his hand to his wrist monitoring the rhythms. Returning home he tied a weight to a string, set it swinging and altered the length of the string until the rate of the swing tallied with the rate of his pulse beat. This experiment led him to the invention and production of *pulsillogies*, which delighted all the apothecaries, who could then take a person's pulse.

The discovery of the pendulum led to the consideration of the laws of falling bodies. It is told that he climbed the leaning tower of Pisa and demonstrated to an audience below how a large and a small stone, released simultaneously, reached the ground together. The demonstration caused not only surprise but roused controversy for it refuted the earlier pronouncements of Aristotle.

Galileo set out to explore the phenomena further. He constructed an inclined plane, marked off a number of equal lengths along it, procured a smooth ball and let it roll down the plane. From a water vessel with a narrow spout he released water while the ball was rolling, caught this water in another vessel and weighed out the varying amounts of water for the varying distances he had let the ball roll. From this he was able to determine the law of gravity and measure the gravitational constant, g. This law of gravity has played a dominant role in the thinking of humanity ever since.

His quest did not stop. Galileo persevered and discovered the laws of inertia and with these the laws of motion.

> I. If no force acts on a body in motion, it continues to move uniformly in a straight line.

> II. If force acts on a body, it produces a change of motion proportional to the force and in the same direction.

> III. When one body exerts force on another, the other reacts with equal force on the one: this is more generally expressed as Action and Reaction are equal and opposite.

Sir Oliver Lodge, in his lectures on Newton, was anxious that the discovery of these laws should be rightly attributed to Galileo.

> For this is Galileo's . . . main glory and title to immortality . . . that he first laid the foundation of mechanics as a firm and secure basis of experiment, reasoning and observation. He first discovered the true laws of motion. . . . They are stated by Newton with unexampled clearness and accuracy, and are hence known as Newton's laws, but they are based on Galileo's works.
>
> Lodge, PIONEERS OF SCIENCE

It is this that makes Galileo not only the father of mechanics but the father of physics and indeed, the scientific age. At the age of twenty-six Galileo was offered the chair of mathematics at the University of Padua, where he remained for eighteen years. It was part of his duty to give instructions in astronomy. For a time

he lectured according to Ptolemy though he himself was convinced that Copernicus was right. Then a remarkable event
occurred in the heavens.

Suddenly, in 1604, a wonderful new star appeared. Galileo gave
three lectures about this star. For the second lecture the auditori-
um, which accommodated a thousand could not hold the audience
so the lecture was given in the open. At the time of the lecture the
star had grown so in brilliance that it outshone Jupiter. But then it
dwindled away. What manner of star was it? Galileo could prove
by the simple method of parallax that it belonged to the distant
heavens. This was as controversial a matter as that of the falling
stones. It had long been held that the heavens were perfect, constant, and immutable. Throwing all caution to the wind, he
declared otherwise and reproved his listeners *for thronging to hear
about an ephemeral phenomenon, while for the much more wonderful and
important truths about the permanent stars and facts of nature they had
but deaf ears.* So the matter rested for about five years.

In 1609 news reached Galileo of a spy glass which had been
invented in Holland, through which the spire of a neighbourhood church appeared much closer but upside down. This
inspired Galileo.

> *First I prepared a tube of lead at the ends of which I fitted the glass lenses,
> both plane on one side while on the other side one was spherically convex
> and the other concave. Then placing my eye near the concave lens I per-
> ceived objects satisfactorily large and near, for they appeared three times
> closer and nine times larger than when seen with the naked eye alone.*
> Stillman Drake, DISCOVERIES AND OPINIONS OF GALILEO

But the objects were now the right way up! This caused great excitement. He was invited to show this marvel to the Venetian Senate.

> *Many of the nobles and senators, although of a great age, mounted more
> than once to the top of the Campanile, the highest church tower in
> Venice, in order to see sails and shipping that were so far off that it was
> two hours before they were seen without my spy-glass, steering full sail
> into the harbor; for the effect of my instrument is such that it makes an
> object fifty miles off as if it were only five.*

The Senators were captivated by the novelty. They saw its benefit
for military purposes and were so impressed that they immediately

renewed Galileo's appointment and increased his salary. Working with his usual assiduity Galileo ground his own lenses, soon improving upon his first instrument.

> *Next, I constructed another one, more accurate, which represented objects as enlarged more than sixty times. Finally, sparing neither labour nor expense, I succeeded in constructing for myself so excellent an instrument that objects seen by means of it appeared nearly one thousand times larger and over thirty times closer than when regarded with our natural vision.*

Here was the instrument with which to view the heavens! Within only ten months of receiving the report from Holland he had already written THE STARRY MESSENGER, a report on his first astronomical discoveries. This and some of his other writings may be researched in an excellent publication, DISCOVERIES AND OPINIONS OF GALILEO, by Stillman Drake. Within two brief months he had made detailed observations of the moon, discovered the earthshine on the moon, uncovered a host of stars never seen before by mortal eyes, found that the nebulae were not diffuse or 'nebulous' stars but clusters of stars, and announced that Jupiter had <u>four</u> moons as compared with earth which had only one. This information caused great perturbation. Two little months against millenniums provided all the physical evidence to prove that Copernicus was right! This rush of revelations by means of a small earthly toy was breath taking but also, to some minds, devastating. It seemed a kind of demonic defiance of what hitherto had been held sacred.

Galileo made and recorded his findings with meticulous care and with enthusiasm at seeing the unmistakable truth before him at last.

> *. . . It is a very beautiful thing, and most gratifying to the sight, to behold the body of the moon, distant from us almost sixty earthy radii, as if it were no further away than two such measures. . . . In this way one may learn with all the certainty of sense evidence that the moon is not robed in a smooth and polished surface but is in fact rough and uneven, covered everywhere, just like the earth's surface, with huge prominences, deep valleys, and chasms.*

Galileo even calculated the height of the mountains on the moon to be four or five thousand feet. He made a careful study of the *secondary light* falling on the moon and proved conclusively that this must come from the earth shining like the other planets by reflection from the sun. This declaration was bitterly opposed.

> *... what is there so remarkable about this? The earth, in fair and grateful exchange, pays back to the moon an illumination similar to that which it received from her throughout nearly all the darkest gloom of night.*

Galileo promised that his SYSTEM OF THE WORLD when completed, would have *a multitude of arguments and experiences* to prove the truth of this to those who argue that the earth is devoid of motion and light.

> *We shall prove the earth to be a wandering body surpassing the moon in splendor, and not the sink of all dull refuse of the universe; this we will support by an infinitude of arguments drawn from nature.*

> *Beyond ... the stars of the sixth magnitude ... a host of stars are perceived through the telescope ... so numerous as almost to surpass belief.*

With the telescope he had been able to scrutinize the Milky Way.

> *The galaxy is, in fact, nothing but a congeries of innumerable stars grouped together in clusters. Upon whatever part of it the telescope is directed, a vast crowd of stars is immediately presented to view. Many of them are rather large and quite bright, while the number of smaller ones is quite beyond calculation.*

Galileo next described the nebulae.

> *.... the stars which have been called "nebulous" by every astronomer up to this time turned out to be groups of very small stars arranged in a wonderful manner.*

Last in THE STARRY MESSENGER, is the announcement about the four moons of Jupiter. He set out his painstaking observations extending from January 4 until March 2, 1610, in a manner intended to remove all doubt and disbelief. As regards his demonstration of Jupiter with its four moons there were some who refused even to look; to them it was sacrilegious to do so.
Galileo to Kepler:

> *Oh, my dear Kepler, how I wish that we could have one hearty laugh together. Here at Padua is the principle professor of philosophy whom I have repeatedly and earnestly requested to look at the moon and the planets through my glass, which he pertinaciously refuses to do. Why are you not here? What shouts of laughter we should have at this glorious folly! And to hear the professor of philosophy at Pisa labouring*

before the grand duke with logical arguments as if with magical incantations, to charm the new planets out of the sky.

Galileo continued his investigations and was able to confirm Copernicus' prediction that Venus must have phases like the moon, which he could clearly follow through his telescope, but again there were those who would not even look.

To another friend he wrote:

You almost make me laugh by saying that these clear observations are sufficient to convince the most obstinate . . . not even the testimony of the stars would suffice, were they to descend on earth to speak for themselves . . of advancing in popular opinion, or of gaining the assent of the book-philosophers, let us abandon the hope and the desire.

The severest blow to earlier belief was that the face of the sun, the most sacred and sublime of heavenly bodies, was marred with spots. The reader may recall Kepler's eulogy. Galileo had to prove, in the face of the most vehement arguments to the contrary, that these spots veritably belonged to the sun itself. He was able to deduce further, from their steady motion across the face of the sun, that the sun must be rotating about an axis once a month.

All these discoveries were achieved within a year. During that same year, following the publication of THE STARRY MESSENGER, Galileo made the ominous decision to forsake Padua in order to return to his native Tuscany, much to the great regret of the Venetian Senate and his closest friends. Venice was a free republic, hostile to even the Papacy. In leaving for Florence he was entering a hot-bed of ecclesiastical intrigue. Under the patronage of the Grand Duke of Tuscany, a former pupil of his, Galileo was welcomed and appointed First Mathematician to the University of Pisa. He was freed from teaching duties and granted the official title of Philosopher to the Duke. An earnest warning from an intimate friend, Sagredo, arrived too late and so the trouble was about to begin.

In 1611 Galileo visited Rome where he was well received by Pope Paul V and other dignitaries. He came away well satisfied. However, he later received warning that his Copernicanism was being seriously questioned in regard to its conflict with the Scriptures. This caused him to write a magnificent letter to the

Duchess of Tuscany, in which he established with force and clarity his views on the relationship between Science and Religion. It was an earnest and valiant endeavour to illucidate that the truths of science and the revelations of the Scriptures need never conflict. Though of little import in his defense, it is of particular interest in showing how these concerns existed for Galileo.

> *The reason produced for condemning the opinion that the earth moves and the sun stands still is that in many places in the Bible one may read that the sun moves and the earth stands still . . .*

He believed that the Holy Bible could never speak untruth but had to be rightly understood. It often expressed itself in images that are not intended to be taken literally, for example that God has feet, hands, and eyes and human emotions such as anger, repentance, and hatred.

> *. . . and sometimes even the forgetting of things past and ignorance of those to come. These propositions uttered by the Holy Ghost were set down in that manner by the sacred scribes in order to accommodate them to the capacities of the common people, who are rude and unlearned . . .*

> *I think that in discussion of physical problems we ought to begin not from the authority of scriptural passages but from sense-experiences and necessary demonstrations; for the Holy Bible and the phenomena of nature proceed from the Divine Word, the former as the dictate of the Holy Ghost and the latter as the observant executrix of God's commands.*

The Biblical words were not to be taken as 'absolute truth' but only as the means of conveying higher truths for 'the understanding of every man.'

> *But Nature, on the other hand is inexorable and immutable; she never transgresses the laws imposed upon her, or cares a whit whether her abstruse reasons and methods of operation are understandable to man.*

Galileo concluded that the testimony of the senses should never be questioned by the testimony of the Bible. The later is not chained to its words and observations as the former is.

> *. . . nor is God any less excellently revealed in Nature's actions than in the sacred statements of the Bible.*

Galileo clinches his argument by quoting Tertullian:

> *We conclude that God is known first through Nature, and then again, more particularly, by doctrine; by Nature in His works, and by doctrine in His revealed word.*

It was none other than Thomas Aquinas, the acknowledged philosopher of the Catholic Church, who made the distinction between Knowledge acquired from below and Revelation granted by Grace from above. Therefore Galileo had a right to feel that his contention was based on acceptable ground. God gave us our common attributes to be used and not to be ignored or denied.

> *But I do not feel obliged to believe that that same God who has endowed us with senses, reason, and intellect has intended to forgo their use and by some other means to give us knowledge which we can attain by them. He would not require us to deny sense and reason in physical matters which are set before our eyes and minds by direct experience or necessary demonstration.*

The fact that the Bible hardly refers to astronomical matters, the only planet mentioned at all being Venus under the name of Lucifer, Galileo accepts as evidence that the Bible had no intention of entering into these questions. He quotes some ecclesiastic as having said, *That the intention of the Holy Ghost is to teach us how to go to heaven, not how heaven goes.*[*]

At times he rebuked his accusers for their 'distorted' interpretations of their biblical questions whether delivered from the pulpit or presented in their writings. All to no avail. His own words are sadly premonitory of the ordeal he would have to face. To command the astronomers themselves to refute their observations *would amount to commanding that they must not see what they see and must not understand what they know . . . and that in searching they must find the opposite of what they actually encounter.*

Opposition was hardening all the time. In 1615, Galileo was summoned to Rome by the Pope to explain his teachings further. His personal visit seemed to be successful but the conspiracy to ban Copernicanism as a heresy continued. So he stayed on in Rome to

---

[*] A marginal note by Galileo assigns this epigram to Cardinal Baronius (1538–1607)

defend the Copernican concepts. *I, as a zealous and Catholic Christian, neither can or ought to withhold that assistance which my knowledge affords.*

All his efforts failed. In 1616, under the ominous threat of worse to follow, he was strictly forbidden ever again to teach that the earth moved. Henceforth he dared refer to Copernicanism only as a hypothesis. This was a terrible disappointment because he aspired to persuade the Church of the validity of these ideas. He continued his work and completed a book on the tides. Writing to a friend: *This theory which I sent you, which is founded on the motion of the earth, I now look upon as a fiction and a dream.*

In 1623 Galileo's hopes were revived when one of his former pupils became Pope. The following year Galileo went to visit Pope Urban VIII, who wrote enthusiastically of their meeting. Much encouraged, Galileo commenced work on his DIALOGUE CONCERNING TWO PRINCIPLE SYSTEMS OF THE WORLD. The book appeared in 1632. The Pope's blatant partiality for Copernicanism immediately raised a storm. Once again Galileo was summoned to Rome, this time for serious interrogation by the Inquisition. In 1634, at the age of 70, he was sentenced to abjuration, to formal imprisonment for life, and to recite the seven penitential psalms every week. Three of the ten Cardinals conducting the case refused to sign the sentence but Galileo nevertheless was obliged to read the Abjuration word for word aloud, upon his knees, and to put his signature to it. Copies were sent to all the universities so that professors could read it publicly. Galileo's calamity was now complete.

> *... because I have been enjoined by the Holy Office altogether to abandon the false opinion which maintains that the sun is the centre and immovable, and forbidden to hold, defend, or teach the said false doctrine in any manner, and after it hath been signified to me that the said doctrine is repugnant with the Holy Scripture, I have written and printed a book, in which I treat of the same doctrine now condemned, and adduce reasons with great force in support of the same, without giving any solution, and therefore have been judged grievously suspected of heresy; that is to say, that I held and believed that the sun is the centre of the universe and is immovable, and that the earth is not the centre and is movable; willing, therefore, to remove from the minds of your*

Eminences, and of every Catholic Christian, this vehement suspicion
rightly entertained towards me, with a sincere heart and unfeigned
faith, I abjure, curse, and detest the said errors and heresies . . .

Since 1616 he had lived in enforced silence. Now he was forbidden
to have visitors without the approval of a Jesuit supervisor.

It was a strange fate that the father of modern science had to end
his days under cover of a lie, even stranger that the science which
he was forced to deny became the scientific materialism that today
rejects the faith Galileo had felt obliged to uphold to the end. What
a tremendous riddle in the struggle for truth! How ironic that
Galileo, who had defended the Scriptures for their higher mysteries, was the one to release a science which declares that there are no
mysteries. To his other afflictions blindness was added.

Alas! Your dear friend and servant is now totally blind. Henceforth this
heaven, this universe, which by wonderful observations had enlarged a
hundred and a thousand times beyond the conception of former ages is
shrunk for me into the narrow space which I myself fill in it. So it pleas-
es God; it shall therefore please me also.

Nothing, however, could break his will for work. In 1638, under
conditions which might have discouraged a lesser man, he completed his DIALOGUE CONCERNING THE NEW SCIENCE. This book
established in final form the basics for the physics of the future.

Remember that it was not just narrow and penurious prejudice that
set up opposition to Galileo's work, nor was it just blind superstition that felt deep uneasiness with his presentations, though prejudice and superstition were certainly powerfully present as they are
at every real step in progress; there must have been enlightened
individuals who, at the time, felt a premonition that something infinitely precious was about be lost for a very doubtful gain. It may
have been no more than an intuition but, if so, history has proved
they were not wrong. The heavens had meant something to
humans from the moment of birth and throughout every moment
of life. This meaning was to be lost and with it, not only the loss of
dignity of the earth but also the loss of dignity of humanity.

The telescope was a splendid toy for watching ships from afar sail-
ing into a distant harbor but to use that same earthly toy to penetrate
the sacred mysteries of the heavens was quite another matter. What

is magnification of 'a hundred or a thousand times' to the magnifications attained today? Beyond beholding the heavens, what is the purpose of accurately directing vessels from earth into space for many millions of miles? What, in truth, has this added to the status of humankind and the meaningfulness of earth existence? The measure of outer dimensions and technological achievements has increased enormously but what of the inner dimensions of mankind?

What can Arthur Eddington tell us in his book, THE EXPANDING UNIVERSE, as compared with the perceived facts of THE STARRY MESSENGER? The spiral nebulae which Galileo was the first to draw are now calculated to be between 1 million and 150 million light years away. That is but one fact only.

> When we have taken together the sun and all the naked-eye stars and many hundreds of millions of telescopic stars, we have not reached the end of things; we have explored only one island . . . one oasis in the desert of space.

The constellation Andromeda is *one of the other islands.*

> A telescope shows many more . . . an archipelago of island galaxies stretching away one behind another until our sight fails. It is these island galaxies which appear to us as spiral nebulae. Each island system is believed to be an aggregation of thousands of millions of stars with a general resemblance to our own Milky Way system.

> The island systems are exceedingly numerous. From sample counts it is estimated that more than a million of them are within reach of our present telescopes. If the theory treated in this book is to be trusted, the total number of them must be in the order of 100,000,000,000. . . . These figures may not be very trustworthy but I think that they give a correct impression.
>
> Arthur Eddington, THE EXPANDING UNIVERSE

And as though these considerations are not sufficient to overwhelm, we are asked to imagine that the universe is expanding with a speed greater than half that of light! This is how far astronomy has reached since the days of the Copernican controversy. Galileo felt he was advancing mankind by sure stages to an ever greater certainty of the truth. Eddington, on the other hand warns us:

> It is better to admit frankly that theory has, and is entitled to have, an important share in determining belief. For the reader resolved to eschew theory and admit only definite observational facts, <u>all</u> astronomical books are banned.

There are no purely observational facts about the heavenly bodies.
Astronomical measurements are, without exception, measurements of
phenomena occurring in a terrestrial observatory or station; it is only by
theory that they are translated into knowledge of a universe outside.

One may wonder what new data will accrue from the present
explorations into outer space. But those investigations are also carried out under imposed terrestrial conditions.

The figure of Galileo as a man of courage, daring, enterprise, and
skill, clearly with a great world mission in the story of humanity,
is not diminished by these later considerations. What his mission
for mankind actually represents has yet to be considered.

GALILEO AND THE HUMAN SENSES

Galileo's work on gravity and the laws of motion, as also his astronomical work in confirming and furthering Copernicanism, have
had far-reaching outer consequences. His third major contribution
in regards to the senses has had an equally profound influence on
man's inner life of soul. His scientific insights literally split that life
in two.

During the terrible Abjuration he was torn apart between his instinctive religious faith, which he dared not question, and his total
reliance on the truth of his observations and mathematical reasoning.
His faith was based on intangible feelings, his science on unmistakable data. Galileo had suffered much from what he regarded as
sheer unreason. His genius lay in his mathematical faculty as
applied to physical phenomena; there, he felt secure. All else was
veiled. This took shape in his life in an unexpected way. He who
had built everything on the validity of his sense perceptions could,
in another respect, totally deny these same sense perceptions any
validity at all. He expressed this somewhat archaically but nevertheless quite clearly.

> . . . I feel myself impelled by the necessity, as soon as I conceived a piece
> of matter or corporeal substance, of conceiving that in its own nature it
> is bounded and figured in such a figure, that in relation to others it is
> large or small, that it is in this or that place, in this or that time, that it
> is in motion or remains at rest, that it touches or does not touch any

other body, that it is single, few, or many; in short, by no imagination can a body be separated from such conditions: but that it must be white or red, bitter or sweet, sounding or mute, of a pleasant or unpleasant odor, I do not perceive my mind forced to acknowledge it necessarily accompanied by such conditions; so that if the senses were not the escorts, perhaps the reason to the imagination by itself would never have arrived at them.

Hence I think that these tastes, odors, colours, etc., on the side of the object in which they seem to exist, are nothing else than mere names, but hold their residence solely in the sensitive body; so that if the animal were removed, every such quality would be abolished and annihilated. Nevertheless, as soon as we have imposed names on them, particular and different from those of the other primary and real accidents, we induce ourselves to believe that they also exist just as truly and really as the latter.   Galileo, THE ASSAYER

Galileo persisted and came to his own consideration of matter as consisting of particles in motion. These particles have 'shapes' which, by impinging on various parts of the sensitive body, produce sensations; however, the reality rests with these mobile particles alone. Still holding to the classical elements, earth, water, air and fire in their descending order of density, he relates them to the four senses, touch, taste, odour, and sound in that same order.

I think that if ears, tongues, and noses were removed, shapes and numbers and motions would remain, but not odours or tastes or sounds. The latter, I believe, are nothing more than names when separated from living beings . . .

Still there remains the sense of sight, or vision that reaches beyond his theory since he cannot create a fifth element for it. Thus, he is obliged to treat sight differently.

And as these four senses are related to the four elements, so I believe that vision, the sense eminent above all others in the proportion of the finite to the infinite, the temporal to the instantaneous, the quantitative to the indivisible, the illuminated to the obscure . . . that vision, I say, is related to the light itself. But of this sensation and the things pertaining to it I pretend to understand but little . . .

In anticipating the modern theory of atoms and molecules, matter resolved itself into particles in motion, thus illustrating how Galileo was in his nature more a forerunner of the future than a representative of his own time.

The life and work of Galileo brings us to the crux of the problem introduced briefly in the opening chapters. We admire his courage, daring, fortitude, intelligence, ingenuity, and practical skill. He stood almost alone in his struggle. He suffered greatly and was so thwarted in his brightest hopes that we sympathize with him in his times of despondency, bitterness, and truculent defiance. But history took a direction through his work that he could not have anticipated. He was to have led humanity out of dependence on unverified claims of truth from the past and set them on an open road to discovery, independence, and new-found freedom. In a way he achieved this. However, the impulses he released also went on working powerfully after him, subsequently leading to a great degree of un-freedom and even greater dependence, if not on God, then on things.

Galileo stands as a great pioneer. Following Copernicus, he effected a great revolution in the thinking of men. What was his historical mission? In effect, he cut the umbilical cord connecting man with the spiritual world. Where has this left man today? It has led from a one-time 'knowing' into a great 'un-knowing.'

· 6 ·

Doubt and Dualism

Though genius may have to walk alone, it rarely occurs singly. The genius of Galileo, father of modern physics, found a complement in Descartes, the father of modern philosophy. In their different ways both evolved a state of dualism in the human soul. The result is that man can no longer find himself in the world; he remains a detached spectator. As indicated, this may prove to be a preliminary step towards inner freedom but, unless transcended, it may equally lead to people coming to regard themselves as mere products of matter. It is necessary, therefore, to determine how the particular influences of Galileo and Descartes affected mankind.

Descartes, probably through his Jesuit upbringing, kept aloof from Galileo. At any rate, the two men never met. Descartes even declared that he had learned nothing from the writings of Galileo. At the age of twenty-eight he passed through Florence where Galileo, then a man of sixty, was greatly renowned, but he chose not to visit him.

Yet Descartes and Galileo had much in common. They were both Catholics, both deeply studied in mathematics, physics, and astronomy and both concerned with wresting the mind free from old established attitudes. What they accomplished has become our own heritage far more than is commonly realised.

There was one point in particular where the fate of Galileo nearly touched Descartes. Descartes had almost completed a work for the

Only if doubt should lead to a new questioning, to new investigation, to new discovery, to new self-knowledge, can it be resolved into new insight leading to a new faith. This is what Descartes attempted to do by means of intellectual reasoning and logic. This is what the whole modern age has tried to do since his time, yet doubt persists still. Descartes was the first to attempt to transcend doubt in the search for real, unquestionable knowledge.

> . . . I was convinced I had advanced no further in all my attempts at learning, than the discovery at every turn of my own ignorance.

This had such an unsettling effect on him that he resolved to abandon all further study, even the mathematics he loved, and to plunge into practical life to gain what he could of knowledge, not by mere learning but through experience.

> I spent the remainder of my youth in traveling, in visiting courts and armies, in holding intercourse with men of different dispositions and ranks, in collecting various experience, in proving myself in the different situations into which fortune threw me, and above all, in making such reflection on the matter of my experience as to secure my improvement.
>
> Descartes, THE DISCOURSE ON METHOD

Doubt, however, continued to possess his soul and would not be allayed. At about age twenty-five he held a commission in the Dutch army for a short while. On the night of November 10, 1619, he retired to his tent, so heavily oppressed with doubt and uncertainty that for relief he felt driven to pray for light. His prayer found an unexpected answer. An idea flashed into his mind which was to serve as his guiding light. This was that the mathematical method in which he had such trust might be applied to all the sciences and to knowledge in general. This was followed by three dreams and an outer sign which further confirmed this guidance.

The sign was that he saw a placard in Dutch and asked a passer-by to translate it for him. It contained a mathematical problem with the challenge to all mathematicians to decipher it. Descartes was able to achieve the solution within a few hours and thereby felt newly encouraged to return to his earlier mathematical interests.

A mathematical process proceeds one step at a time each step being deduced from the previous one each being thoroughly tested with nothing extraneous allowed to enter so that at the resolution the whole ground covered is directly surveyable from beginning to end and remains transparently clear in thought. Following this procedure, he set out to investigate and test the grounds of knowledge so that no detail should escape his intellectual scrutiny. Not the slightest detail was left to lingering doubt. With new-born hope and zeal he commenced his quest.

> *Like one walking in the dark, I resolved to proceed so slowly and with such circumspection, that if I did not advance far I would at least guard against falling.*

The philosopher, like the mathematician, must have his starting point. It must be as clear as any axiom in geometry.

> *The first principles are given by intuition alone . . . each individual can have intuitions of the fact that he exists, and that he thinks that a triangle is bounded by three lines only; a circle by a single superficies, and so on.*

Next, Descartes established the 'rules' to be followed strictly.

The first:

> *. . . never to accept anything for true which I did not clearly know to be such; that is to say, carefully to avoid precipitancy and prejudice, and to comprise nothing more in my judgment than what was presented to my mind so clearly and distinctly as to exclude all ground for doubt.*

The second:

> *To divide each of the difficulties under examination into as many parts as possible, i.e., as might be necessary for its adequate solution.*

The third:

> *To conduct my thought in such order that, by commencing with objects the simplest, i.e., easiest to know, I might ascend by little and little, and, as it were, step by step, to the knowledge of the more complex; assigning in thought a certain order even to these objects which in their own nature do not stand in a relation to antecedence and sequence.*

The fourth and the last:

> *In every case to make enumerations so complete and reviews so general, that I might be assured that no thing was omitted.*

In his search for a knowledge that was totally free from doubt Descartes held strictly to thought alone. He knew that knowledge must comprise experience as well but he considered even the most elementary experiences too complicated to ensure against initial errors. Therefore he kept to the intuitional idea and to what could be deduced from it. Intuition and deduction he regarded as *the most certain routes to knowledge*. Thus he excluded everything that did not arise strictly from within himself. The results, and the successive stages by which he arrived at them, he published in his DISCOURSE ON METHOD. Having, as he thought, reached his goal, his mind was, nevertheless, assailed with doubt as regards himself.

In his essay on Descartes in THE GREAT THINKERS, Rupert Lodge described the situation:

> *He had published a method for banishing doubt, and yet doubt refused to be banished. . . . He concentrated, brought all his mental powers to bear, as he reviewed point by point, what he had written and published and, indeed, successfully used. . . . 'I am constrained,' he writes, 'at last to avow that there is nothing at all that I formerly believed to be true of which it is impossible to doubt, and that not through thoughtlessness or levity, but from cogent and maturely considered reasons.' An idea could be both clear and distinct, so much so as to exclude all doubt. But, after all, was not this subjective rather than objective certainty? For instance, as he meditated, he would sometimes drop off into sleep, and would dream that he was meditating, would dream that he was awake and concentrating. His idea of himself would be clear and distinct. He would have no doubt as to its certainty. But then he would wake up and would find that he had really been dreaming. It was thus possible to have ideas which were clear and distinct, but false, out of touch with the order of nature, not conveying imagination which was objectively reliable. Even in the field of mathematics, where it had seemed to him that doubt was absolutely excluded, he could now see that it was possible to be sincerely in error. He needed, in a word, something more than his own powers of clear and distinctive intuition to be assured that his thinking was objectively true. It might be that 'some malignant demon' delighted in deceiving him, in encouraging him to think clear and distinct ideas which were false.*

Descartes set to work all over again. After much labour, not only testing his own thoughts in every way he could but inciting criticism from the most competent thinkers he knew, he came to one single conclusion. There was just one fact and one only which was indisputably beyond doubt . . . the fact that he doubted! No one could ever question that. His long and ardent quest was revealed; now he had his starting point.

What is of principle importance is that in Descartes a new type of consciousness was emerging, one which is typical of today. His abstract mind informed him that anything we know or think we know may be illusion, all except the one certain fact of doubt. With this secure though negative fact he felt he could now go further.

I know that I doubt. How do I know that I doubt? Only through thought. Therefore, Descartes deduced from the initial *I doubt* the conclusion *I think*. But how am I able to think? Only through the fact that I exist . . . *I am*. He deduced from *I think* the conclusion *I am*. Hence, the famous formula, <u>*Cogito ergo sum*</u> (<u>I think therefore I am</u>).

The full sequence reads: *I know that I doubt, from which I deduce that I think, from which I further deduce that I am.* The sequence here is most important. He did not say, 'I exist, and, that I think, is one fact of my existence' but the other way round, 'Through the fact that I think I deduce that I exist: I infer from my thinking that I am.'

The fact that he doubted needed no further explanation but what exactly did he mean by thought? Descartes defined what he meant.

> *By the word thought I understand all that of which we are conscious as operating in us. And that is why not only understanding, willing, imagining, but also feeling are here the same thing as thought.*
>
> Descartes, THE DISCOURSE ON METHOD

This is equivalent to saying that we are only thought conscious: whatever enters our consciousness we apprehend as thought and nothing else. He does not ask what pre-conditions exist to lift the various experiences of feeling, willing, or even doubt into consciousness. He is concerned only with the content of consciousness itself and our consciousness is one of thought.

Having defined thought, the next question to be considered was the thought, 'I am.' What am I?

> *Thinking is an attribute of the soul which properly belongs to myself. This alone is inseparable from me. I am — I exist: this is certain; but how often? As often as I think. I am, precisely speaking, a mind, understanding, or reason, a thinking thing.*

What then is a thinking thing? Is it a thing (undefined) which thinks, or is it a thing composed only of thought? To the thinker who merely thinks, 'I am' is merely a thought like any other thought entering consciousness.

> *What am I? A thinking thing, it has been said. But what is a thinking thing? It is a thing that doubts, understands (conceives), affirms, denies, wills, refuses, that imagines also, and perceives.. Assuredly it is not little, if all these properties belong to my nature.*

Still observing himself in thought only, Descartes continued.

> *But why should they not belong to it? Am I not that very being who now doubts of almost everything; who, for all that, understands and conceives certain things; who affirms one alone as true and denies others; who desires to know more of them, and does not wish to be deceived; who imagines many things, sometimes even despite his will; and is likewise percipient of many, as if through the medium of the senses.*

Descartes observes all this taking place in his consciousness, but he perceives it only as thought — part of his thought. It is through thought that he seeks to ratify the fact of his own existence — thought is the only primal reality which he can acknowledge.

> *Is there anything of all this as true as that I am, even although I should be always dreaming, and although he who gave me being employed all his ingenuity to deceive me? Is there also any one of these attributes that can properly be distinguished from my thought, or that can be said to be separate from myself? For it is of itself so evident that it is I who doubt, I who understand, and I who desire, that it is here unnecessary to add anything by way of rendering it more clear. And I am as certainly the same being who imagines; for, although it may be (as I before supposed) that nothing I imagine is true, still the power of imagination does not cease really to exist in me and to form part of my thought.*

So far Descartes has referred to experiences which arise within his consciousness. He views them as part of his thought and from his capacity to think them he deduces that he is. What then of the world of impressions which reach him through the senses? In so far as they also enter his consciousness and he apprehends them in thought, they form part and parcel with all the foregoing.

> *In fine, I am the same being who perceives, that is, who apprehends certain objects as by the organs of sense, since, in truth, I see light, hear a noise, and feel heat. But it will be said that these presentations are false, and that I am dreaming. Let it be so. At all events it is certain that I seem to see light, hear a noise, and feel heat; this cannot be false, and this is*

what in me is properly called perceiving (sentire), which is nothing else than thinking. From this I begin to know what I am with somewhat greater clearness and distinctiveness than before.

Descartes began by declaring that intuition and deduction were the only true roads to knowledge. Thus, the whole perceptual world becomes no more than his thought of it or his dream of it. Is this the end for which he set out?

To summarize briefly, knowledge is arrived at through the mental imagery of thought. Yet into this there enters doubt. Never to have doubted and merely to accept naively whatever declares itself to the mind cannot lead to true knowing. Doubt makes the thinker critically awake to himself and to all that may meet him. Only then does conscious life begin. Yet is this conscious life confined only to images and thoughts as these arise in the mind? How then does this isolated state of consciousness relate to the world of experience which promotes these thoughts, the world which engenders both the thinker and his thoughts? How is one to pass from <u>the idea</u> of existence to <u>the reality</u> of existence of which one is no less a part?

This dilemma stood before Descartes and has remained ever since a concern for modern philosophy. Over-reliance on the idea perceived in the mind has led to various forms of idealism, transcendentalism, and abstraction. Over-reliance on the senses has led to what has claimed the name of realism and, eventually, materialism.

Whether through one-sided idealism or one-sided realism, the conclusions he had achieved were no more than speculative theory, a compromise between life in its totality and our own intrinsic existence. However, Descartes' quest was for the certainty of knowledge. He would not submit to the thought that this was unattainable. Having justified to himself the thought <u>I am</u>, how should he insert this concept into the world process? Here he followed a remarkable course, the only possibility his previous reasoning could evolve. He did not turn to the world of common experience . . . the world of nature, he took instead a direct leap from <u>I am</u> to God. From the <u>I am</u> he inferred that God is, and from <u>God is</u> he turned to God's Creation. He inferred Creation from the existence of God, the Creator, and not, as is usually done, God the Creator from his Creation.

He had arrived at the certainty of his I am beginning from the negative factor of Doubt. By a further negative he arrived at what for him was the compensating positive. Reflecting on his I am he was obliged to acknowledge his limitations but then, in that moment of reflection, conceived of the idea of the Illimitable. He could not know what the Illimitable or the Perfect might comprise. His finite mind could not contain the Infinite. But how could what was limited conceive of the Illimitable, what was imperfect conceive of the Perfect, what was finite conceive of the Infinite, unless they had existence, though their nature was beyond the scope of human knowing? Such thoughts could not be born of himself but only of God. It followed that God exists, that God is.

> When I make myself the object of reflection, I not only find that I am an incomplete (imperfect) and dependent being, and one who increasingly aspires to something better and greater than he is; but, at the same time, I am assured likewise that he upon whom I am dependent possesses in himself all the goods after which I aspire (and the ideas which I find in my mind) and that not merely indefinitely and potentially, but infinitely and actually, and that he is thus God. And the whole force of the argument of which I have here availed myself to establish the existence of God, consists of this, that I perceive I could not possibly be of such a nature as I am, if God did not in reality exist.

For Descartes this was proof enough. Even though he did not *comprehend the infinite* and even though it was not possible to *compass by thought* what God was, this idea of the existence of God at which he had arrived was for him *the most true, clear and distinct of all the ideas* in his mind. Why, if this solution was so simple and direct, was not all the world equally convinced? For Descartes to have pursued his inquiry further in regard to God would have made no sense. In that direction he had reached a limit. The only further course was to observe God's creation, the perceptual world. The philosopher had now to turn scientist. The mind derived from God was to contemplate a world which was not mind; what was not mind was body. Here Descartes' dualism declares itself. Even as a person has a mind distinct from the body, so God was to be sharply distinguished from Creation.

Descartes reasoned that surely God would not have given him a mind in order to deceive him; neither then would what the God-given senses transmitted to his consciousness all be illusion. It was for him to determine how much was illusion and how much was verifiable truth.

Here Descartes the mathematician joins hands most closely with Galileo. In regard to the senses Descartes decided that only what was mathematically verifiable by reason could be held to be true. The sensations of warmth and cold, smoothness and hardness, light and dark, and all the other sensations were only subjective and therefore secondary. The primary qualities, being independent of the subject, alone were real. These he reduced to two: extension in space and movement. *Give me extension and movement and I will construct the world.*

Even this differentiation he developed further. Extension alone belonged properly to body. Though bodies moved, they could not have originated their movement — they must have been made to move and only mind could do that. It was the mind of God that set the planets in motion. Descartes conceived that God had, from the beginning, put a given amount of motion into the world. There was thus a sum-total of motion and there could be neither more nor less; whatever was lost in motion in one place was gained in another.

With great ingenuity, Descartes constructed on this his vortex theory. Whereas Copernicus, Galileo, Kepler, and Tycho Brahe were concerned with how the planets moved, Descartes was the first to propound a theory of why they moved. The Ptolemaic view attributed the motion of the planets to the Divine Intelligences inhabiting them hence the harmony of the spheres. Descartes' theory was that the original impetus was given by God through an act of Infinite intelligence and the same momentum had continued ever since. However, this did not explain what maintained the planets in their orbits nor why there were irregularities in their motions.

An example of how a mind, divorced from reality, can evolve abstraction on abstraction, convinced that it is building on solid ground, making whatever theoretical assumptions it chooses in order to maintain itself, is illustrated in James Jean's description of Descartes' theory.

> *He proceeds to argue that, as extension is the fundamental property of matter, extension without matter is unthinkable . . . a strange argument*

for a philosopher who claimed to accept nothing that could not be estab-
lished with certainty.

Sir James Jeans, PHYSICS & PHILOSOPHY

A parallel argument would be that as motion is the fundamental property of a locomotive, ergo motion without a locomotive is unthinkable.

> *Thus, all space must be occupied by matter of some kind or another. 'A vacuum or space in which there is absolutely no body is repugnant to reason.' He accordingly imagines that all those parts of space which are not occupied by solid matter of our experience are occupied by other 'primary' matter consisting of very fine particles which make no impression on our senses.*

> *When a fish swims though the sea it pushes particles of water away from in front of itself, while other particles close in from behind to fill the gap vacated by the fish. 'All natural motions are in some way circular.' In the same way, Descartes thought, when ordinary gross matter pushes its way though the sea of particles, this must move in closed circuits, and so may be pictured as a series of vortices.*

> *On this foundation, Descartes built his famous theory of vortices. The vortices were whirlpools in a sea of particles: ordinary material objects were like floating corks which revealed how the currents were flowing in the whirlpools. The finest particles of all, which were rubbings or filings from the coarser kind, were drawn towards the centre of the vortices. The planets were corks carried in the whirlpool of the sun and whirled around its centre, while a falling leaf was a smaller cork drawn towards the centre of the earth's whirlpool. In a later elabouration, there was supposed to be so much agitation at the centre of a large whirlpool that objects became luminous; this explained why the sun and the stars shone.*

There are two additional points to be mentioned. The interference of the interlocking whirlpools with one another was considered responsible for the apparent, slight irregularities in the courses of the planets. Still more notable was Descartes' attempt through his theory to resolve the vexing question of whether the earth moved or not. It will be recalled that he abandoned his book, THE WORLD, because it was pronouncedly Copernican. In his Vortex theory he argued that since the earth merely was resting on its whirlpool; it could, in a sense, be considered not to be moving. This exposition did not save his theory from censure by the Church but he managed to escape personal persecution. An important fact to be noted is that side by side with his idea of a perfect God Descartes produced the first mechanical explanation Vortex theory was uncritically adopted and continued to be taught in universities all over Europe until well into the eighteenth century. In England, notably at Oxford, it was taught long after Newton's PRINCIPIA was published. This indicates that there were many minds in tune with Descartes' mode of thinking.

It is most extraordinary the way Descartes came to apply his dualism to the animal kingdom. He divided God's living kingdom into two orders of substance, thinking substance and extended substance; what was not thinking substance or mind could only be extended substance or body. That being so, since animals had no minds, they could only be bodies; nothing but cleverly constructed machines. Animal cries were compared to the creaking of machines, which led to the most horrifying vivisection practices, and all in the name on science. According to Descartes and his followers, the animals were mere automata, denied all consciousness, sensation and feeling. Since the animal possessed no thinking-substance but had motion, it could only be a machine. Abstraction could lead this far.

The human body was no less a machine. Descartes' anatomical description made that clear. However, mankind was the sole exception in possessing thinking-substance as well as extended-substance, mind or soul as well as body. How, then, could mind function in a machine? Descartes' answer was that this was possible through the constant intervention of God. He even indicated the very spot where this intervention took place, namely the pineal gland, which he declared to be the seat of the soul. This he seemed to take totally for granted from its central position in the brain and its undivided nature. The machine-body conveyed impressions to this gland by way of nerves and fluid pressures. Within this gland functioned the soul, comprised of thinking, feeling, imagining, perceiving, and all the rest. How mechanical transmission was translated, in the case of an individual, into psychical response or, how the mind or soul could order and direct the body, was simply referred back to the inexplicable intervention of God. Under what injunction Descartes chose to ignore the fact that the pineal gland is an organ which mankind has in common with every vertebrate down to the humblest fish is not known. He chose to disregard it, though with all the dissections he performed, it is hardly credible that this could have been through ignorance.

Descartes' own mind or soul seemed to have been ruled by a strange kind of logical-illogicality. With logical insistence he adhered to his mind-contra-body conception, converting all phenomena in nature, including the human body, into mechanical terms. His reasoning was interspersed with large-scale, unwarranted assumptions — a practice which, in his philosophical treatise, he felt most sternly bound to reject.

That motion is an attribute of mind; that nature abhors a vacuum; that space is filled with a fine, 'primary' matter; that the pineal gland is the seat of the soul; that the eye projects a shaft of light with which it senses objects as the blind feel them through a cane; that the blood on reaching the heart effervesces and thus propels itself by its own force into the arteries; and that the sun and the stars grow to luminosity according to the indications in his Vortices theory; such statements he advanced without misgivings and without the slightest attempt at explanation, regarding them apparently as genuine intuitions. How strange this is from someone who felt from the outset that even the simplest intuition 'I exist' was subject to doubt. We know that his rational waking life was powerfully influenced by the irrational life of dreams. It was out of a dream, like an atavistic echo of a long-forgotten teaching, that he arrived at his theory about the pineal gland.

What stands out most strongly in Descartes' life and work is his dualism.

First there is the contrast of his Christian belief in the Divine and his philosophical Deism. His philosophical Idea of God holds no trace of the Christian Trinity the creative might and moral profundity of the Father, the compassionate and enduring love of the Son, and the fiery language and illumination of the Holy Spirit. His philosophic God is an Infinite Intelligence and Mind-God, creator of a mathematically conceived, mechanical and soul-less universe, except for the limited mind of man. It is a God who neither evokes awe, nor moves to deeds of sacrifice, nor contains the force of

prophecy. Despite this, Descartes was anxious to retain communion with his Church and thankful to die in the Catholic faith.

Descartes' Mind-God was kept strictly apart from his Creation,
with the one imaginary link, the pineal gland, the one and only evidence in this whole vast world of something that is non-machine.
This dualism has persisted even if terms and images have changed.
In later times Descartes' Mind-God ended as mindless Nature.

Creation itself was divided between two distinct and irreconcilable
types of substance, thinking-substance and extended-substance, in
its final form the cleavage between mind and body.

Descartes discriminated in the perceptual world between the primary and secondary qualities — the former alone being objective
and real, and the latter subjective and unreal — thus giving direct
support, though in different terms, to the division introduced by
Galileo and adopted by the world at large.

Even the primary qualities were resolved into two, motion pertaining to mind, and extension to body. Today this dualistic attitude has
reached the point where it is no longer mind which orders and
directs the body but where, for certain schools of thought, it is body
that rules and determines whatever is called mind.

Descartes remains the master-mind of dualistic thinking. But he
also brought the whole question of doubt into prominence for our
day. Doubt that is no longer only a thought in the mind but is a
reflection in the mind of the deepest need of our modern age to
both understand and to be understood. It is far more than an intellectual need. Of itself doubt can only undermine and even destroy.
To conquer doubt can lead to reconciliation and the greatest good.

Involved as we are in the world process, the questioning doubt
enables us to gain detachment from that process and from ourselves. That is our human prerogative; that the truly godly reaches into man, enabling him by conquering doubt, to arrive at
greater freedom.

To reach this goal was Descartes' most genuine striving and it
made his life, like Galileo's, a great historic event. They articulated
the problem for a later age to solve.

press when he heard of Galileo's recantation. This news came as a great shock to him.

> . . . if the opinion of the earth's movement is false, all the foundations of my philosophy are also . . . It is so bound up with every part of my treatise that I could not sever it without making the remainder faulty; and although I consider all my conclusions based on very certain and clear demonstrations, I would not for all the world sustain them against the authority of the Church.

His book, THE WORLD, was abandoned and never published. Its contents were incorporated in later works but by then Descartes had developed his own theory about the planets, describing himself as a disciple of Tycho Brahe, not of Copernicus.

Descartes, the philosopher, was also a brilliant mathematician. He was the founder of Analytical Geometry which, according to Sir Oliver Lodge, brought geometry into regions of which we have and can have no direct conception, because we are deficient in sense organs for accumulating any kind of experience in connection with such ideas.

In other words, through Analytical Geometry, we are brought by concrete stages to the borderland of a concrete reality, though one lying beyond the grasp of our limited faculties. In his philosophy, too, Descartes arrived at the borderland of direct knowledge but, by following his reasoning one step further, he came to the absolute conviction that God exists. This is even more remarkable because his Cartesian philosophy is based essentially on doubt.

Doubt in its most pronounced form entered history with Descartes. Doubt in one form or another has held sway ever since. The moment thought becomes abstract we begin to doubt the validity of both our thinking and our sense perceptions. We doubt about God, about all we behold and about one another. Modern life is beset with doubts. Descartes from the first made doubt the starting point in his quest for knowledge. Doubt implies taking nothing on authority or anything for granted. It requires the need for testing all experience, inner and outer, on the ground of reason, after first freeing reason itself from all partiality.

The mediaeval world was built on faith. Doubt entered with the birth of the abstract intellect. The old faith cannot withstand it.

· 7 ·

Newton's Triumph

It would be difficult to find a more striking example of dualism and its resulting divided state of soul than Isaac Newton. He was a fervent adherent of the Bible, especially the prophetic Book of Daniel, yet he firmly believed that all natural phenomena would one day be explained mechanistically. While his mathematical genius introduced a view of universal gravitation which was accepted for hundreds of years, he was actually more intent, with the help of his oven, in his quest to produce the elixir of life. So while Galileo and Descartes had divided human experience into two separable parts, outer and inner, quantitative and qualitative, primary and secondary, these counterpoints already existed side-by-side within Newton and caused him no difficulty. His public achievement brought him great fame.

Stillman Drake's DISCOVERIES & OPINIONS OF GALILEO draws up a vivid picture comparing Newton and Galileo, both in character and circumstance.

> Galileo's work had gone counter to every accepted tradition of his age; Newton fitted intimately into the spirit of his time. Newton shrank from controversy and declined even to answer ignorant critics; Galileo was nothing if not combative, and used the most obstinate opponents as foils for his own purposes. Newton cared little for society, particularly that of women. Galileo thrived on companionship, and his mistress bore him three children. Newton tended to be abstemious, while Galileo delighted in wine, which he called 'light held together by moisture' — and even when under close arrest he insisted on having a well-stocked cellar. Whenever he could find the time he diverted himself by gardening, and

he loved to observe the growth of plants; Newton, though he took an occasional turn in his garden, could not abide the sight of a weed there. Galileo took pleasure in conversing with artisans and applying his science to their practical problems; Newton preferred the precisely designed problems; the deductive application of scientific laws. While Newton spent much of his life in alchemical pursuits and theological speculations, Galileo (almost alone in his age) ridiculed the alchemists, and ventured into theology only when it encroached upon his science. Galileo was personally skilled in art, talented in music, and devoted to literature; to Newton these appear to have remained passive enjoyments. In Galileo it is hard to say whether the qualities of the man of the Renaissance were dominant, or those of our scientific age. Of Newton this question cannot be asked.

Galileo was a sunny Catholic Italian in contrast to Newton an austerely puritanical Englishman. While Galileo was a popularizer and wrote his works in the vernacular, Newton was exceptionally reticent and wrote in Latin for the educated few. Galileo sent his STARRY MESSENGER to every court in Europe. Newton kept his discoveries locked up until they were drawn out of him. There is little unknown about Galileo's private life while Newton's remains very private.

Newton (1642–1727) was born prematurely on Christmas Day of the year Galileo died. He was a posthumous child, named Isaac after his deceased father. His birth was anything but auspicious.

He was so small at birth that his mother said she could have put him in a quart pot, and so lacking in vitality that the two women who went to fetch a 'tonic medicine' for the poor child were surprised to find him still alive when they returned.

At his village school he made little impression. Unlike Descartes, he was not precocious. Outside school he loved making working models of the simple machines around him. At the age of twelve his mother sent him to live with an apothecary friend so that he could attend the famous King's School, founded by Henry VIII, which was located at Grantham, just seven miles away.

The excellent Mr. Clark allowed and encouraged him to spend school holidays 'entirely in knocking and hammering in his lodging room,' with little saws, hatchets, hammers, and all sorts of tools. He made a model of a new windmill that had recently been built at Grantham. He put the model on the roof of the house to catch wind and in it was a mouse 'which he called the miller.' The mechanism was so arranged that the mouse could set the mill going at any moment and Isaac 'would joke, too upon the miller eating corn that was put in.' He made a water-clock four feet high . . . He made kites, which he flew at night, with lamps tied to their tails, 'which at first frightened the country people exceedingly, thinking they were comets.'

Mr. Clark had a little step-daughter who, at the time, became Isaac's closest friend. Miss Storey recalled that Isaac

was always a sober, silent, thinking lad, and was never known scarce to play with the boys abroad, at their silly amusements; but would rather chose to be at home, even among the girls and would frequently make little tables, cupboards, and other utensils for her and her play fellows, to set their babies and trinkets on.

Their friendship continued through the years. She was the only women he thought of marrying, but never did. In her old age he still visited her from time to time, gave her presents, even money if she needed it, but that was the extent of his romance.

Mr. Clark also possessed many chemicals and scientific books which initiated and inspired Newton's passion for alchemy.

At King's school he attracted no more notice then at his previous school. He gained greatest fame by thrashing an older boy for kicking him. This incident seemed to rouse him in other ways and he became more industrious and eventually rose to be top of the school, though he was not outstanding in his abilities. An unusual glimpse pictures him at the age of sixteen, jumping with and against a strong wind and thereby ascertaining its velocity. His toy models and his moderate scholastic success are the only indications of any promise shown during childhood and youth. Even in his first undergraduate years at Trinity College, Cambridge, there was nothing to indicate what lay ahead. He showed no signs of any special interest in science until a book on astrology caught his attention.

For in it he found a geometrical diagram which he could not understand and he then bought a 'Euclid' and set to work to learn geometry. Having mastered this book with ease, he went on to study the far more difficult Geometry *of Descartes, which seems to have given him a real interest in mathematics and a taste for science.*

This newly discovered interest was enhanced by his tutor, the renowned Isaac Barrow, who, the following year, procured him a scholarship at Trinity. It was then that his genius not only awoke, it shot into being. At that moment a terrible plague broke out and work at Cambridge was suspended. For the greater part of 1665 and 1666 Newton lived in quiet retirement at his country home at Woolthorpe. This turned out to be the wonder-period of his life, which he described in writing half a century later.

> In the beginning of the year 1665, I found the method for approximating series, and the rule for reducing any dignity (i.e., any power) of any binomial of such a series.*
>
> The same year in May I found the method of tangents of Gregory and Elusius, and in November had the direct method of fluxions.**
>
> And in the next year, in January had the theory of colours, and in May following I had entrance into the inverse method of fluxions (i.e., the integral calculus) and in the same year, 1666, I began to think of gravity extending to the moon . . . from Kepler's rule of the periodic times of the planets, I deduced that the forces which keep the planets in their orbits must be reciprocally as the squares of their distances from the centres about which they revolve; and thereby compared the force requisite to keep the moon in her orbit with the force of gravity at the surface of the earth, and found the answer pretty nearly. All this was in the two plagues years of 1665 and 1666, for in those days I was in the prime of my age for invention, and minded mathematics and philosophy more than at any time since.
>
> Isaac Newton, BIOGRAPHY
>
> Thus, before he was twenty-four years old, he had already thought out a programme for a larger part of his life's work.
>
> Jeans, PHYSICS AND PHILOSOPHY

This brief and sudden burst of intense activity is all the more astonishing because the rest of what he did may well be regarded as no more than a postulate, much detail but no new inspiration. In fact Newton's life falls into three clear phases: the first, his slow incubation and flare up of unparalleled activity; the second, until age of forty five, he elaborated and completed the 'programmeme'

---

* This is the famous binomial theorem.
** This is the differential calculus, the most famous and important of Newton's mathematical discoveries

commenced in these two rare years — a period of twenty-one years ending with the publication of his PRINCIPIA; the third, a long lapse of forty years up to his death at the age of eighty-five, in which, apart from an occasional flash, his production work as a scientist was virtually ended.

Astonishing, too is his remarkable reticence. Once he had worked something out, he would lay it by and trouble no further about it until a request from someone on one point or another led him to pull open a drawer and hunt out a paper which might have lain there unthought of for years.

By age forty-five his METHOD OF FLUXIONS was not yet published, his OPTICS only imperfectly; and his PRINCIPIA had passed its first edition but only because an impecunious young astronomer, Edmund Halley, had persistently urged him to do so. In the end Halley paid for the publication out of his scant purse although Newton had a comfortable salary and a private income.

In 1667 Newton returned to Cambridge to be made a Fellow of his College. In 1669 Barrow, wishing to engage in other work, resigned his chair in favor of Newton. Thus at the age of twenty-seven, though unpublished, Newton was a full professor with a good income, a light programme, and unlimited time at leisure to pursue his scientific work.

> He had to give only twenty-four lectures a year, and hold twice as many conferences with his students. Often no one came to his lectures. He used to wait around the lecture room for a few minutes, and if no one came, return to his study.

He had twenty years before him of collegiate life, much of it was spent on his alchemy and Bible studies. In 1679 he wrote to Hooke, a contemporary scientist, that for years he had been trying *to bend himself from philosophy to other studies* and that he *'grutched'* the time spent on his science *except perhaps at idle hours sometimes as a diversion.* That same year he had a shed fitted out with furnaces and other equipment for his chemical or alchemical studies.

There were times when Newton's thinking was so intense that it made him oblivious to all else around him. This seems to have been particularly the case during the two years before completing his PRINCIPIA.

> *During those years he lived but to calculate and think. . . . Thus, for instance, when getting up in a morning, he would sit on his side of the bed, half dressed, and remain like that till dinner time. Often he would stay at home for days together, eating what was taken to him, but without apparently noticing what he was doing.*

At this same time Newton had as his amanuensis a young man, Humphery Newton (no relation), who years later recorded his impressions of him. *I cannot say I ever saw him laugh but once.* The occasion was when a friend had said that he could not see the benefit of learning Euclid, *Upon which Sir Isaac was very merry.*

According to Humphery Newton, his master led a secluded life, rarely went out, rarely had visitors, never took exercise or recreation, never went to bed until two or three in the morning or even later and never stayed in bed for more than four or five hours.

> *. . . at spring and the fall of the leaf . . . he used to employ about six weeks in the labouratory, the fire scarcely going out day or night, he sitting up one night, and I another, till he had finished his chemical experiments, in the performance of which he was the most accurate, strict, exact . . .*

> *He would sometimes tho' very seldom, look into an old mouldy book which lay in his labouratory, I think it was titled, <u>Agricola de Metallis</u>, the transmuting of metals being his main design.*

Humphery Newton also described how he would sometimes appear *with shoes down at heels, stockings untied, surplice on, and his head scarcely combed.* He would sometimes, when taking a turn around his very neat garden with its little square beds, *suddenly rush up to his room to note something down, doing so standing as though he had not had time to sit down.*

His fervour for his biblical studies, so remote from his 'science' and his alchemy, also occupied him deeply and devoutly. He could write with puritanical zeal:

> *The authority of Emperors, kings, and princes, is human. The authority of councils, synods, bishops, and presbyteries, is human. The authority of prophets is divine, and comprehends the sum of religion, reckoning Moses and the Apostles among the prophets; and if an angel from heaven preach any other gospel, than what they have delivered, let him be accursed.*

Such passionate expression did not come out of a sudden ebullition of feeling but was nurtured through a lifetime.

He identified the Book of Daniel particularly with the Christian religion, *for this religion is founded upon his prophecy concerning the Messiah.* He strongly rejected the concept of the Trinity.

The following is a description of Newton:

> *In appearance he was rather short, and in his youth, slight. His jaw was square, and his features rather sharp. His brow was broad and his eyes, which protruded, were brown. His luxurious hair turned white before he was thirty. He had a very long nose. His early portraits show great force of expression, with a fierce mouth. Later ones reveal an apprehensive, suspicious look. The latest represent him as a pink, portly, amiable old man.*

The portraits showing 'great forces of expression' are what we would expect of the younger man. The ones with the 'apprehensive, suspicious look' recall the fact that, shortly after the publication of his PRINCIPIA, he suffered for a brief spell from mental aberration and 'persecution mania.' The last description corresponds to his affluent later years, no longer the active scientist but now, strangely enough, Master of the Mint. In 1703 he became the President of the Royal Society until his death in 1727.

This illustrates Newton's divided nature. He was a master-mind in a thinking style that grasped the future, and a lonely groper after mysterious practices of the past. His often quoted words were written in his old age.

> *I do not know what I may appear to the world, but to myself I seem to have been only a boy playing on the seashore, and diverting myself in now and then finding a smoother pebble or a prettier shell than ordinary, whilst the great ocean of truth lay all undiscovered before me.*

Returning once again to the year 1666, the second year of the plague, which kept Newton at home in Woolthorpe, we find him sitting in his garden one day, pondering deeply on the question of what it was that held the planets in their orbits round the sun and the moon in its orbit around the earth. While he sat there deep in thought, an apple fell from a tree. This simple occurrence gave him the clue that he needed. A thought entered his mind which was to become the ruling thought about the universe for at least two hundred years.

What were the data which preceded this thought? The Ptolemic system was for Newton a thing of the past. He was fully convinced, with Galileo, that the earth, like the other planets, moved around the sun. He had not only made Galileo's laws of motion his own but had re-formulated them. Conceived under terrestrial conditions they could not be tested or realised because of this constant presence of gravity. How would the same laws apply to celestial bodies?

Newton had been brought up on Descartes' theory of vortices. With this theory he tried to surmount the idea of one body influencing another body across empty space. There must surely be a primary matter filling space! He also had arrived at the idea, stated by Descartes but first expressed by Galileo, that motion, having once been imparted to a body (God in the beginning), could never be lost.

> ... neither was the idea new that motion tended to persist in the absence of all force. We have seen that Leonardo declared that 'every body has weight in the direction in which it is moving,' while Plutarch had put the thing even more clearly when he wrote (A.D. 100) that 'everything is carried along by the motion natural to it, if it is not deflected by something else.' But Galileo was the first to establish the principle experimentally; where others had conjectured, Galileo proved.
>
> Yet, strangely enough, he never announced the principle with perfect clearness. Perhaps Descartes was the first to do so when he wrote (1644): 'When a body is at rest, it has the power of remaining at rest and of resisting everything which could make it change. Similarly, when it is in motion, it has the power of continuing in motion with the same velocity and in the same direction.' Thirty years later, Huygens restated it in the form 'If gravity did not exist, nor the atmosphere obstruct the motion of bodies, a body would maintain for ever, with equable motion in a straight line, the motion one impressed on it.' In 1687, Newton again restated it in his Principia and made it the foundation of his whole system of dynamics. But the main credit for the law which was to revolutionize the whole of mechanical science must go to Galileo and his experiments.

Newton's formulation reads:

> Law I. Every body persists in its state of rest or of uniform motion in a straight line, unless it is compelled to change that state by impressed forces.

For Newton, unlike Descartes, the concept of empty space presented no difficulty. Descartes would have stated that the apple fell
because it was sucked to the earth by the earth's vortices. Newton
was later to disprove the whole vortices theory on the basis of
Kepler's three famous laws, which he regarded not as theories but
as mathematically demonstrated laws.

> His (Kepler's) book *Astronomia Nova* (1609), which announced the
> results of his labour, enunciated the two laws:
>
> 1) The planet (Mars) moves in an ellipse which has the sun as one of its
> foci.
>
> 2) The line joining the sun to the planet sweeps out equal areas in equal
> times.
>
> Nine years later (1631) Kepler published another book, *Epitome
> Astronomica Copernicus*, in which he extended those laws to the other
> planets, to the moon, and to the four newly discovered satellites of
> Jupiter. In his *Harmonica Mundi* (1619), he announced yet another law
> of planetary motion, now commonly known as Kepler's third law:
>
> 3) The square of the time which any planet takes to complete its orbit is
> proportional to the cube of its distance from the sun.
>
> These three laws covered all aspects of planetary motion. The first spec-
> ifies the path in which a planet moves, while the second specifies how it
> moves on this path, i.e., the way in which the speed varies. As the plan-
> et moves nearer to the sun, the sweeping arm — the line joining the sun
> to the planet —becomes shorter, so that the planet must move faster to
> sweep out areas at the same rate as before; the nearer a planet is to the
> sun, the greater its speed of orbit. The third law tells us how the times
> compare which the different planets require to complete their various
> orbits . . . we find that Saturn's year must be equal to 29.5 of our years.
> In general, the nearer a planet is to the sun, the faster it moves.
>
> These three laws of Kepler have been confirmed by innumerable obser-
> vations. We know now they are not absolutely correct but they are so
> exact that no error was found in them for more than 200 years.

The third law suggests a mystery not directly comprehensible. It is
remarkable to note in what terms Kepler himself related to it.

> Using the Pythagorean relation between the lengths of strings and the
> musical notes they produced, he represented the motions of the planets in
> their orbits by a group of musical notes, the harmony of the spheres —
> and the same *Harmonica Mundi* which announced Kepler's third law of

planetary motions also announced the chords which the planets must sing as they moved in their paths round the sun.

This goes to show that Kepler's laws were least of all mechanically conceived. The third law clearly held a connection for him with the ancient Music of the Spheres.

It is interesting to note that Newton of all people should have been seeking to reach the alchemical mysteries of the transmutation of metal, for these, too, were connected with the planets and the spheres. The central mystery related to gold, the earthy representative of the sun sphere.

Both in Kepler and Newton, though differently expressed, there were still echoes from the past playing into the awakening consciousness of a new age.

Newton was fully familiar with Kepler's laws. They described wonderfully how but not why the planets moved as they did. It was the why that concerned him.

Kepler conceived:

> *that the planets were moved on their course by a sort of virtue which streamed out of the sun. . . . He once called this force an affluvium magneticum.*

In his thinking, Newton combined the mechanics of Galileo with the mathematical conceptions of Kepler. On the assumption of empty space, it was clear from the first law of motion that the planets needed no force to keep them in motion. Then why did they not proceed for ever in the same direction? What Newton was looking for was not a propelling but a deflecting force. Since the deflection of the planets was always towards the sun, there must be such a force emanating from the sun. It was clear that, by the third law of motion, each planet would be held centripetally by the force in question. As for the second law of motion requiring a planet to sweep out equal areas of space in equal periods of time, Newton could show conclusively that this was valid only if there were a force controlling the planet from the sun. Newton knew that such a force also existed between Jupiter and its satellites, and between the earth and its moon. It was with all this in his mind that he sat in the garden on that fateful day when he saw the apple fall.

Then suddenly came the thought: may not the force simply be gravity? Why should not the same force which attracted the apple to the earth also be attracting the moon in its orbit? Why should not that force of gravity apply equally to Jupiter and its satellites or to the sun and the planets?

Immediately Newton set to work to apply this hypothesis to the earth and the moon. He knew what the gravitational pull was at the earth's surface and that the pull of gravity diminished inversely as the square of the distance. The moon was sixty radii away; therefore the pull of the earth on it would be diminished by 60 x 60. He arrived at the figure of 16 feet per minute per minute, i.e., in each minute as the moon sped along on a would-be straight course, the earth pulled the moon towards itself 16 feet. To confirm this formula he needed to know the size of the earth. The figure available was that one degree of the earth's circumference was about sixty miles. Working with this figure, he arrived not at 16 feet as he had expected, but at 13.9 feet. Therefore, either the force in question was not the same force of gravity, or else some other influence was at work — maybe the vortices of Descartes had to be considered after all.

There was nothing further Newton could explain. True to character, he laid the whole matter aside, breathing not a word about it to anyone. Only years later news reached him of a report given to the Royal Society which set the measurement of the degrees closer to seventy miles, not sixty as he had been given to suppose. He dug out his previous calculations, substituted the new figure, and lo, the answer came perfectly as he had previously expected, 16!

Now he had the proof that the deflecting force he had been looking for was indeed none other than the force of gravity. He could apply this now also to Jupiter and its four moons, to the sun and the planets, in fact to the entire universe. This law of earth was also the law of the heavens. He had discovered the Law of Universal Gravitation. A multitude of supplementary calculations followed; everything seemed to fall neatly into place. Even the fleeting comets no longer needed to be looked at as mysterious messengers of portent. They, too, obeyed the one universal law of gravitation, moving in long elliptical orbits. Their periodicity could be calculated like all planetary movements. All mysteries were now resolved. The whole universe could be resolved by the one simple law of gravity, or, to put it more generally, by the one single principle, that:

> . . . *every particle of matter attracts every other particle with a force directly proportional to the mass of each and to the inverse square of their mutual distance.*

Newton felt answered. He put his papers back in his drawer and said nothing. It was not until 1684, through a visit from Edmund Halley, that this whole matter of Newton's discovery came to light.

Newton had discovered that the world was a machine of smoothly running interlocking parts — a world of inertia ruled by gravity. But he kept silent. He hated controversy. His OPTICS on which he had reported to the Royal Society, had led to disputes. He wrote to the Secretary of the Royal Society:

> *I see I have made myself a slave to philosophy, but if I get free of the present business I will resolutely bid adieu to it eternally, except what I do for my private satisfaction or leave to come out after me; for I see a man must either resolve to put out nothing new, or to become a slave to defend it.*

And again in a letter to Leibnitz:

> *I have been so persecuted with discussions arising out of my theory of light that I blamed my own imprudence for parting with so substantial a blessing as my quiet to run after a shadow.*
>
> *So he locked up the first part of his* Principia *in his desk, doubtless intending it to be published after his death.*

The way that the PRINCIPIA finally came to be published is a little story in itself. It happened that in 1684 Robert Hooke and Edmund Halley were offered a prize by a fellow member of the Royal Society, Sir Christopher Wren, if they could bring him within two months evidence 'that the path of a planet subject to an inverse square law would be an ellipse.' After seven months had gone by with no result forthcoming, Halley, having kept close contact with Newton, decided to visit him at Cambridge. He went directly to the point with Wren's problem.

> *Newton at once replied, 'an ellipse.' 'How on earth do you know?' said Halley in amazement. 'Why I have calculated it,' and he began hunting for the paper. He actually couldn't find it just then, but sent it him*

shortly by post, and with it much more . . . in fact what appeared to be
a complete treaty on motion in general.

This is how Newton's work on his PRINCIPIA first became known. The Royal Society commissioned Halley to persuade Newton to have his work published. Under Halley's persistent prompting Newton set about completing his work, adding a great number of further developments. Even so, for the book to appear, Halley, much Newton's junior and a poor man, had to defray all the expenses himself. Newton, writing to Halley, even referred to it as 'your book.'

The first appearance of the PRINCIPIA led to a dispute with Hooke on matters of priority. Though Newton eventually acknowledged Hooke's claim, at the time he was so disturbed that he decided to suppress the third book which later became the most popular, dealing with the total system of the world.

He wrote to Halley:

Philosophy is such an impertinently litigious lady that a man had as
good be engaged in a law-suit as have to do with her. I found it so for-
merly, and now I am no sooner come near her again but she gives me
warning. The two books without the third will not so well bear the title
Mathematical Principles of Natural Philosophy, and therefore I have
altered it to this, On the Free Motion of Two Bodies; but on second
thought I retain the former title: 'twill help the sale of the book — which
I ought not to diminish now 'tis yours.

Halley persuaded him, nevertheless, to publish all three books which appeared in their final form in 1687. Newton was then forty-five years of age with forty years more to come.

Do you realise the tremendous stride in knowledge — not stride, as
Whewell says, nor yet a leap, but a flight — which has occurred between
the dim gropings of Kepler, the elementary truths of Galileo, the fascinating
but wild speculations of Descartes, and this magnificent and comprehensive
system of ordered knowledge. To some his genius seemed almost divine.

Lodge, PIONEERS OF SCIENCE

Nature and Nature's laws lay hid at night.
God said, Let Newton be, and all was light.

Alexander Pope

Copernicus had displaced the earth from its central place in the heavens — that was the first act in the story. Newton then took the terrestrial fact of gravity, and, by projecting this into the heavens, determined the basis of universal order by earthly law — that was the second act, a strange and unforeseen reassertion of the earth in regard to the heavens. The universe became a mechanical extension of the mechanics of the earth, a mechanical interpretation based on the play of inert matter. Newton believed that all phenomena, including living nature, would also one day find their mechanical explanation. History played no part in his picture and natural evolution had not yet been conceived. He held quite literally to the biblical view that the world was created about 6,000 years ago. As for irregularities that must arrive in his system as time went on, he felt assured that God would himself intervene to set things right, a view expressed by Newton and scornfully ridiculed by Leibnitz. Where God had his home, if not in the mechanical universe, was a mystery left unexplored.

Newton's work was not confined to gravity alone. He arrived at an equally mechanical view in regard to light. He had the conception of a tennis ball on the spin, and he thought of light as consisting of particles in motion. The passage of light through a refracting medium gave the particles a kind of spin. The particles, not being identical in their rates of motion, received varying degrees of spin on entering the refracting medium. The effect was a fanning out of the particles into the range of the spectrum colours. These colours, he considered, were contained within the original white light which was clearly not single but compound. By interposing into the band of colours another refracting prism the opposite way round to the first, the particles would be despun and the fan of colours could be gathered up again into white light. Further, each colour zone within the spectrum could be fanned out still further by more prisms but it yielded no additional colours. There were just the seven as he enumerated them: violet, indigo, blue, green, yellow, orange, and red.

The effect of Newton's colour theory was also to regard light as something material and subject to mechanical law. The theory, supported by well-thought-out experiments, agreed perfectly with the theories of Galileo and Descartes that colours were secondary phenomena, namely, the results of particles in motion playing upon the sense of vision but nothing in themselves. Newton was not concerned with the <u>experience</u> of colour but only with determining a mathematical scale, which he could accomplish perfectly. The Newtonian theory of colour became as universally adopted as his law of universal gravitation. His science of OPTICS appeared before his PRINCIPIA.

It lay in the trend of the times to think mechanically and materialistically.

> . . . had Newton not lived we should doubtless, by the labour of a long chain of distinguished men, beginning with Hooke, Wren, and Halley, have been now in possession of all the truths revealed by the <u>Principia</u>. We should never have had them stated in the same form, nor proved with the same marvellous lucidity and simplicity, but the facts themselves we should by this time have arrived at.

> The material universe consists of radiation and matter. . . . When Newton discovered how to treat light mathematically he brought . . . one half of the universe under the reign of mathematical law. He (then) proceeded to deal with the other half, the matter in the universe.

That light in its own nature is invisible, that gravity as a force is inscrutable, that both alike remain concealed behind the effects they produce seemed not to be considerations at that time. Langdon-Davies, writing on the effect of Newton's work on human outlook asks three questions in particular.

1. What has been the effect on man's view of the universe?

> He (Newton) had substituted for the chaos of many unrelated things an order based upon law. . . . But what a different kind of order from that of the Middle Ages! Then order existed, but upon the basis of moral law; now there was no moral law involved in the picture, but physical law only.

2. What had Newton done to God?

> . . . the mediaeval God had beauty, perfection, goodness as attributes . . . . . Newton's God was nothing at all except a good mathematician.

3. What of Newton himself?

> . . . While one part of his mind showed him a God who prevented comets from wrecking the solar system, a task undertaken to preserve the piece

of machinery of which its inventor was rightly proud, another part showed him a Deity to whom he could pray, of whom he might be afraid, with whom he might have life after death.

And here we have a clear example of what the scientific adventure did to humanity: it split the human mind into separate compartments—more or less water-tight or idea-tight — and hereby made the picture of God, the attitude to life, the idea of the universe, inconsistent and muddled.

According to Langdon-Davies, the situation of the man of today may be summed up as follows:

Most of us are content to admit the incompatibility of the scientific view with other views and to see that in this particular we are poorer than the Middle Ages. . . . To go back to the harmony of mediaevalism is cowardly obscurantism; to look forward to a new harmony, a new synthesis between the measurable and the un-measurable in the far future is only common sense.

Langdon-Davies, MAN & HIS UNIVERSE

William Blake, born thirty years after Newton's death, portrayed Newton as:

The figure of a handsome youth, quite naked, drawing something in the sand . . . which the next tide would completely erase,

to which Blake adds:

may God us keep
From single vision and Newton's sleep.

Blake sees in this single vision, which reduces everything to mathematical terms, the devil tempter in the wilderness:

Come hither into the desert and turn these stones to bread. Vain foolish man! Wilt thou believe without experiment?

Blake saw the withering force of a teaching which reduced everything to terms of death:

A mighty spirit leaped from the land of Albion,
Named Newton: he seized the trump and blow'd the
*   enormous blast!*
Yellow as leaves of autumn, the myriads of Angelic hosts
Fell through the wintry skies seeking their graves,
Rattling their hollow bones in howling and lamentation.

And what of Newton, the Bible scholar, the disciple of prophecy who had written a treatise on Daniel and the Book of Revelation:

Both read the Bible day and night,
But thou readst black where I read white.

William Blake, THE PORTABLE BLAKE

What then is Langdon-Davies' conclusion about the effect of science on man? He sees. . .

> . . . *the unified spirit of humanity split in two . . . and become Newton and Blake, two irreconcilable opposites. The clearer the picture that Newton painted, the less it showed about the things that interested Blake the most.*

He sees in each human being *a Blakian part and a Newtonian part*, and the result of science has been to create *conflict and contradiction* between the two. Langdon-Davies concludes his comparison with the following paragraphs which carry the sadness and sense of helplessness we experience as we confront the abyss of today.

> *To get to know accurately about life, it has become necessary to strip life of all these things that we most like about life. Mediaevalism offered us an explanation of all in one: God, the sparrow, and the stone illuminated and explained one another; but hence-forth the more we know of stones and sparrows, the less do we know of God, the less does God seem knowable, the less does God seem worth knowing.*

> *The modern man is in a more difficult position than Newton, because Newton came too early to realise what science must finally do to his God. He could worship a <u>deus ex machina</u>, he could interpret the prophets and argue about the Trinity, he could even find a place and evidence for God in his own mechanical picture of the Universe. But as time went on, the cleavage grew greater, for science made the mediaeval idea of God ridiculous; but the idea of God which it could substitute seemed more absurd.*

Langdon-Davies, MAN & HIS UNIVERSE

From Copernicus to Newton via Galileo, Kepler, and Descartes was a straight line progression. To begin with an all-powerful Church forbade the new-born science. Little did its founders realise they were promoting an all dominant doctrine that would one day totally banish all religion. The displacement of the earth lead to the displacement of God and therefore also the displacement of man. What declared itself as the dualism of mind and matter resolved itself into an all-inclusive materialistic monism so that man and matter became totally identified and the poetry of earlier times became a wayside dream. This identification was to go much further before there could be the beginning of an awakening to new self-recognition and with it a new demand for the recognition of man as the bearer of an inborn morality. Without this awakening and without this recognition, the elimination of God may well lead to the elimination of man.

· 8 ·

Meaning in Question

The division between quantitative and qualitative formulated by Galileo came to be generally adopted. Henceforth, whatever could be submitted to mathematical treatment was to be regarded as real, primary, objective and all other elements of experience as non-real, secondary, and subjective. This view was to dominate science for centuries to come and, to all intents and purposes, does so still.

> Scientific method, as we see from the work of its founders, Copernicus, Kepler, Galileo, began by quite consciously and deliberately selecting and abstracting from the total elements of experience. From the total wealth of impressions received from nature these men fastened upon some only as being suitable for scientific formulation. These were the elements that possess quantitative aspects. Between these elements mathematical relations exist, and these men were convinced that mathematics is the key to the universe.
>
> With Galileo this separation of the mathematical from the other qualities became a perfectly clear and definite doctrine. Kepler had supposed that the non-mathematical qualities actually did belong to bodies, but that they were somehow less real. Galileo went further than this and stated that the non-mathematical properties are all entirely subjective. They have no existence at all apart from our senses. Thus colours, sounds, odours, and so on exist, as such, wholly in our minds. They are, in reality, motions of some kind or another in the external world, and these motions, impinging on our senses, give rise to these sensations of colour, sound, and so on. It is the mind that peoples the world with the songs of birds, the colours of the senses, etc. In the absence of mind the universe would be a collection of masses of various sizes, shapes, and weights, drifting, without colour, sound, or odour, through space and time.
>
> Sullivan, LIMITATIONS OF SCIENCE

This approach, once adopted, led to a totally different conception of time from that held in the Middle Ages:

> The purpose of everything was to reach to a higher state of being, culminating in union with God. The whole of the past, up to the present moment, was the ground already won, as it were. As the process continues, the ground won increases, the future is being drawn into the present. This process goes on until the final culmination is reached, when time stands still. We see how different is this notion of time from the mathematical time introduced by Galileo. Time, as it appears in science, may be likened to an ever-moving mathematical point. The present moment, which has no finite duration, is merely a boundary point between a vanished past and a non-existent future.

According to this view, all inner purpose and direction vanishes from the world we are in and, if they exist at all, must be relegated, as was the case with Galileo, Newton, and their subsequent followers, to some other existence outside this one.

> With this change in the notion of time comes a corresponding change in the notion of cause. When all things were regarded as moving towards union with God, then union with God was regarded as the final cause of all change. The cause of a process was to be found in the purpose, the happening served. With the new notion of time the future, being non-existent, had no influence on present happenings. The cause of anything happening now was to be found in its immediate past. Further, all that really happens is motions — motions of the constituent particles of the bodies forming the real world. And these motions are themselves the products of preceding motions.

Sullivan sums up what he calls Galileo's 'amazing revolution of thought' as follows:

> The vivid world of the mediaevalist, a world shot through with beauty and instinct with purpose, a world having an intimate relation to his own destiny and an intelligible reason for existing in the light of that destiny, is dismissed as an illusion. It has no objective existence. The real world, as revealed by science, is a world of material particles moving in accordance with mathematical laws, through space and time.

It is this 'real world' that Sir Arthur S. Eddington also felt called upon to examine. An outstanding scientist pursuing the methods of science, at heart he was always a Quaker with a great concern for his fellow human beings. He saw all too clearly how science and morality were drifting ever further apart, that the quantitative had totally outstripped the qualitative to the great endangerment of mankind. He suffered from the dualism which he could not of himself overcome, though he gave clear expression to it in his books, THE NATURE OF THE PHYSICAL WORLD and THE PHILOSOPHY OF PHYSICAL SCIENCE. Whatever science might provide, it offered nothing to support man in his search for a sense of reality of his own existence. Yet it seemed imperative that man should not abandon his quest for inner reality. For Eddington it became a moral issue to share this concern with his layman readers, at least to strip bare the illusion that science as we know it has the answers. His genius was able to translate basic problems into 'lay terms.' Scientific method has proceeded on its way but the human problem has grown ever more acute. Here is a characteristic piece of his somewhat whimsical yet deeply felt writing.

> Let us then examine the kind of knowledge handled by exact science. If we search the examination paper in physics and natural philosophy for the more intelligible questions we may come across one something like this: 'An elephant slides down a grassy hill-side. . . .' The experienced candidate knows that he need not pay much attention to the this; it is only put in to give an impression of realism. He reads on: 'the mass of the elephant is two tons.' Now we are getting down to business: the elephant fades out of the problem and a mass of two tons takes its place. What exactly is this two tons, the real subject matter of the problem? It refers to some property or condition which we vaguely describe as 'ponderosity,' occurring in a particular region of the external world. But we shall not get much further that way; the nature of the external world is inscrutable, and we shall only plunge into a quagmire of inscrutables. Never mind what two tons refers to; what is it? How has it actually entered in so definite a way into our experience? Two tons is the reading of the pointer when the elephant was placed on a weighing machine. Let us pass on. 'The slope of the hill is 60 degrees.' Now the hillside fades out of the problem and the angle of 60 degrees takes its place. What is 60 degrees? There is no need to struggle with mystical conceptions of direction; 60 degrees is the reading of a plumb-line against the divisions of a protractor. Similarly for the other data of the problem. The softly yielding turf on which the elephant slid is replaced by a coefficient of friction which, though perhaps not directly a pointer reading, is of a kindred nature. No doubt there are more roundabout ways used in practice for determining the weights of elephants and the slopes of hills, but these are justified because it is known that they have the same results as direct pointer readings.

And so we see that the poetry fades out of the problem, and by the time the serious application of exact science begins we are left only with point-er readings. If then only pointer readings or their equivalents are put into the machine of scientific calculation, how can we grind out anything but pointer readings? But that is just what we do grind out. The question pre-sumably was to find the time of descent of the elephant and the answer is a pointer reading on the seconds' dial of our watch.

The triumph of exact science in the foregoing problem consisted in establishing a numerical connection between the pointer reading of the weighing machine in one experiment on the elephant and the pointer reading on the watch in another experiment. And when we examine critically other problems of physics we find that this is typical. The whole subject matter of exact science consists of pointer readings and similar indications. . . . The essential point is that although we seem to have very definite conceptions of objects in the external world, those conceptions do not enter onto exact science and are not in any way con-firmed by it. Before exact science can handle a problem they must be replaced by quantities representing the results of physical measurement.

Leaving out all aesthetic, ethical, and spiritual aspects of our environ-ment, we are faced with qualities such as massiveness, substantiality, extension, duration, which are supposed to belong to the domain of physics. In a sense they do belong; but physics is not in a position to handle them directly. The essence of their nature is inscrutable; we may use mental pictures to aid calculations, but no image in the mind can be a replica of that which is not in the mind.

And so in its actual procedure, physics studies not these inscrutable fac-ulties, but pointer-readings which we can observe. The readings, it is true, reflect the fluctuations of the world — qualities but our exact knowledge is of the readings, not of the qualities. The former has as much resemblance to the latter as a telephone number has to the subscriber.

Eddington, The Nature of the Physical World

With Eddington there is no question of belittling the value of these pointer-readings. They coordinate accurately certain types of phenomena in so far as they have purely physical or mechani-cal attributes, and on this depends the greatness of modern tech-nology. Yet how remote this is from the world of actual, colourful, vital experience! Physics, on which all the other sciences have built, has led to a manipulation of world processes on a vast and even terrifying scale; and yet it is dealing all the time with formu-lae which are no more than mental images of inscrutables. From penetration into the real nature of these inscrutables, physics seems forever excluded. Hence Eddington speaks of 'The Cyclic Method of Physics,' illustrated in the following.

> Einstein's law in its analytical form is a statement that in empty space certain qualities called <u>potentials</u> obey certain lengthy differential equations. . . . What are potentials? They can be defined as quantities derived by simple mathematical equations from certain fundamental qualities called intervals. . . . What are intervals? They are relations between pairs of events which can be measured with a <u>scale</u> or a <u>clock</u> or with both. . . . What are scales or clocks? . . . A scale is a graduated strip of matter. . . . What is matter? Matter may be defined as the embodiment of those related physical quantities, <u>mass</u> (or energy), <u>momentum</u>, and <u>stress</u>. What are 'mass,' 'momentum,' and 'stress'? It is one of the most far-reaching achievements of Einstein's theory that it has given an exact answer to this question. They are rather formidable looking expressions containing the <u>potentials</u> and their first and second derivatives with respect to their coordinates. What are potentials? Why, that is just what I have been explaining to you. The definitions of physics proceed by the method immortalized in 'The House the Jack built.' This is the potential, that was derived from the interval, that was measured by the scale, that embodied the stress, that . . .

Well, then what about Jack? At this point Jack becomes Mr. X, who has been listening carefully. He knows nothing about physics but he believes he really knows what matter is.

> Very well, matter is something that Mr. X knows. Let us see how it goes. This is the potential that was derived from the interval that was measured by the scale that was made from the matter that Mr. X knows. Next question: What is Mr. X.?

> Well, it happens that physics is not all anxious to pursue the question, what is Mr. X.? It is not disposed to admit that its elabourate structure of a physical universe is 'The House that Jack Built.'

> It looks upon Mr. X that <u>knows</u> — as a rather troublesome tenant who at a late stage of the world's history has come to inhabit a structure which inorganic nature has by slow evolutionary progress continued to build. And so it turns aside from the avenue leading to Mr. X — and closes up its cycle <u>leaving him out in the cold</u>.

What is it prompts Arthur Eddington, an accomplished astrophysicist, to write in this way? It is written in great earnestness out of his profound sympathy for Mr. X, who has not only been left out in the cold but has been cold-shouldered out into the darkness of the night. Mr. X is the Everyman of the twentieth century. The mediaeval Everyman was warned by Death not to forget the life hereafter. The modern Everyman is brushed aside like an insubstantial shadow. His existence is at best no more than a dream of matter. To what conclusions can all this lead?

> The early creators of science did not assume that this real world was purposeless. Although God was no longer invoked as the final cause of phenomena, he was still given an important role as the initiator of the whole process. But, having made matter with its properties, he then left the world to develop according to the laws of mathematical necessity. In the course of time it came to be considered unnecessary to invoke God even for this purpose, and the way was clear for thorough going materialism. That this doctrine was made plausible by scientific researches is the greatest possible testimonial to the 'humanistic' importance of science. We have seen what the mediaeval outlook was in essentials. The essentials of the materialistic outlook may be given in the words of Bertrand Russell.
>
> Sullivan, LIMITATIONS OF SCIENCE

> That man is the product of causes which had no prevision of the end they were achieving; that his origin, his growth, his hopes and fears, his loves and beliefs, are but the outcome of accidental collocations of atoms; that no fire, no heroism, no intensity of thought and feeling, can preserve an individual beyond the grave; that all the labourers of the ages, all the devotion, all the inspiration, all the noonday brightness of human genius, are destined to extinction in the vast death of the solar system, and that the whole temple of man's achievements must inevitably be buried beneath the debris of a universe in ruins — all these things, if not quite beyond dispute, are yet so nearly certain, that no philosophy which rejects them can hope to stand.
>
> Bertrand Russell, MYSTICISM AND LOGIC

Taken historically, these words, quoted from Bertrand Russell's MYSTICISM AND LOGIC, acquire monumental significance because they mark the total divorce between the world within and the world without; and they attribute abiding reality only to the latter with its bareness and barrenness. In THE SCIENTIFIC OUTLOOK, Russell is bitterly against religion. He rails against the mystic tendencies which appear to him to be infiltrating into the scientific outlook. To him the tendency towards this is not the early dawn, possibly of a new faith, but a decline of faith in the scientific method, a form of defeatism — and in part he may be right. Yet the picture he himself gives of a world organized on scientific principles is devastating in its unlimited futility. Despite this, he can still speak of human values, of love, and beauty, without which science must drive mankind to utter inhumanity. In turning towards these, he plays rebel to himself; for love, beauty, and the values of life are indefinables, entering human consciousness from subjective sources, strangers to his scientific world. Bertrand Russell pinned his faith on Pavlov's experiments on the salivary flow of dogs and conditioned reflexes. He also accepted the Freudian theory of repression. He would not admit that a philosophy based on such evidence is incompatible with one that upholds love, beauty, and human values as indispensable realities. With a jealous regard for the inconsistencies of others, he seemed to ignore his own inconsistency in appraising the inhuman while deploring the resulting inhumanity. This dichotomy in his own nature points to the tragic state of dichotomy of the whole age.

In so far as science enters our lives we all become part of that dichotomy. Eddington opens The Nature of the Physical World with two descriptions of the same table, the one of a solid structure as this appears to the robust life of the senses, the other in what is now the familiar picture of innumerable jouncing and bounding, infinitely minute particles whose total volume is only the tiniest fraction of the otherwise empty space they occupy. The former picture is to be taken as hypothetical and illusionary, the latter as real. A summation of the stage we have reached since the time of Galileo follows:

> This astonishing change in outlook has been brought about by assuming that, of all the elements of our total experience, only those elements which acquaint us with the quantitative aspects of material phenomena are concerned with the real world. They alone refer to an objective world. None of the other elements of our experience, our perception of colour, etc., our response to beauty, our sense of mystic communion with God, have objective counterparts. All these things, which are ultimately products of the motions of little particles, are illusory in the sense that they do not acquaint us with the nature of objective reality.
>
> Eddington, The Nature of the Physical World

What then is the nature of the knowledge on which our scientific age builds?

> Concerning this knowledge, Eddington had a phrase . . . which is highly suggestive. In the acquisition of such knowledge, he suggests, it is as

though we had used only a single sense of sight which is 'colourless and non-stereoscopic.' What this means in the words of Ernst Lehrs (In his book Man or Matter), is that the physicists have exercised the faculty of quantitative abstraction to the point of looking at the world as though they had only one eye (nonsteroscopic) and as if this single eye were colour-blind. They have constructed a kind of imaginary world composed of the abstract shadows of what is ordinarily regarded as real — the world of molecules and atoms, which are mostly empty space; the electrons, which as a basis for physical matter, are hypothetical and physically non-existent. Man is thus led into an infinite and alien emptiness which chills his imagination and defies his experience. This emptiness contains nothing that he knows, nothing with which as a man, he is familiar — no colour, no sound, no smell, no feeling, and no beauty. Its ultimate criteria are statistical, amoral, and purposeless. Not only is it unlike anything he experiences in a sensory way, it is unlike anything he desires or aspires to. There exist in the vast interstices of this world of abstraction not a single spark of love, or mercy, or awe, or magnanimity, or hope. The works of the artist are as much out of place in it as the judgements of the moralist. And the revelations of the religious prophet echo and re-echo through its interminable equations, and vanish into nothing.

And, indeed, once man had embarked upon a quantitative spirit of inquiry, this denouement could not be avoided. The greatest realities of the quantitative world were only the bloodless phenomena of matter, which could be dealt with mathematically. Each of these realities became increasingly abstract with the advance of science, until they have passed beyond the limits not only of human experience, but of imagination itself. . . . Matter is now judged to be composed of entities, the nature of which no one can define, except to say that they are not material in any sense that the ordinary human being can recognize.

This is the kind of world that results from the vision of a single, colour-blind eye.

Davenport, DIGNITY OF MAN

H. G. Wells was a scientist by training. As an author he could escape into a world of phantasy of his own, in WHEN THE SLEEPER AWAKES, for example, where the divided nature of man finds expression in two distinctly contrasting types of human progeny for the distant future, reminiscent of the contrasting figures of Ariel and Caliban in Shakespeare's TEMPEST, without a Prospero to hold the balance. Wells could also conjure up the scene of a spiritual seance in which one of those present grows convinced that he is a reincarnation of Akhnaton, returned with a mission to save mankind. We see him

standing on the steps of St Paul's Cathedral calling to the multitude
below him — until a kindly policeman removes him to a place of
safety, an asylum. Such visions found a scope in his life of imagination but his sense of realism took another shape. His brief history of
the world is thoroughly materialistic in conception from end to end;
maybe that accounts for the deep pessimism that filled his later
years. This comes to expression in a small booklet written at the age
of seventy-nine, shortly before his death, entitled MIND AT THE END
OF ITS TETHER. It reads like his parting testament.

> The end of everything we call life is close at hand and cannot be evad-
> ed. Our universe is not merely bankrupt; there remains no dividend at
> all; it has simply liquidated; it is going clean out of existence leaving
> not a wrack behind. The attempt to trace a pattern of any sort is
> absolutely futile.
>
> A series of events have forced upon the intelligent observer the realiza-
> tion that the human story has already come to an end, and that Homo
> Sapiens, as he has been pleased to call himself, is in his present form,
> played out. The stars in their courses have turned against him and he
> has to give place to some other animal better adapted to face the fate that
> closes in more and more swiftly upon mankind. There is no way out for
> man but steeply up or steeply down. Adapt or perish now as ever is
> Nature's inexorable imperative.
>
> The rotation of the earth and its annual circulation in its orbit is slow-
> ing down.
>
> The writer sees the world as a jaded world devoid of recuperative power.
> Ordinary man is at the end of his tether. Only a small highly adaptable
> minority of the species can possibly survive.
>
> H. G. Wells, MIND AT THE END OF ITS TETHER

The question arises whether it is 'mind' that is at the end of its
tether or only the type of mind that chooses to be ruled by the logic
of materialism. What may well add to the pessimism of Wells is the
thought that the world of mathematical abstraction has released
powers capable of totally annihilating the world of the familiar
real. It is no longer a case of awaiting a natural end such as Wells
presupposes, but of confronting an immanent threat of present disaster. It is here that the challenge meets man just because he has a
mind which thinks.

What is mind? What reliance can one place on mind? What has the mind to offer?

> *Thought is one of the indisputable facts of the world. I know what I think with a certainty which I cannot attribute to any of my physical knowledge of the world.*
>
> Eddington, THE NATURE OF THE PHYSICAL WORLD

Eddington goes on to reflect, however, that the brain with which he thinks consist of atoms, electrons and all the other inscrutables with which physics deals by its pointer-reading method. Reality remains an 'unknown background' to this. However, since he thinks with the brain and the brain itself is produced out of this 'unknown background' of existence, he is led to the question: *Why not accept that this background has a nature capable of manifesting itself as mental activity?* The conclusion he is brought to is that *stuff of the world is mind-stuff.* But such a conclusion is too facile to carry conviction. He feels obliged to add:

> *By 'mind' I do not exactly mean mind and by 'stuff' I do not at all mean stuff. The mind-stuff of the world is of course something more general than our individual conscious mind.*

The nineteenth century came to regard mind as a derivative of matter. In Eddington's statement there is a tendency towards mentalism, that is placing mind or some form of consciousness anterior to matter, but there the enquiry seems to end. The mind, however, refuses to lie dormant but is forever seeking some new form of expression or interpretation.

Sir James Jeans, in his PHYSICS AND PHILOSOPHY, takes a bold step forward.

> *The physical theory of relativity has now shown that electric and magnetic forces are not real at all; they are mere mental constructs of our own, resulting from our rather misguided effort to understand the motion of particles. It is the same with the Newtonian force of gravitation, and with energy, momentum, and other concepts which are introduced to help us understand the activities of the world — all prove to be mere mental constructs, and do not even pass the test of objectivity. If the materialists are pressed to say how much of the world they now claim as material, their only possible answer would seem to be 'matter itself.' Thus their whole philosophy is reduced to a tautology, for obviously matter must be material. But the fact that so much of what was*

thought to possess an objective material existence now proves to consist of <u>subjective mental constructs</u> must surely be counted a pronounced step in the direction of mentalism.

The classical physics seemed to bolt and bar the door leading to any sort of freedom of the will, the new physics hardly does this it almost seems to suggest that the door may be unlocked — if only we could find the handle. The old physics showed us a universe which looked more like a prison than a dwelling-place. The new physics shows us a universe which looks as though it might conceivably form a suitable dwelling-place for free men, and not a mere shelter for brutes — a home in which it may at least be possible for us to mould events to our desires and live lives of endeavour and achievement.

He will not admit this is a final conclusion —

The plain fact is that there are no conclusions. If we must state a conclusion, it would be that many of the former conclusions of the nineteenth century are once again in the melting pot.

Jeans, PHYSICS AND PHILOSOPHY

The circle has gone full round! Science, from the time of Galileo on, set out to achieve an objective view of the world. Now, after centuries of pursuing the principles they laid down, the same science declares that *so much of what used to be thought to possess an objective physical existence now proves to consist only of subjective mental constructs.* Physicist has answered physicist!

Jeans also explains that the old duality of mind and matter is reflected for the physicist in the new duality of waves and particles. To one mode of calculation matter resolves itself into particles but their appearance in the field of observation is 'unpredictable'; to another mode of calculation matter resolves itself into waves whose motions can be determined but they remain just waves! He says in the new duality there is no longer antagonism: waves and particles are complementary. The waves control the particles — the mental controls the material: another argument for mentalism. It is the law of indeterminacy, first pronounced by Heisenberg, that opens the way to a new freedom. The iron law that all is predictable has broken down. There is a loophole for escape from bound necessity — there is room for freedom after all. This offers a slender hope that the future may be different. Strange that it should come through physics, hitherto the most fast-bound science of all.

Sullivan recalls how Newton, in line with his predecessors,

> dispensed with final causes, and found the cause of a phenomena in the
> immediately preceding conditions. Also, he proceeded as though science
> formed a self-enclosed system, that is to say, as if a complete account of
> phenomena could be given in the terms mass, velocity, force, etc., which
> science had isolated, and without bringing in such concepts as beauty,
> purpose, etc., which do not form part of the scientific outlook. It is not pos-
> sible to say that Newton held these opinions dogmatically, since he him-
> self said that science, in the mathematical form it had assumed, was an
> adventure, which might have to be replaced by a truer method. But for
> practical working purposes he certainly made these assumptions, and his
> immense success caused these assumptions to be unquestioningly accept-
> ed by the whole scientific world. Newton also accepted the doctrine of the
> subjectivity of secondary qualities.
>
> . . . what is called the modern 'revolution' in science consists in the fact
> that the Newtonian outlook, (which dominated the scientific world for
> nearly two hundred years) has been found insufficient. It is in process
> of being replaced by a different outlook. . . .
>
> Sullivan, LIMITATIONS OF SCIENCE

Technically the change came about with the transition from Newton to Einstein, who abolishes all the previously held notions of
mass, gravity, and so on. Sullivan, however, is concerned with a
change which he foresees coming, touching the whole of life, a radical change of human outlook — nothing less than the reuniting of
inner and outer, of the qualitative and the quantitative, and the
overcoming of the split between mind and matter, between man
and his world.

It is the artist in Sullivan that comes to his aid. Having demonstrated the one-sidedness of modern science, its selective attitude
towards phenomena, its self-imposed limitations, he envisions a
science of the future which will take equal cognizance of <u>all</u> phenomena. He awaits a new awakening to bring art and religion, no
less than science, within the scope of objective truth. Thus he can
write with self assurance:

> Science has become self conscious and comparatively humble. We are no
> longer taught that the scientific mode of approach is the only valid
> method of acquiring knowledge of reality. Eminent men of science are
> insisting, with what seems a strange enthusiasm, on the fact that sci-
> ence gives us but a partial knowledge of reality, and we are no longer

required to regard as illusionary everything that science finds itself able to ignore. But the enthusiasm with which some men of science preach that science has limitations is not really surprising.

For the universe of science, if accepted as the final reality, made of man an entirely accidental by product of a huge, mindless, purposeless, mathematical machine. And there are men of science sufficiently human to find such a conclusion disconcerting. Even the sturdy Victorians who preached the doctrine betray at times a despairing wish that things were not so. We need not be surprised, therefore, to find that the discovery that science no longer compels us to believe in our essential futility is greeted with acclamation, even by some scientific men.

We are no longer required to believe that our response to beauty, or the mystic's sense of communion with God, have no objective counterpart. It is perfectly possible that they are, what they so often have been taken to be, clues to the nature of reality. Thus our various experiences are put on a more equal footing, as it were. Our religious aspirations, our perceptions of beauty, may not be the essentially illusionary phenomena they were supposed to be. In this 'new scientific universe' even mystics have a right to exist.

Somewhere Sullivan further declares that the scientist however admirable he may be, is nevertheless only half a man. Yet it is not by merely adding the other half, the qualitative to the quantitative, that we arrive at the whole. Rather we need to start from the whole and see how, where, and why diversity arises. Sullivan declares his awareness of this as a need and he is not alone. Consider also C. E. M. Joad:

There is a certain vague consciousness of the fact that materialism is losing ground, and that the closed circle of the mechanist universe of the Nineteenth Century has been broken: but there is no clear conception of what has come to take its place.

There is a general sense of new beginnings such as, I imagine, must have been felt at the time of the Renaissance. The Nineteenth Century view seems to have been that we were within reasonable distance of attaining a complete understanding of man and the universe. It is only now that we are coming to realise our comparative ignorance of both. Most of the knowledge previously obtained is seen to be misleading and, where the old methods have failed, there is a willingness to experiment with new ones. The Nineteenth Century regarded European Civilization as mature and late, the final expression of the human spirit; we are now beginning to realise that it is young and childish.

We have come, in fact, to a definite break in the tradition of our civilization. The Nineteenth Century was the end of an epoch; we, it is increasingly evident, are at the beginning of another. Not only is there scepticism as to the conclusions reached, but doubt as to the proper methods of reaching them. Hence, men are not only more willing to explore different avenues of possible understanding of the universe, art as well as science, religious ecstasy as well as common sense, but within the boundaries of science itself they are continually trying new experiments. As Sir William Bragg says, 'We use the classic theory on Monday, Wednesday, Friday, and the Quantum Theory on Tuesday, Thursday, Saturday.'

C.E.M. Joad, GUIDE TO MODERN THOUGHT

Assuming from the foregoing that science, in broad and in large, admits of the need for a new art of investigation, the question still remains how this is to proceed. How are we truly to integrate the *secondary qualities* so as to arrive at a totality of outlook? How is Mr. X to find his way in again — no longer left out in the cold? As for Sir William Bragg's interesting division of the days, it is not in a trivial mood that the question arises, *What, then of the Sunday?*

So we see that we are not wholly lost in matter, there are wakeful spirits standing on the threshold for a new departure, though the way is still obscure.

· 9 ·

Only a Cosmos

We have seen how Newton extended the terrestrial mechanics of Galileo to include the heavens. In his PRINCIPIA he wrote: *. . . from the same principles, I now demonstrate the frame of the system of the world*. So confident was he of his procedure that he could write: *I wish we could derive the rest of the phenomena of nature by the same reasoning from mechanical principles* and he continues:

> *for I am induced by many reasons to suspect that they all depend upon certain forces by which the particles of bodies, by causes hitherto unknown, are either mutually impelled towards each other and cohere in regular figures, or are repelled and recede from each other; which forces being unknown, philosophers have hitherto attempted the search of nature in vain.*

Newton conceived of the ultimate particle of matter as consisting of an inner core with a surrounding part: ordinary chemical change he attributed to the outer part, radical change or 'transmutation' to alterations in the nuclear core. He thus almost forestalled the later conception of the atom. His bent was to reduce all natural phenomena to 'calculables.' It is here his genius shone.

Combined with his predisposition for the mechanical, he maintained an unswerving belief in an all-ruling Deity. The harmony of the arrangement that all the planets moved in the same direction round the sun and that all satellites moved in the same direction around their respective planets was for him proof positive of a supernal divine mind — God in the beginning. Conversely, perceiving that there were certain recurring irregularities amongst the planets and, in particular, disturbances caused by the periodic intrusions of the comets, he feared lest the cumulative effects of these might wreck the system. But he reassured himself with the thought that God, whose handiwork all this was, would surely intervene to avert any such catastrophe. Leibnitz, no great friend of Newton, scornfully reacted to this notion of divine benevolence:

> Sir Isaac Newton and his followers have also a very odd opinion concerning the work of God. According to their doctrine, God Almighty wants to wind up his watch from time to time, otherwise it would cease to move. He had not, it seems, sufficient insight to make it a perpetual motion. Nay, the machine of God's making is so imperfect according to these gentlemen, that he is obliged to clean it now and then by an extraordinary concourse, and even to mend it as a clock-maker mends his work; who must consequently be so much the more unskillful a workman, as he is oftener obliged to mend his work, and set it right.

With Pierre Simon Laplace (1749–1827), described as the French Newton, God finally faded out of the universe. Laplace, like Newton, was also a youthful prodigy. At the age of twenty-two he promised the world *a complete solution of the great mechanical problem presented by the solar system*, and this he did to the full satisfaction of his own generation and for a long time after. Newton had been concerned with how the solar system worked, Laplace primarily with how it had come into being. This new paradigm is the famous Kant-Laplace nebular theory. (Kant, the philosopher, was likewise a notable mathematician and arrived at the same theory independently.)

> He [Laplace] *imagined that the sun had begun as a nebulous mass in a state of rotation. This gradually cooled, and as it cooled, it shrank. The Newtonian mechanics required it to rotate ever faster and faster. Laplace had shown that the orange-shaped flattening of the earth and planets resulted from their rotations — the faster a planet rotated, the flatter it would become. So he supposed that as the sun rotated ever faster, its shape became ever flatter, until it assumed a disc-like shape. Then it could flatten no further, but broke into pieces by shedding ring after ring of matter from its protruding equator. He supposed that these rings of matter finally condensed and formed the present planets. These, too would start as masses of hot rotating gas, and would go through the same series of changes as their parent sun before them; they too, would cool, shrink, flatten in shape, and finally throw off rings of matter which in time condensed, thus forming the satellites of the planets. It was now*

easy to see why the planets and satellites were all revolving and rotating
in the same direction; the direction was that in which the primeval mass
had rotated.

Jeans, PHYSICS AND PHILOSOPHY

This is Jeans' description of the theory. He then proceeds to give
two reasons why it had to fail. Firstly, had the planets been cast off
from a shrinking sun, our present sun ought to be rotating very
rapidly. In point of fact it is rotating very slowly; according to
Galileo, there was one rotation in the course of a month; more
recent figures indicate once in twenty-five days.

Secondly, according to the properties of matter as known today . . .

Laplace's mass of hot gas would cool and shrink so slowly that it would
throw off matter only in driblets. Calculation shows that the masses
thrown off in this way would merely scatter though space, and so could
not condense into planets.

Quite apart from these two points, this theory offers no explanation of what caused the original rotation.

Sir James Jeans himself propounded a famous hypothesis known
as the 'tidal theory.' He considered that while a nebular theory
might account for an entire galaxy such as our Milky Way, it was
mathematically inconceivable that it could apply to something so
small as a solar system. He concluded that since the planets could
not have been thrown off from the sun perhaps they were sucked
away or torn from it by the gravitational pull of another star passing unusually close to it.

Arthur Eddington in his book, THE EXPANDING UNIVERSE, gives a
modern astronomical scale for measuring the heavens — what he
calls a *celestial multiplication table.*

We start with a star as the unit most familiar to us, a globe comparable
to the sun. Then . . .

A hundred thousand million stars make one Galaxy;
A hundred thousand million Galaxies make one universe.

These figures may not be very trustworthy, but I think that they give a
correct impression.

But then Eddington, with his characteristic sense of consequence,
warns us:

It is better to admit frankly that theory has, and is entitled to have, an important share in determining belief. For the reader resolved to eschew theory and admit only definite observational facts, <u>all</u> astronomical books are banned.

<u>*There are no purely observational facts about the heavenly bodies.*</u> *Astronomical measurements are, without exception, measurements of phenomena occurring in a terrestrial observatory or station; it is only by theory that they are translated into knowledge of a universe outside.*

How then do we actually read the heavens? Eddington concludes with an unexpected parable.

A slight reddening of the light of distant galaxies, an adventure of the mathematical imagination in spherical space, reflection on the underlying principles implied in all measurements, nature's curious choice of certain numbers such as 137 in her scheme — these and many other scraps have come together and formed a vision. As when the voyager sights a distant shore, we strain our eyes to catch the vision. Later we may more fully resolve the meaning. It changes in the mist; sometimes it is rather a vista leading on and on till we wonder whether aught can be final.

Once more I have recourse to Bottom the Weaver . . .

'I have had a most rare vision. I have had a dream past the wit of man to say what dream it was: man is but an ass, if he go about to expound this dream. . . . Methought I was, — and methought I had, — but man is but a patched fool if he will offer to say what methought I had. . . . It shall be called Bottom's Dream, because it hath no bottom.'

Shakespeare's Bottom was transformed into Faery. There, with an ass's head clapped onto his shoulder, he was wooed and loved by fair Titania. Later, restored to his common lot with the other mechanicals, the sweetness of his past vision and his present confusion assail him together. Modern speculation also has its enchantments, but into what world does it translate us? What queen of pleasures greets us there? And when we awaken, if we awaken, what sweet delirium of the past soothes us in our present dilemma between fact and theory?

Surveying the universe presented by modern astronomy, we see that the vast majority of the bodies in it seem to exist without any reference to the seeds of life and consciousness. The vast extent of the universe, both in space and time, is, from the human point of view, aimless. These immense lumps of matter, in their millions of millions, incessantly pouring out an inconceivably furious energy for millions and millions of years, seem to be completely pointless. For a fleeting moment man has been permitted to stare at this gigantic and meaningless display. Long before the process comes to an end, man will have vanished from the scene and the rest of the performance will take place in the unthinkable night of the absence of all consciousness. This revelation is startling. It is still more startling, almost incredible, when we reflect that this amazing panorama sprang suddenly into existence a finite time ago. It emerged, full-armed, as it were, out of nothing, apparently for the sole purpose of blazing its way to an eternal death. This is the scientific account. It seems to be true as far as it goes, but we can not believe that it is the whole truth. We prefer to believe that the present scientific method has its limitations.

Sullivan, LIMITATIONS OF SCIENCE

Sullivan turns ever and again to that side of nature which cannot be taken hold of by formulae and equations, which is there, immensely real, but which remains incalculable.

It is suspected that many of the difficulties and puzzles we meet with in science today are due simply to the way we think about things. It is very possible that some of the questions we are putting to nature are meaningless. It is this fact that makes the present stage of science so peculiarly interesting. We are living, not merely in an epoch of fresh discoveries, but at the birth of a new world outlook.

What that 'new world outlook' is to be he does not say except that it will be arrived at only when art and religion can find their legitimate entry into science, to make for a wholly human outlook. This he puts forward, not merely as an article of faith but because these other faculties, born of reverence for life and a sense for beauty, are alive in him even as is the disciplined mind of the mathematician-scientist. It is with all three that he contemplates nature and the world in all its variety of expression.

We now move to an article which appeared in the Feb. 12, 1961 SUNDAY OBSERVER written by science correspondent, John Davy. First he refers to the progress in cosmic measurement:

... our scale of cosmic distance has stretched vertiginously. By the turn of the century, the nearest star was known to be four 'light years' away, or 2,352,000 million miles By 1930, it was agreed that the diameter of our galaxy is about 100,000 light years while a neighbouring galaxy in Andromeda is nearly one million light years away. By 1936 the American, Edwin Hubble, was speaking of galaxies 500 million light years away, but in 1952 Walter Reade re-interpreted the observation

and blithely multiplied the size of Hubble's universe by two. Subsequent corrections have again tripled this, and distances of several thousand million light years are now commonplace.

The idea of light speeding thorough space at 186,300 miles in every second since the world began is not really comprehensible, and the scales of measurement in millions of light years become mere number tokens for vaster incomprehensibles. They are totally remote from any significance touching the immediate life of man.

Davy then brings forward an alternative to so-called 'steady state' theories.

> *But the most startling discovery has been that all these distant galaxies appear to be hurtling away from us — and the farther away they are, the faster they hurtle. This is the starting point for all modern conclusions.*

It is this most startling discovery which led to the 'big bang' theory.

> *. . . if the galaxies are getting further apart, they must originally have been closer together. By measuring the speed of expansion and reversing it, one can calculate a time in the past when all the galaxies were packed close together.*
>
> *At this time, it was supposed, the universe may have consisted of a 'primeval atom' of incredibly concentrated energy. This 'atom' then blew apart, and the universe has been expanding like a bomb ever since. In the future, it may simply disperse and run down like a clock — or it might start to contract into another primeval atom.*

Since the light which is reaching us now from the most distant galaxies must have left them *thousands of millions of years ago*, it follows that we are not seeing them as they are now but as they once were.

> *If the big bang theory is right, the most distant galaxies we see should be close together . . . since we are seeing them as they were nearer to the time of the bang. But if the 'steady state' theory is right, the distant galaxies should be distributed in the same way as the near ones.*

The 200-inch telescope at Mount Palomar could only begin to *probe the regions where there should be a detectable difference between an evolving and a steady state universe.* 'Evolving' here means speeding away from the effects of the big bang. The more recent use of radio telescopes confirms the big bang theory and reveals a considerable number of 'radio stars' that suggest that the 'hurtling away' is at accelerating speeds — speeds exceeding the speed of light!

All the incredible labours of controlled observational methods with ever more perfected instruments, and the equally incredible calculations based on the most advanced mathematical reasoning aided by computers, lead to the alternatives of either an exploded primeval atom or a steady state of spontaneous creation of hydrogen out of non-space into space. Both bring us to a kind of end for either way, the universe we contemplate is no more than a mathematical-mechanical construction of the mind.

The concept of non-space also meets us in another connection. The modern view of the atom is of a nuclear core, a proton, with one or more electrons circling around it at the speed of light. The electrons move in concentric rings, so many negatively charged electrons around a positively charged proton. The transmission of an electron from one such ring or orbit to another should bring about a change of composition and therefore of substance. It has been determined, however, that there can be no such transposition of an electron from one orbit to another across the intervening space. The electron would have to vanish from space in order to reappear in space in its new position. We have the remarkable circumstance that the speed of light is our basic unit of measurement both for the infinitely great, the cosmos at large, and equally for the infinitely small, the electron. And at both extremes we meet with the phenomenon of non-space, except that, with the electron there is a vanishing into non-space as well as a reappearance out of it.

It should be noted that in measuring space in terms of light years, space and time have been amalgamated to the point of being indistinguishable; also that in all this range of reasoning, we remain strictly bound to the quantitative as the decisive element. Mr. X is even more lonely and out of place in this most recently conjectured picture of the world.

Here we have reached the present day limits to calculation as regards the universe we look out on daily as an extension of the original Newtonian outlook. The next step is to depart from Newtonian to Einsteinian, from mechanical to quantum physics, and to a total shift of view regarding the primary factors of mass, space, motion, and time on which Galileo and Newton built their theories.

· 10 ·

The Consequences of Liberating Science

Up to the beginning of the present century, physical science sought for an explanation of the universe in mechanical terms.

Sullivan, LIMITATIONS OF SCIENCE

In 1905, with the publication of Einstein's first paper on relativity, *the mechanical explanation of the universe was definitely abandoned.*

In the scientific world a new era had dawned. In the world at large this was hardly noticed for Newtonian physics continued to reign as securely as ever.

The two schemes of Einstein and Newton are poles asunder in their physical interpretations, but it would be a mistake to think of the Newtonian scheme as nothing but an accumulation of error. The quantitative error in Newton's law of gravitation is so small that nearly two hundred years elapsed before any error was discovered, or even suspected. Indeed, the difference between the laws of Newton and Einstein depend on the square of the small ratio, v/c, where v is the speed of the moving planet and c is the speed on light. Even for the fastest moving planet, Mercury, this square is only .00000003; throughout the whole solar system the two theories differ quantitatively only by this minute fraction or less. And when we come down from the heavens to the earth, we find a science of everyday life which is entirely Newtonian; the engineer who is building a bridge or a ship or a locomotive does precisely what he would have done if Einstein's challenge to Newton had never appeared and so does the computer who is preparing the Nautical

Almanac, and the astronomer who is discussing the general motion of
the planets

Jeans, Physics and Philosophy

Einstein deals with the outermost limits of the material world, with the vast compass of the rolling universe on the one hand and the infinitesimal states of matter on the other. From these remote boundaries of knowledge Einstein views the Newtonian world picture as a limited aspect of his own. In Einstein's universe man and his world are totally uncentred, and out of the atom have emerged the greatest destructive forces the earth has known. Thus, psychologically and factually, the later physics has come powerfully to rule our lives.

In 1927, the bicentenary of Newton's death, Einstein wrote:

> *It is just two hundred years ago that Newton closed his eyes. We feel impelled at such a moment to remember this brilliant genius who determined the course of Western thought, research, and practice like no one else before or since. . . . The figure of Newton has, however, an even greater importance than his genius warrants because destiny placed him at a turning point in the history of the human intellect. . . . Actual results of a kind to support the belief in the existence of a complete chain of physical causation hardly existed before Newton.*

We have seen that Newton, though a deeply religious man, was not prevented by his religion from regarding all observable effects in nature as springing from purely physical and material causes. When his God finally disappeared out of science it left his system quite impaired. Einstein too, by his own confession, was not without religion though averse to doctrine. His system of non-mechanical physics subscribes equally to *the belief in the existence of a complete chain of physical causation.* In this respect there is nothing to choose between them. Both Einstein and Newton esteemed moral experience as the highest attribute of human nature, yet morality lay quite outside their system, which remained exclusively materialistic. Moral idealism and so-called scientific realism remained as separate in Einstein as in Newton. In any question of overcoming materialism, Einstein's materialism being more subtle, is the more challenging. Further on in his essay on Newton, Einstein wrote:

It is the combination,
Law of Motion plus Law of Attraction
which constitutes the marvelous edifice of thought which makes it pos-
sible to calculate the past and the future states of a system from the state
obtaining at one particular moment, in so far as the events take place
under the influence of the forces of gravity alone.

Strange that it is just this 'marvelous edifice' that Einstein demol-
ished; his Special Theory disposed of Newton's Law of Motion and
his General Theory superseded Newton's Law of Attraction. It is just
this which represents Einstein's advance over Newton.

The idealism of Einstein finds expression in the following answers
to questions of a Japanese scholar:

I. It is difficult to attach a precise meaning to the term 'scientific truth.'
Thus the meaning of the word 'truth' varies according to whether we
deal with a fact of experience, a mathematical proposition or a scientific
theory. 'Religious truth' conveys nothing clear to me at all.

II. Scientific research can reduce superstition by encouraging people to
think of things in terms of cause and effect. Certain it is that a convic-
tion, akin to religious feeling, of the rationality or intelligibility of the
world lies behind all scientific work of a higher order.

III. This firm belief, a belief bound up with deep feeling, in a superior
mind that reveals itself in the world of experience, represents my con-
ception of God. In common parlance this may be described as 'pantheis-
tic'(Spinoza).

IV. Denominational traditions I can only consider historically and psy-
chologically; they have no other significance for me.

Albert Einstein, ON SCIENTIFIC TRUTH (1929)

And further . . .

The ideals which have lighted my way, and time after time given me
courage to face life cheerfully, have been Kindness, Beauty, and Truth.
Without the sense of kinship with men of like mind, without the occu-
pation with the objective world, the eternally unattainable in the field of
art and scientific endeavours, life would have seemed to me empty. The
trite objects of human efforts . . . possessions, outward success, luxury
. . . have always seemed to me contemptible.

Let every man be respected as an individual and no man idealized. It is an
irony of fate that I myself have been the recipient of excessive admiration
and reverence from my fellow beings, through no fault, and no merit of

my own. The cause of this may well be the desire, unattainable by many, to understand the few ideas to which I have with my feeble powers attained through ceaseless struggle.

How vile and despicable seems war to me! I would rather be hacked in pieces than take part in such an abominable business.

The most beautiful experience we can have is the mysterious. It is the fundamental emotion which stands at the cradle of true art and true science. Whoever does not know it and can no longer wonder, no longer marvel, is as good as dead and his eyes are dimmed. It was the experience of mystery — even if mixed with fear — that engendered religion. A knowledge of the existence of something we cannot penetrate, our perceptions of the profoundest reason and the most radiant beauty, which only in their primitive forms are accessible to our minds — it is this knowledge and this emotion that constitutes true religiosity; in this sense, and in this alone, I am a deeply religious man.

Einstein, THE WORLD AS I SEE IT (1931)

What is the meaning of human life, or, for that matter, of the life of any creature? To know an answer to this question means to be religious. You ask: Does it make any sense, then to pose the question? I answer: The man who regards his own life and that of his fellow creatures as meaningless is not merely unhappy but hardly fit for life.

The true value of a human being is determined primarily by the measure and the sense in which he has attained liberation from the self.

. . . . the scientist is possessed by a sense of universal causation. The future, to him, is every whit as necessary and determined as the past. There is nothing divine about mortality; it is a purely human affair. His religious feeling takes the form of a rapturous amazement at the harmony of natural law, which reveals an intelligence of such superiority that, compared with it, all the systematic thinking and acting of human beings is an utterly insignificant reflection. This feeling is the guiding principle of his life and work, in so far as he succeeds in keeping himself from the shackles of selfish desire. It is beyond question closely akin to that which has possessed the religious geniuses of all ages.

Einstein, MEIN WELTBILD (1934)

. . . science can only ascertain what is, but not what should be, and outside of its domain value judgments of all kinds remain necessary. Religion, on the other hand, deals only with evaluations of human thought and action; it cannot justifiably speak of facts and relationships between facts.

. . . science can only be created by those who are thoroughly imbued with the aspiration towards truth and understanding. This source of feeling, however, springs from the sphere of religion.

. . . Science without religion is lame, religion without science is blind.
Einstein, SCIENCE, PHILOSOPHY, AND RELIGION (1941)

It is not enough to teach a man a specialty. Through it he may become a kind of useful machine but not a harmoniously developed personality. It is essential that the student acquire an understanding of and a lively feeling for values. He must acquire a vivid sense of the beautiful and the morally good. Otherwise, he — with his specialized knowledge — more closely resembles a well trained dog than a harmoniously developed person. He must learn to understand the motives of human beings, their illusions, and their sufferings in order to acquire a proper relationship to individual fellow-men and to the community.

These precious things are conveyed to the younger generation through personal contact with those who teach, not — or at least in the main — through textbooks.
Einstein, EDUCATION FOR INDEPENDENT THINKERS (1952)

The foregoing passages reveal Einstein as a man of high moral responsibility for his thoughts and actions, with a deep concern for his fellow human beings. It is important to take note of this in view of the heavy destiny that lay upon him. Science he regarded as the attempt to understand by rational means what pertained to natural law in the world accessible to the senses. Religion concerned the strivings for human beings of *super-personal values*; such strivings, free from personal motives, should belong to the character of true scientists. In addition to devotion for truth in the scientific sense, and to superpersonal values in the religious sense free from all dogmas, art and beauty were for him a continuous source of enrichment and ennoblement.

There is a revealing anecdote about Einstein's early childhood. When he was about five years old, his father gave him a magnetic compass. He was not merely fascinated by it as any child might be, but was overcome by a sense of awesome wonder at this mysterious working, even trembled and felt cold. He is said to have recalled this later as his first meeting with the electromagnetic field which was to occupy and determine this life's work. Could he, at that early age, have had a premonition of a fearful moment in which he would have every reason to tremble and feel cold? In his essay on Newton, quoted earlier, he adds that it was the failure to explain along Newtonian principles, the 'dynamic interaction' within the 'electromagnetic field' which led to a *gradual shift in our fundamental notions.*

The new physics, which has affected human life so powerfully, is based fundamentally on a changed conception of the nature of matter.

> *All of these things being considered, it seems probable to me that God in the Beginning formed matter in solid, massy, hard, imponderable, moveable Particles of such Sizes and Figures, and with such other Properties and in such Proportion to Space as most conduced to the End for which he formed them; and that these primitive Particles being Solids, are incomparably harder than any porous Bodies composed of them; even so very hard, as never to wear or to break in Pieces; no ordinary Power being able to divide what God Himself made one in the first Creation.*
>
> Isaac Newton, OPTICS

It was John Dalton (1766–1844) who first established the theory for modern times, namely, that all matter consisted ultimately of indivisible particles or atoms. He distinguished between elementary and compound substances and attributed to each elementary substance its particular type of atom. It became the object of research to explore the nature of these ultimate particles. This led to the systematic classification of the elements according to their 'atomic weights,' hydrogen, the lightest element known, being given the atomic weight of one. The atomic weights were expressed as ratio figures in relation to hydrogen as 1.

> *This analysis of matter into atoms was considered to be ultimate, although it was certainly felt as vaguely disturbing that there should be ninety-two different kinds of atoms. It was even surmised that atoms had not, perhaps, the simple structure they were supposed to have, for certain groups of elements were found to have marked affinities with certain other groups, suggesting that their atoms were constructed on very much the same plan.*
>
> Sullivan, LIMITATIONS OF SCIENCE

The idea of the solid particle vanished with the investigation of the electrical structure of matter.

. . . the modern era may be said to have begun about the year 1895. Between that year and the year 1900 those researches were begun which have changed our whole conception of the meaning and purpose of physical science. So great a revolution in scientific thought has not occurred since Copernicus showed that the earth went round the sun.
                                    Sullivan, LIMITATIONS OF SCIENCE

Are we led by a light which leaves us in the dark?

The great difference between the 'mechanical physics' of Newton and the 'non-mechanical' physics at which we have arrived ultimately, with Einstein, is that the former remained in the field of naively perceived phenomena and the world still had a solid feel about it. On the other hand, the new physics engages us in a world which is truly hidden or occult. This new though hidden world, conceived as an interrelated field of mutually active elements, has more the character of an organism: it can evince untold power yet in fact it is remote, dead, and dangerous. Man has come into possession of it but morality has no part in it —— that is where the greatest danger lies.

Newton had the work of Copernicus and Galileo behind him. Einstein enters upon the scene when the very substance that constitutes this world, the nature of matter, is in question.

To the question, 'What is the ultimate substance of the Universe?' which had puzzled science form the time of Thales on, it at last appeared possible to give the answer — the one word 'electricity.'
                          Jeans, PHYSICS AND PHILOSOPHY (1947)

How subtle this whole question has become and how far reaching in consequence is brought clearly to the fore by Einstein's famous laws of the Equivalence of Mass and Energy. He himself set out a popular explanation of this law in a 1946 article for SCIENCE ILLUSTRATED.

The science of mechanics distinguishes between potential and kinetic energy, the simplest example being that of the pendulum. Imagine the bob of a pendulum swinging to and fro. At the highest point on either side it is momentarily at rest. At its lowest point it has acquired its maximum motion. The distance through which it falls, and therefore its maximum motion, is determined by the length of string to which it is attached, for, like any other falling body, its speed accelerates during its fall. In the same measure, the bob will decelerate during its ascent.

In its moment of rest it possesses its greatest potential energy. This is determined by three factors, the mass of the bob, the height through which it may fall, and the force of gravity which causes it to fall.

The most finely constructed pendulum, however, even if suspended in a vacuum, must eventually come to rest due to an inevitable amount of friction, however small, at the point of suspension. This friction gradually robs the system of its available energy. What then happens to this energy? Friction always engenders heat. The energy is translated into a corresponding quantity of heat.

> *The physicists were for long unable to account for this kind of heat 'production.' Their difficulties were overcome only when it was successfully established that, for any given amount of heat produced by friction, an exactly proportional amount of energy had to be expended. Thus did we arrive at a principle of the 'equivalence of work and heat.' With the pendulum, for example, mechanical energy is gradually converted into heat.*

This led to the concept of <u>Conservation of Energy</u>. Later, in addition to mechanical energy, were added chemical energy, magnetic energy and electrical energy.

> *It appeared that in our physical system there was a sum total of energies that remained constant through all changes that might occur.*

Einstein, in his article, next turns to a consideration of <u>mass</u>. He draws attention to a fact which plays directly into his General Theory of Relativity. Physics speaks of <u>inert mass</u> and <u>heavy mass</u>. <u>Inert mass</u> is defined by *the resistance that a body opposes to its acceleration, and* heavy mass *is measured by its weight.*

> *That these two radically different definitions lead to the same value for the mass of a body is, in itself, an astonishing fact.*

For the moment, however, he is concerned only with the concept held by earlier physicists of <u>Conservation of Mass</u>.

> *. . . the mass seemed to be the essential (because unvarying) quality of matter. Heating, melting, vaporization, or combining into chemical compounds, would not change the total mass.*

This principle of <u>Conservation of Mass</u>, Einstein adds,

> *proved inadequate in the face of the special theory of relativity. It was therefore merged with the energy principle — just as, about sixty years before, the principle of the conservation of mechanical energy had been combined with the principle of the conservation of heat. We might say that the principle of the conservation of energy, having previously swallowed up that of the conservation of heat, now proceeded to swallow up that of the conservation of mass . . . and holds the field alone.*

This equivalence between mass and energy he expressed in a formula: $E=mc^2$. In this formula, m represents mass and c the constant speed of light. The term E , Einstein defines as *the energy that is contained in a stationary body of mass m.*

In other words,

> *The energy that belongs to the mass $\underline{m}$ is equal to this mass, multiplied by the square of the enormous speed of light, which is to say, a vast amount of energy for every unit of mass.*

Since the value of c is constant in the above formula the values of mass, m, and the energy, E, are directly equated. It may further be seen that the slightest increase or decrease in the value of m must involve an enormous change in the value of E. This becomes more graphic when, taking the speed of light, c, at 186,000 miles per sec., we realise that the square of this is 34,596,000,000.

> *For a mass increase to be measurable, the change of energy per mass unit must be enormously large. We know of only one sphere in which such amounts of energy per mass unit are released: namely, the radioactive disintegration*

We can now begin to see how Einstein's equation relates to the release of energy in atomic fission.

> *An atom of the mass $\underline{M}$ splits into two atoms of mass $\underline{M'}$ and $\underline{M''}$, which separate with tremendous kinetic energy. If we imagine these two masses as brought to rest — that is, if we take this energy of motion from them — then, considered together, they are essentially poorer in energy than was the original atom. According to the equivalence principle, the mass sum $\underline{M'} + \underline{M''}$ of the disintegrating products must also be somewhat smaller than the original $\underline{M}$ of the disintegrating atom — in contradiction to the old principle of the conservation of mass. The relative difference of the two is in the order of one-tenth of one percent.*

Now we cannot actually weigh the atoms individually. However, there are indirect methods for measuring their weights exactly. We can likewise determine the kinetic energies that are transferred to the disintegration products M' and M". Thus, it has become possible to test and confirm the equivalence formula. Also, the law permits us to calculate in advance, from precisely determined atomic weights, just how much energy will be released with any atomic disintegration we have in mind. The law says nothing, of course — as to whether or how — the disintegration reaction can be brought about.

Whilst it is true that the law, in itself, did not give the method for effecting atomic disintegration, it provided clues for future experimenters in this field.

Einstein in his article goes on to explain why, if there was so much energy in even a gram of matter, it was not observed earlier.

The answer is quite simple: so long as none of the energy is given off externally, it cannot be observed. It is as though a man who is fabulously rich should never spend or give away a cent; no one could tell how rich he was.

This miser divides his fortune between his two sons, M' and M", on the strict condition that a small amount, less than one-thousandth of the whole estate (energy or mass) must go to the community. Einstein concludes very pointedly:

But the part given to the community, though relatively small, is still so enormously large (considered as kinetic energy) that it brings with it a great threat of peril. Averting that threat has become the most urgent problem of our time.

Now consider how bombardment with neutrons can set up an almost instantaneous chain reaction of disintegrating atoms with a corresponding avalanche of enormous energy release, and you can grasp the enormity of the problem — a problem which, by its very nature, becomes in the highest degree, a moral one. This was the path towards the most devastating single event in documented history.

In 1938 Hahn and Strassman in Germany discovered *the phenomenon of uranium fission.* The thought that Nazi Germany might be the first in the field with atomic weaponry was unacceptable; and therefore American scientists, some who were refugees from Germany, did their utmost to urge their governmental authorities to promote similar research without delay. In the end they sent their leader, Szillard, to see Einstein, the father of the Law of Equivalence of Mass and Energy, in the hope that he might be able to influence President Roosevelt to take action. This led to the famous letter which Einstein sent to the President just one month before the Second World War began. He wrote:

> Some recent work by E. Fermi and Szillard . . . leads me to expect that the element uranium may be turned into a new and important source of energy in the near future. Certain aspects of the situation which has arisen seem to call for watchfulness and if necessary, quick action on the part of the administration.

But then he added what the effect of an atom bomb might be. If introduced into a port and exploded, it *might well destroy the whole port, together with the surrounding territory.*

The necessary research was quickly begun with the result that America, not Germany, was the first to acquire the atom bomb. No scientist, least of all Einstein, believed that the bomb would ever be used as more than a deterrent to Hitler. They were horrified when it was eventually used against the Japanese. It had a shattering effect, not only physically but morally.

Einstein, engaged in the disinterested pursuit of scientific knowledge, had led the way into the fearsome depths of matter, providing man with a power equaled only by the apprehension which now possesses him.

> Through the release of atomic energy, our generation has brought into the world the most revolutionary force since prehistoric man's discovery of fire.

> Today, everything that has been acquired with such effort seems a razor in the hands of a child of three.

In 1945 he opened an address at a Nobel Peace Prize celebration dinner with the following words:

> Physicists find themselves in a position not unlike that of Alfred Nobel. Alfred Nobel invented the most powerful explosive ever known up to his time, a means of destruction par excellence. In order to atone for this, in order to relieve his human conscience, he instituted his awards for the promotion of peace and for achievements of peace. Today, the physicists who participated in forging the most formidable and dangerous weapon of all times are harassed by an equal feeling of responsibility not to say

guilt. And we cannot desist from warning, and warning again, we cannot and should not slacken in our efforts to make the nations of the world, and especially their governments, aware of the unspeakable disaster they are certain to provoke unless they change their attitude towards each other and toward the task of shaping the future. We helped to create this weapon in order to prevent the enemies of mankind from achieving it ahead of us, which, given the mentality of the Nazis, would have meant inconceivable destruction and the enslavement of the rest of the world. We delivered this weapon into the hands of the American and the British people as trustees of the whole of mankind as fighters for peace and liberty. But so far we fail to see any guarantee of peace, we do not see any guarantee of the freedoms that were promised to the nations in the Atlantic Charter. The war is won but the peace is lost.

His one hope, which he advocated tirelessly, was the formation of a One-World Government. In the same year, 1945, still regarding Soviet Russia as an ally, he wrote for the ATLANTIC MONTHLY, urging that *The secret of the bomb should be committed to a world government* consisting of the United States, Great Britain, and the Soviet Union . . . *the only three powers with great military strength.*

In that same article, he also wrote:

Do I fear the tyranny of a world government? Of course I do . . . But a world government is preferable to the far greater evil of wars, particularly with their intensified destructiveness.

He was certain that America would not hold the secret of the bomb for long, that other nations with the will to do so could make the same discovery; therefore, *If war is to be averted, it must be done quickly.*

Of himself he wrote:

I do not consider myself the father of the release of atomic energy. My part in it was quite indirect. I did not in fact, foresee that it would be released in my time. I believed only that it was theoretically possible. It became practical through the accidental discovery of chain reaction, and this was not something I could have predicted. It was discovered by Hahn in Berlin, and he himself misinterpreted what he discovered. It was Lise Meitner who provided the correct interpretation and escaped from Germany to place the information in the hands of Niels Bohr.

In 1948, he wrote:

We scientists, whose tragic distinction has been to help in making the methods of annihilation more gruesome and more effective, must consider

*it our solemn and transcendent duty to do all in our power in prevent-
ing these weapons from being used for the futile purpose for which they
were invented. What task could possibly be more important for us?
What social aim could be closer to our hearts?*

In 1950, writing to the Italian Society for the Advancement of
Science, he describes the present position of the scientist.

> *. . . the man of science as we can observe with our own eyes, suffers a
> truly tragic fate. Striving in great sincerity for clarity and inner inde-
> pendence, he himself, through his sheer superhuman efforts, has fash-
> ioned the tools for which are now being used to make him a slave and to
> destroy him also from within . . .*

In 1950, in a television programme arranged by Mrs. Roosevelt,
he said:

> *The armament race between the U.S.A. and the U.S.S.R., originally
> supposed to be a preventative measure, assumes hysterical character.
> On both sides, the means to mass destruction are perfected with fever-
> ish haste — behind the respective walls of secrecy, The hydrogen bomb
> appears on the horizon as a probably attainable goal. Its accelerated
> development has been solemnly proclaimed by the President [Truman].
> If it is successful, radioactive poisoning of the atmosphere and hence
> annihilation of any life on earth has been brought within the range of
> technical possibilities. The ghostlike character of this development lies
> in its apparently compulsory trend. Every step appears as the unavoid-
> able consequence of the preceding one. In the end, there beckons more
> and more clearly general annihilation.*

There is pathos in the following. It is part of a message in a
Japanese magazine in autumn 1952.

> *My part in producing the atomic bomb consisted in a single act: I signed
> a letter to President Roosevelt, pressing the need for experiments on a
> large scale in order to explore the possibilities of an atomic bomb.*

> *I was fully aware of the terrible danger to mankind in case this attempt
> succeeded. But the likelihood that the Germans were working on the same
> problem with a chance of succeeding forced me to this step. I could do
> nothing else, although I have always been a convinced pacifist. To my
> mind, to kill in war is not a whit better than to commit ordinary murder.*

A few days before his death in 1955, Einstein signed a declaration,
together with Bertrand Russell and a number of prominent scientists, to warn the world of the danger to humanity attending the
use of the hydrogen bomb. This was his last message.

· 11 ·

The Abolition of the Absolute

Isaac Newton at the age of sixteen set out to measure the velocity of the wind by using the inertia of his own body. Einstein, at the same age, was occupied with the thought: what would it be like to pursue light at its own speed? For him no fleeting thought for in it lay the germ of his future theory, known today as Einstein's Theory of Relativity.

Einstein was twenty-six years old and had not yet met a single leading scientist. He was married and living a contented, inconspicuous life as one of twelve clerks in the Swiss Patent Office. His duties required an eight-hour day but he found he could fulfill them in half that time. The rest he spent on private calculations, making jottings on pieces of paper which he would hurriedly hide away when anyone entered the room. There came a culminating five weeks of such feverish intensity of concentration that it left him prostrate for two weeks, but the result was a thirty-page paper which was to become a world-historical document. It contained his Theory of Relativity, known as the Special Theory to distinguish it from the General Theory which followed ten years later.

The sequence of developments was as follows: his preoccupation with the spread of light and the electromagnetic field; the publication of his Special Theory in 1905; the publication of his Law of Equivalence shortly after; and then his crowning achievement, the publication of his General Theory in 1916 when still a man only in his thirties.

Sullivan, in his chapter, 'The Web of Reason,' provides an excellent approach to a subject which is technically beyond the scope of most of us. He begins his chapter with a consideration of motion.

> . . . to the Greeks different bodies had different natural motions. Thus the natural tendency of flame was to fly upward, seeking its natural place in the heavens. The natural tendency of heavy bodies was to sink downwards. The heavenly bodies naturally moved in circles for the Greeks were greatly impressed by the aesthetic properties of the circle, and regarded it as the most perfect of all figures, and thus peculiarly appropriate to heavenly bodies.
>
> Sullivan, LIMITATIONS OF SCIENCE

Galileo altered all this. He declared that it was natural for a moving body to continue in the same direction and at the same speed forever unless interfered with by an outside force. This view was ultimately accepted by science as the only 'natural motion' of a body. Yet, as Sullivan points out, this condition has never been observed and can never occur; *for if all other forces be removed, gravitation remains.* Why then should scientific men have chosen *as the foundation for reasoning about motion, a law that can never be certified by observation?* His answer is *because it was the most convenient possible law to choose.*

> For it must be remembered that what scientific men mean by truth is, in the last resort, convenience. Scientific men are pragmatists in practice, whatever they may think they are in theory.

Galileo, however, went further.

> He knew, like everybody else, that a stone, in its fall towards the earth, falls faster and faster. But he claims to have been the first man to ask himself at what rate the speed increased. This problem, he tells us, had never occurred to any other philosopher . . . Galileo, by simple and ingenious experiments, found out the law of increase. By these and other experiments he was the first to put the study of motion on a really scientific basis. And Newton, born the same year that Galileo died, showed that in this study lay the key to the material universe.

Sullivan wishes to emphasize how *complete order and harmony* were established by Newton for the solar system and then by later astronomers on the same Newtonian principles, *throughout the heavens.* With subsequent development, however, the Newtonian principles, so thoroughly established, came to be questioned and discarded. Sullivan asks, for example, what precisely Newton meant by the statement that *two bodies* <u>*attract*</u> *one another.*

> We know that two people who 'attract' one another may 'will' to come together, but we can hardly imagine such a relation existing between the sun and the planets.

The idea of attraction between bodies turned out to be merely an assumption.

The theory of attraction further assumed that there would be *direct action at a distance.* Newton himself was uneasy about this, yet his theory was based on it. And this force acted instantaneously. *Newton's formula for gravitation takes no account of time.*

Newton himself had said

> that his formula merely described the way in which bodies behaved; it did not profess to say anything about the causes of this behaviour. Indeed, he did not think that science could say anything about ultimate causes, for ultimately, Newton thought, everything happens by the will of God. But the mathematicians after Newton . . . created direct action at a distance into a fundamental principle. They dowered matter with a variety of attractions, electric, magnetic, gravitational, and a few repulsions. All these acted instantaneously at a distance.

Light, however, remained a mystery, It was not propagated instantaneously as had once been believed, but traveled with a definite velocity.

> The idea that light is something that moves with a definite velocity is, when one comes to think of it, a very queer idea, That we should <u>see</u> when we open our eyes seems the most natural thing in the world. It seems strange to apply to light, this circumambient something, the notion of distance and velocity.

Yet, the speed of light has been definitely determined at about 186,000 miles a second. Did light then consist *of little particles shot out from the visible objets* or was it carried in waves through space? If the latter was the case then space would not be empty — *space was filled with a vast jelly-like substance called ether.*

> The wave theory of light, which is really the ether theory, is one of the most amazing instances in science of a theory which is developed with enthusiasm by extremely gifted men, which goes on from success to

success until it secures the universal assent of the scientific world and yet which turns out to be wrong.

But then Sullivan continues:

An even more startling instance is provided by Newton's theory of gravitation, which was regarded for two hundred years as 'the most perfect, and perfectly established, of scientific laws.' Its accuracy and perfection became proverbial; it was the ideal by which all other scientific theories were judged. And great mathematicians have been unanimous that Newton's discovery and development of it was the supreme achievement of human genius. Yet, today the whole method of thought on which it reposes has been abandoned, root and branch.

And now Sullivan passes on to consider the three fundamentals of Newtonian physics: matter, space, and time.

We can imagine, or think we can, completely empty space. The fact that space has material bodies existing in it is, it appears, quite irrelevant to the nature of space. We imagine space being spread out before the material universe appeared, and we imagine it continuing even if the material universe were annihilated.

Similarly, with time. We <u>measure</u> time by events, it is true. We watch the successive swings of a pendulum or the movements of the heavenly bodies. But these events, it seems, occupy time very much as a body occupies space. Time, in its own nature, seems to be independent of events. . . . But can we imagine time going on in the absence of all space? If there were no space, if the whole universe shrank to a point, would time still exist? This is not so easy to answer. We have an uneasy feeling that the question is meaningless. We become obscurely aware that space and time are, in some way, interconnected. . . . A third reality is matter. . . . We cannot conceive of a piece of matter that does not occupy space or that exists for no time at all. But matter is a separate reality in the sense that it is, in its own nature, something utterly different from space and time. It is an extraneous something embedded, as it were, in space and time.

Add to matter, space, and time the

subsidiary concepts of attractive and repulsive forces, stresses and strains, cohesion, gravitation, etc., and out of this particular set of ideas scientific men bound themselves, as it were to explain — everything.

However, the new physics, which found its consummation in the work of Einstein, altered the view of all these concepts. One of the first things to go was the ether theory.

The ether theory was an attempt to explain the phenomena of light mechanically. A vast medium was supposed to fill all space, and the mathematicians set themselves the task of working out what properties this medium must possess in order that its vibrations should constitute light. . . . As the mathematicians piled ingenuity on ingenuity the ether became more and more fantastic. . . . In the end, the ether became more like the nightmare dream of a mad engineer than a physical reality. Space became filled with an incredible complex of gyroscopes, driving bands, pulleys, cog-wheels, and what not. . . . Einstein showed that there was no reason to suppose that an ether existed. The whole of this effort to explain light had been a misdirection of energy. <u>Light is not to be explained in mechanical terms</u>.

A dispute about the supposed ether, whether it remained stationary as the earth moved through it or whether the earth, in its motion, carried some of the ether along with it, led, in 1887, to the famous experiment of Michelson and Morely, which yielded a totally unexpected and highly improbable result. This result was to be to Einstein what the apple falling from the tree had been to Newton. It gave him the clue for the reconstruction of the whole universe. The experiment has been carried out many times since but always with the same result.

Michelson and Morely considered that if the earth were moving through a stationary ether, then, whether it was moving towards a source of light or away from it, or whether the light was approaching the earth from an equally distant source but from some other direction, say at right angles to the path of the earth's motion, there should be detectable differences in the apparent speed of light. By rough analogy, if a car of speed 60 miles an hour is approaching another car of speed 40 miles an hour, it will appear (to the 40 mph car) to be approaching at 100 miles an hour. If, however, the cars are moving in the same direction, the apparent speed of the faster car will be only 20 miles an hour.

But, although the experiment has often been repeated, no difference has ever been found, although in some of these experiments the apparatus has been so delicate that a difference one hundred times less than the difference expected could have been measured. Michelson concluded from the negative result of his experiment, that the earth carries the ether along with it. This conclusion, however, is quite opposed to certain very trustworthy astronomical observations.

Einstein not only abolished the ether once and for all, but he set up a mathematical proof that:

> ... the velocity of light is always the same, whether we measure the velocity from a system which is in motion or a system that is at rest.

This seems utterly contrary to common sense, for it is equivalent to saying that the faster car in the above instance passes the slower car at the same speed whether approaching in the opposite direction or in the same direction. Einstein claimed that at the speed of light this is just what did happen, and on this statement, coupled with his Law of Equivalence whereby the mass of a body changes with its speed of motion or kinetic energy, he based his theory of relativity. He treated the observer with his instruments as the varying mass — thus no observation could ever be alike for any two observers.

> Einstein asserts ... that our measures of length and of time vary with our motion. A stationary observer, watching our measuring instruments as we moved past him, would judge that our yard sticks had contracted, and that our clocks were running slow. Curiously enough, if we watched his measuring instruments we would make exactly the same judgments about them. These extraordinary phenomena have never, of course, been observed, because they do not become measurable, even by the finest observation, except at enormous speeds comparable with the velocity of light itself.

We have seen how the idea of mass fell away. What had been first observed in connection with electrified bodies in an electromagnetic field, Einstein applied to all bodies. Mass and energy became quantitatively interchangeable.

Now we see also the abolition of absolute space and time. In Einstein's picture, if the constancy of light under all circumstances is taken to be an observed fact, then:

> Two events which are simultaneous for one observer, ... are not simultaneous for an observer who is moving with a different motion. There is no such thing as the time or the distance between two events. Different observers reach different results. And no one observer is more privileged than any other.

In any case, how is motion to be determined at all? In every-day experience we determine the speed of a body by the rate at which it passes something stationary, but in the heavens nothing is stationary.

We have no means of arriving at an absolute speed or velocity —
all motion is relative, and so too are mass, space, and time relative.
There are no absolutes left.

At this point Einstein introduces Minkowski, who had been one of
his mathematics teachers as a student at the Zurich Polytechnic.

> *The real significance of Einstein's theory was not realised until*
> *Minkowski gave his celebrated address in 1908. Minkowski gave an*
> *astonishing beauty and symmetry to Einstein's doctrine of the relativi-*
> *ty of space and time as being aspects of a more fundamental reality . . .*
> *the fourth dimensional space-time continuum.*
>
> *Henceforth, space by itself, and time by itself, are doomed to fade away*
> *into mere shadows, and only a kind of union of the two will preserve an*
> *independent reality.*

According to Minkowski, the way we ordinarily regard space and
time is no more than *a psychological peculiarity of ours.*

> *There is nothing absolute about space and time. As we have seen, differ-*
> *ent observers make different estimates of the space and of the time sepa-*
> *rating two events. But there is a certain relation that they are all agreed*
> *on — a relation referring directly to the four-dimensional reality. This*
> *relation is called the* <u>interval</u>. *It is a spatio-temporal relation, and is*
> *obtained by each observer combining his space and time measurements*
> *in a certain way. Different observers will disagree as to the space sepa-*
> *rating two events. They will disagree as to the time separating the two*
> *events. But they will all agree on the interval between these events.*

Sullivan now introduces something which to non-mathematicians
must seem obscure. He draws attention to the fact that today there
are many types of geometry, not only Euclidean, and that, in fact,
each investigator can select or create the type that serves him best.
We are led to infer that there could be as many geometries as there
are investigators.

> *Each geometry has its own particular mathematical expression for a*
> *length. No two geometries are alike in this respect, and from this one*
> *expression the mathematician can deduce all the characteristics of a*
> *geometry. Now if we regard the* <u>interval</u> *as a length in a four dimen-*
> *sional continuum we can, by studying its mathematical expression, find*
> *what sort of geometry it indicates for the four-dimensional continuum.*
>
> *The result is very interesting. We find that the geometry in question is not*
> *Euclidean, and one of the most striking facts about it is that, according to*

this geometry, a <u>critical velocity</u> must exist. There must be a velocity that appears the same to all observers whatever their relative motions may be. The fact that we have already discovered such a velocity in the velocity of light is a strong indication, therefore, that we are on the right track.

Minkowski did, in fact, create a geometry suited to Einstein's theory. A number of other results deduced from this geometry could be confirmed by experiment, thus establishing its validity.

We see that what would seem to us to be singular and arbitrary laws of nature are really consequences of the fact that the four-dimensional space-time continuum is governed by a certain type of geometry. <u>We replace laws of nature by geometry</u>, as it were.

From this there is born a comment, typical of Sullivan, to make us ponder, weigh and consider what the significance of all this may be.

This fact throws a strange light on the scientific picture of the universe. We see that that picture is much more of a mental creation than we had supposed.

We quoted Einstein's reference to the Newtonian construction 'Law of Motion plus Law of Attraction' as 'a marvelous edifice of thought.' The Law of Motion includes mass, space, and time which, under Einstein's Special Theory of Relativity are radically changed, therefore also the concept of motion. There is left still to be considered the Law of Attraction or, more specifically, Gravitation, which, for Newton, was the ground basis for his view of the universe.

The force of gravitation had always been a puzzle. In certain respects it stands quite alone amongst all the forces of nature. The gravitational force between two bodies is not affected in the least, for example, by their physical or chemical conditions. Also, there is the puzzling fact that it seems to act instantaneously. Light, as we know, takes time to travel. So does every other form of radiant energy.

Another singular fact about gravitation is that nothing acts as a screen to it. We have substances that stop light, that stop heat, that stop the electric and magnetic forces, that stop even X-rays, but we know of nothing that stops gravitation. A body held up in the air weighs just as much however many bodies we interpose between it and the surface of the earth. The pull of the earth on it is not affected in the slightest.

All these facts are very puzzling if we conceive gravitation as a force like the other natural forces. But Einstein showed that it is not a force at all. That bodies 'gravitate' to one another is a straight forward consequence of the fact that we live in a non-Euclidean universe. A four-dimensional continuum governed by Riemannian geometry will possess a certain kind of curvature in the neighbourhood of matter. This curvature manifests itself to us as 'gravitation.' We can thus understand its omnipresence and unalterability, for it is inherent in the very structure of space-time.

It appears that for this further development of Einstein's theory, the Minkowski geometry was no longer adequate. It required the more complicated geometry of Riemann. Einstein, however, regarded his theory as a simplification; it not only gave him more accurate results but some which Newtonian thinking could not reach, and yet it eliminated the law of gravity. The great ideal of science, often reiterated by Einstein, was to cover the phenomena with the minimum number of laws. This is the great achievement of the General Theory.

Sullivan then describes two triumphs of this theory. The one concerns the movements of Mercury, the planet nearest the sun, which Newtonian calculations could not wholly account for. Einstein's theory *clears up the whole matter — this formula, when applied to Mercury, gives exactly the motion as observed.*

> *An even more spectacular result is Einstein's prediction of the deflection of light. We have already said that Einstein makes gravitation an inherent property of space-time. The planets, for instance, move in the way they do because they are pursuing the easiest path through the space-time continuum that surrounds them. It is not that they are acted upon by a force; the path they follow is the natural 'straight line' path in a region governed by that particular kind of non-Euclidean geometry.*

Einstein predicted that the same must be true of light — that light, too, *entering what we call a gravitational field,* for example *passing near the sun* would appear to be deflected. This prediction, too, was confirmed, in 1919, by observations of a solar eclipse.

We have previously seen the greatest human catastrophe that had ever occurred, arising out of Einstein's work. Now, by contrast, we see him in his moment of greatest triumph. His laws of relativity played a decisive part in both. Despite his moral pleadings, the instruments of destruction have reached far more fearful potentials. Over against this we have yet to evaluate, in terms of human progress, Einstein's expressed ideal of reducing the phenomena of the world to their simplest possible terms. This he thought he had achieved in physical terms. It means transferring all familiar values into a four-dimensional space-time continuum accessible to certain types of mathematical reasoning which find confirmation in a particular geometric system but one which are totally remote from common experience. All things are to be considered relative to one another — but in their sum-total, relative to what?

By the Law of Equivalence mass and energy are interchangeable, so there is no longer an absolute mass or an absolute energy or an absolute position. And, therefore, there is no longer an absolute space or absolute time. Now, finally, gravity, on which the world of Newton was founded, has been abolished. To understand this fully we need, at the least, to be advanced mathematicians, at home with Riemanninan geometry.

In this new world-conception all phenomena are related to one another. Each conditions and is in turn conditioned by the others, so that the world becomes an integrated whole — an integrated unity of interdependent parts. There is a condition that pertains quite certainly to any living organism, a condition without which life is inconceivable. Thus far the new conception is suggestive and attractive; yet nowhere in the system as set out, whether Newtonian or Einsteinian, is there the slightest trace indicative of life of any kind. For ordinary living both systems remain mental abstractions arrived at through mathematical symbols and formulae, entirely quantitative in character. The qualities of living are left to go their own way. The law of equivalence has largely invaded the inner life so that all inner values have tended to become merely relative. There are no longer any norms, be they of truth, beauty, goodness, love, or morality to which one may refer. Outside is the threat of annihilation; inside, the danger of moral extinction. A science that is all relative and uncentred offers no ground for constructing any kind of human future.

In December of 1953, at a commemorative evening at Columbia University to honour the memory of Copernicus four hundred years after his death, Einstein opened his brief address with the words:

We are honouring today, with joy and gratitude, the memory of a man who, more than almost anyone else, contributed to the liberation of the mind from the chains of clerical and scientific dominance in the Occident.

Imagine the sincerity with which Einstein pronounced these words. How impressive they must have been to his listeners. Our quest has followed the liberating force of science for four hundred years. How is it possible, then, on another public occasion, that Einstein, the most recent of the great giants of science, humbly confessed to the fearful burden of shame he felt in the face of life? He was addressing an audience enthusiastic for a one world order — in fact, he was at that occasion to receive the One World Order Award. A most strange circumstance! Liberating science had brought man to a pass where the greatest scientist of the day, and the other outstanding scientists with him, pled for the creation of supranational power to safeguard life and moral freedom.

What freedom can we hope to have until we have created a science capable of perceiving not only measurement but meaning, until the joys and sorrows of men become at least as significant as numbers, until they become at least as valid in the search for truth as abstract considerations of mass, space, time, energy, and motion?

In 1959, Professor Michael Polanyi, in appreciation of his books, Personal Knowledge and The Study of Man, received the Award of the Lecomte du Noüy Foundation. He acknowledged what we owe to 'Scientific Rationalism' which for a hundred and fifty years had been *the main guide to intellectual, moral, and social progress.* Then, in reviewing where we had reached since, he felt obliged to utter the sharp, uncompromising words, *the ideals of science are nonsensical.* He went on to explain. . .

Current biology is based on the assumption that you can explain the processes of life in terms of physics and chemistry. And of course, physics and chemistry are both to be represented ultimately in terms of the forces acting between atomic particles. So all life, all human beings, and all words of man including Shakespeare's <u>Sonnets</u> and Kant's <u>Critique of Pure Reason</u>, are also to be so represented. The ideal of science remains what it was in the time of Laplace: to replace all human knowledge by a complete knowledge of atoms in motion. In spite of much that is said to the contrary, quantum mechanics makes no difference at all in this respect. A quantum mechanical view of the universe is just as empty of meaning as a mechanical theory.

This is the heart of the matter. This is the origin of scientific obscurantism under which we suffer today. This is why we corrupt the conception of man, reducing him either to an insentient automaton, or to a bundle of appetites. This is why science denies us the possibility of acknowledging personal responsibility. This is why science can be invoked in support of totalitarian violence: why science has become, as I have said before, the greatest source of dangerous fallacies today.

The question is: Can we get rid of all this terrible nonsense without jettisoning the beneficial guidance which science still offers us in other respects? I think it is very difficult. That is why it has not yet been done. For dissatisfaction with the blatant absurdities of the scientific approach is widespread and efforts to remedy the situation are not infrequent. Yet they remain on the whole ineffectual.

That the scientific impulse is related to the problem of human freedom can scarcely be doubted. Nevertheless, the one-sidedness which has entered human thinking has brought its heavy penalties and threatens worse. Einstein showed with tragic concern, and Polyani and many others equally, that conscience, a new conscience, has come knocking at the door.

Thus the course of physical science has been traced since its first inception with Copernicus and Galileo, through to the concepts of Einstein. Now the focus turns to the science of living nature and its development.

· 12 ·

Finding the Circle

William Harvey (1578–1657), through his discovery of the circulation of the blood, is ranked among the great pioneers of the modern era, with its bias towards the mechanical. He was educated at the medical school at Padua where Galileo, fourteen years his senior, had also studied. Harvey makes no reference to Galileo in his works. Nor does he mention Descartes, another contemporary, whose vivisection practice Harvey utilized. He describes this in the Introduction to his ANATOMICAL EXERCISES ON THE GENERATION OF ANIMALS.

> . . . it is a new and difficult road in studying nature, rather to question things themselves than, by turning over books, to discover the opinion of philosophers regarding them, . . . Nature is herself to be addressed; the paths she showed us are to be boldly trodden; for thus, and whilst we consult our proper senses, from inferior to superior levels, shall we penetrate at length to the heart of her mystery.

George Ent, who undertook the publication of this work, quotes Harvey further:

> It is true, the examination of the bodies of animals has always been my delight; and I have thought that we might thence not only observe an insight into the lighter mysteries of nature, but there perceive a kind of image or replica of the Omnipotent Creator himself.

An impression of the times in which Harvey lived may be gleaned from the manner in which he dedicated his earlier and more famous work, MOTION OF THE HEART AND BLOOD IN ANIMALS, to Charles I.

Most Illustrious Prince!

The heart of animals is the foundation of their life, the sovereignty of everything within them, the sun of their microcosm, that upon which all life depends, from which all power proceeds. The King, in like manner, is the foundation of his kingdom, the sun of the world around him, the heart of the republic, the fountain whence all power, all growth doth flow. . . . The knowledge of his heart, therefore, will not be useless to a Prince, as embracing a kind of Divine example of his functions . . .

The language of this dedication, still the imagery of the mediaeval age, is typical of Harvey. His feelings were still suffused with impressions of that earlier time even though he was totally intent on new discovery. That the heart may be regarded as the sun-organ in the body was a piece of ancient wisdom which Harvey never seemed to query, even though, in order to arrive at his results, he had *frequent recourse to vivisection.*

Vivisection was the practice of the day, utilized not only by Harvey but by Descartes and his followers seemingly without compunction. Harvey enumerates among the 'colder animals' he examined, toads, frogs, serpents, small fishes, crabs, shrimps, and shell-fish; of the warm-blooded creatures, he mentions in particular the dog and the hog. But he was also familiar with surgery as a practicing physician. His writings give a faithful record of his observations and reflections. There was nothing hasty about his work. He arrived at his conclusions only after the painstaking labour of years. His greatest preoccupation was with the heart and the blood.

I have occasionally observed, after the heart and even the right auricle had ceased pulsating, when it was in articule mortis *in short, that an obscured motion, an undulation or palpitation, remained in the blood itself which was contained in the right auricle, this being apparent so long as it was imbued with heat and spirit.*

Contrary to the general view nowadays, Harvey was convinced that pulsation began in the blood and was then transmitted to the heart. For this reason, the heart, being born of the blood, was, from the very first, a pulsating organ.

Thus nature, ever perfect and divine, doing nothing in vain, has neither given a heart where it was not required, nor produced it before its office had become necessary; but by the same stages in the development of every animal, passing through the constitutions of all, as I may say (ovum, worm, foetus), it acquires perfection in each. These points will be found elsewhere confirmed by numerous observations on the formation of the foetus.

There are two points to be noted here. When Harvey describes nature as *perfect and divine* we may take it that he means this literally. This reverent view never forsakes him. He was also remarkably free from prejudice in arriving at a judgment. He was a firm exponent of Epigenesis, namely, the view that each organism has to be built up and shaped anew — a view which many held to be contrary to the Scriptures as described in Genesis.

The most cryptic remark in this respect, concerning the relationship of the heart to the blood, occurs in Exercise I of Harvey's work on THE GENERATION OF ANIMALS.

... the blood is the prime part that is engendered, and the heart the mere organ destined for its circulation.

In the same exercise Harvey elabourates further on the nature of the blood.

... in whatever part of the body heat and motion have their origin, in this also must life take its rise, in this be the last extinguished; and no one, I presume, will doubt there are the lares and penates of life enshrined, that there the vital principle (anima) itself has its seat.

The life, therefore, resides in the blood (as we are also informed in our sacred writing, Leviticus 17.11.14) because in it life and the soul first show themselves, and last become extinct. ... Everyone may perceive that the blood ... this author of pulsation and life ... longest retains its heat: for when this is gone, and it is no longer blood, but gore, so is there, then, no hope of a return to life ...

From this it clearly appears that the blood is the generative part, the fountain of life, the first to live, the last to die, and the primary seat of the soul; the element in which, as in a fountainhead, the heat first abounds and flourishes; from whose influxive heat all the other parts of the body are cherished, and obtain their life; for the heat, the companion of the blood, flows through and cherishes and preserves the whole body, as I formerly demonstrated in my work on the motion of the blood.

Harvey's writings exemplify his great regard for accuracy and his determination to interpret phenomena so that it truly accords with actual experience. He writes confidently of heat as a vital principle and of anima or soul as though these were self-evident. In the transition period in which Harvey lived it is difficult to determine how far such terms were used literally, how far figuratively. Does 'anima' exist in itself or is it only on appearance in the body? Is fire really of divine origin? What actual value attaches to the four elements of antiquity? Is a corporeal substance like the blood an actual embodiment of higher principles or merely a semblance suggestive of them?

In the following passage taken from his GENERATION OF ANIMALS (Exercise 71) Harvey seems to be wrestling with traditional terminology to determine how it relates to the factual data before him. It is as though he is striving to see how far he can justify the authority of the ancients in the light of his knowledge and experience based on perception through the physical senses. The weight of tradition with its background of spiritual values was still strong and the new spirit of enquiry as seen in the physical sciences scarcely begun. Even as God faded out from the physical universe for the physicists, how was it to be for the living or organic sciences? Where does the old life of religion meet the new world of scientific enquiry?

> There are three bodies — simple bodies — which seem especially entitled to receive the name, at all events, to perform the office of 'spirit,' viz., fire, air, and water, each of which, by reason of its ceaseless flux and motion, expressed by the words flame, wind, and flood, appears to have the property of life, or of some other body. Flame is the flow of fire, wind the flow of air, stream or flood the flow of water. Flame, like an animal, is self-motive, self-nutrient, self-augmentative, and is the symbol of life. It is therefore that it is so universally brought into requisition in religious ceremonies; it was guarded by priestesses and virgins in the temples of Apollo and Vesta as a sacred thing, and from the remotest antiquity has been held worthy of divine worship by the Persians and other ancient nations; as if God were most conspicuous in flame, and spoke to us from fire as He did to Moses of old. Air is also appropriately spoken of as 'spirit,' having received the title from the act of respiration. Aristotle himself admits, 'that there is a kind of life, and birth, and death of the winds.' Finally we speak of a running stream as 'living water.'
>
> These three, therefore, inasmuch as they have a kind of life, appear to act superiorly to the forces of the elements, and to share in a more divine nature; they were, therefore, placed among the number of the divinities by

> the heathen. When any excellent work or process appeared, surpassing
> the powers of the naked elements, it was held as proceeding from some
> more divine agent. 'To act with power superior to the power of the ele-
> ments,' therefore, and on that account 'to share in the properties of some
> more divine thing, which does not derive its origin from the elements,
> appear to have the same significance.'

All this is pure description from the past. Such qualifying phrases
as, 'a kind of life,' and 'seem especially entitled,' and, 'appear to
act superiorly,' imply the questioning of how these things are in
actuality. Considering his findings on blood, Harvey perceived a
fluid which combined all three of the foregoing qualities: it acted
in a manner 'surpassing the powers of the naked elements' and
with infallible wisdom as though it were itself divine. What then is
blood really?

> The blood, in like manner, 'acts with powers superior to the powers of
> the elements' in the fact of its existence, in the forms of primordial and
> innate heat, in semen and spirit, and its producing all the other parts of
> the body in succession; proceeding at all times with such foresight and
> understanding, and with definite ends in view, as if it employed rea-
> soning in its acts. Now this it does not, in so far as it is elementary, but
> in so far as it is possessed of plastic powers and endowed with the gift
> of the vegetative soul, as it is the primordial and innate heat, and the
> immediate and competent instrument of life. . . . The blood, therefore, by
> reason of its admirable properties and powers is 'spirit.' It is also celes-
> tial; for nature, the soul, that which answers to the essence of the stars,
> is the inmate of the spirit, in other words, it is something analogous to
> heaven, vicarious of heaven.

There is nothing to suggest that this is not Harvey's genuine conclusion, a veritable hymn of praise. It is difficult to understand,
therefore, how and why it has been asserted that Harvey
approached his task with the eyes of a mechanist and that he
regarded blood as a mechanical fluid. At the least there is implied a
choice of viewpoint. For Harvey, *all natural objects*, that is to say, *all
things subject to generation by birth, and to death and decay*, might be
regarded simply at their face value, or they might be viewed *as the
instruments of some more noble agent and superior power*. Whether one
chose to think the one way or the other neither detracted from nor
added to the excellencies which the eye could directly perceive. In
this subtle manner does Harvey suggest a possible distinction

between the object as nakedly perceived and that which endows the subject with cause for veneration and worship. Freed from any kind of dogma, the choice is left to each individual. Therefore, he writes that the natural objects _seem to participate with another and more divine body, and to surpass the powers of the ordinary elements._ In his terminology, Nature, the Sun, God, become synonymous: it is as though he saw in nature the divine directly incorporated — therefore, the distinction between nature and the divine becomes more theoretical than real. Insofar as this might raise a question, the answer touches mysteries beyond the scope of common observation and reason. But science must be based on perception, not on belief. Harvey, out of an earlier background, still perceives nature as divine and interprets it accordingly; thus, he is unequivocal when he writes of the blood:

> In the same way, too, is the blood the animal heat, in so far, namely, as it is governed in its action by the soul; for it is celestial as subservient to heaven; and divine because it is the instrument of God.

He asserts, that blood _is_ the animal heat, it _is_ celestial, it _is_ divine — it manifests these qualities directly and therefore it _is_ all these. Yet the matter does not rest quite as simply as that. Harvey does not, like Descartes, make a distinction between thinking substance and extended substance, thus splitting experience into mind and body. Nor does he, like Galileo, divide off the secondary qualities from the rest and dismiss them as subjective illusions. As a biologist he relies essentially on these secondary qualities — it is they and not the primary qualities which declare the language of nature to him. He is, therefore, least of all a mechanist. Nevertheless, as a scientist he is obliged to hold to the facts as he sees them — he may not willfully interpolate agencies to account for the facts as was commonly done. Either nature was divine or only material. The fact that he chose to regard it as divine in no way altered the fact.

In considering the motion of the blood and the fact that it flowed, he was concerned with a physical phenomenon and, in terms of pure sense experience, with nothing else. His demonstration of the blood flowing made no actual call on a divine element lying outside and beyond the fact as simply displayed. Therefore it could as easily be interpreted materialistically and mechanically without recourse to anything higher. This is what eventually came about. Thus, in spite of Harvey's own personal outlook and conviction, his discovery came to be viewed as laying the foundation for a mechanistic view, not only of the motion of the blood but of the whole of physiology. That this came about has to be attributed to the general trend of the times to adopt the new physics as the ground for the study of all natural phenomena. It was not the researcher, Harvey, but the mood and character of the new era with its mathematical-mechanical bias which determined that blood was to be regarded as a 'mechanical fluid,' propelled by mechanical causes. This did not come about all at once.

Harvey's work on the circulation of the blood was the more remarkable because there was as yet no microscope to help him. The existence of capillaries and the whole capillary system throughout the body was wholly unknown. Venous and arterial blood were seen as separate natures and theories were rife to explain their difference and also the manner of functioning of the lungs. Popular imagination abounded with intervening agencies and spirits. Therefore, Harvey had to rely on the sheer force of his own reasoning to counter the confusion in these matters and to surmount the serious gaps in the available information. Despite the care and circumspection of his statements, there were few who were ready and willing to follow him. Thus he writes:

> To those, therefore, whom I hear denying that the blood, aye, the whole mass of the blood, may pass through the substance of the lungs, even as the nutritive juices percolate the liver, asserting such a proposition to be impossible, and by no means to be entertained as credible, I reply, with the poet, that they are of that race of men who, when they will, assent fully readily, and when they will not, by no manner of means; who, when their assent is wanted, fear, and when it is not, fear not to give it.

The crowning passage on this theme occurs in Chapter VIII of his MOTION OF THE HEART AND BLOOD IN ANIMALS. It may be regarded as the counterpart in regard to physiology of Galileo's announcements in his STARRY MESSENGER and had as startling an effect.

> But what remains to be said upon the quantity and source of the blood which thus passes is of so novel and unheard-of character, that I not only fear injury to myself from the envy of a few, but I tremble lest I have mankind at large for my enemies, so much doth want and custom,

that become as another nature, and doctrine once sown and that hath struck deep roots, and respect for antiquity influence all men: still, the die is cast, and my trust is in my love for truth, and candour that inheres in cultivated minds. And sooth to say, when I surveyed my own evidence, whether derived from vivisections, and my various reflections on them, or from the ventricles of the heart and the vessels that enter into and issue from them, the symmetry and the size of these conduits, — for nature doing nothing in vain, would never have given them so large a relative size without a purpose — or from the arrangement and intimate structure of the valves in particular, and of the other parts of the heart in general, with many things besides, I frequently and seriously bethought me, and long resolved in my mind what might be the quantity of blood which was transmitted, in how short a time its passage might be effected, and the life: and not finding it possible that this could be supplied by the juices of the ingested aliments without the veins on the one hand being drained and the arteries on the other being ruptured through the excessive change of blood, unless the blood should somehow find its way from the arteries to the veins, and so return to the right side of the heart: I began to think whether this might not be a Motion, as it were, in a circle. Now this I afterwards found to be true.

What a complicated and involved preamble leading to the abrupt assertion at the end, like a hammer, long suspended, being suddenly let fall! And so the hammer did indeed fall, but England being a country of greater restraint than Italy in the case of Galileo, and the protection of the Monarch being mighty, the fall was scarcely damaging. Indeed, Hobbes, a friend of Harvey, declared that Harvey was *the only one I know who has overcome public odium and established a new doctrine during his own lifetime.*

The phrase, 'in a circle' had an added meaning in those days. Harvey relates it to 'Aristotle on circular motion.' The circle as the symbol of perfection was applied also to the perfect motion of the heavens. The heart, then, occupying the central position in the circulation of the blood, and thus best serving all the members of the body, could well be likened to the sun, the centre and the regulator of all heavenly motions.

The heart, consequently, is the beginning of life; the sun of the microcosm, even as the sun in his turn might well be designated the heart of the world . . . it is the household divinity which, discharging its function, nourishes, cherishes, quickens the whole body, and is indeed the foundation of life, the source of all action.

> *The heart which contains in itself blood, life, sensation, motion, Harvey*
> *described as a kind of internal creature . . . the prince in a kingdom . . .*
> *the original and foundation from which all power is derived, on which*
> *all power depends in the animal body.*

Such a description hardly suggests that the heart is a kind of mechanical engine. Yet Harvey, no less than the physicists, stood at the parting of the ways. The shadow of the dualistic creed fell upon him also. This may be detected in such a statement as the following:

> *all natural bodies fall to be considered under a twofold point of view,*
> *viz., either as they are specially regarded, and are comprehended within*
> *the limits of their own proper nature, or are viewed as the instruments*
> *of some more noble agent and superior power.*

This 'either . . . or' recurs a number of times. It implies a choice. In this may be detected the beginning of the cleavage which is to grow so pronounced later, the cleavage between scientific determinism and the impulse to freedom referred to in the opening chapters. It began in the seventeenth century for the few and has since affected life as a whole.

It is too easily assumed that men in the past saw less than they do today. In regard to material knowledge this is true, but not in regard of moral and aesthetic perception, gifts of an inward seeing. If we turn with unprejudiced minds to the time preceding the scientific era, we may see that physical and moral perception still went hand in hand. Something of this still lingered on in Harvey. He wrote as he saw and, seeing as he did, he was still able to hold Nature and God together as one. The dualism that invaded human thinking drove Nature and God ever further apart until, the quantitative prevailing over the qualitative, the calculable alone came to be held as true and other values as merely illusionary. The wavelength for a particular tone of green was real, the actual perception of that green an illusion. Harvey did not yet see the blood as a mechanical fluid and the heart as a mechanical engine but his successors with their dualistic outlook did.

· 13 ·

The Mechanical Invades
the Living

The dominant character of the New Age lay in the exploration of the kingdoms of nature and their interpretation by physical causes. It led to experimentation of every kind in every field. Over time it led to a vast accumulation of external data, but only more recently has the search begun for deeper causes lying within the phenomena we survey. Men were simply fascinated from the beginning of this age with experiment and experimented with living creatures as readily as with the non-living.

One of the early problems was that of the origin of life. This eventually led to the current belief in *spontaneous generation*. Life was conceived as having been generated at some time from the lifeless much as spontaneous combustion can arise in a haystack.

Today physics declares that the world originated from atomic dust or the spontaneous creation of hydrogen atoms out of non-space into space; then chemistry builds up the atoms into molecules. Biology, taking a new start from physics and chemistry, conceives that certain molecules increase in complexity, grow into macromolecules and thence into living protoplasm. Thus the belief in *spontaneous generation* has been shifted from primeval mud to primeval atoms. A complete understanding of the origin of *life* remains an unresolved problem.

Genesis taught, or so it was interpreted, that the various creatures sprang into being fully-created, straight from the mind of God. This belief in pre-creation in the spirit underlay the idea of preformation in the material body.

As discovery followed discovery, there were those who marveled at the grandeur of God's pre-visioned plan and others who wondered at the infinite scope of his mechanical ingenuity. Both parties felt they were hot on the trail of solving mysteries. With accumulating knowledge, questions grew more precise but faith in higher intervention diminished as speculation increased.

La Mettrie (1709–51), born a hundred years before Darwin, was the first unequivocal and outspoken materialist among the natural philosophers (as scientists were called then). His first book, L'HISTOIRE NATURELLE DE L'AME, published in 1745, was publicly burned and he was forced to flee from France to Holland. In this book, *he traced all knowledge to sensation and all mental events to bodily changes.* His next book, L'HOMME MACHINE, published in Holland three years later, obliged him to flee from that country also. He found refuge in Germany under the protection of Frederick II, and there published a third book, L'HOMME PLANTE, which was as mechanistic in theory as its predecessors. La Mettrie was willing to risk his life for his atheism. He might be regarded as the first of the free thinkers. In his own day he shocked many. By the end of the nineteenth century his type of philosophy, materialistic monism, had millions of adherents.

Linnaeus (1707–78), La Mettrie's contemporary, the genius of all classifiers, continued quite untroubled in his religious faith. His Linnaean Order, a superb achievement of taxanomy, covered all three kingdoms below man. He was a firm believer in the 'fixity of species.'

> In Linnaeus' view, each species represented the descendants of an original entity, or pair of entities, individually created at the beginning of the world. Its flora and fauna had always been exactly as they are now, and hence the concept of species was justified . . . by common descent from a unique created form, just as humanity was defined by common descent from Adam.

Towards the end of his life there was enough new evidence accruing to make Linnaeus waver in his view, but he hardly dared admit it. To withdraw the belief in *fixity of species* was to cast doubt on the thought of *special evolution,* and thus to the question also *the special creation of man,* the very keystone of religious faith. Whatever Linnaeus himself may have thought at the end of his life, his followers were dogmatic in upholding the belief in *fixity of species.* They were stubborn opponents when the time arrived for the introduction of the idea of evolution.

The idea of natural evolution was struggling through but only gradually. Most of the naturalists in the eighteenth century were catastrophists. The most orthodox of them held strictly to the account in Genesis: creation had taken place in a series of days, a day being the usual twenty-four hours; and the various types or species were still as they had been on the day they were created. There were other catastrophists who admitted to changes but held to the idea of special creation: for example, the existing creatures were descendants of the paired animals of Noah's ark and they of the animal types in Genesis. The more progressive of the catastrophists were willing to admit that there must have been a number of catastrophic of sudden events, the Flood probably being the last of these. At each such event, life was exterminated except for a few survivors who, in course of time, repopulated the earth. Thus the continuity of the original types were essentially maintained though each catastrophe brought some degree of change.

For Aristotle, the elaboration of the successive parts of the organism was the unfolding and fulfillment of a spiritually existing Idea. Harvey saw in the same phenomenon the fulfillment of a natural law in which nature and God were still indivisibly one. The Epigeneticists of later date were more concerned with physical nature alone. They saw how the complex arose from the simple and the heterogeneous, more advanced types out of more primitive ones. Not only in the single organism did the later emerge from the earlier in this way; the same might be said of mutations in general with the emergence of ascending types. Thus did epigenesis and mutation prepare the way for evolution. Nature came to be regarded as self-sufficient, needing no God or supernatural Idea to explain it: the material phenomenon was the primal cause. And so, even while the evolutionary idea was struggling to come to light, human

thought was steadily inclining towards materialism. The two culminating figures leading up to Darwin were Lamarck (1744–1829),
and Cuvier (1769–1832) and they held strongly divergent views.

Lamarck's first major work was published in 1809, the date of
Darwin's birth.

> Lamarck, who has been called with considerable justification, the founder
> of evolution, published his view on the subject just fifty years before the
> appearance of the Origin. He was sixty-five years old when he first put
> forward his views publicly and he lived for another twenty, during
> which he revised his original ideas but added little to them. Their publi-
> cation passed unnoticed. It is an extraordinary fact that while Darwin
> and Lamarck both put forward revolutionary views leading to the new
> conception of evolution, those of Darwin conquered the scientific world
> while those of Lamark, for all the effect they produced in the first fifty
> years of the century, might just as well never have been written.
>
> H. Graham Cannon, THE EVOLUTION OF LIVING THINGS

Lamarck believed that the animal kingdom represented one continuous line of descent stretching over an immense period of time
— in fact, so continuous that were the fossil records complete,
there would be no clear distinction left between species and genera. He saw that, throughout this period of time, there must have
been progressive mutations. In the first place, he attributed this to
an innate capacity in living nature to adapt itself to a changing
environment; in fact, this capacity was the essential distinguish-
ing quality of life itself. Beforehand, the main interest had been in
establishing the differences between existing types or species. But
what was responsible for those differences? What was it that controlled mutation?

Lamarck attributed the primal cause of mutation to the changing
environment. A living organism, out of an inner need or feeling,
which pervaded not a part or parts of an organism but its entire
being, was impelled by its very nature to strive evermore to relate
itself to its environment in the way that was most harmonious to
itself. In the course of doing so and in accordance with this interi-
or need, it modified its existing organs or created new ones. This it
accomplished with infallible certainty. The classifiers distinguished the different species by their particular organs. However,
it was not the separate features or organs which determined the

character of a particular organism but the innate character of the organism as a whole, with all its interrelated parts, which determined the detailed characteristics and the organs. This was a working from the whole to the parts, or the principle of holism, as this came to be regarded later.

A protracted change in the conditions of the environment evoked new needs, which gave rise to new habits, which produced a modification of existing structures and, possibly, the creation of new ones. This form of description, which on the basis of pure observation is very suggestive, is not easy to refute. However, Lamarck added a clause which spelt disaster. He suggested that these modifications or *acquired characters* were transmitted through heredity. This became popularized into the familiar picture of the giraffe which, through countless generations of stretching upwards to reach the upper leaves of trees, arrived at its exceptional and permanent long neck. The name of Lamarck became synonymous with the theory of *the inheritance of acquired characters* by outer physical adaptation, and on this basis his theory was condemned.

Lamarck's fate was indeed a sad one, for his main teaching has been grossly misrepresented and misunderstood. During his lifetime his fundamental ideas were ignored, to be treated with contumely after his death.

> *Lamarck died blind and in great poverty in 1829 and, as a distinguished member of the French Academy, was entitled to a eulogy. This was delivered by the popular and successful zoologist Cuvier, and what a eulogy it was. As one of the successors to Lamarck's professional chair remarked, 'et quel eloge!' It was so scurrilous and full of abuse that the Academy would not allow its publication until after Cuvier's death and, even then, only published an expurgated edition from which most of the offensive remarks had been deleted.*

Nor did Lamarck fare much better at the hands of Darwin.

> *Now it might be asked, since Lamarck's views had been published to the scientific world fifty years before, why does not Darwin take account of them in his <u>Origin</u> and either publicly accept them or reject them. There is no doubt that he was aware of them. In his work for the monograph on barnacles . . . he must have referred to Lamarck's monumental work on the natural history of invertebrates published in 1815. In this work*

> Lamarck put forward to the general public his first account of his evo-
> lutionary ideas in their most complete and precise form. But it was so
> large a book of seven volumes and Darwin detested bulky tomes and so
> perhaps he only referred to the chapter immediately concerning him and
> did not read any of the general conclusions. However, he must have
> obtained an idea of Lamarck's views somehow because he condemns
> them so strongly in his correspondence. But here is the puzzle. In his
> earlier published works he does not mention Lamarck, while in the sixth
> edition of his Origin which contains an historical sketch as a preface, he
> refers to Lamarck as 'this justly celebrated naturalist.' And yet in his
> letters he refers to 'Lamarck's nonsense' as 'veritable rubbish!' To anoth-
> er correspondent he says that he read one of Lamarck's 'wretched books'
> and got not a thing from it.

Lamarck was a great naturalist with a clear vision of natural evolution. In his own day he disagreed with the religious catastrophists'
ideas of pre-formation and fixity of species. Equally he disap-
proved of the later evolutionists for the reasons stated previously.
He was an intuitive, not a mechanistic, thinker. For him life was
larger than the mechanical.

Living nature he felt to be imbued with an innate power of
response, present at all levels, and to this he attributed the evolutionary process. He addressed himself to the inwardness of life
rather than to the direct cause and effect principle of the physicists.
Life had subtleties calling for a finer sense of comprehension. He
beheld nature as perpetually changing, moulding, producing, and
engendering new types; always responding and adapting itself,
now contracting and now expanding, while evolving to nobler,
more expressive forms created out of interior necessities or needs,
yet always infallible in its reaction to given circumstances. This is
a mobile, plastic, artistic mode of perceiving life. Lamarck thereby
offended the traditionalists and failed to gain the appreciation of
the modernists. It may well be that his day has yet to come.

As for Cuvier, who out of his orthodoxy passed such bitter judgments, his practical achievements still hold good but as a theorist
he has faded out completely. He was a catastrophist in outlook; he
believed there had been several upheavals but that, in the intervals
between, species had remained fixed and immutable. He believed
that with each catastrophe life was well-nigh exterminated but

that always some region was spared from which repopulation could take place again. He accepted that, in keeping with the story of Noah's Ark, the animal types had been created from the beginning and then continued a parallel existence surviving all disasters. This continuity of type applied also to man in his descent from Adam.

Cuvier has been described as *the first man to enjoy the luxury of a bird's-eye view of the whole of life spread out backwards in time, as well as around in space.* He undoubtedly saw much, but with limited vision.

Meanwhile there were the catastrophists holding to their view of 'original creation,' taking Genesis literally as their text. God created heaven and earth, the plants, the animals, and lastly man; the world was populated much as it is, from the beginning, with subsequent changes being of a minor character and following the mechanical principle of outer cause and effect. There were others who divorced the idea of mutation from religious doctrine, adhering to mechanical principles to account for change.

Lamarck (his actual name was Jean Baptiste de Monet) arrived at a clear conception of evolution. He saw as the *prime characteristic of the living state* the power of response through inner needs. This power of response became for him the active, directive principle in evolution, reaching beyond chance and mechanical law.

Approaching the time of Darwin there was still the hereditary principle to be formulated, which set itself in opposition to Lamarck's concept of environment, and, along with heredity, the idea of *struggle for existence.*

The last word in this transitional picture comes from Immanuel Kant who has been described as the 'philosopher of philosophers.' He was a mathematician and, in his own degree, a 'natural philosopher.' He invented a nebular theory so closely akin to that of Laplace that it took the name of the Kant-Laplace Nebular Theory. Despite his profound conviction of a moral world order he was a confirmed mechanist in regard to outer creation, and surpassing even Descartes, the master of dualistic thinking. In fact, he was the first to formulate a completely mechanistic statement of evolution. The following quotation is taken from his CRITIQUE OF PURE JUDGMENT, published in 1787, over thirty years before Lamarck's first publication.

> It is desirable to examine the great domain of organized beings, by means of comparative anatomy, in order to see whether we may not find in them something resembling a system, and indeed something in accordance with the principle of generation. Otherwise we would have to be content with a mere consideration of things as they are — which gives us no insight into their generation — and, in despair, give us all hope or claim of natural insight into this field. The agreement of so many genera of animals in a certain common plan of structure . . . so that with an admirable simplicity of original outline, a great variety of species has been produced by the shortening of one member and the lengthening of another, the involution of this part and the evolution of that — allows a ray of hope, however faint, to penetrate into our minds, that some results might be obtained here by the application of the principle of the mechanism of Nature, without which there can be no natural science at all. This analogy of forms, which with all their differences seem to have been produced according to an original common type, strengthens our surmise of an actual relationship among them in their procreation from a common parent, through the gradual approximation of one animal-genus to another — from that genus in which the principle of purposiveness seems best authenticated, namely man, down to the polyp, and again from this down to the mosses and lichens, and finally to the lowest form of Nature, observable to us, namely to raw matter. And so the whole technique of Nature, which, as perceived in organized beings is so incomprehensible to us that we feel ourselves compelled to think a different principle for it, seems to have been derived from matter and its powers according to mechanical laws (like those which are operative in the formation of the crystal).

This vista of progressive evolution as it appeared to the mind's eye of Kant, was to be attributed to the workings of 'mechanical law' beginning with 'raw matter.' Yet Kant recognized that, in his moral intuition, man is related to a world-order remote from the mechanical, designated that of God. In his dualism we see Kant wholly at one with Newton.

· 14 ·

The Impact of Darwinism

It was in December, 1831, that Darwin set out on an exploration which was planned to last two years but lasted five, his now famous VOYAGE OF THE BEAGLE. His task was to bring back observations, particularly of flora and fauna, to serve the interests of science. He was able to visit islands in the Atlantic and the Pacific, both coasts of South America and also New Zealand and Australia. An untried young man of twenty-two when he left, with scant knowledge and minimal experience, he believed in *the permanence of species*. Though *vague doubts occasionally flitted* across his mind, it was not until two or three years after his return home that Darwin came to the conclusion that *species were mutable*. This idea was forced upon him through his many observations, for he proved to be a most keen observer. It was not until many years later that his book, ORIGIN OF SPECIES, was to take the world by storm. His theory of evolution did not cause a major stir for that had been taking shape quite specifically in a number of minds. It was his theory of natural selection based on chance variation which drew attention because it seemed to undercut the ground of all previous beliefs in any form of preordained creation.

From Darwin's AUTOBIOGRAPHY, written in the first place for his family, and from his staunchest defendant Thomas Huxley's brief but vivid account, it is possible to retrace the steps that led up to his appointment on the Beagle and the main developments that followed.

Darwin was born at Shrewsbury in 1809. His mother died when he was a little over eight. He *can remember hardly anything about her except her death-bed, her velvet gown, and her curiously constructed work-table.* He was attending a local day-school at the time. A schoolfellow recalls him *bringing a flower to school and saying his mother had taught him how, by looking at the inside of the blossoms, the name of the plant could be discovered.*

Darwin was a born collector. Already at this early age he *collected all sorts of things, shells, seals, franks, coins, and minerals.* He writes:

> *The passion for collecting, which leads a man to be a systematic naturalist, a virtuoso or a miser, was very strong in me, and was clearly innate, as none of my sisters or brothers ever had that taste.*

At the age of nine, Darwin became a boarder at the Shrewsbury Grammar School. Of the seven years spent at this school, Darwin writes:

> *Nothing could have been worse for the development of my mind than Dr. Butler's school, as it was strictly classical, nothing else being taught except a little ancient geography and history. The school as a means of education to me was simply a blank.*

To his schoolmasters he was *no better than a dunce.* His headmaster even on one occasion rebuked him publicly *for wasting his time on such a contemptible subject as chemistry.*

There being so little to engage him at school, Charles directed his energies all the more to *athletic amusements and sports,* so much so that his father was once constrained to say to him: *You care for nothing but shooting, dogs, and rat-catching, and you will be a disgrace to yourself and all your family.* But Darwin in his autobiography adds the following apologetic note for his *father who was the kindest man I ever knew, and whose memory I love with all my heart and who must have been angry and somewhat unjust when he used such words.*

Darwin was a chronic invalid for the last forty years of his life. Though he suffered almost constantly and was sometimes incapacitated, *no physician could find an organic cause.* The puzzle was never solved during his lifetime. The tendency since has been to seek for *neurotic and psychotic causes.* The mildest statement made is that Darwin suffered from *poor nervous heredity on both sides.* One authority sees in his illness *depressive, obsessional, anxiety, and hysterical symptoms* which are a *distorted expression of the aggression, hate, resentment, felt at an unconscious level, by Darwin toward his tyrannical father.* Another discovered signs of a suppressed emotion, *compounded of fear, guilt, and hate,* all due to his relationship with his father.

The cause is always sought externally; and never considered that, in the course of his long years of internal struggle to substantiate a theory which, at the least, must cause great controversy, there may have been an anxiety factor to contend with; or even that, at certain times he may have felt out of accord with himself. It is all too easy to ascribe things to heredity and in this case, to ascribe it to a father who inspired hate, though Darwin claims he loved him with all his heart. Nevertheless it is important to realise that Darwin suffered so greatly from ill health in his later life. He was healthy enough in childhood, youth, and early manhood. His illness began after his return from the voyage when he was *occasionally unwell and so lost time.* In the end he could write that his illness had *annihilated several years* of his life.

Perhaps this is the best moment to introduce Darwin's noted grandfather, Dr. Erasmus Darwin. It has been claimed that he was the first true evolutionist, and that his theory, as propounded in his book, ZOONOMIA, closely resembles that of Lamarck and anticipates it by fifteen years.

> *Years before Charles was born, Coleridge coined the word 'darwinising' to describe the wild theorising of Erasmus, . . . though some of these ideas had affected Coleridge deeply in his youth, when still in sympathy with scientific adventure. It was only in his later years of disillusionment and antagonism to contemporary materialism that he came to oppose all that Erasmus Darwin stood for and cried: 'O Mercy, the blindness of the man!' . . . he stigmatised Dr. Darwin's philosophy in* Zoonomia *as the 'State of Nature or Orang Outang theology of the human race, substituted for the first chapters of the Book of Genesis';' . . . a strange foreshadowing of the outraged protests that followed on the publication of the* Origin of Species *two generations later.*

Darwin, too, had little use for ZOONOMIA, though for different reasons: *the proportion of speculation being so large to the facts given.*

But to return to the narrative of Darwin's personal history, he was doing so little at school that, at sixteen, his father decided to send him to join his brother at the medical school in Edinburgh but there he fared little better. From his own account:

> The instruction at Edinburgh was altogether by lectures, and these were intolerably dull, with the exception of those on chemistry by Hope. . . . Dr. Duncan's lectures on Materia Medica at 8 o'clock on a winter's morning are something fearful to remember. Dr. Munro made his lectures on human anatomy as dull, as he was himself, and the subject disgusted me.

> During my second year in Edinburgh I attended Jameson's lectures on Geology and Zoology, but they were incredible dull. The sole effect they produced on me was the determination never as long as I lived to read a book on Geology or in any was to study the science.

> I was also a member of the Royal Medical Society, and attended pretty regularly, but as the subjects were exclusively medical I did not care much about them. Much rubbish was talked there, but there were some good speakers.

Darwin, AUTOBIOGRAPHY

Two college acquaintances introduced him to marine zoology. There his reaction was quite different.

> I also became friends with some of the Newhaven fishermen, and sometimes accompanied them when they trawled for oysters, and thus got many specimens. But from not having had any regular practice in dissection, and from possessing only a wretched microscope my attempts were very poor. Nevertheless I made one interesting little discovery and read, about the beginning of the year 1826, a short paper on the subject to the Plinian Society. This was that the so-called ova of Flustra had the power of independent movement by means of cilia, and were in fact larvae. In another paper I showed that the little globular bodies which had been supposed to be the young state of Fucus loreus were the egg-cases of the worm-like Pontobdella muricate.

The only other noteworthy matter during his time in Edinburgh was that he heard *some interesting discourses on the habits of N. American birds* by Audubon and that he met a Negro who, *for payment,* taught him to stuff birds. *I used often to sit with him, for he was a very pleasant and intelligent man.*

Darwin's summer vacations at this time *were wholly given up to amusements* and his autumns *were devoted to shooting.*

My zeal was so great that I used to place my shooting boots open by my bed-side, so as not to lose half-a-minute in putting them on in the morning.

After two years it was clear that Darwin would never make a doctor, the more so as he *could not bring himself to endure a dissecting room* and *fled from operations.* His father's next and last suggestion was that he should try for the Church.

Charles Darwin found the proposal agreeable, none the less, probably, that a good deal of natural history and a little shooting were by no means held, at that time, to be incompatible with the conscientious performance of the duties of a country clergyman.

Accordingly, having first sought means to satisfy himself that *his religious opinions left nothing to be desired on the score of orthodoxy,* Charles went up to Cambridge, where he did, indeed, obtain a degree, though he could, nevertheless, write:

During the three years which I spent at Cambridge my time was wasted as far as the academical studies were concerned, as completely as at Edinburgh and at school.

He was, however, able to indulge his *passion for shooting and hunting* together with dining, drinking, jolly singing, and playing at cards. He had also *friends of a widely different character,* one of whom inoculated him with *a taste for pictures and good engravings* and others, with a *strong taste for music.* In retrospect he marvels how, being *utterly destitute of an ear* and unable to *perceive a discord, or keep time and have a tune correctly,* he nevertheless could have taken *pleasure from music.*

There was still one other outstanding interest:

. . . no pursuit at Cambridge was followed with nearly so much eagerness or gave me so much pleasure as collecting beetles. It was the mere passion for collecting.

There was no sign in this of any particular zeal for science itself. There were public lectures on science he could have attended, but he was too *sickened with lectures at Edinburgh* to do so. There was a single great exception which played deeply into his life.

I attended, however, Henslow's lectures on Botany, and liked them much for their extreme clearness, and the admirable illustrations; but I did not study botany.

It was Henslow whom he later called his *dear old master in Natural History* who finally set Darwin on his course. Henslow took his pupils and others on field excursions *on foot, or in coaches to distant places, or in a barge down the river,* lecturing on the rarer plants and animals they came across. Henslow also kept open house one evening a week for students interested in science and these Darwin attended regularly.

> *Before long I became well acquainted with Henslow, and during the latter half of my time at Cambridge took long walks with him on most days; so that I was called by some of the dons 'the man who walks with Henslow.'*

Henslow was well versed in *botany, entomology, chemistry, mineralogy, and geology.* Henslow made it possible for Darwin to accompany Sedgwick on a geological excursion in Wales, so that he gained *a certain amount of practical instruction in geology.* Through Henslow he came to read the recently published first volume of Lyell's Principles of Geology; but Henslow being a deeply religious man and a catastrophist cautioned *on no account to adopt Lyell's general views.* In short, Henslow became young Darwin's friend, guide and mentor. Eventually he procured Darwin's appointment to the <u>Beagle</u>, not as *a finished naturalist, but as amply qualified for collecting, observing, and noting anything worthy to be noted in Natural History.*

Darwin was keen to go but first had to gain his father's approval. This was flatly refused with the words, *If you can find any man of common sense, who advises you to go, I will give my consent.* To find such a person seemed so improbable that Darwin wrote that night to refuse the offer. The very next day however, an unexpected supplicant, his uncle, Josiah Wedgewood appeared on his behalf. His father considered Josiah *one of the most sensible men in the world;* so without further ado, the consent was given *in the kindest manner.*

But now another obstacle presented itself: his interview with Captain Fitz-Roy of the <u>Beagle</u>.

> *He was an ardent disciple of Lavater, and was convinced that he could judge a man's character by the outline of his features; and he doubted whether anyone with my nose could possess sufficient energy and determination for the voyage.*

Out of such unpromising beginnings, Darwin was launched on his career. According to Huxley:

> His ambition hardly rose above the hope that he should bring back materials for the scientific 'lions' at home of sufficient excellence to prevent them from turning and rending him.

As yet, he had no inkling of what his ultimate mission would be. Later he wrote, *I have always felt that I owe to this voyage the first real training or education of my mind.* During the course of the voyage, his real interest in science first awoke. With Lyell's volume beside him, his first intention was *to write a book on the geology of the various countries visited [and this made me thrill with delight]* but as time went on his main interest turned to the variation of species.

> During the voyage of the <u>Beagle</u> I had been deeply impressed by discovering in the Pampean formation great fossil animals covered with armour like that on the existing armadillos; secondly, by the manner in which closely-allied animals replace one another in proceeding southwards over the continent; and thirdly, by the South American character of most of the productions of the Galapagos Archipelago, and more especially, by the manner in which they differ slightly on each island of the group; some of the islands, appearing to be very ancient in a geological sense . . .

> It was evident that such facts as these, as well as many others, could only be explained on the supposition that species gradually became modified; and the subject haunted me.

Existing theories included: the adherents to Genesis; the theory of spontaneous creation which Huxley described as *the creative hypothesis with the creator left out*; and the evolutionists, whose opinions Darwin regarded as more speculative than real. Even though modification of species had become manifestly clear for him, he could discover no working hypothesis to support the facts so the subject remained conjectural. He focused his study on those cases of modification which might best be accounted for, and he pursued this *with a thoroughness to which none of his predecessors even remotely approximated.*

> After my return to England it appeared to me that by following the example of Lyell in Geology, and by collecting all facts which bore in any way on the variation of animals and plants under domestication and nature, some light might perhaps be thrown on the whole subject.

My first notebook was opened in July 1837. I worked on true Baconian principles, and without any theory collected facts on a wholesale scale, more especially with respect to domesticated productions, by printed enquiries, by conversation with skillful breeders and gardeners, and by extensive reading. When I see the list of books of all kinds which I read and abstracted, including whole series of Journals and Transactions, I am surprised at my industry.

I soon perceived that the selection was the keystone of man's success in making useful races of animals and plants. But how selection could be applied to organisms living in a state of nature remained for some time a mystery to me.

This last was the crucial question on which all depended. After much pondering without result the answer came to him through a phrase in a book and its attendant argument.

In October 1838, that is, fifteen months after I had begun my systematic enquiry, I happened to read for amusement Malthus on <u>Population</u>, and being well prepared to appreciate the struggle for existence which everywhere goes on from long-continued observation of the habits of animals and plants, it at once struck me that under these circumstances favourable variations would tend to be preserved, and unfavourable ones to be destroyed. The result of this would be the formation of new species. Here, then, I had at last got a theory by which to work. . . .

For the remaining forty-four years of his life Darwin applied this theory with unremitting labour to an ever-increasing multitude of facts; he called it the *Theory of Natural Selection.*

From that moment on, the source of Darwin's inspiration became a veritable taskmaster in his life. Thomas Malthus (1766–1834), began his career as a curate but soon left this to devote his life to economics. In 1798 he published a short work entitled, AN ESSAY ON THE PRINCIPLE OF POPULATION AS IT AFFECTS THE FUTURE IMPROVEMENT OF SOCIETY, WITH REMARKS ON THE SPECULATIONS OF MR. GODWIN, MR. CONDORCET, AND OTHER WRITERS. He wished to challenge the optimism of these other writers and to confront their speculative idealism with facts.

Malthus produced what he deemed to be hard facts. He claimed that population was increasing at a faster rate than the means of subsistence, population in geometric proportion, subsistence only in arithmetic proportion. Thus there was always a surplus population for the amount of food available, and if this were not checked, it must inevitably lead to a struggle for existence. How could this be corrected so as to reduce misery in the world, thus to ameliorate the struggle for existence? That was his question.

There were certain *positive checks* on population such as:

> ... all unwholesome occupations, severe labour and exposure to the seasons, extreme poverty, bad nursing of children, large towns, excesses of all kinds, the whole train of common diseases and epidemics, war, plague and famine.

Yet all these together, and others that he mentioned (for example, *vicious methods* to keep families down), were insufficient to solve the problem of excess population.

Malthus had little to propose as remedy beyond the appeal to reason, which men possessed and nature did not. His appeal was for *moral restraint*, to marry at a later age, to refrain from having large families, but he could attach little hope for this and his outlook remained pessimistic.

At the time when Malthus wrote this paper the French Revolution was still a recent event, the industrial revolution was on its way and questions concerning the social future were acquiring a quite new impetus.

The concept of population increase versus means of subsistence struck Darwin strongly. While plants produced seeds prolifically and animals their young at a prodigious rate, only a fraction survived. Fantastic figures were worked out to demonstrate this. Those who survived must be better favoured in some way. Then came the further thought: whatever had proved to their advantage would be transmitted by heredity to their descendants. Variations were known to occur in nature constantly. What caused the variations was something Darwin never went into. Once a favourable variation occurred, however slight the advantage over the common stock, it would be perpetuated in the succeeding generations. In the course of immense periods of time, new species would build up, and older and less favoured ones would grow extinct.

Three strands of thought became interwoven: Malthus' struggle for existence, Herbert Spencer's survival of the fittest, for this formulation belongs to him, and Darwin's natural selection. Darwin believed he had solved the riddle; modification through descent was the key to evolution.

> I was so anxious to avoid prejudice, that I determined not for some time to write even the briefest sketch of it. In June 1842 I first allowed myself the satisfaction of writing a very brief abstract of my theory in pencil in thirty-five pages; and this was enlarged during the summer of 1844 into one of two hundred thirty pages, which I had fairly copied out and still possess (1876).
>
> Darwin, AUTOBIOGRAPHY

> Darwin was so fully convinced of the importance of his work, as it then stood, that he made special arrangements for its publication in case of his death. But it is a singular example of reticent fortitude, that, although for the next fourteen years the subject never left his mind, and during the latter half of that period he was constantly engaged in amassing facts bearing upon it . . . only two or three friends were cognisant of his views.
>
> Thomas Huxley

Thus Darwin read Malthus in 1838, waited four years before he wrote the first, very brief abstract, another two years before he enlarged this, and twelve further years before he began seriously to prepare his material for publication.

> Early in 1856 Lyell advised me to write out my views pretty fully, and I began at once to do so on a scale three of four times as extensive as that which afterwards followed in my Origin of Species; yet it was only an abstract of the materials I had collected, and I got through about half the work on this scale.
>
> Darwin, AUTOBIOGRAPHY

And thus Darwin continued to work in privacy, guarding his secret, to be divulged when all the preparations had been completed and he felt the time was ripe. But then something sudden and dramatic happened; he received a document from Malay.

> But my plans were overthrown, for early in the summer of 1858, Mr. Wallace who was in the Malay archipelago, sent me an essay On the Tendency of Varieties to depart indefinitely from the Original Type. This essay contained exactly the same theory as mine.

In a letter written at the time, Darwin added:

If Wallace had my MS sketch written out in 1842 he could not have made a better short abstract! Even his terms stand now as heads of my chapters . . . So all originality, whatever it may amount to, will not be deteriorated; as all the labour consists in the application of this theory.

It is greatly to Darwin's honour that he intended to have Wallace's essay published immediately without any regard to himself. This was prevented by his friends, Lyell and Hooker, who arranged, instead, for a joint reading of Wallace's essay and extracts from Darwin's manuscript of 1844. The reading was scheduled to take place before the Linnaean Society in July, 1858, under the common title, ON THE TENDENCY OF SPECIES TO FORM VARIETIES AND ON THE PERPETUATION OF VARIETIES AND SPECIES BY NATURAL MEANS OF SELECTION. *The theory*, as Wallace writes, *received little attention till Darwin's great and epoch-making book appeared at the end of the following year.*

What led Wallace to arrive at *exactly the same theory?* Writing many years later, he tells us:

Relying mainly on the well-known facts of geographical distribution and geological succession, I deduced from them the law, or generalization, that, 'Every species has come into existence coincident in Space and Time with a Pre-existing closely allied Species'; and I showed how many peculiarities in the affinities, the succession and the distribution of the forms of life, were explained by this hypothesis, and that no important facts contradicted it.

Thus Wallace had arrived independently at his perception of what Darwin called *modification through descent.* This led him to the same problem that confronted Darwin.

Even then, however, I had no conception of how and why each new form had come into existence with all its beautiful adaptions to its special mode of life; and though the subject was continuously being pondered over, no light came to me till three years later, under somewhat peculiar circumstances.

Modification had grown obvious, but what conditioned or controlled it? Wallace continues:

I was then living at Ternate in the Moluccas, and was suffering from a rather severe attack of intermittent fever, which prostrated me for several hours each day during the cold and succeeding hot fits. During one of these fits, while again considering the problem of the origin of species, *something led me to think of Malthus' <u>Essay on Population</u> (which I had read ten years before), and the 'positive checks' . . . war, disease, famine, accidents, etc., . . . which he adduced as keeping all savage populations nearly stationary. It then occurred to me that these checks must also act upon animals, and keep down their numbers, and as they increase so much faster than man does, while their numbers are always very nearly or quite stationary, it was clear that these checks in their case must be far more powerful, since a number equal to the whole increase must be cut off by them each year. While vaguely thinking how this would affect any species, there suddenly flashed upon me the idea of the <u>survival of the fittest</u> . . . that the individual removed by these checks must be, on the whole, inferior to those that survived. Then, considering the <u>variations</u> continually occurring in every fresh generation of animals or plants, and the changes of climate, of food, of enemies always in progress, the whole method of specific modifications became clear to me, and in the two hours of my fit I had thought out the draft on a paper; in the two succeeding evenings I wrote it out, and sent it by the next post to Mr. Darwin. I fully expected it to be as new to him as it was to myself. . . . I was therefore surprised to find that he had really arrived at the very same theory as mine long before (in 1844) . . .*

The coincidence now explains itself. Unknown to each of them, both had derived the theory from the same source. Malthus wrote his book out of quite other considerations, concerned with the social welfare of mankind and seeking methods to overcome the 'positive checks.' This then was applied to a theory concerning the entire field of living nature, including man. In the Introduction to his ORIGIN OF THE SPECIES Darwin acknowledges this quite clearly: *This is the doctrine of Malthus, applied to the whole animal and vegetable kingdoms.*

The doctrine, as presented, builds the whole of evolution on the basis of chance variation, with its counterpart in physics of chance and probability; and likewise, natural selection becomes an automatic process, again akin to the physicist's notion of physical cause and effect. There is no ground left for inwardness of any kind. Since man is a consequence of this same process, therefore, what he might term inwardness in his own experience belongs, as the physicists declared it, to the secondary qualities and is illusory. To this extent has the materialistic trend in the physical sciences influenced and determined the biological sciences. It is important to recognize that influence when placing Darwin and Malthus into the historical framework of their time. It is understandable, considering the initial shock caused by this doctrine, why Darwin hesitated so long in making it public; and he took great pains to make his meaning clear.

Let the endless number of slight variations and individual differences occurring in our domestic productions, and, in a lesser degree, in those under nature, to be borne in mind; as well as the strength of the hereditary tendency. Under domestication, it may truly be said that the whole organization becomes in some degree plastic. But the variability which we almost universally meet with in our domestic productions, is not directly produced . . . by men; he can neither originate varieties, nor prevent their occurrence; he can only preserve and accumulate such as do occur . . . can it, then, be thought improbable, seeing that variations useful to man have undoubtedly occurred, that other variations useful to each being in the great and complex battle of life, should occur in the course of many successive generations? If such do occur, can we doubt (remembering that many more individuals are born than can possibly survive) that individuals having any advantage, however slight, over other, would have the best chance of surviving and of procreating their kind? On the other hand, we may feel sure that any variation in the least degree injurious would be rigidly destroyed. This preservation of favourable individual differences and variations, and the destruction of those which are injurious, I have called Natural Selection, or the Survival of the Fittest. . . .

Several writers, have misapprehended or objected to the term Natural Selection. Some have even imagined that natural selection induces variability, whereas it implies only the preservation of such variations as arise and are beneficial to the being under its condition of life.

Others have objected that the term selection implies conscious choice in the animals which become modified; and it has even been urged that, as plants have no volition, natural selection is not applicable to them!

It has been said that I speak of natural selection as an active power of Deity; but who objects to an author speaking of the attraction of gravity as ruling the movements of the planets? Everyone knows what is meant and is implied by such metaphorical expressions; and they are almost necessary for brevity. So again it is difficult to avoid personifying the word Nature; but I mean by Nature, only the aggregate action and product of many laws, and by laws the sequence of events as ascertained by us.

We have good reason to believe . . . that changes in the conditions of life give a tendency to increased variability . . . and this would manifestly be variable to natural selection, by affording a better chance of the occurrence of profitable variations. Unless such occur, natural selection can do nothing.

Man can act only on external and visible characters: Nature, if I may be allowed to personify the natural preservation or survival of the fittest, cares nothing for appearances, except in so far as they are useful to any being. She can act on every internal organ, on every shade of constitutional difference, on the whole machinery of life. Man selects only for his own good: Nature only for that of the being which she tends.

Under nature, the slightest differences of structure or constitution may well turn the nicely-balanced scale in the struggle for life and so be preserved. How fleeting are the wishes and efforts of man! how short the time! and consequently how poor will be his results, compared with those accumulated by Nature during whole geological periods! Can we wonder, then, that Nature's productions should be far 'truer' in character than man's productions; that they should be infinitely better adapted to the most complex conditions of life, and should plainly bear the stamp of far higher workmanship?

It may metaphorically be said that natural selection is daily and hourly scrutinizing, throughout the world, the slightest variations; rejecting those that are bad, preserving and adding up all that are good; silently and insensibly working <u>whenever and wherever opportunity offers</u>, at the improvement of each organic being in relation to organic and inorganic conditions of life. We see nothing of these slow changes in progress, until the hand of time has marked the lapse of ages, and then so imperfect is our view into long-past geological ages, that we see only that the forms of life are now different from what they formerly were.

Always it is assumed that nature works 'insensibly' and that intelligence is to be found only in mankind. Nature, without mind, has produced the well-nigh miraculous organizations and adaptations, skills, qualities, and beauties of an ever advancing range of plants and creatures, including the gift of human intelligence. Her method is one and the same at all levels, the method of natural selection, and it is this which fills his book. As Darwin said, *All the labour consists in the application of the theory . . .*

Following the meeting with the Linnaean Society in July, 1858, Darwin determined to complete a book for publication in the shortest time possible. He must have worked under high pressure. In March 1859 he wrote in a letter:

I am weary of my work. It is a very odd thing that I have no sensation that I overwork my brain; but facts compel me to conclude that my brain was never formed for such thinking.

On November 19th, only five days before THE ORIGIN OF THE SPECIES was to appear, he wrote to a friend:

> When I think of the many cases of men who have studied one subject for years, and have persuaded themselves of the truth of the foolishest doctrines, I feel sometimes a little frightened, whether I may not be one of these monomaniacs.

It is to be remembered that for twenty-one years he had been serving an idea borrowed from Malthus, and then applied to his vast field of observations, but not born as a direct intuition out of those observations. Therefore it is not surprising that before the great moment of the publication had arrived, he should have felt invaded by doubt and apprehensions about the absolute validity of it all.

Despite the uproar which the book caused, or maybe because of it, the book sold astonishingly well. Writing in retrospect in 1876, Darwin recalls:

> The first small edition of 1,250 copies was sold on the day of the publication, and a second edition of 3,000 copies soon afterward. Sixteen thousand have now been sold in England; and considering how stiff a book it is, this is a large sale. It has been translated into almost every European tongue, even into such languages as Spanish, Bohemian, Polish, and Russian. . . . Even an essay in Hebrew has appeared on it, showing that the theory is contained in the Old Testament! The reviews were very numerous . . .
>
> Darwin AUTOBIOGRAPHY

Considering the much smaller reading public of those days, this is even more remarkable. Darwin offers his own explanation:

> It has sometimes been said that the success of the <u>Origin</u> proved that 'the subject was in the air,' or 'that men's minds were prepared for it.' I do not think that this is strictly true, for I occasionally sounded not a few naturalists, and never happened to come across a single one who seemed to doubt about the permanence of species. Even Lyell and Hooker, though they would listen with interest to me, never seemed to agree. I tried once or twice to explain to able men what I meant by natural selection, but signally failed. What I believe was strictly true is that innumerable well-observed facts were stored in the minds of naturalists, ready to take their proper places as soon as any theory which would receive them was sufficiently explained.

Elsewhere he observed, *Nothing is more remarkable than the spread of skepticism or rationalism in the [last] half of my life.* The roots of this skepticism were already apparent so that his reliance focused increasingly on the outer factors alone. There is no doubt that in Darwin's time the general trend was to try and reduce all the complexities of life to a few simple formulae based on common reason. Darwin's theory was of that order, a simple formula to explain the whole of evolution. Here was a theory free from all articles of faith, claiming to stand on perceptible facts alone. From the section on morphology:

> What can be more curious than that the hand of a man, formed for grasping, that of a mole for digging, the leg of the horse, the paddle of the porpoise, and the wing of the bat, should all be constructed on the same pattern, and should include similar bones, in the same relative positions? . . .

> Nothing can be more hopeless than to attempt to explain this similarity of pattern . . . by utility or by the doctrine of final causes. . . . On the ordinary view of the independent creation of each being, we can only say that so it is; . . . that it has pleased the Creator to construct all the animals and plants in each great class on a uniform plan; but this is not a scientific explanation.

> The selection is to a large extent simple on the theory of the selection of successive slight modifications, . . each modification being profitable in some way to the modified form, but often affecting by correlation other parts of the organisation. In changes of this nature, there will be little or no tendency to alter the original pattern, or to transpose the parts. . . . If we suppose that an early progenitor . . . the archetype as it may be called . . . of all animals, birds, and reptiles, had its limbs constructed on the existing general pattern, for whatever purpose they serve, we can at once perceive the plain signification of the homologous construction of the limbs throughout the class.

> Darwin, ORIGIN OF THE SPECIES

In THE ORIGIN OF THE SPECIES, Darwin is cautious in his references to mankind though his *belief that man must come under the same law* is implicit and occasionally peeps through. The most he allowed himself to state was that by this method *light would be thrown on the origin of man and his history.* It was not until 1871, by which time his general theory had been widely accepted, that he published his DESCENT OF MAN. The following passage, excerpted from his later book, shows graphically where THE ORIGIN was leading:

The early progenitors of man must have been once covered with hair, both sexes having beards; their ears were probably pointed, and capable of movement; and their bodies were provided with a tail, having the proper muscles. Their limbs and bodies were also acted on by many muscles which now only occasionally reappear, but are normally present in the Quadrumana. . . . Still earlier, the progenitors of man must have been aquatic in their habits; for morphology plainly tells us that our lungs consist of a modified swim-bladder, which once served as a float. . . . In the lunar or weekly recurrent periods of some of our functions we apparently still retain traces of our primordial birthplace, a shore washed by tides. . . . These early ancestors of man, thus seen in the dim recesses of time, must have been as simply, or even still more simply organized than the Lancelet or amphioxus.

Darwin, Descent of Man

The challenge which such a statement represented when it first appeared has to be imagined. It seemed to leave no room for disputation. These were the declared facts; to seek beyond the facts could only be regarded as sheer folly.

Man may be excused for feeling some pride at having risen, though not through his own exertions, to the very summit of the organic scale; and the fact of his having thus risen, instead of having been aboriginally placed there, may give him some hope for a still higher destiny in the future.

These later statements were implicit in The Origin though not yet so openly stated. Man was, like his humblest progenitors, the involuntary product of natural selection; and there the matter must end, unless further favourable variations should arrive to enable natural selection to develop further. By implication, this was the obvious bearing of his thought process. At no point in his evolutionary chain is there any room for a single conscious step. It is all handed over to material nature working insensibly all the way. That was the situation Darwin had arrived at in his own mind and the one which, through his work, he was inviting the world to adopt.

In 1859, when The Origin was published, Thomas Huxley, who described himself as a 'sort of sub-nurse' of the book, wrote:

That this most ingenious hypothesis enables us to give a reason for many apparent anomalies in the distribution of living things in time and space, and that it is not contradicted by the main phenomena of life and organization appear to us to be unquestionable; and, so far, it must be admitted *to have an advantage over any of its predecessors. But it is quite another matter to affirm absolutely either the truth or falsehood of Mr. Darwin's views at the present stage of the enquiry. Goethe has an excellent aphorism defining that state of mind which he calls 'Tatige Skepsis' . . . active doubt. It is doubt which so loves the truth that it neither dares rest in doubting, nor extinguish itself by unjustified belief; and we commend this state of mind to students of species, with regard to Mr. Darwin's or any other hypothesis, as to their origin. The combined investigations of another twenty years may, perhaps, enable naturalists to say whether the modifying causes and the selective power, which Mr. Darwin has satisfactorily shown to exist in Nature are competent to produce all the effects he ascribes to them; or whether, on the other hand, he has been led to over-estimate the value of the principle of natural selection, as greatly as Lamarck over-estimated his <u>vera causa</u> of modification by exercise.*

Here there is a healthy note of caution in forming a judgment. A year later, at the height of the controversies, he comes strongly to Darwin's defense:

Everybody has read Mr. Darwin's book, or, at least, has given an opinion upon its merits and demerits; pietists, whether lay or ecclesiastic, decry it with vigorous invective; old ladies of both sexes consider it a decidedly dangerous book, and even savants, who have no better mud to throw, quote antiquated writers to show that its author is no better than an ape himself; while every philosophical thinker hails it as a veritable Whitworth gun in the armoury of liberalism; and all competent naturalists and physiologists, whatever their opinions as to the ultimate fate of the doctrines put forth, acknowledge that the work in which they are embodied is a solid contribution to knowledge and inaugurates a new epoch in natural history.

Huxley's complaint is against prejudiced judgments. By 1880 Darwin's *general doctrine of evolution* had grown so far popular that Huxley felt constrained on the contrary, to utter a warning against overcredulity.

History warns us, however, that it is the customary fate of new truths to begin as heresies and to end as superstitions; and, as matters now stand, it is hardly rash to anticipate that, in another twenty years, the new generation, educated under the influences of the present day, will be in danger of accepting the doctrines of the <u>Origin of Species</u> with as little reflection, and it may be with as little justification, as so many of our contemporaries twenty years ago, rejected them.

Against any such a consummation, let us devoutly pray. . .

On Darwin's death in 1882, Huxley wrote an appreciation of him for NATURE. This essay ends as a requiem.

> *There is a time for all things — a time for glorying in our ever-extending conquests over the realm of Nature, and a time for mourning over the heroes who have led us to victory.*
>
> *None have ever fought better, and none have been more fortunate, than Charles Darwin. He found a great truth trodden underfoot, reviled by bigots, and ridiculed by all the world; he lived long enough to see it, chiefly by his own efforts, irrefragably established in science, inseparably incorporated with the common thoughts of men, and only hated and feared by those who would revile, but love not. What shall a man desire more than this?*
>
> *'The hour of departure has arrived, and we go our ways — I to die and you to live. Which is the better, God only knows.'*

Huxley, in his praise of Darwin, epitomizes the fervour of the scientific spirit in his day. Men were idealists, even as materialists, in their eagerness to carry discovery further. It is remarkable that he felt he could make a comparison between Darwin and Socrates whose every endeavour, as described particularly in the Apologia, was to wrest himself free of dependence on the life of the senses in his striving to reach a higher world of real and abiding values. Death meant for him entering into that higher life. For Socrates, like Goethe, the earth was nothing if not a school for educating immortal spirits.

In the latter part of the nineteenth century, the process begun with the physicists in the sixteenth and seventeenth centuries reached a culminating point. Human thinking appeared to die to inner causes and become wholly externalized. Darwin, with unfailing honesty, describes this dying process in himself though he would not have used this term. The following passage is quoted from the section in his autobiography, RELIGIOUS BELIEF.

> *Whilst aboard the <u>Beagle</u> I was quite orthodox, and I remember being heartily laughed at by several of the officers (though themselves orthodox) for quoting the Bible as an unanswerable authority on some point of morality.*

Later he comes to reflect:

> *. . . that the clearest evidence would be requisite to make any sane man believe in the miracles by which Christianity is supported, . . . that the more we know of the fixed laws of nature, the more incredible do miracles become. . . .*

A thinking which builds only on 'the fixed laws of nature,' that is exclusively on physical laws, cannot with honesty relate itself to 'miracles' or events of a supernatural kind. But Darwin did not resign his religious belief without a struggle.

> *. . . I can well remember often and often inventing day-dreams of old letters between distinguished Romans and manuscripts being discovered at Pompei or elsewhere which confirmed in the most striking manner all that was written in the Gospels. But I found it more and more difficult, with free scope given to my imagination, to invent evidence which would suffice to convince me. Thus disbelief crept over me at a very slow rate, but was at last complete.*
>
> Darwin, Autobiography

Thus a source of experience which was native to him slowly faded out. What then is left of all creation? Can it be without plan or purpose? Darwin feels obliged to answer:

> *The old argument from design in nature, as given by Paley, which formerly seemed to me so conclusive, fails, now that the law of natural selection has been discovered. We can no longer argue that, for instance, the beautiful hinge of a bivalve shell must have been made by an intelligent being, like the hinge of a door by man. There seems to be no more design in the variability of organic beings and in the action of natural selection, than is the course which the wind blows. Everything in nature is the result of fixed law.*

How different from the words of St. John, *The wind bloweth where it listeth.* That wind is no longer felt or perceived — it does not come under the aegis of scientific law.

Darwin considers the question of suffering, *the suffering of millions of the lower animals throughout almost endless time.* How can one reasonably relate this suffering to an *intelligent first cause?* Yet, the presence of suffering *agrees well with the view that all organic beings have been developed through variation and natural selection.* Darwin considers that since natural selection always works toward a heightened capacity for enjoyment with each advancing organism, there is probably a preponderance of pleasure over suffering in the world. No God need be invoked for this, insensible nature can cope with it all.

Of what account are the feelings of exaltation which arise in the contemplation of nature? Of what do they give evidence, if anything at all? The following passage is noteworthy as reflecting Darwin's inner state of mind.

> In my Journal I wrote that whilst standing in the midst of the grandeur of a Brazilian forest, 'it is not possible to give an adequate idea of the higher feelings of wonder, admiration, and devotion which fill and elevate the mind.' I well remember my conviction that there is more in man than the mere breath of his body. But now the grandest scenes would not cause any such convictions and feelings to rise to my mind.

Experience the tragedy contained in this text. The journal continues:

> It can truly be said that I am like a man who has become colourblind, and the universal belief by men of the existence of redness makes my present loss of perception of not the least value as evidence. This argument would be a valid one if all men of all races had the same inward conviction of the existence of one God; but we know that this is far from being the case. Therefore I cannot see that such inward convictions and feelings are of any weight as evidence of what really exists. The state of mind which grand scenes formerly excited in me, and which was intimately connected with a belief in God, did not essentially differ from that which is often called the sense of sublimity; and however difficult it may be to explain the genesis of this sense, it can hardly be advanced as an argument for the existence of God, any more than the powerful though vague and similar feelings excited by music.

Despite this, Darwin does not yet wholly abandon the idea of God. He is seeking for an objective ground on which to base belief.

> Another source of conviction in the existence of God, connected with reason and not with the feelings, impresses me as having much more weight. This follows from the extreme difficulty or rather impossibility of conceiving this immense and wonderful universe, including man with his capacity of looking far backwards and far into futurity, as the result of blind chance and necessity. When thus reflecting I feel compelled to look for a First Cause having an intelligent mind in some degree analogous to that of man; and I deserve to be called a Theist.

> This conclusion was strong in my mind about the time, as far as I remember, when I wrote the Origin of Species; and it is since that time that it has very gradually with many fluctuations become weaker.

Against this last reasoned attempt to hold on to the probability of there being an Intelligent First Cause to existence, there rose the argument for natural selection.

> . . . can the mind of man, which has, as I fully believe, been developed from a mind as low as that possessed by the lowest animal, be trusted when it draws such grand conclusions? May not these be the results of the connection between cause and effect which strikes us as a necessary one, but probably depends merely on inherited experience?

It is not now the feelings but the mind itself which is being questioned, and if that is the resultant of an inevitable process of automatic cause and effect, then all further questioning grows useless. In place of mind there is brought forward what today is termed 'the conditioned reflex.'

> Nor must we overlook the probability of the constant inculcation in a belief in God on the minds of children producing so strong and perhaps an inherited effect on the brains not yet fully developed, that it would be as difficult for them to throw off the belief in God, as for a monkey to throw off its instinctive fear and hatred of a snake.

An alarmingly powerful simile at the end! It disturbed Darwin's wife so deeply that she begged their son, Francis Darwin, on first editing the AUTOBIOGRAPHY to omit this passage from the text,

> . . . partly because your father's opinion that all morality has grown up by evolution is painful to me; but also because where this sentence comes in, it gives one a sort of shock — and would give an opening to say, however unjustly, that he considered all spiritual beliefs no higher than hereditary aversions or likings, such as the fear of monkeys towards snakes.

Yet this is precisely what Darwin did think or allowed his theory to persuade his to think. His theory requires that all human attributes shall find their incipient beginnings in the lower creatures: it leaves no room for a single exception, if as a theory it should not fall to the ground.

> I cannot pretend to throw the least light on such abstruse problems. The mystery of the beginning of all things is insoluble by us; and I for one must be content to remain an Agnostic.

The Oxford Dictionary defines an agnostic as *one who holds that nothing is known, or likely to be known, of the existence of a God or of anything beyond the material phenomena.*

Whence then does what we call 'moral' enter into life? How does Darwin, with his reasoning, account for it. The argument goes as follows.

A dog acts from instinct to acquire what will give him the greatest satisfaction or pleasure and does so blindly. A man need not act so blindly; he can think about his experiences and compare them. Though thought or the intellectual faculty is also, strictly speaking, evolved on the principle of natural selection, man nevertheless possesses this faculty of reflection and he can use it. It may lead him to the conclusion, *in accordance with the wisest men,* that he obtains his greatest satisfaction from following his social instincts. That way he will be approved by those around him and loved by those nearest him and thus enjoy *the highest pleasure on this earth.*

These higher impulses, once they are acquired, *may be almost called instincts,* so that to act at a lower level, *to obey his sensuous passions,* becomes intolerable to him. Should he act at any time in contradiction to the opinion of others *whose approbation he will then not receive,* he still has *the solid satisfaction of knowing that he has followed his innermost guide or conscience.*

Thus Darwin attempts to construct a continuous line from the behaviour of a dog, who follows his instincts blindly for the greatest satisfaction of his desire, to the reasoned action of a man who, obedient to the highest instinct of all, his conscience, is ready to face not only the misery of being rejected by his fellows, but, if need be, martyrdom itself. In all this argument nothing is admitted that could in any way exceed the bounds of natural selection. This way there is no distinction to be made between the instinctive and the moral — the impulse which prompts a dog and the conscience which directs a man. There are no virtues which are really virtuous, and no vices which are really vicious: there are certain factors, derived from the instincts of primitive races and their animal progenitors, called social instincts, acquired over great stretches of time through the indifferent law of natural selection.

It becomes a question of whether Darwin had possession of his theory or whether his theory, stage by stage, gained possession of him. Insofar as he, through his myriads of painstaking observations, confirmed the truth of evolution as an incontrovertible fact, the greatness of his contribution must live for all time. It offered release from various fixations of thought and thus served for a notable expansion of human outlook. In so far as he confined the whole of this newly conceived outlook to the one dominant thought of natural selection based on chance variation (supplemented further by his theory of sexual selection, developed more particularly in THE DESCENT OF MAN) — in so far as he bound the whole of evolution to this one law, the resolution was a scene of interminable strife without a goal in view, without a glimmer of light for anything called freedom. It is this lack which takes away whatever Darwin may have intended as a kind of consolation by the closing paragraph of his ORIGIN.

> It is interesting to contemplate a tangled bank, clothed with many plants of many kinds, with birds singing on the bushes, with various insects flitting about, and with worms crawling through the damp earth, and to reflect that these elabourated, constructed forms, so different from each other, and dependent on each other in so complex a manner, have all been produced by laws acting around us. These laws, taken in the largest sense, being Growth and Reproduction; Inheritance which is almost implied by reproduction; Variability from the indirect and direct action of the conditions of life, and from use and disuse; a Ratio of Increase so high as to lead to a Struggle for Life, and as a consequence to Natural Selection, entailing Divergence of Character, and the Extinction of less-improved forms. Thus, from the war of nature, from famine and death, the most exalted object which we are capable of conceiving, namely, the production of the higher animals, directly follows. There is grandeur in this view of life, with its several powers, having been originally breathed by the Creator into a few forms or into one; and that, whilst this planet has gone cycling on according to the fixed law of gravity, from so simple a beginning endless forms most beautiful and most wonderful have been, and are being evolved.
>
> Darwin, ORIGIN OF SPECIES

Darwin, at this stage, still permits himself to use the term Creator, but leaves us in the dark as to his interpretation of it. From the foregoing final paragraph it may be regarded as no more than a figure of speech.

We know from our everyday experience how thought and feelings interact, how there are thoughts which can enhance our feelings and enliven us, and others that can subdue our feelings and benumb our sense of life. This persistent setting aside of everything that is most precious to human life, reducing the 'grandeur' of what we behold to the gray monotony of an endless chain of insensible cause and effect, induces an impression of sinking away into a kind of darkness. It is astonishing that Darwin, with all the power and clarity of his faculty of impartial observation, could leave us the following picture of something akin to a dying process in himself.

> *I have said that in one respect my mind has changed during the last twenty or thirty years. Up to the age of thirty, or beyond it, poetry of many kinds, such as the works of Milton, Gray, Byron, Wordsworth, Coleridge, and Shelley, gave me great pleasure, and even as a schoolboy I took intense delight in Shakespeare, especially the historical plays. I have also said that formerly pictures gave me considerable, and music very great delight. But now for many years I cannot endure to read a line of poetry; I have tried lately to read Shakespeare, and found it so intolerably dull that it nauseated me. I have also lost my taste for pictures and music. Music generally sets me thinking too energetically on what I have been at work on, instead of giving me pleasure. I retain some taste for fine scenery, but it does not cause me the exquisite delight which it formerly did. . . . My mind seems to have become a kind of machine for grinding general laws out of large collections of facts, but why this should have caused the atrophy of that part of the brain alone, on which the higher tastes depend, I cannot conceive. A man with a mind more highly organized or better constituted than mine, would not, I suppose, have thus suffered; and if I had to live my life again, I would have made a rule to read some poetry and listen to some music at least once a week; for perhaps the parts of my brain now atrophied would thus have been kept active through use. The loss of these tastes is a loss of happiness, and may possibly be injurious to the intellect, and more probably to the moral character, by enfeebling the emotional part of our nature.*
>
> Darwin, AUTOBIOGRAPHY

We admire and must be grateful for this testimony. Has not the world in general been living in Darwin's kind of thinking, drawing his kind of conclusions, living by what has become the common practice of *grinding out general laws out of large collections of facts*, statistical laws, economic laws, genetic laws, salesmanship laws, every kind of law supposed to have some bearing on natural and human circumstances and conditions? Has not the same kind of thinking entered our medical, psychological and social sciences does it not largely rule in our educational methods? In our modern science, is a man of more account in the universe than his dog or his cat or the rabbit that runs across his field? What is happening to enhance or to deaden the 'higher tastes' in the cultural life of today, and do we, or do we not, see a falling off in many respects in 'moral character'?

Sir Julian Huxley is as stout a defender of Darwin's theory in this century as ever his grandfather, Thomas Huxley, was in the last. He writes

> . . . it is to Darwin and to Darwin alone that honour is due for the first full proof of evolution, and for the demonstration that it could be accounted for, not in supernatural or mystical terms, but in those of natural law.

In his introductory remarks to his synopsis of Darwin's main works, he states:

> When Darwin wrote, the state of biological ignorance on many important subjects was enormous, and sometimes total. Darwin's views on the mechanism of heredity bore no resemblance to ours — for the reason that the elementary principles of the subject had not yet been discovered; even the distinction between what variations were heritable and what were not, was still completely vague. The microscope had not yet revealed the basic facts concerning the chromosomes and their behaviour. Paleontology was still in its childhood, so that one of the chief supports of the evolutionary view, in the shape of long series of fossils exhibiting gradual and progressive change, was not yet available. The greatest triumphs of comparative embryology had not yet come to the aid of biology, either for the study of variation, or for giving a quantitative basis to the theory of natural selection.

These advances, in Sir Julian Huxley's final judgment, while confirming some of the earlier views and rejecting others, in their sum total go to show *that Darwin was in principle correct.* Yet the effect of Darwin's theory has been to draw man so far into the web of animal existence that the distinction between man and animal has grown even more blurred as time has gone on, and this has had, and is having, its effects.

Sullivan gives Darwin full credit for all the evidence he assembled, both geologically and geographically, to support the view of *modification by descent* as opposed to the belief in *special creation.* And yet the whole subject is loaded with questions.

> Again and again we have the feeling that the primary concepts used by biologists are inadequate to their most important problems.

> The great theory of natural selection, for example, is full of lacunae. Instead of the natural and ready assent one gives to a demonstration in

physics, for example, one has to make a really immense effort to believe, even for a moment, that the whole evolution of living forms on this planet has come about by 'random variations' and the struggle for existence. It does not in the least explain the most obvious fact about the whole process, that is, the upward tendency of living forms. If mere survival is the sole desideratum, then it would seem that some rudimentary type of organism would be all that is needed. And there would seem no reason why even a rudimentary type of organism should appear, since it could not hope to rival in longevity the everlasting rocks.

We have the impression that it is only by an extraordinary act of faith that biologists can suppose that the actual progress of life can be explained in the terms that they adopt.

Sullivan, LIMITATIONS OF SCIENCE

There are scientists who have introduced such ideas as vital force, entelechy, and others but these are all too indefinite for scientific purposes — they merely *testify to the conviction that the present primary concepts are inadequate.*

Darwin's ORIGIN took the world mightily by surprise. Nothing similar had occurred since Galileo startled Europe with his STARRY MESSENGER. First the face of the world was changed by Galileo, then Darwin altered the status of man. To agree with Huxley that all who objected strongly were bigots, pietists, and *old ladies of both sexes* would be wrong. There were deeply thinking, knowledgeable men, who could well appreciate the genius contained in Darwin's work, yet who could not reconcile themselves to his conclusions. Just as the physicists had dismissed God from the heavens, so this new theory threatened belief in the latent divinity in man; henceforth mankind was to be registered as belonging to the beasts. Evolution might proceed further, but without influence from the will of man and dependent on the chance variations of organic matter. Morality could only be a derivative of matter. The same applied to aesthetics, art, poetry, religion, and to all that constituted the so-called 'higher life of man,' The outer physical facts were magnificently portrayed but were there not other experiences to be apprehended as facts, only inwardly? Between the outer and the inner there no longer was any bridge; it seemed the outer had claimed the inner as its own.

The idea of natural selection on which Darwin built all his theories is by no means proven yet.

· 15 ·

Transhumanism

It must have been shortly after the Second World War, a time of general depression, that there appeared in a popular magazine, THE ILLUSTRATED, a brief article by Julian Huxley the gist of which was that unless man had a worthwhile goal to strive for he must sink into apathy or despair. He disclaimed religion in its accepted sense of relying on some higher world. Still less did he approve of ideology. The phrase *apathy or despair* was written, clearly, out of deep concern, demanding a positive answer. Years later Huxley presented a possible answer in RELIGION WITHOUT REVELATION. It reveals the sincere honesty and earnest striving of a prominent contemporary scientist, who bases hypothesis on his intellectual grasp of the phenomena of nature irrespective of all else. In its own degree it stands as a witness of man's striving to endow life, and particularly human life, with meaning. One must admire and honour the rectitude of Huxley's endeavour to solve the problem he had postulated; yet he rejected all evidence that he could not call his own. He declared his position on the opening page of his book, RELIGION WITHOUT REVELATION (the 1967 New Edition):

> 'Mind' and 'matter' appear as two aspects of our unitary mind-bodies. There is no separate supernatural realm: all phenomena are part of one natural process of evolution. There is no basic cleavage between science and religion; they are both organs of evolving humanity.
>
> This earth is one of the rare spots in the cosmos where mind has flowered. Man is a product of nearly three billion years of evolution, in whose person the evolutionary process has at last become conscious of

itself and its possibilities. Whether he likes it or not, he is responsible for
the whole further evolution of our planet.

This comes as the conclusion of a lifetime of work and study.

Huxley, in his book, set out to solve a personal problem. He needed to determine for himself the ground he stood on. It turned out
that the greater part of the Western world, certainly of the scientific world, shared that same ground with him. That is what makes
his book one of special interest.

He tells how, as a child, he went to church only on festival occasions.
Even at that early age the combination of mysteriousness and the
feeling of sanctity and awe, produced in him an interior puzzle-
ment, an unsatisfied sense of emotional and intellectual mystery.

> . . . *this remained an unresolved complex, growing with me and with-*
> *in me like a thought-tumour, part of my being and yet not assimilated*
> *into the rest of my mental life.*

Easter Day took a special hold on him. He looked back on this later
as a good example of *natural religion.*

> *The holy day became, as it were, a lightning-conductor on to which*
> *could be concentrated those apprehensions which a child may have of*
> *something transcendent in the beauty of nature, that dim and vague*
> *sense of what can best be called holiness in material things.*

Later, at Eton, he was *one of the comparatively few boys who enjoyed*
the chapel services. Yet this had nothing to do with *belief in the ordi-*
nary sense.

> *The whole Christian scheme, theologically considered, remained wholly*
> *incomprehensible. . . . I could not for the life of me understand how any-*
> *one with the background of the time could come to accept it. And yet*
> *there was the patent fact that the great majority of those around me did*
> *accept it. . . . This made me feel that there must be some difference*
> *between me and the others, a difference which eluded me but . . . made*
> *me feel mentally uncomfortable . . .*
>
> *In spite of my intellectual hostility, the chapel service gave me some-*
> *thing valuable, and something which I obtained nowhere else in pre-*
> *cisely the same way.*

Huxley recalls the beauty of the chapel . . . the anthems, the organ
voluntaries, the poetry of the psalms and the lessons.

But, once the magic doors were opened and my adolescence became aware of literature and art and indeed the whole emotional richness of the world, pure lyric poetry could arouse in me much intenser and more mystical feelings than anything in the church service; a Beethoven concerto would make the highest flights of the organ seem pale and one-sided, and other buildings were found more beautiful than the chapel.

. . . so here in later boyhood I was confronted with a place, a liturgy and a ritual which presented themselves to my mind inevitably as wearing a mantle of reverence, bathed in a special atmosphere, or, to put it most unequivocally, as in some immediate way possessing holiness, through the fact that so many individual people had in that place experienced awe, found in that liturgy an outlet for their desires of righteousness, expressed their inner religious feelings in the physical acts of ritual.

For Huxley there grew up a state of increasing tension between his emotional and intellectual life,

. . . a mood of permanent and unsatisfied questioning by the unacceptability, to my growing intellectual interest, of any Christian theology proffered to me, and the failure of any person or any book to come to the rescue with any more intelligible or more acceptable scheme.

He began to reflect once again *on the religious problems which were still constantly at the back of my mind.* Again the questions presented itself — was he differently constituted from others, and if so, in what way?

I was determined to get to the bottom of this if I could. It was impossible that the problem which for nineteen centuries Christian theologians had been discussing could have no meaning whatever.

Huxley began to read a number of theological writings to see how much of them he could grasp in terms of the *evolutionary-naturalistic scheme* towards which he was moving. This led on to a wide study of the religions of the world.

He understood what it was to reach moments of transcendent beauty, of holiness, of sacredness, moments as of a religious sense, but he needed no church for that.

Suddenly, for no particular reason, without apparent connection with other thoughts, a problem and its solution flashed across my mind. I had understood how it was how two views or courses of action could not only both be sincerely held as good, but both actually could be good — and yet when the two came into contact, the one could both appear and be evil. . . .

> *Ideas and facts, particular examples and their general meaning, the*
> *tragedy of bitter conflict between two fine realities, two solid honesties,*
> *all jostled each other in my mind in that moment of insight, and I had*
> *made a new step towards that peaceful basis for action which is*
> *expressed by the French proverb 'Tout comprendre, c'est tout pardon-*
> *ner' (To understand all, is to forgive everything).*

This experience lived strongly in Huxley's later endeavours to resolve the conflict between science and religion.

This sudden flashing in upon the consciousness he compares with moments

> *... when one is suddenly transported to a complete peace and satisfac-*
> *tion by some sudden view of distant hills over plain; or by a sudden*
> *quality of light — 'the light that never was on sea and land,' and yet is*
> *suddenly here, transforming a familiar landscape; or by a poem or a pic-*
> *ture or a face.*

> *But only once before had I had such a complete sense of outside given-*
> *ness in an experience — the only occasion on which I had had a vision*
> *of a non-hallucinatory but amazingly real sort.*

He refers to the mystic visions of St. Theresa, and adds,

> *This of mine had no connexion with morals or religion; it was a sensing*
> *with the mind, a seeing of a great slice of this earth and its beauties, all*
> *compressed into an almost instantaneous experience. Mozart describes*
> *something of the same sort with music, when, after finishing the com-*
> *position of a symphony, he would experience an intense pleasure, the*
> *intensest which he knew, in an interior 'hearing' of the whole work*
> *almost instantaneously.*

> *It is, I suppose, a realization, by means of the intuitive faculty, of a great*
> *deal which the conscious mind has been striving towards but has never*
> *yet held all at one time, an indivisible whole, in its grasp.*

> *These two experiences, in two different fields of the mind, made me realize,*
> *perhaps incompletely, the quality of mystic vision, whether artistic or reli-*
> *gious; they drove me to read a great deal on mysticism and the descriptions*
> *given by visionaries of their own experience; and made me realize how stu-*
> *pid it was to dismiss all such happenings with the word 'pathological.'*

In this particular study of the religions, Huxley held strictly to the method of Natural Science; thus his refusal to accept things on authority; and insistence on the study of facts and the inductive reasoning derived from them. His quest was to find what types of gods actually are being or have been worshipped; to classify and compare these gods and these ideas; to analyse them in terms of sociology, history, psychology, plus the non-human sciences; and, as a result, to try to understand what it was that man <u>has</u> actually experienced in his religious moments.

All this Huxley carried out with utmost conscientiousness, posing questions as he went along and seeking rational an-swers. For example, the gods the Greeks worshipped have now been set aside as *poetical fancies or allegories.* Why then should there be a higher status for the legends of saints and divinities of later times?

Huxley knew what he himself had experienced as *the sense of holiness or sacredness.* All the more did he question such statements as, *the essential of religion is belief in God.* There were religions, notably Buddhism, that made no mention at all of God. It is knowledge and not belief to which mankind must pin its faith; knowledge, that is, of the physical which is present for them.

> *I propose therefore to leave the idea of God on one side for the present, as an interpretation or explanation by theology of certain ultimate and irreducible facts which we may call the facts of religious experience.*

As regards, coming to an actual knowledge *we know directly no human consciousness but our own.* The crux of the matter remains, namely, *the question of the reality at the basis of religion.*

The prominent thinkers he turned to left him unsatisfied. In the end, what is it one is trying to express?

> *Is it not the sense of sacredness? And is not this sense of sacredness, like the feeling of hunger, or the emotion of anger, or the passion of love, something irreducible, itself and nothing else, only to be communicated by worlds to others who have the same capacity, just as the sensation of colour is incommunicable to a blind man?*

> *One thing is clear, . . . that feeling, action and belief, all three, must be, or at least usually are, involved in religion.*

> *What makes religious emotion religious and not merely aesthetic? What makes us say that one motive or reaction is religious, another moral? What is it that brings one piece of ceremonial or ritual within the pale of religion and leaves another out? Why is it that we call one belief scientific and another religious?*

For Huxley, the origin of religion has nothing whatever to do with belief in a God or gods, or with abstract good against abstract evil, or with the salvation of souls, or with obedience to this or that revelation. All these he regards as later growths, carrying division, controversy and conflict which have hindered progress, both scientific and social.

Must there be conflict, for example, between science and religion?

> *Conditions drawn from sacred science or theology overflow into everyday life and demand application to quite ordinary objects, while natural science, pursuing its humdrum methods, eventually comes to apply them to objects regarded as sacred as well as the ordinary ones.*

How to bring harmony into this is one of Huxley's great aims. He had once come across a sentence by Lord Morley which struck him deeply.

> *The next great task of science will be to create a religion for humanity.*
>
> *... if religion is not essentially belief in a god or gods and obedience to their commands or will, what then is it? It is a way of life, an art like other arts of living, and an art which must be practised like other arts if we are to achieve anything good with it.*

Huxley concludes:

> *... it is our duty ... to place our whole tumultuous life of feeling and will under the joint guidance of reverence and reason.*

Unless this can be accomplished, extending reverence and reason to encompass religion and science, man must continue to be *a house divided against itself.*

> *And the choice remains with us.*

Huxley, in his survey of religion, remains ever the scientist.

> *Comparative religion is the study of the religious beliefs and practices of mankind, conducted in the same spirit as comparative anatomy, which is the comparative study of the structure and plan of animals and plants. It notes the facts, the differences and the resemblances between one religion and another; it seeks to trace the family history of beliefs and rites, their evolutionary origins; to explain the presence of this or that practice as a survival from past times; to correct the theorizing of those who lay down what religion ought to be by showing them what it actually and in hard fact is.*

A great transition comes into modern civilization with the rise to dominance of the scientific spirit.

> *The chief ways in which the scientific spirit is making its influence felt are its uncompromising hostility to all the magical, semi-magical or superstitious elements in religion; its insistence upon natural law, both in inorganic and organic nature . . . its achievements in controlling nature . . . as an earnest of fuller and more general control to come, with a consequent greater emphasis on the role of religion in this life to the detriment of concern in another life; its successful appeal to the authority of fact in opposition to all other authoritarianism, which has naturally weakened all religious appeals to the sacred books or revealed codes of conduct or miracles and of tradition in general; and, finally, in its narrowing down the field of the supernatural to its vanishing point.*

Huxley outlines a whole progression of mental states, based on his reading of the writings of mystics.

At the best,

> *. . . the mystic experience . . . represents a raising of the level in regard to another aspect of mental life, namely the embracingness of the experience, the comprehension of many aspects of reality in one mental act, the integrated resolution of conflict.*

Then come

> *. . . visions and auditions . . . and the worshipper usually goes through an experience known as a mystical conversion in which the struggle between the individual's own will and all those other tendencies described as the Will of God comes to resolution through the total submission of the individual.*

But there are other ways of reaching spiritual enrichment.

> *It should also not be forgotten that for many people art and literature help nowadays to accomplish many of the functions of meditative prayer. Good music to many listeners brushes away all the cobwebs of every day, and opens the ivory gates of meditation, whilst at the same time, 'taking the mind with beauty,' imposing a dominant loveliness and reverence of the spirit.*

The idea of the Fall and redemption, coming either through *supernatural grace* or through the *unique redemptive power of Jesus*, is something to which Huxley cannot reconcile himself at all.

The doctrine of original sin is a theological perversion of natural fact. It is a fact that all human beings begin life with an equipment of instincts, impulses, and desires, at war with one another and often out of harmony with the realities of the physical, social, and spiritual world.

Sin and the sense of sin will always be with us, to torture and weigh down; but . . . the religion of the future will try to prevent men's being afflicted with the sense of sin, rather than encourage it, and then attempt to cure it.

The diffusion of thought and ideas is a means of spreading suggestion further afield. At first this was confined to the spoken word, then came writing, and then printing, and now all the resources of mass media. In those earlier times the Church was a centre of culture and religion was a great socializing force.

But now industrialism, universal education, improved transport and communications, and the progress of invention are putting a different complexion on affairs.

What then is left of organized religion today? What purpose does it serve?

Why go to church and listen to familiar prayer and to a prosy sermon, when you could stay at home and receive new knowledge and deeper thoughts from a book? Goethe, Emerson, Wordsworth, Blake, Carlyle, Dante, Sir Thomas Browne, Shelley, and the rest of the assembly of immortal spirits — they jostle each other on your shelves, each waiting only to be picked up to introduce you to his own unique and intense experience of reality.

Huxley continues with enthusiasm:

The Origin of Species is today a good deal more profitable as theology than the first chapter of Genesis, and William James's Principles of Psychology will be a better commentary on the Decalogue than any hortatory sermon. The poetry of Herbert or Donne or Vaughan, of Francis Thompson or Walt Whitman, will introduce you to new ways of mystic feeling; Trevelyan's History of England is likely to be a more salutary history lesson, because nearer home, than the historical books of the Old Testament; Whitehead's Science and the Modern World is more likely to help the perplexed mind of a twentieth-century Englishman than the apocalyptic visions of Revelations or the neo-Platonic philosophy of the Fourth Gospel, to sacrifice a score of Sundays to making acquaintance with the ideas of other great religions like Buddhism might be very much preferable, even from the purely religious point of view, to continuance in the familiar round and familiar narrowness of one's own church.

Religion, as Huxley sees it, unstructured and free from all doctrinal traditions, resting solely and alone on its own 'sense of sacredness,' leaves room for all.

> We need poets as we need artisans; we need visionaries as much as hard-headed business men; we need the man who devotes all his energy to invention; we need the artist and the man of science; we need the saint; we need achievement and we need character.

What we do not need is any kind of belief or reliance on a supernatural.

> One of the most vital things is to have singleness of heart. If religion be an art, it must be unified, like a great work of art.

For Huxley, a science

> . . . of the future must have as its basis the consciousness of sanctity in existence — in common things, in the events of human life, in the gradually comprehended interlocking whole revealed to the human desire for knowledge, in the benedictions of beauty and love, in the catharsis, the sacred purging, of the moral drama in which character is pitted against fate and even deepest tragedy may uplift the mind.

What greater idealism can there be than that which rests solely and simply upon the nature of man, as he is, waiting to be realised by his own effort and growing. Here is purest humanism.

Whence do these qualities arise which make human life human and generate religion, in a universe which is totally indifferent to man's existence . . . and yet these gifts and qualities are there.

> [A] developed religion should definitely be a relation of the personality as a whole to the rest of the universe, one into which reverence enters, and one in which the search for the ultimate satisfaction of discovering and knowing truth, experiencing and expressing beauty, and ensuring the good in action, all have the freest possible play.

Huxley asserts and reasserts the ideals which the great established religions have ever proclaimed. The difference is only one of source-origin. All these high qualities of truth, beauty, goodness, reverence, love, have their source not in a divine world order but in brute matter.

> No one who will turn his eyes upon himself and his own being, and contemplates the spectacle in a spirit of detachment from practical details of every day, so far as possible sub specie aeternitatus, but will feel

something of reverence at what we may call the miracle of the mere exis-
tence of such an organization of material and mental qualities. If he has
had some scientific training, his sense of wonder will be increased.

All this has been self-engendered and self-evolved, and has been
accepted as simply natural and factual.

This man is a small block of the general substance of which the whole
universe is formed, just as in a stone or a stream or a piece of bread.

This piece of world-stuff possesses not only form and movement, but the
capacity of knowing about other parts of the world, even stars a thou-
sand light-years off, events ten million years ago. It possesses the capac-
ity for will, and with will and knowledge working together has learnt to
control in notable degree both outer nature and its own nature. In some
ways most extraordinary of all, it possesses the capacity for feeling, and
for feeling in such a way that before some emotions all practical consid-
erations fall away as unimportant; through feeling, the sentient portion
of the world-continuum may be exalted to states which have value high-
er than anything else in the same world-continuum, and are often
regarded as having absolute value.

The wonder does not cease.

Here is a man of a few kilograms, of substance that is indivisibly one
(both in matter and spirit), by nature and by origin, with the rest of the
universe, which can weigh the sun and measure light's speed, which can
harness the tides and organize the electric forces of matter to its profit,
which is not content with huts or shelters, but must build Chartres or
the Parthenon; which can transform sexual desire into the love of a
Dante for his Beatrice; which can not only be raised to ineffable heights
at the sight of natural beauty or find thoughts too deep for tears in a
common flower, but can create new realms and even heavens of its own,
through music, poetry, and art, to which it may be transcended, albeit
temporarily, from this practical world; which is never content with the
actual, and lives not by bread alone; which is always not only sur-
mounting what it thought were the limitations of its nature, but, in
individual and social development alike, transcending its own nature
and emerging in newness of achievement.

Is this a poet writing or a scientist? It is a scientist, an evolutionist,
who based his whole evolutionary picture on the basic fact of an
undifferentiated world-stuff from the beginning, and yet, is in
search of a religion worthy of a free spirit.

Any conflict which prevents the personality from attaining wholeness is
a hindrance: all taboos against considering any part of the universe in

relation to man and his destiny are hindrances; so, too, are all restrictions upon the free use of reason, or the free appeal to conscience.

In other words, any religion which is not an affirmation of the ultimate value of truth and knowledge, beauty and its expression, and goodness and moral action, which ever sets itself up against these, is in that respect a false, low and incomplete religion.

The great difference between today and the past is that

the present is the first period in the long history of the earth in which the evolutionary process, through the instrumentality of man, has taken the first step towards self-consciousness. In becoming aware of his own destiny, man has become aware of that of the entire evolutionary process of this planet: the two are interlocked. This is at once an inspiring and a sobering conception.

This fact of self-consciousness places a new and immense responsibility on the conduct of human life. On the face of it there still may be conflict between science and existing religious systems, but there cannot and may not any longer be conflict between science and religion itself. Religions are nothing but creations of the human mind. The new concept of science fully recognizes the need for a religious life, so now science is responsible in ways that could never have been possible previously, to actually further the progress of religious life . . . that is, a religious life free from all traditional creeds and beliefs.

The picture of the universe provided by modern science is of a single process of self-transformation, during which new possibilities can be realised. There has been a creation of new actualities during cosmic time; it has been progressive, and it has been a self-creation.

The entire universe, in all its appalling vastness, consists of the same world-stuff. Following William James, I use this awkward term deliberately in place of matter, *because 'matter' is commonly opposed to 'mind,' whereas it is now apparent that the world-stuff is not restricted to material properties. When organized in certain ways — as, for instance, in the form of human bodies and brains — it is capable of mental as well as material activities.*

It is now that the phenomenon of mind is properly placed within the naturalistic view — we can no longer say materialistic view — of the evolutionary process. There can be no such thing as mind divorced from what we have been accustomed to call matter.

... it is now clear that minds, in the sense of all activities with an obvious mental component, have evolved just as much as have material bodies; mental activities of every kind, from awareness and knowledge to emotion, memory and will, have become increasingly intense and efficient, and mental organization has reached ever higher levels. Through sense organs and brains, the mind-like potentialities of the world-stuff have been progressively intensified and actualized ...

How to define the unique position of man more clearly?

During evolution, the onward-flowing stream of life breaks up into a vast number of branches or trends, each resulting in improvement of one sort or another.

This same logic accounts also for mind.

If the self-creation of novelty is the basic wonder of the universe, this eliciting of mind from the potentialities of world-stuff, and its intensification and increasing importance during evolution, is the basic wonder of life.

All this in anticipation of what is yet to come.

When we look at the actual course of the evolutionary process, we find that general biological advance has been achieved in a series of steps, through the emergence of a series of dominant types. Each new type possesses some improvement in general organization, which enables it to spread and multiply at the expense of the previously dominant group from amongst whole less specialized members it has evolved.

It is thus perfectly proper to use terms like <u>higher</u> and <u>lower</u> to describe different types of organism, and <u>progress</u> for certain types of trend. A higher organism is one which has realised more of the inherent possibilities of living substance, and biological progress denotes those trends which do not restrict the further realization of those possibilities.

This leads on to Huxley's crowning statement.

The next fact of importance is that during evolutionary time the avenues of possible progress have become progressively restricted, until today only one remains open.

The only avenue of major advance left open was through the improvement of brain and mind. This was the line taken by our own ancestors, and it was this advance which enabled man to become the latest dominant type in evolution. His rise to dominance is very recent — an affair of less than a million years — but its later course, in the short period since the waning of the last phase of glaciation, has been spectacularly rapid, and it has been by marked decline and widespread extinction of the previously dominant mammals, as well as by a radical transformation of the environment by man. Furthermore, it is clear that man is only at the beginning of his period of evolutionary dominance, and that vast and still undreamt-of possibilities of further advance still are before him.

We now reach the very purpose of Huxley's book.

Biology, I repeat, has thus revealed man's place in nature. He is the highest form of life produced by the evolutionary process on this planet, the latest dominant type, and the only organism capable of further major advance or progress. Whether he knows it or not, whether he wishes it or not, he is now the main agency for the further evolution of the earth and its inhabitants. In other words, his destiny is to realise new possibilities for the whole terrestrial sector of the cosmic process, to be the instrument of further evolutionary progress on this planet.

On what is he to depend?

. . . notably his properties of reason, imagination and conceptual thought, and his unique capacities of accumulating, organizing, and applying experience through a transmissible culture and set of ideas.

That man has come to possess these higher faculties marks the transition from evolution in general to what Huxley calls evolutionary humanism, evolution that is in the hands of man. And knowing man also in his frailties, more than ever is he in need of a religion in which knowledge can be combined with ideals and imaginatively fused with our deep spiritual emotions to form a stable framework of sentiments and beliefs, which in turn will influence behaviour and help to determine moral and practical action.

Again there arises the question of religion . . . *the idea of religion as an organ of destiny.*

It is clear, as I suggested earlier, that twentieth-century man needs a new organ for dealing with destiny, a new system of beliefs and attitudes adapted to the situation in which he and his societies now have to exist, and thus an organ for the better orientation of the human species as a whole. . . . a new religion.

One that is born of science.

. . . it will at the outset be expressed and spread by a small minority.

Science as a system of discovering, organizing and applying shared knowledge is already unified and universal in principle.

. . . It remains for man to unify and universalize his religion.

It must be a religion . . .

> *. . . centred on the idea of fulfillment. Man's most sacred duty, and at the same time his most glorious opportunity, is to promote the maximum fulfillment of the evolutionary progress on this earth; and this includes the fullest realization of his own inherent possibilities.*

What form that religion will take ultimately, what rituals or celebrations it may evolve, whether it develops a professional body or a priesthood, what buildings it will erect, what symbols it may adopt, . . . Huxley does not venture to suggest. It must rest with the evolutionary impulse in man . . .

> *that is something which no one can prophesy. Certainly it is not a field on which the natural scientist should venture. . . . what science can do is to . . . aid in the building up of a fuller and more accurate picture of reality in general and of human destiny in particular and thus help to make possible the emergence of a more universal and more adequate religion.*

What name could this new religion have, born of the scientific impulse and totally free of any direct association with any preexisting religions?

> *The human species can, if it wishes, transcend itself . . . not just sporadically, an individual here in one way, an individual there in another way, but in its entirety, as humanity. We need a name for this new belief. Perhaps transhumanism will serve: man remaining man, but transcending himself, by realizing new possibilities of and for his human nature.*

> *I believe in transhumanism: once there are enough people who can truly say that, the human species will be on the threshold of a new kind of existence, as different from ours as ours is from that of Peking man. It will at last be consciously fulfilling its real destiny.*

With these words, Sir Julian Huxley brings his remarkable book to a close; remarkable as the testimony of a man who fostered the highest hopes and ideals for humanity; and who conceived of immense possibilities of further development through the evolving mind of man. He marveled at the accomplishments of science which is still so young, and did not pause to consider the perilous state which this same science had created for man and life on earth. Determined to remain positive, he spoke of the duty men owe to their own further progress and that of their fellows.

Grasping within his own mind an absolute of truth, beauty, good-ness, harmony, and unity, he still ascribed this entire vast and won-derful adventure of earth evolution to an original conscious-less world-stuff whose beginnings no one can know but whose end must lapse into endless nothingness and night. Huxley seemed to stoically accept this fate, yet focused his attention on the miracu-lous fact of the evolutionary process as he had come to perceive and know it. He was obliged out of the sense of his own integrity to regard all past witness of a divine world order out of which cre-ation is born as self-delusion and mere dream. Yet he believes whole-heartedly that creation can be carried further in human terms, if man has the will for it.

As a biologist he has come to the conclusion that natural evolution in an outer sense has reached its outside limit. He has declared that there is only one channel left open for further progress and that is in the mind of man. As he most eloquently declared, outer natural evolution passes over into inner moral evolution. If this is put as a question, the only reply is that there is only one evolution; that the moral arises where man transcends his natural self through a con-sciousness which is itself an unaccountable product of that same nature that was from the very beginning of whatever that begin-ning might have consisted.

· 16 ·

The Non-Man

Huxley dismissed the heavens and their gods as being non-exis-tent but he placed great reliance on mankind whose 'second duty' it was to further evolution. With B. F. Skinner, in his book, BEYOND FREEDOM AND DIGNITY, this human vanished from sight; that is, man as we thought we knew him with ideas and ideals springing up from an original source within himself. Since such a human does not exist, to speak of 'freedom' and 'dignity' is mere spinning of words. Skinner wages war against all who do so, be they ecclesiastics, philosophers, psychologists, psychotherapists, governmental reformers, teachers, or anyone else. With their antiquated notions of inner independence they are the obstructionists of progress.

The driving force in Skinner's work is his view of a world in decline. His opening sentence tells of *the terrifying problems that face us in the world of today.* The basic problem is that of human behaviour. All appeals to feeling and to common sense have proved useless. To avert *the catastrophe towards which the world seems to be inexorably moving,* there has to be a vast change in human behaviour; and for this, nothing short of a new science, a technology of behaviour, will serve. He envisions in the successful technologies of physics and biology something that inspires hope.

> *An experimental analysis shifts the determination of behaviour from autonomous man to the environment — an environment responsible for the evolution of the species and for the repertoire acquired by each member . . .*
>
> B. F. Skinner, BEYOND FREEDOM AND DIGNITY

. . . that is, a repertoire of built-in resources out of which to meet the exigencies of life as these occur.

> *Environmental contingencies now take over functions once attributed to autonomous man.*

> *Is man then abolished?*

Skinner replies to his own question:

> *Certainly not as a species or as an individual achiever. It is the autonomous man who is abolished, and that is a step forward.*

By 'autonomous man' is meant man as the original author of his own thoughts, feelings, and actions. In debunking the idea of autonomous man Skinner sees himself in the role of a liberator. The world is in a state of rapid decline, and he feels that he holds in his hand the only workable solution.

It was Descartes who first made use of terms such as stimulus, response, and reflex. Pavlov, in the nineteenth century, was able to show in his experimental work on dogs that new reflexes could be built up through conditioning . . . hence the idea of the conditioned reflex. This has been evolved into *a full-fledged stimulus-response psychology, in which all behaviour came to be regarded as reactions to stimulus.*

The implication of this was not properly understood so long as there still persisted the idea of *something like an inner man to convert a stimulus into a response.* With the eventual realization that the environment exercises *a selective force similar to that of natural selection though on a very different scale,* there opened up a new interest in environment.

> *A scientific analysis reveals unsuspected controlling relations between behaviour and environment . . .*

. . . a discovery which was innovative and novel.

> *The role of natural selection in evolution was formulated a little more than a hundred years ago, and the selective role of the environment in shaping and maintaining the behaviour of the individual is only beginning to be recognized and studied.*

> *As the interaction between organism and environment has come to be understood, however, effects once assigned to states of mind, feelings*

*and traits are beginning to be traced to accessible conditions, and a
technology of behaviour may become available.*

As a consequence, autonomous man becomes increasingly dispos-
sessed of all that was accorded to him and ideas of freedom and
dignity lose all meaning.

> *Man's struggle for freedom is not due to a will to be free, but to certain
> behavioural processes characteristic of the human organism, the chief
> effect of which is the avoidance of or escape from aversive features of
> environment, especially any due to other human beings.*

This raises the question of control by some men of others. The literature of freedom regards all controls, being contrary to freedom,
as bad. Yet without certain measures of control society would end
in chaos. The step to be realised *is not to free men from control but to
analyse and change the kinds of control to which they are exposed* and this
the technology of behaviour can deal with. So, the question of inner
moral freedom is no longer a question . . . it does not exist.

As with freedom, so with dignity, the approach is purely an external one.

> *Any evidence that a person's behaviour may be attributed to external
> circumstances seems to threaten his dignity or worth.*

If freedom is conceived of as born of aversive circumstances, dignity is seen to depend on *positive reinforcements*, applause, praise,
and admiration being examples. *A man wins respect by gaining
notice, and we have no respect for any who are 'beneath our notice.'* In
general, the literature of dignity is concerned with preserving the
credit. Therefore it opposes the advance of a technology of
behaviour with its scientific analysis, which, by continual reference to environmental influence, robs an individual of the claim
for credit.

In Skinner's view personal praise or blame no longer comes into
question. All is accounted for by the interplay between an inherit-
ed organism and its given environment. There is no room in this
for autonomous man.

Behaviour and maintaining social order involve questions of punishment. The same principle applies.

What must be changed is not the responsibility of autonomous man but the conditions, environment and genetic, of which a person's behaviour is a function.

In the pre-scientific view, . . . a person's behaviour is at least to some extent his own achievement. He is free to deliberate, decide and act, possibly in original ways, and he is to be given credit for his successes and blamed for his failures.

In the scientific view . . . a person's behaviour is determined by a genetic endowment traceable to the evolutionary history of the species and by the environmental circumstances to which as individual he has been exposed. As we learn more about the effects of the environment, we have less reason to attribute any part of human behaviour to an autonomous controlling agent.

Admittedly the traditional belief in autonomous man is hard to change but *the environment can be changed, and this we are learning to do and we are learning how to change it.*

Since there is no autonomous man, the emphasis falls mainly on social environment.

The great individualities so often cited to show the value of personal freedom have owed their successes to earlier social environments.

Even those who stand out as revolutionaries are almost wholly the conventional products of the systems they overthrow.

The struggle for freedom and dignity has been formulated as a defense of autonomous man rather than as a revision of the contingencies of reinforcement under which people live. A technology of behaviour is available which could more successfully reduce the aversive consequences of behaviour, approximate or deferred, and maximize the achievements of which the human organism is capable. The defenders of freedom oppose its use.

They bring forward such questions as:

Who is to decide what is good for man? How will a more effective technology be used? By whom and to what end? What constitutes a culture at all? How does it arise and what maintains it? What role does the individual play in it?

A child is born a member of the human species with a genetic endowment showing many idiosyncratic features, and he begins at once to acquire a repertoire of behaviour under the contingencies of reinforcement to which he is exposed as an individual. Most of these contingencies are arranged by other people. They are, in fact, what is called a culture, although the term is usually defined in other ways.

The individual is the resultant of the interplay between genetics and environment. A culture is recognized by the way its people live, rear their young, form their diet, shape their buildings, choose their attire, play or interact, and govern themselves.

These are the customs, the customary <u>behaviours</u> of a people.

Contingencies arise through the physical environment and the genetic history. So social contingencies arise, and these and the resulting behaviours are the ideas, and establish the common values.

A culture corresponds to a species. We describe it by listing many of its practices, as we describe a species by listing many of its anatomical features. . . . The practices of a culture, like the characteristics of a species, are carried by its members, who transmit them to other members. In general, the greater the number of individuals who carry a species or a culture, the greater its chances of survival.

Cultures can mix with one another. *Explicit design* is introduced to promote, improve, advance, and accelerate the evolutionary process of culture. A change brought about by a science and technology of behaviour would correspond to a biological 'mutation' towards the better.

If there is any purpose or direction in the evolution of a culture, it has to do with bringing people under the control of more and more of the consequences of behaviour.

The term 'control' raises awkward questions. Who is to control whom? What is the relationship between the controller and the controlled? This brings us to the vital question of counter-control.

The scientist who designs a cyclotron is under the control of the particles he is studying. The behaviour with which a parent controls his child, either aversively or through positive reinforcement, is shaped and maintained by the child's responses. A psychotherapist changes the behaviour of his patient in ways which have been shaped and maintained by his success in changing the behaviour. A government or religion prescribes and imposes sanctions selected by their effectiveness in controlling the citizen or communicant. An employer induces his employees to work industriously and carefully with wage systems determined by their effect on behaviour. The classroom practices of the teacher are shaped and maintained by the effects on his students. In a very real sense, then,

the slave controls the slave driver, the child the parent, the patient the
therapist, the citizen the government, the communicant the priest, the
employee the employer and the student the teacher.

Thus the question turns on itself.

Although cultures are improved by people whose wisdom and compassion
may supply clues to what they do or will do, the ultimate improvement
comes from the environment which makes them wise and compassionate.

The great problem is to arrange effective counter-control and hence to
bring some important consequences to bear on the behaviour of the
controller.

Yet, the final determining cause, whether genetic or cultural, is
never an ethical or moral one, but always leads back to the environment. The world is a large-scale laboratory. Both the controller and
the controlled are subject to conditioning. All life is a conditioning.

As a science of behaviour adopts the strategy of physics and biology,
the autonomous agent to which behaviour has traditionally been
attributed is replaced by the environment – the environment in which
the species evolved, and in which the behaviour of the individual is
shaped and maintained.

This applies as much to the controller as to the controlled and there
must be control.

The intentional design of a culture, and the control of human behaviour
it implies, are essential if the human species is to continue to develop.

This applies to the scientist of technological behaviour as much as
to anyone else.

The published results of scientists are subject to rapid check by others,
and the scientist who allows himself to be swayed by consequences that
are not part of his subject-matter is likely to find himself in difficulties.
To say that scientists are therefore more moral or ethical than other
people, or that they have a more finely developed ethical sense, is to
make the mistake of attributing to the scientist what is actually a fea-
ture of the environment in which he works.

It is a mistake to think at all of man having an inborn ethical or
moral sense.

Man has not evolved as an ethical or moral animal. He has evolved to the
point at which he has constructed an ethical or moral culture. He differs

from the other animals not in possessing a moral or ethical sense but in having been able to generate a moral or ethical social environment.

The designer of a culture is not an interloper or meddler. He does not step in to disturb a natural process, he is part of a natural process.

The designer, like all others, is subject to the compensating forces of counter-control.

There still is the question of the self. There is no doubt that every normal human being lives with a feeling of self. On what is this based? Skinner also asked this question and supplied an answer. It is in the nature of an experimental analysis of human behaviour that it should strip away the functions previously assigned to autonomous man and transfer them one by one to the controlling environment. The analysis leaves less and less for autonomous man to do. But what about man himself? Is there not something about a person which is more than a living body? Unless something like a self survives, how can we speak of self-knowledge and self-control? To whom is the injunction 'Know thyself' addressed?

Self-knowledge and self-control imply two selves in this sense. The self-knower is almost always a product of social contingencies but the self that is known may come from other sources. The controlling self (the conscience or super-ego) is of social origin, but the controlled self is more likely to be the product of genetic susceptibilities to reinforcement (the id, or the Old Adam). The controlling self generally represents the interests of others, the controlled self the interests of the individual.

This distinction is a fundamental factor in the thesis of our quest. This eliminates all thought of what we have been prone to call a *real* self!

The picture which emerges from a scientific analysis is not of a body with a person inside, but of a body which <u>is</u> a person in the sense that it displays a complete repertoire of behaviour.

There arises the question of how self, self-awareness, and consciousness generally can manifest themselves in a non-autonomous man. Skinner writes:

Man is said to differ from the other animals mainly because he is 'aware of his own existence.' He knows what he is doing; he knows that he has had a past and will have a future; he 'reflects on his own nature'; he alone follows the classical injunction 'Know thyself.'

The question is not whether a man can know himself but what he knows when he does so.

The problem arises from the indisputable fact of privacy: a small part of the universe is enclosed within a human skin. It would be foolish to deny the existence of that private world, but it is also foolish to assert that because it is private it is of a different nature from the world outside. The difference is not in the stuff of which the private world is composed but in its accessibility. There is an exclusive intimacy about a headache or a heartache or a silent soliloquy.

Once again, it is the environment that promotes this kind of exchange and kindles consciousness, hence the startling conclusion:

Consciousness is a social product. It is not only <u>not</u> the special field of autonomous man, it is not even within range of a solitary man.

This removes all ground from any theory, *which attributed human behaviour to an observable inner agent.* And now one step further.

. . . perhaps the last stronghold of autonomous man is that complex 'cognitive' activity called thinking. Because it is complex, it has yielded only slowly to explanation . . .

There comes the theological question of sin.

Does man sin because he is sinful, or is he sinful because he sins? . . . The sin assigned as an inner possession (the sin a person 'knows') is to be found in a history of reinforcements. (The expression 'God-fearing' suggests such a history, but piety, virtue, the immanence of God, a moral sense or morality does not. As we have seen, man is not a moral animal in the sense of possessing a special trait or virtue; he has built a kind of social environment which induces him to behave in moral ways.)

Skinner, in the course of his book surveys a number of subjects: freedom, dignity, punishment, social values, the evolution and the design of a culture. We have done little more than to touch on them as contributory to the main thesis . . . the abolition of all ideas of the existence of an autonomous man. The logic of the book rests on this assumption. One needs to grow accustomed to his chosen vocabulary, terms such as aversive, reinforcers, reinforcements good and bad, contingencies, and contingencies of reinforcement. In the form of a parenthesis he offers a partial explanation.

(The reader may have been inclined to dismiss frequent references to contingencies of reinforcement as a new fashion in technical jargon, but it is not simply a matter of talking about old things in new ways. Contingencies

are ubiquitous; they cover the classical fields of intention and purpose, but in a much more useful way, and they provide alternative formulations of so-called 'mental processes.' Many details have never been dealt with before, and no traditional terms are available in discussing them.)

He knows his terms present difficulties and, to use his own words, are aversive to some, but this applies equally to his whole behavioural approach, which provokes ridicule or indignation or, at the least, a deep concern at a view which so aligns cultural with natural evolution. The heroic image of mankind sinks back into a kind of nature-creature whose thoughts, feelings, and actions are least of all his own.

What is it then that makes a man a man?

The picture which emerges from a scientific analysis is not of a body with a person inside, but of a body which is a person in the sense that is displays a complex repertoire of behaviour.

The man thus portrayed is a stranger, and from the traditional point of view he may not seem to be a man at all.

Is there just one traditional point of view? Is not the above conclusive statement a direct challenge to every other point of view, based as it is on the behaviourist's laboratory exercises in conditioning animals which are now extended to include man? The above description of a 'person' could, in its formulation, hold equally for an animal; just as the description of a cultural environment makes it out to be no more than an offshoot of a natural environment.

Skinner is armed against all criticism; and, being so very confident of his own view, attributes any such criticism to *a kind of blindness to the current state of science.* He quotes some of his critics with seemingly unperturbable equanimity. Arthur Koestler was most outspoken. He referred to behaviourism as 'a monumental triviality'; as 'question-begging on a heroic scale' which has spun psychology into 'a modern version of the Dark Ages.' He speaks of the behaviourist use of 'pedantic jargon' and of reinforcement as 'an ugly word.'

According to the Behaviourist doctrine, all learning occurs by the hit-and-miss or trial-and-error method. The correct response to a given stimulus is hit upon by chance and has a rewarding or, as the jargon has it, reinforcing effect; if the reinforcement is strong or repeated enough, the response will be 'stamped in' and an S-R bond, a stimulus and response link is formed.

Arthur Koestler

All such criticisms he dismisses as based on ignorance. The fact is, though, that all the phenomena he offers in his description of man fall short, singly or in their sum-total, of what others perceive a man to be. His statement that 'man is not a body with a person inside but that the body is the person' inevitably calls out a chorus of protests, and these he also quotes.

For at least one hundred years, we have been prejudiced in every theory, including economic determinism, mechanistic behaviourism, and relativism, that reduces the stature of man until he ceases to be man at all in any sense that the humanists of an earlier generation would recognize.

Joseph Wood Krutch

. . . the empirical behavioural scientist. . . . denies, if only by implication, that a unique being, called Man, exists.

Matsen

What is now under attack 'is the being' of man.

Maslow

Man is being abolished.

C. S. Lewis

What, in fact, is being abolished?

The human species may indeed abolish itself, through disease, famine, pollution, or a nuclear holocaust, but that is not what Lewis meant. Nor are individual men growing less effective or productive. We are told that what is threatened is 'man qua man' or 'man in his humanity' or 'man as Thou not It' or 'man as a person not a thing.'

With regard to C. S. Lewis and his use of the word 'abolition,' we may recall that he wrote a phantasy tale, THAT HIDEOUS STRENGTH. In it he portrays a war between two orders of men. In the one, its members are obliged without demur to carry out the injunction of their master, an excised human brain made somehow to function as a bloodless, humanless, spectre. In the other, we meet the last defenders of inner moral freedom, that is, of the true being of man. It could be described as a war between the automatic and the autonomous. Of course, Lewis still has sufficient hope and optimism to give victory to the latter.

His small book, THE ABOLITION OF MAN, stands as a warning. Skinner's insistent reply to his own question forms the essential message of the book.

> What is being abolished is autonomous man. . . . the inner man, the homunculus, the possessing demon, the man defended by the literature of freedom and dignity.

> His abolition has been long overdue. Autonomous man is a device used to explain what we cannot explain in any other way. He has been constructed from our ignorance, and as our understanding increases, the very stuff of which he is composed vanishes. Science does not dehumanize man, it de-humunculizes him; and it must do so if it is to prevent the abolition of the human species. To man qua man we readily say good riddance. Only by dispossessing him can we turn to the real causes of human behaviour. Only then can we turn from the inferred to the observed, from the miraculous to the natural, from the inaccessible to the manipulable.

There is little more to add, maybe one or two questions and surmises. May not the continued scientific analysis of the non-human lead by contrast to the knowledge of what is essentially human? How far will the machine dispossess man even further? As controls increase and grow more efficient, will not man be reduced to a mere spectator, and come to a dead end in his long struggle to control his own destiny?

Answer:

> It is only autonomous man who has reached a dead end.

> The physical environment of most people is largely man-made . . . the social environment is obviously man-made.

Comes the voice of Lewis again:

> . . . the power of man to make himself what he pleases . . . means . . . the power of some men to make other men what they please.

To which Skinner replies:

> The controlling self must be distinguished from the controlled self, even when they are both inside the same skin. . . .When a person changes his physical or social environment 'intentionally' . . . that is, in order to change human behaviour, possible including his own . . . he plays two roles: one as a controller, as the designer of a controlling culture, and another as the controlled, as the product of a culture. There is nothing inconsistent about this.

The question of how man will change further cannot be known. *He has introduced new practices which serve as cultural mutations,* and he is now moving in the direction of designed genetic mutation.

> *... there are no limits to perfection. The human species will never reach a final state of perfection before it is exterminated ... 'some say in fire, some in ice' and some in radiation.*

The book ends with the words:

> *A scientific view of man offers exciting possibilities. We have not yet seen what man can make of man.*

Whatever else may be said of the book, it will always hold a unique place in the progressive story of scientific outlook. It may be considered a masterpiece of its kind. In it man divests himself totally of anything hitherto called human and he can never be called to account for good or evil.

The question might arise, does such a creature live or merely exist? This brings us back to the beginning of the book, a world in imminent danger of chaos and destruction. Skinner offers what he ardently believes is the hope of surviving the pending crisis ... it cannot be said with an enlightened humanity, but with one that would be better conditioned than the humanity of today; and better might lead to still better.

· 17 ·

From Abstract to Concrete

Galileo was the first to split experience into what came to be known as primary and secondary qualities. Descartes made a similar division between mind and body. Bacon kept his science of nature strictly to the evidence of sense observation held entirely free from all speculative thinking and religious considerations. All this led to the dualistic outlook of the eighteenth century, of which the philosopher Kant was the master exponent. In the nineteenth century as scientific thinking became predominant and religion receded, this resolved itself into scientific materialistic monism.

The twentieth century has produced increased questioning of the nineteenth-century materialistic doctrine as exemplified in such scientific thinkers as Sullivan, Jeans, Eddington, Joad, and Alfred Whitehead. Whitehead's book, Science and the Modern World, has gone through many printings since it first appeared in 1926 and still stands as a classic. To him the mechanistic view of the world was not only unsatisfactory but misleading. The opening chapter, 'The Origin of Modern Science,' he examines what he regarded as the main contributory factors in the shaping of the scientific outlook.

> The sixteenth century of our era saw the disruption of Western Christianity, and the rise of modern science. It was an age of ferment. Nothing was settled, though much was opened — new world and new ideas.

Whitehead takes as two representative figures of that century Copernicus, who in his De Revolutionibus Coelorum presents a new system of the heavens with the sun and not the earth as centre, and Vesalius, who in his DE HUMANI CORPORIS opens up for the first time a complete anatomy of the human body. Both these books which look in opposite directions, the one towards the heavens, and the other into the human body, were published in 1543. Whitehead also makes mention of Giordano Bruno, who was burned at the stake in 1600 for his unorthodox views. He regards this dour event as *having ushered in the first century of modern science in the strict sense of the term.*

In his own unique fashion, Whitehead sets out three antecedent influences that instigated the formation of the modern scientific mind.

He looks first to the great Greek tragedians, Aeschylus, Sophocles, and Euripides, with

> . . . *their vision of fate, remorseless and indifferent, urging a tragic incident to its inevitable issue. Fate, in Greek tragedy, becomes the order of nature in modern thought . . . the laws of physics are the decrees of fate.*

The second influence he ascribes to

> . . . *the inexpungible belief of the mediaevalists, that every detailed occurrence can be correlated with its antecedents in a perfectly definite manner.*

Without the faith *that there is a secret that can be unveiled* science would have lacked the motive power for its research. This *faith* he perceives as *an unconscious derivative from mediaeval theology.*

His third source of influence is even more unexpected. He sees in Gregory the Great and St. Benedict,

> . . . *the two outstanding men who, in the Italy of the sixth century, laid the foundations of the future. . . . Gregory and Benedict were practical men, with an eye for the importance of ordinary things; and they combined this practical temperament with their religious and cultural activities. In particular we owe it to St. Benedict that the monasteries were the homes of practical agriculturalists, as well as saints, artists, and men of learning. The alliance of science and technology, by which learning is kept in contact with 'irreducible and stubborn facts' — a phrase he borrowed from William James — owes much to the practical bents of the early Benedictines. Modern science derives from Rome as well as from Greece, and this Roman strain explains its gain in an energy of thought kept closely in contact with the world of facts.*

Whitehead also saw how life in and with nature found expression in art. *The whole atmosphere of every art exhibited a direct joy in the apprehension of the things which lie around us.*

Giotto, Chaucer, Wordsworth, Walt Whitman, and the New England poet Robert Frost *are all akin to each other in this respect. . . . The simple immediate facts are the topics of interest, and these reappear in the thought of science as the* irreducible stubborn facts. *. . . The mind of Europe was now prepared for its new venture in thought.*

He adds that science is essentially anti-rationalistic.

> *Science repudiates philosophy — it has never cared to justify its faith or to explain its meanings. But that can no longer be the case.*

> *The progress of science has now reached a turning point. The stable foundation of physics has now broken up: also for the first time physiology is asserting itself as an effective body of knowledge, as distinct from a scrap-heap. The old foundations of scientific thought are becoming unintelligible. Time, space, matter, material, ether, electricity, mechanism, organism, configuration, structure, pattern, function all require reinterpretation. What is the sense of talking about a mechanical explanation when you do not know what you mean by mechanics?*

> *If science is not to degenerate into a medley of* ad hoc *hypothesis, it must become philosophical and must enter upon a thorough criticism of its own foundations.*

The following is Whitehead's main point of contention:

> *There persists, however, throughout the whole period the fixed scientific cosmology which presupposes the ultimate fact of an* irreducible brute matter, *or material, spread throughout space in a flux of configurations. In itself such a material is senseless, valueless, purposeless. It just does what it does do, following a fixed routine imposed by external relations which do not spring from the nature of its being. It is this assumption that I call* scientific materialism. *Also it is an assumption which I shall challenge as being entirely unsuited to the scientific situations at which we have now arrived.*

Whitehead concedes that scientific materialism has succeeded admirably within its own abstracted limitations.

> *But when we pass beyond the abstraction, either by more subtle employment of our senses, or by the request for meaning and for coherence of thoughts, the scheme breaks down at once. The narrow efficiency of the scheme was the very cause of its supreme methodological success.*

Thought, he writes, *is abstract; and the intolerant use of abstractions is the vice of the intellect.* He regards the faith referred to earlier, which made science possible, as a particular example of a deeper faith. *It springs not from abstractions but from our own immediate experience in all its aspects as it meets us.*

Here there sounds forth a new voice.

> *To experience this faith is to know that in being ourselves we are more than ourselves; to know that our experience, dim and fragmentary as it is, yet sounds the utmost depth of reality; to know that detached details merely in order to be themselves demand that they should find themselves in a system of things; to know that this system includes the harmony of logical rationality, and the harmony of aesthetic achievement; to know that, while the harmony of logic lies upon the universe as an iron necessity, the aesthetic harmony stands before it as a living ideal moulding the general flux in its broken progress towards finer, subtler issues.*

Whitehead requires us to take the whole of our humanity with us in our investigation of nature and, above all, of man's place in nature. It is scientific materialism that has to be overcome. He traces its origin back to the strong mathematical bias of the seventeenth century.

> *... the idea of functionality in the abstract sphere of mathematics found itself reflected in the order of nature under the guise of mathematically expressed laws of nature. .... Mathematics supplied the background of imaginative thought with which men of science approached the observation of nature. Galileo produced formulas; Descartes produced formulas; Huyghens produced formulas; Newton produced formulas.*

It is here that number began to take precedence over everything else, turning life itself into a mechanism. Whitehead quotes from Descartes' DISCOURSE ON METHOD:

> *... the variety of movements performed by the different automata, or moving machines fabricated by human industry, and that with the help of but few processes, compared with the great variety of bones, muscles, nerves, arteries, veins, and other parts that one finds in the body of each animal — such persons will look upon the body as a machine made by the hand of God, which is incomparably better arranged, and adequate to movements more admirable than any machine of human invention.*

Man, too, is a machine of this kind though curiously endowed with a mind. The general influence of mathematics continued its rule in the eighteenth century but began to lessen in the nineteenth.

The romantic movement in literature, and the idealistic movement in philosophy were not the products of mathematical minds. Also, even in science, the growth of geology, of zoology, and of the biological sciences generally, was in each case entirely disconnected from any reference to mathematics.

Whitehead follows closely every phrase of scientific progress in its bearing on human outlook. For example, he presents the particular problems raised by the quantum theory which we have touched on already. According to this theory, *an electron does not continuously traverse its path in space.* It proceeds in jumps appearing and disappearing successively. We have to reconcile *this discontinuous existence in space* with *the continuous existence of material bodies as we know them,* for electrons and their related protons *are now conceived as being the fundamental entities out of which the material bodies are composed.* This theory of discontinuity obliges us *to review all our notions of the ultimate character of natural existence.* A continuous colour is explained, by analogy, as due to vibrations in the ether. What vibratory action or energy can be sought for as underlying the continuity of a material body? And further, *What are the ingredients which form the vibratory organism?* What is matter per se, and what is living matter? In dealing with this latter question, Whitehead foresees the possibility *for introducing some new doctrine of organism* to replace that of the materialism with which science *has saddled philosophy* since the seventeenth century.

Now the scientific philosophy of the seventeenth century was dominated by physics . . . as a matter of fact, these concepts are very unsuited to biology, and set for it an insoluble problem of matter and life and organism with which biologists are now wrestling.

Given *the root idea of the seventeenth century* of the locomotion of matter in space, how is this to apply to living organisms? Having kept clear of mathematics, what did Bacon have to offer? Whitehead quotes from Bacon's SILVA SILVARUM.

It is certain that all bodies whatsoever, though they have no sense, yet they have perception for when one body is applied to another, there is a kind of election to embrace that which is agreeable, and to exclude or expel that which is ingrate, and whether the body be alterant or altered, evermore a perception precedeth operation; for else all bodies would be like to one another. And sometimes this perception, in some kind of bodies, is far

> *more subtle than sense; so that sense is but a dull thing in comparison of it; we see a weatherglass will find the least difference of the weather in heat or cold, when we find it not. And this perception is sometimes at a distance, as well as upon the touch, as when the lodestone draweth iron; or flame naphtha of Babylon, a great distance off. It is therefore a subject of a very noble enquiry, to enquire of the more subtle perceptions; for it is another key to open nature, as well as the sense; and sometimes better. And besides, it is a principal means of natural divination; for that which in these perceptions appeareth early, in the great effects cometh long after.*

Whitehead finds:

> *. . . a great many points of interest about this quotation . . . note the careful way in which Bacon discriminates between <u>perception</u>, or <u>taking account of</u>, on the one hand, and <u>sense</u>, or <u>cognitive experience</u>, on the other hand. In this respect Bacon is outside the line of thought which finally dominated the century.*

> *Later on, people thought of passive matter which was operated on externally by forces. I believe Bacon's line of thought to have expressed a more fundamental truth than do the materialistic concepts which were then being shaped as adequate for physics. We are now so used to the materialistic way of looking at things, which has been rooted in our literature by the genius of the seventeenth century, that it is with some difficulty that we understand the possibility of another mode of approach to the problems of nature.*

Whitehead notes in this regard,

> *The explicit realisation of the antithesis between the deductive rationalism of the scholastics and the inductive observational methods of the moderns must chiefly be ascribed to Bacon, though, of course, it was implicit in the mind of Galileo and of all the men of science of those times. But Bacon was one of the earliest of that group and had the most direct apprehension of the full extent of the intellectual revolution which was in progress.*

Then as though in parenthesis, Whitehead refers to *the artist Leonardo Da Vinci* who lived almost exactly a century before Bacon and who *most completely anticipated Bacon and the whole modern point of view.* Leonardo illustrated what was one of Whitehead's most favoured themes:

> *. . . that the rise of naturalistic art was an important ingredient in the formation of our scientific mentality. Indeed, Leonardo was more completely a man of science than Bacon.*

Induction has proved to be a somewhat more complex process than Bacon anticipated. Nevertheless *Bacon remains as one of the great builders who constructed the mind of the modern world.* Contrary to Bacon's view is the statement, *Induction presupposes metaphysics. In other words, it rests upon an antecedent rationalism.* It is as though Bacon was blind to this.

On the other hand, Whitehead notes that Bacon's quotation is purely qualitative:

> *Science was becoming and has remained primarily quantitative. . . . Bacon ignores this role of science which has led to the triumphs of Galileo, and supremely of Newton.*

In what did these triumphs consist? How did Whitehead himself view them? For example, in regard to the question of light,

> *. . . there is the particle theory of Newton, the wave theory of Huyghens, and the more recent attempt in connection with radiation to arrive at a kind of combination of both.*

To what has this led?

Whichever theory you choose, there is no light or colour as a fact in external nature. There is merely motion of material. Again, when the light enters your eyes and falls on the retina, there is merely motion of material. Then your nerves are affected and the brain is affected, and again this is merely motion of material. The same line of argument holds for sound, substituting waves in the air for waves in the ether, and ears for eyes. *What of the scent of the nose?* According to Galileo, *apart from eyes, ears, or noses, there would be no colours, sounds, or smells.*

And Descartes concludes, *that by our senses we know nothing of external objects beyond their figure (or station), magnitude and motion.*

It is Locke who

> *. . . elaborates a theory of primary and secondary qualities in accordance with the state of physical science at the close of the seventeenth century. The primary qualities (including mass) are the essential qualities of substances whose spatio-temporal relationships constitute nature. The orderliness of these relationships constitute nature. The occurrences of nature are in some way apprehended by minds, which are*

associated with living bodies. Primarily, the mental apprehension is aroused by occurrences in certain parts of the correlated body, the occurrences in the brain, for instance. But the mind, in apprehending, also experiences sensations which, properly speaking, are qualities of the mind alone. These sensations are projected by the mind so as to clothe appropriate bodies in external nature. Thus the bodies are perceived as with qualities which in reality do not belong to them, qualities which in fact are purely the offspring of the mind. Thus nature gets credit which should in truth be reserved for ourselves; the rose for its scent; the nightingale for its song; and the sun for its radiance. The poets are entirely mistaken. They should address their lyrics to themselves, and should turn them into odes of self-congratulation on the excellency of the human mind. Nature is a dull affair, soundless, scentless, colourless, merely the hurrying of material, endlessly, meaninglessly.

However you disguise it, this is the practical outcome of the characteristic scientific philosophy which closed the seventeenth century.

In the first place, we must note its astounding efficiency as a system of concepts for the organization of scientific research. In this respect, it is fully worthy of the genius of the century which produced it. It has held its own as the guiding principle of scientific studies ever since. It is still reigning. Every university in the world organises itself in accordance with it. No alternative system of organising the pursuit of scientific truth has been suggested. It is not only reigning but it is without a rival. And yet it is quite unbelievable.

And now comes the following key sentence:

This conception of the universe is surely framed in terms of high abstractions and the paradox only arises because we have mistaken our abstractions for concrete realities.

The enormous success of the scientific abstractions, yielding on the one hand matter with its simple location in space and time, on the other hand mind, perceiving, suffering, reasoning, but not interfering, has foisted onto philosophy the task of accepting them as the most concrete rendering of fact.

Thereby, modern philosophy has been ruined. It has oscillated in a complex manner between three extremes. There are the dualists who accept matter and mind on an equal basis, and the two varieties of monists, those who put mind into matter and those who put matter inside mind. But this juggling with abstractions can never overcome the inherent confusion introduced by the ascription of misplaced concreteness to the scientific scheme of the seventeenth century.

Whitehead is emphatic in his statement that *the scheme of scientific ideas of the seventeenth century, has dominated thought ever since*. It certainly ruled the thinking of the eighteenth century.

> *It involves a fundamental duality, with <u>material</u> on the one hand, and on the other hand <u>mind</u>. In between there lie the concepts of life, organism, function, instantaneous reality, interaction, order of nature, which collectively form the Achilles heel of the whole scheme.*

The concept, <u>simple location</u>, meaning that a piece of matter can exist at a given point in space and at a given moment of time without further reference to surrounding space and the passage of time may satisfy the physicist in pursuing a particular problem but in reality, *there is no element whatever which possesses this character* — it is abstracted from the total reality and remains an abstraction. So, there is no mind simply *perceiving suffering, reasoning but not interfering*, divorced and isolated in this way from all that sustains it, serves it, and maintains it. The error lies in what Whitehead calls *The Fallacy of Misplaced Concreteness*.

Bacon's weakness lay in his rejection of all philosophical thinking in regard to phenomena. Whitehead, on the contrary, claims that we cannot think without abstractions, and therefore, all the more do we need a philosophy to serve as *the critic of abstractions. A civilization which cannot burst through its current abstractions is doomed to sterility after a very limited period of progress.*

Of the eighteenth century he writes:

> *It was the age of reason, healthy, manly, upstanding reason; but, of one-eyed reason, deficient in its vision of depth. We cannot overrate the debt of gratitude which we owe to these men. For a thousand years Europe had been a prey to intolerant, intolerable visionaries. The common sense of the eighteenth century, its grasp of the obvious facts of human suffering, and of the obvious demands of human nature, acted on the world like a bath of moral cleansing.*

The triumph of materialism was in the rapid progress of the physical sciences, but, *In this century the notion of the mechanical explanation of all the processes of nature finally hardened into a dogma of science.* He passes by the idealistic philosophy of the nineteenth century as being *too much divorced from the scientific outlook*. The way lies between one-sided realism and one-sided idealism.

> *My point is that a further stage of provisional realism is required in which the scientific schema is recast, and founded upon the ultimate concept of <u>organism</u>.*

After all, that is the main objective of Whitehead's book. He is looking for *a system of thought basing nature upon the concept of organisms and not upon the concept of matter.* He turns to literature because it is there

> *. . . that the concrete outlook for humanity receives its expression. Accordingly it is to literature we must look, particularly in its more concrete forms, namely in poetry and in drama if we hope to discover the inward thoughts of a generation.*

As a scientist Whitehead resorted to the humanities, after first noting the great inconsistency that has arisen in Western thinking.

> *A scientific realism based on mechanism is conjoined with an unwavering belief in the world of man and of the higher animals as being composed of self-determining organisms.*

As regards the literary world, to a great extent *science might never have been heard of,* and yet, *the indirect influence of science has been considerable.* He illustrates this by comparing the sequence of *four great, serious poems in English literature.*

Milton, in PARADISE LOST, was untouched by the influence of scientific materialism.

Pope, in his ESSAY OF MAN, coming sixty years later:

> *. . . represents the popular thought . . . the assured triumphs for the scientific movement.*

Wordsworth, in EXCURSION:

> *. . . was not bothered by any intellectual antagonism. What moved him was a moral repulsion. He felt that something had been left out, [something that] comprised everything that was important.*

Tennyson, in IN MEMORIAM:

> *. . . is the mouthpiece of the waning romantic movement, in its attempt to come to terms with science.*

This opens up the significant issue as to what truth we live by.

Tennyson stands in this poem as the perfect example of the distraction which I have already mentioned. There are opposing visions of the world, and both of them command his assent by appeals to ultimate intuitions from which there seems no escape. Tennyson goes to the heart of the difficulty. It is the problem of mechanism which appalls him.

'The stars,' she whispers, 'blindly run.' This line states starkly the whole philosophic problem implicit in the poem. Each molecule blindly runs. The human body is a collection of molecules. Therefore, the human body blindly runs, and therefore there can be no individual responsibility for the actions of the body. If you once accept that the molecule is definitely determined to be what it is, independently of any determination by reason of the total organism of the body, and if you further admit that the blind run is settled by the general mechanical laws, there can be no escape from this conclusion. But mental experiences are derivative from the actions of the body, including of course its internal behaviour. Accordingly, the main function of the mind is to have at least some of its experiences settled for it, and to add such others as may be open to it independently of the body's motions internal and external.

There are then two possible theories as to the mind. You can either deny that it can supply for itself any experience other than those provided for it by the body, or you can admit them. If you refuse to admit the additional experiences, then all individual moral responsibility is swept away. If you do admit them, then a human being may be responsible for the state of his mind, though he has no responsibility for the actions of his body. The enfeeblement of thought in the modern world is illustrated by the way this plain issue is avoided in Tennyson's poem. There is something kept in the background, a skeleton in the cupboard. He touches on almost every religious and scientific problem, but carefully avoids more than a passing allusion to this one.

Either the bodily molecules blindly run, or they do not. If they do blindly run, the mental states are irrelevant in discussing the bodily actions.

This is the unresolved situation resulting from dualism. What then can Whitehead offer towards a solution, for this is the very problem he is wrestling with. What is mind and what is body? What is organism and what is mechanism? How do they relate? How does one reconcile the abstract and the concrete so that life grows meaningful?

Whitehead offers the following as an attempt at a solution.

The doctrine which I am maintaining is that the whole concept of materialism only applies to very abstract entities, the products of logical discernment. The concrete, enduring entities are organisms, so that the plan of the whole influences the very characters of the various subordinate organisms which enter into it.

The electron blindly runs either within or without the body; but it runs within the body in accordance with its character within the body, that is to say, in accordance with the general plan of the body, and this plan includes the mental state. But the principle of modification is perfectly general throughout nature and represents no property peculiar to living bodies.

The statement thus far still does not achieve what Whitehead is aiming for, *The abandonment of the traditional scientific materialism, and the substitution of an alternative doctrine of organism.* He introduces a new concept, the theory of organic mechanism.

In this theory, the molecules may blindly run according to the general laws, but the molecules differ in their intrinsic characters according to the general organic plans of the situation in which they find themselves.

Following Whitehead's theory leads us to a greatly extended view of organism since this reached right down to include the play of electrons and protons of the new physics. Whereas Descartes translated organism as mechanism, it is as though Whitehead would wish to seek in every manifestation of nature some aspect of organism.

The discrepancy between the materialistic mechanism of science and the moral intuitions, which are presupposed in the concrete affairs of life, only gradually assumed true importance as the centuries advanced.

Whitehead illustrates this in the following very striking sequence.

Milton ends his introduction with a prayer,
> *'That to the height of this great argument*
> *I may assert external Providence*
> *And justify the ways of God to men'*

So, too, in <u>Samson Agonistes</u>,
> *'Just are the ways of God*
> *And justifiable to man.'*

This is not merely a question of belief. *It is the swansong of a passing world of untroubled certitude.*

Sixty years later, Pope addressed himself not to God but to Lord Bolingroke:

Awake my St. John! leave all meaner things
To low ambition and the pride of kings.
Let us (since life can little more supply
Than just to look about us and to die)
Expatiate free o'er all this scene of man;
A mighty maze but not without a plan.

Whitehead asks us to compare *the jaunty assurance of Pope's 'A mighty maze but not without a plan,'* to Milton's *Just are the ways of God.*

Then comes the opening line of Wordsworth's EXCURSION:

Twas summer, and the sun had mounted high.

And Whitehead adds:

Thus the romantic reaction started neither with God nor with Lord Bolingbroke, but with nature. We are here witnessing a conscious reaction against the whole tone of the eighteenth century. That century approached nature with the abstract analysis of science, whereas Wordsworth opposes to the scientific abstractions his full concrete experience.

We are led on to the opening lines of Tennyson's IN MEMORIAM.

Strong son of God, immortal Love
Whom we, that have not seen Thy face,
By faith, and faith alone, embrace,
Believing where we cannot prove.

The note of perplexity is struck at once. . . . The importance of Tennyson's poem lies in the fact that it exactly expressed the character of its period. Each individual was divided against himself.

Then Whitehead recalls the *mood of individual distraction* with the closing line of Arnold's DOVER BEACH:

And we are here as on a darkling plain
Swept with confused alarms of struggle and flight,
Where ignorant armies clash by night.

Is one to ascribe this loss of certainty as humanity moves forward in time to the influence of science which is so triumphant in its own field? Whitehead returns to Wordsworth:

He [Wordsworth] alleges against science its absorption in abstractions. His consistent theme is that the important facts of nature elude the scientific method.

What was it that Wordsworth found in nature that failed to receive expression in science? The answer is essential to our whole consideration of the subject. While being so deeply in sympathy with Wordsworth, Whitehead nevertheless will not abandon science and holds away the thought 'that the abstractions of science are irreformable and unalterable.' But then, what <u>are</u> the important facts of nature that elude the scientist?

Whitehead himself answers:

> It is the brooding presence of the hills which haunt him. . . . He dwells on the mysterious presence of surrounding things, which imposes itself on any separate element that we set up as an individual for its own sake. He always grasps the whole of nature as involved in the tonality of the particular instance. That is why he laughs with the daffodils and finds in the primrose thoughts too deep for tears.

This concrete experience totally escapes the abstract mind. Is science doomed to rest in abstractions? Has the quantitative view of nature excluded the qualitative, or the calculable the incalculable, or the starkly logical the intuitive? But cannot the latter in each case be seen to include the former? Whitehead quotes a passage from Wordsworth's greatest poem . . . The Prelude . . . pervaded by this sense of haunting presences of nature.

> Wordsworth is a poet writing a poem, and is not concerned with dry philosophical statements. But it would hardly be possible to express more clearly a feeling for nature, as exhibiting entwined prehensive unities, each suffused with modal presences of others.

> > 'Ye presences of Nature in the sky
> > And on the earth! Ye Visions of the hills!
> > And Souls of lonely places! can I think
> > A vulgar hope was yours when ye employed
> > Such ministry, when ye through many a year
> > Haunting me thus among my boyish sports,
> > On caves and trees, upon the woods and hills,
> > Impressed upon all forms the characters
> > Of danger or desire; and thus did make
> > The surface of the universal earth,
> > With triumph and delight, with hope and fear,
> > Work like a sea!'

> . . . the point I wish to make is that we forget how strained and paradoxical is the view of nature which modern science imposes on our thoughts.

Wordsworth, to the height of genius, expresses the concrete facts of our apprehension, facts which are distended in the scientific analysis.

Must then science always be what it has so far become?

Is it not possible that the standardised concepts of science are only valid within narrow limitations, perhaps too narrow for science itself?

Whitehead turns to Shelley almost as to a kindred spirit:

Shelley's attitude to science was at the opposite pole to that of Wordsworth. He loved it, and is never tired of expressing in poetry the thoughts which it suggests. It symbolises to him joy, and peace and illumination. What the hills were to the youth of Wordsworth a chemical laboratory was to Shelley. It is unfortunate that Shelley's literary critics have, in this respect, so little of Shelley in their own mentality. They tend to treat as a casual oddity of Shelley's nature what was, in fact, part of the main structure of his mind, permeating his poetry through and through.

He quotes the following line from PROMETHEUS UNBOUND:

The vaporous exultation not to be confined! and transcribes this into the expansive force of gases.

The following from the Earth's stanza:

*I spin beneath my pyramid of night
Which points into the heavens, — dreaming delight,
Murmuring victorious joy in my enchanted sleep;
As a youth lulled love-dreams faintly sighing,
Under the shadow of his beauty lying.
Which round his rest a watch of light and warmth doth keep.*

Of this Whitehead writes,

This stanza could only have been written by someone with a definite geometrical diagram before his inward eye — a diagram which it has often been my business to demonstrate to mathematical classes. . . . [N]ote especially the last line which gives poetical imagery to the light surrounding night's pyramid. This idea could not occur to anyone without the diagram. But the whole poem and other poems are permeated with touches of this kind.

For Shelley nature retains its beauty and its colour — is in its essence a nature of organisms, functioning with the full content of our perceptual experience. To Shelley, to separate off the secondary qualities as being merely subjective would have been totally unreal. Shelley is entirely at one with Wordsworth as to the interfusing of the Presence in nature.

From Shelley's MONT BLANC:

> The everlasting essence of Things
> Flows through the Mind, and rolls its rapid waves
> Now dark — now glittering — now reflecting glooms —
> Now lending splendours, where from secret springs
> The source of human thought its tribute brings
> Of waters — with a sound but half its own
> Such as a feeble brook will oft assume.

Whitehead has framed the word <u>prehensive</u> to mean precognitive awareness, *a prehensive unification as constituting the very being of nature,* yet there is a significant distinction between Shelley's quality of awareness and Wordsworth's.

> Shelley thinks of nature as changing, dissolving, transforming as it were at a fairy's touch. The leaves fly before the West Wind. 'Like ghosts from an enchanter fleeing.' The subject of the poem is the endless, eternal, elusive change of things, 'I change but I cannot die.' It is 'a change of inward character.'

> Wordsworth, by contrast, was haunted by the enormous permanence of nature. For him change is an incident which shoots across a background of endurance 'Breaking the silence of the seas / Among the farthest Hebrides.'

To these two factual aspects of nature, <u>change</u> and <u>endurance</u>, Whitehead adds a third, <u>eternality</u>. A mountain may endure for a period of time, but then changes, may pass away, may be replaced by another mountain. Here changes and endurance play their natural roles. On the other hand,

> A colour is eternal. It haunts time like a spirit. It comes and goes but where it comes, it is the same colour. It neither survives nor does it live. It appears when it is wanted.

Whitehead is striving to arrive at *an objective philosophy adapted to the requirements of science and to the concrete experience of mankind.* The mechanistic view of nature has no room in it for *aesthetic intuitions* or intuitions of any kind. This raises the whole question of objectivity and subjectivity in regard to human experience. The mechanist views himself as a detached observer of the world. What he surveys, including his observation of himself as a spatio-temporal object stripped of all human values, he calls objective. What he experiences within himself as aesthetic or moral experience, through art or religion he regards as merely subjective, having no real existence. What he perceives of the world through his senses, the sensory qualities of experience, is likewise only subjective. He is left with a cognitive mind, stripped of all human values. That way life itself grows valueless. It is this view of things, born of the seventeenth century and persisting into our time, that Whitehead is questioning. This may hold good for a machine but not for an organism. An organism lives by growth, by processes of change, by powers of generation, by its interfusion with other organisms and with its environment, also by its 'mental state' in which is vested the unifying principles pervading all its parts and subdivisions, rising in man to the <u>conscious mental state</u>, to self-awareness, and with this self-awareness to advance further by directed effort.

It is the inner values by which men live that give meaning to life. As the Romantic Movement faded out in the nineteenth century, the values took on powerful outer materialistic forms.

> *Value is an element which permeates through and through the poetic view of nature. We have only to transfer to the very texture of realisation in itself that value which we recognise so readily in terms of human life. This is the secret of Wordsworth's worship of nature . . . the romantic reaction was protest on behalf of value.*

> *What is peculiar and new to the century, differentiating it from all its predecessors, is its technology.*

> *The greatest invention of the nineteenth century was the invention of the method of invention. . . . The prophecy of Francis Bacon has been fulfilled; and man, who at times dreamt of himself as a little lower then the angels, has submitted to become the servant and the minister of nature.*

In reviewing the changes that changed human life and outlook in the nineteenth century, Whitehead speaks of *four great novel ideas* — *introduced into theoretical science.*

> *One of the ideas is that of a field of physical activity pervading all space, even where there is an apparent vacuum.*

Here he is referring to Maxwell's theory of electromagnetism. The *second great notion* was that of <u>atomicity</u>.

The living cell is to biology what the electron and the proton are to physics. Apart from cells and the aggregates of cells there are no biological phenomena. The cell theory was introduced into biology contemporaneously with, and independently of Dalton's atomic theory. The two theories are independent exemplifications of the same idea of 'atomism.'

Louis Pasteur carried over these same ideas of atomicity still further into the region of biology . . . for they introduced the notion of organisms into the world of minute beings. The remaining pair of new ideas — are — connected with the notion of transition or change.

The doctrine of energy has to do with the notion of quantitative permanence underlying change. The doctrine of evolution has to do with the emergence of novel organisms as the outcome of chance. The theory of energy lies in the province of physics. The theory of evolution lies mainly in the province of biology.

And now Whitehead gives a vivid picture of the effect of these four ideas, and how they

. . . transformed the middle period of the century into an orgy of scientific triumph. Clear sighted men, of the sort who are so clearly wrong, now proclaimed that the secrets of the physical universe were finally disclosed. If only you ignored everything that refused to come into line, your powers of explanation were unlimited. On the other hand, muddle-headed men muddled themselves in the most indefensible positions. Learned dogmatism, conjoined with ignorance of the crucial facts, suffered a heavy defeat from the scientific advocates of new ways. Thus to the excitement derived from technological revolution, there was now added the excitement arising from the vistas disclosed by scientific theory. Both the material and the spiritual bases of social life were in the process of transformation. When the century entered upon its last quarter, the three sources of inspiration, the romantic, the technological, and the scientific had done their work.

The period of the last twenty years was efficient, dull, and half-hearted. It celebrated the triumph of the professional man. . . . It was an age of successful scientific orthodoxy, undisturbed by much thought beyond the conventions.

We will not pursue Whitehead's elaboration of this particular theme further but pass on to the two closing chapters of his book, 'Science and Religion,' and 'Requisites for Progress.' These give a concluding summation up of points bearing most directly on the needs and conditions of humanity which have arisen out of the history of the scientific age up to the present.

When we consider what religion is for mankind, and what science is, it is no exaggeration to say that the future course of history depends upon the decision of this generation as to the relations between them. We have here the two strongest general forces (apart from the mere impulse of the various senses) which influence men, and they seem to be set one against the other — the force of our religious intuitions, and the force of our impulse to accurate observation and logical deduction.

. . . there has always been a conflict between religion and science — and both religion and science have always been in a state of continual development.

Science is concerned with the general conditions which are observed to regulate physical phenomena; whereas religion is wholly wrapped up in the contemplation of moral and aesthetic values. On the one side there is the law of gravitation, and on the other the contemplation of the beauty of holiness. What one side sees, the other misses and vice versa. Consider, for example, the lives of John Wesley and of St. Francis of Assisi. For physical science you have in these lives merely ordinary examples of the operation of the principles of physiological chemistry, and of the dynamics of nervous reactions: for religion you have lives of the most profound significance in the history of the world. Can you be surprised that, in the absence of a complete and perfect phrasing of the principles of science and of the principles of religion which apply to these special cases, the accounts of these lives from divergent standpoints should involve discrepancies? It would be a miracle if it were not so.

Religion is the vision of something that stands beyond, behind, and within, the passing flux of immediate things; something which is real, and yet waiting to be realised; something which is a remote possibility, and yet the greatest of present facts; something that gives meaning to all that passes, and yet eludes apprehensions, something whose possession is the final good, and yet is beyond all reach; something which is the ultimate ideal, and the hopeless quest.

It is the one element in human experience which persistently shows an upward trend. It fades and then recurs. But when it renews its force, it recurs with an added richness and purity of content. The fact of the religious vision, and its history of persistent expansion, is our one ground for optimism. Apart from it, human life is a flash of occasional enjoyments lighting up a mass of pain and misery, a bagatelle of transient experience.

The vision claims nothing but worship; and worship is the surrender to the claim for assimilation, urged with the motive force of mutual love. The vision never overrules. It is always there, and it has the power of *love presenting the one purpose whose fulfillment is eternal harmony. Such order as we find in nature is never force, it presents itself as the one harmonious adjustment of complex detail.*

*Evil is the brute motive force of fragmentary purpose, disregarding the eternal vision. Evil is overruling, retarding, hurting. The power of God is the worship He inspires. The worship of God is not a rule of safety —
it is an adventure of the spirit, a flight after the unattainable. The death of religion comes with the repression of the high hope of adventure.*

Reflections drawn from the closing chapter, 'Requisites for Social Progress':

The general conceptions introduced by science into modern thought cannot be separated from the philosophical situation as expressed by Descartes. I mean the assumption of bodies and minds as independent individual substances, each existing in its own right apart from any necessary references to each other.

But in the nineteenth century, when society was undergoing transformation into the manufacturing system, the bad effects of these doctrines have been very fatal. The doctrine of minds, as independent substances, leads directly not merely to private worlds of experiences, but also to private worlds of morals. The moral intuition can be held to apply only to the strictly private world of psychological experience. Accordingly, self-respect, and the making the most of your own individual opportunities, together constituted the efficient morality of the leaders among the industrialists of that period. The western world is now suffering from the limited moral outlook of the three previous generations.

Also the assumption of the bare valuelessness of mere matter led to a lack of reverence in the treatment of natural or aesthetic beauty. . . .

Wisdom is the fruit of a balanced development. It is this balanced growth of individuality which it should be the aim of education to secure.

My own criticism of our traditional educational method is that they are too much occupied with intellectual analysis, and with the acquirement of formularized information. What I mean is that we neglect to strengthen habits of concrete appreciation of the individual facts in their full interplay of emergent values, and that we merely emphasize abstract formulations which ignore this aspect of the interplay.

At present our education combines a thorough study of a few abstractions, with a slighter study of a larger number of abstractions. We are too exclusively bookish in our scholastic routine. In the Garden of Eden, Adam saw the animals before he named them; in the traditional system, children named the animals before they saw them.

When you understand all about the sun and all about the atmosphere and all about the rotation of the earth, you may still miss the radiance of the sunset. There is no substitute for the direct perception of the concrete achievement of a thing in its actuality. We want concrete fact with a high light thrown on what is relevant to its preciousness.

What I mean is art and aesthetic education. It is, however, art in such a general sense of the term that I hardly like to call it by that name. Art is a special example. What we want is to draw out habits of aesthetic appreciation.

For example, the mere disposing of the human body and the eyesight so as to get a good view of a sunset is a simple form of artistic selection. The habit of art is the habit of enjoying vivid values.

But, in this sense, art concerns more than sunsets. A factory with its machinery, its community of operatives, its social service to the general population, its dependence upon its organizing and designing genius, its potentialities as a source of wealth to the holder of its stock is an organism exhibiting a variety of vivid values. What we want to train is the habit of apprehending such an organism in its completeness.

This fertilization of the soul is the reason for the necessity of art. A static value, however serious and important, becomes unendurable by its appalling monotony of endurance. The soul cries aloud for release into change. It suffers the agonies of claustrophobia. The transitions of humour, irreverence, play, sleep and above all — of art are necessary for it. Great art is that arrangement of the environment so as to provide for the soul vivid, but transient, values. . . . The great art is more than a transient refreshment. It is something which adds to the permanent richness of the soul's self-attainment. It justifies itself both by its immediate enjoyment and also by its discipline of the inmost being. Its discipline is not distinct from enjoyment, but by reason of it. It transforms the soul into the permanent realization of values extending beyond its former self.

This element of transition in art is whose by the restless exhibit in its history. An epoch gets saturated by the masterpieces of any one style. Something new must be discovered. The human being wanders on. Yet there is a balance in things. Mere change before the attainment of adequacy and achievement either in quality or output is destructive of greatness. But the importance of a living art, which moves on and yet leaves its permanent mark, can hardly be exaggerated.

Mankind has wandered from the trees to the plains, from the plains to the sea-coast, from climate to climate, from continent to continent, and from habit of life to habit of life. When man ceases to wander, he will cease to ascend in the scale of being. Physical wandering is still important but greater still is the power of man's spiritual adventure, — adventures of thought, adventures of passionate feeling, adventures of aesthetic experience. A diversification among human communities is essential for the provision of the incentive and the material for the Odyssey of the human spirit. Other nations of different habits are not enemies; they are godsends. Men require of their natures something sufficiently akin to understand, something sufficiently different to provoke attention, and something great enough to command admiration.

Modern science has imposed on humanity the necessity of wandering. Its progressive thought and its progressive terminology make the transition through time, from generation to generation, a true migration into uncharted seas of adventure. The very benefit of wandering is that is it dangerous and needs skills to avert evils. We must expect therefore, that the future will disclose dangers. It is the business of the future to be dangerous and it is among the merits of science that it equips the future for its duties.

In the immediate future there will be less security than in the immediate past, less stability. It must be admitted that there is a degree of instability which is inconsistent with civilization. But on the whole, the great ages, have been unstable ages.

If we review in brief the main features which come to light in Whitehead's contribution we may, perhaps, summarize as follows:

The dualism of the seventeenth and eighteenth centuries has to be superceded.

This is achieved by reintroduction of the qualitative values which carry the full reality of human experience. Here true objectivity has to be sought contributing to human life and growth.

The mechanistic view is abstract and justified for its limited ends.

The evolutionary view demands the concept of organism which Whitehead traces, according to the new physics, to the innermost character of substance or matter.

Beyond the logic concerned with things, education must provide the possibility of awakening and cultivating moral aesthetic intuitions. It is the neglect of these higher values that has reduced life to a mere struggle for existence and to the detriment of social and human values in economic and political life.

With the advance of science from a mechanist to an organic view of the world, these higher possibilities become attainable. The ultimate appeal is for a right integration and orientation of science, art, and religion, which leads to a new humanitarianism, inclusive of all, in the conduct of life.

All these elements are contained in Whitehead's text and must be regarded as a pioneering endeavour to bring a new sanity into the world.

If we regard materialism as a modern kind of Hades, as adventure which has carried men down into realm of darkness and death, then one may perceive in Whitehead a pioneer leading an upward trend towards a beckoning light with promise of a renewing life. Certainly his striving was an endeavour for the reunification of religion, art and science in their actual threefold unity of being, — a uniting that gives encouragement and hope for the future — when humankind needs it most.

· 18 ·

A Biologist Testifies

J. S. Haldane, a foremost biologist of the century, wrestled in his own way with the scientific materialism which has so greatly dominated Western thought and its perceptions of living nature up to mankind. He, like Whitehead, traced its source to the dualism of the seventeenth century, which carried forward into our time. Of the several figures he quoted, Descartes and Kant were outstanding; Descartes for his division into mind and body; and Kant for his two worlds which never meet, an outer phenomenal world mechanistically conceived, and an invisible noumenal world of ethic and aesthetics.

Haldane, in his THE PHILOSOPHY OF A BIOLOGIST, intended to rescue the mind from its enslavement to matter and to arrive at a one-world view comprising both. His approach was to build on the common sense values of practical experience.

He surveyed experience in four stages, moving from physical-mineral science to living nature and the evidences of biology, thence to conscious nature or psychology, and finally, in a quite unexpected way, to the subject of religion, directly concerning the human in us.

Haldane refers to the ruling concept of matter as particles in motion, a view of inner chaos, of chance and probability leading by its logic to the second law of thermodynamics and the leveling down of all energies to a state of entropy or heat death.

He contrasts this with the more ordered findings of the newer physics with its promise of further development ahead.

> One discovery after another has shown that what was previously taken as inert matter is in reality a centre of intense activity.

This leads to the further thought:

> The science of physics appears to possess at present no definite word to describe the new facts of observation which are now forced upon it, and perhaps it may become necessary to go to biology in search of a word.

The underlying question is whether there might not be something concealed in the inner constitution of matter as a precondition of the emergence of living nature. For Haldane the term 'co-ordinated activity' carries a very special magic with it.

> Mechanical conceptions are still of the utmost practical use in physics, but in fundamental matters, physics can no longer be said to be a mechanical science. The modern conception of relativity cuts across the idea that the universe can be regarded as consisting of a self-existent matter and separate events. In all its aspects the universe of recent physical interpretations implies unity. On the other hand, the distribution of what is happening has taken on a measure of co-ordination which was absent in the older conception. The happenings in an atom, electron, proton, or light quantum appear as no longer chaotic, or dependent on mere chance, but inherent and co-ordinated . . . from the newer statement co-ordinated activity is inherent in matter.

Haldane saw it as the task of philosophy *to bring together in some way or other the physical interpretation of the world with those of biology and psychology,* and he adds, *For the new physics the gap appears no longer one which can never be bridged. If, in this respect, we seek for anything fundamental along the narrow lines of the old physical conceptions, we can only meet with disappointment.*

> There are no simple sense-data or isolated elements in our experience. What we may take as simple sense-data unrelated to the rest of experience are only imaginary entities, the ghosts of the old conception that mind and body are related to one another in a manner similar to that in which two inert bodies are related to one another according to the old mechanistic physics.

Haldane hoped that the science of physics may be brought into *direct touch with experience which has not hitherto been interpreted physically.*

Can the science of physics ever be brought into a direct relationship with the organic sciences or must we forever regard the higher manifestations in nature as having their origin in what Whitehead called 'brute matter'?

> We can accept the physically interpreted world as a partial representation of reality, sufficient for certain practical purposes, but quite insufficient in other respects.

The questions always arise: how could the living have arisen from the non-living; and how does an organism, once arrived, maintain its life?

Descartes' theory of the body as a machine evoked a reaction which gave rise to the theory of vitalism, that is, of a vital principle or vital force active within the organism. Each species of organism was regarded as having its own vital principle which disappeared at death.

> Life implies constant activity, and the vital principle was accordingly regarded as something essentially active, constantly controlling and therefore interfering with physical tendencies towards disintegration of organic structure, and building up new organic structure in the process of nutrition and reproduction.

In the course of the nineteenth century the theory of vitalism faded out, largely because of the rise of the evolutionary theory; but also, in Haldane's view, because it regarded each organism as a self-contained and isolated entity. According to Haldane there were two dominant facts to be considered: the coordinated life within an organism; and equally decisive and not to be separated from it, the sustaining forces of the environment.

> The life of an organism, with all its characteristic peculiarities, can be shown by an ever-increasing body of experimental evidence to be dependent on the nature of its environment, which was interpreted physically and chaotically by vitalists and non-vitalists alike. Human life ceases at once if the oxygen supply to the central nervous system is cut off, or if the latter is reached by some very poisonous substance in quite small concentration. Facts such as these, which may be multiplied indefinitely, make vitalism an altogether inconsistent hypothesis.

Then there developed a belief that life must be generally regarded as no more than a complicated physico-chemical process. However, this view Haldane was most concerned to combat.

Whenever the attempt to form any detailed conception of what sort of physico-chemical process could, on the prevailing mechanistic conception of physics and chemistry, correspond with the characteristic functions of life, the attempt breaks down completely. We can form no conception on these lines of how it is that a living organism, presuming it, as we must on the mechanistic theory, to be an extremely complex and delicately adjusted piece of molecular machinery, maintains and adjusts its characteristic form and activity in face of a varying environment, and reproduces them indefinitely often.

That the new physics, not being of a mechanistic nature might have something to offer towards a solution of the riddle is a haunting thought. How does the lifeless translate into the living, if indeed it ever does? All the more must we study as closely as possible what living nature can tell. Haldane describes this explicitly.

In the development and the maintenance of a living organism the coordination is very clear. The development of each part can be shown to be dependent on that of other parts, including the immediate environment; and the more closely development and maintenance are studied, the more evident does this become. But the particular manner in which the parts and the environment influence one another is such that the specific structure and activities of the organism are maintained. They are unmistakably developed and maintained as a whole, and this is what we mean when we say that the organism lives a specific life. The conception of its life enables us to predict the general behaviour of its parts so long as it is alive, and in particular it enables us to predict the general manner of its reproduction from a rudimentary part of the same organism. . . . it is this co-ordinated maintenance that we call life.

Haldane gives a striking example of such co-ordination in connection with the circulation of the blood. Contrary to the generally maintained view from Harvey *that blood is simply pumped round mechanically by the action of the heart,* Haldane puts forward the directly opposite view:

. . . that the circulation is everywhere co-ordinated locally and generally with what is required locally for the maintenance in structure and activity of each part of the body, so that the blood, propelled by each beat if the heart, as well as the frequency of beat, is determined in this way. Special stimuli of inhibitions, acting locally, bring this about, and it is the requirement of the tissues, and not primarily the action of the heart, which determines the rate of circulation of each part.

This is a remarkable statement born, not of theory, but of genuine biological insight. It is the same insight that leads him to declare:

> The maintained co-ordination is present, just as much between organism and environment as in the relations between the parts of an organism itself. We cannot separate in space the phenomena of life from those of the environment.

The manifestation of life depends absolutely on the active interrelationship of both. To illustrate this at its most intimate level, he takes up the crucial question of what constitutes subjective and objective experience. Haldane can not accept the divisive view of the dualists of a subjective world contained within man and an objective world wholly detached from him. He gave a lengthy description, based on experimental evidence as to what is involved in the act of vision, in the experience of brightness and darkness and then in the perception of colour. He wished to demonstrate that what one actually saw arose through an interaction between the perceiving eye and the phenomenon perceived; that it is impossible, in the act of seeing, to separate the subjective from the objective. The experience of the subject involved not a state of mere passivity but also outgoing activity towards the object. This totally contradicts the Kantian view that with our senses we can never perceive *the thing in itself*. This would mean that we are ever confined to our own world of subjective impressions conditioned by the nature of our sense organs: what is out there actually we can never know; all we can know are the effects induced in us.

This is a view that Haldane wholly rejects. What is experienced arises through the interplay between organism and environment, an interplay which fulfills the coordinating activity that is the expression of life.

> When we realise, for example, that in our 'observing' the blue sky, we are also making it blue, our attitude to the 'nature' that we see around us becomes very different,

> When we realise, as a good artist does in practice, that in what we see around us, we ourselves are always present, and we are not mere 'observers' of what is outside us, our visual environment becomes in reality not merely something much nearer the truth, but of far greater personal interest. The oppression produced by the idea of a perceived world in which we have no part disappears.

Haldane extends this to all the other senses. Whether we choose to measure a thing in grams or pounds is of the least importance. What takes place between us and the object is pressure and counter-pressure, action and reaction.

> *It is, for instance, in our sense of effort that we experience what is called inertia and the force required to overcome it. A mere observer is only a convenient figment. Our own sense-experiences are experiences of life, and are embodied in all we perceive.*

Again and again Haldane stressed the difference between a merely physical and a biological interpretation.

> *From the standpoint of the traditional physical sciences, a living organism appears as a complex aggregation of separable units of matter associated causally with one another in separate events. From the biological standpoint, on the other hand, the apparently separable units of matter and events are seen to be not actually separable, but, in their relationships with one another, to be taking part in the manifestation of the co-ordinated and persistent whole which is called a life, and which has no spatial limits. Thus the separable units and events of physical interpretation are seen to be illusory, but the same phenomena become intelligible in so far as they can be interpreted as phenomena of life. It is the maintenance of co-ordination that we are considering in biology.*

Life is a fact of experience, and when we make that our starting point it leads us to a deeper insight than can be gained through physico-chemical considerations.

> *We have just as good a right to consider the biologically interpreted world to be a directly perceived world of common sense as we have to consider the physically interpreted world in this manner . . . the nature of what we discover in biology is incapable of being expressed in physical terms.*

> *. . . there is no limit to the discoveries which could be included under the general headings of bio-physics or bio-chemistry. But when we put these discussions together as mere physics and chemistry, they are always indefinite, since they do not tell anything about the fact that the phenomena they refer to are co-ordinated and maintained. The more amazing and unintelligible from a physical and chemical standpoint do the co-ordination, maintenance, and reproduction become.*

A consistent study of the phenomena of life must reject the idea that *life has originated out of mechanical conditions.*

A thought about death:

> We must, I think, regard the normal death as a feature characteristic of
> life. Normal death is sometimes regarded as a wearing out of the
> machinery of life; but it is evidently a quite unsuitable metaphor, since
> living structure, when we consider it closely, can easily be seen to be
> constantly renewing itself, so that it cannot be regarded as mere
> machinery which necessarily wears out. Normal death must apparently
> be regarded from the biological standpoint as a means by which room is
> made for further more definite development of life.

The next seemingly unbridgeable question is how does life give
rise to consciousness? Haldane is not concerned with building
bridges but only with experience directly perceived. He does not
stay to survey the great range of varying consciousness in the animal world at all, but goes directly to the human being, to himself in
fact, where the experience of consciousness meets him at first hand.

> When we attribute conscious experience to a living organism we do so
> for a very good reason, which is that the behaviour of the organism
> exhibits retrospect and foresight . . . as can be verified easily in our own
> experiences . . . what in other respects might be regarded as a mere
> organism perceives, or forms ideas, of what is around it, and respond to
> these ideas. What it responds to embodies direct relations to a past and
> future of its own and of what is around it, as well as to an immediate
> present, in which it is now a centre of specifically arranged 'objects' and
> 'events in time.'

Haldane goes on. Perceptions awake interests, give rise to motives
for action, to values implying choice, and so we arrive at the concept of personality. If we could imagine a physical universe which
is not perceived, hereness and nowness would have no meaning.

> It is, however, the perceived and willed universe of a person that we deal
> with in scientific or other observation, so that what is here and now has
> an intelligible meaning.

It was at one time customary, perhaps still is, to speak of 'biological memory' from the fertilized ovum on. Haldane is not ready to
accept this.

> To attribute this maintenance to the memory of past behaviour of the
> race does not add to our understanding of mere life, but only introduces
> obscurity. Memory is indeed a meaningless word apart from conscious
> experience of a past in personal relation to a present.

*It is concrete personality . . . which is embodied in conscious experi-
ence. Reality now appears as concrete personality. In psychology, the
conception of personality is just as fundamental as the conception of
life in biology.*

Considering the building up of the concept of personality, Haldane
felt obliged to repudiate the idea of a physico-chemical origin.

*We perceive, not mere physical or biological phenomena, but a world of
our own interests and personalities and those of others; and when we see
persons, it is persons with their interest that we see, and not mere physical objects or living organisms. For Descartes, with his mistaken separation of mind from matter, the persons and living organisms we see
were necessarily no more than physical objects, and this idea still persists in much of present day science and literature.*

*In all that we may interpret as mere, blind biological instinct entering
into conscious experience, personality with its accompanying responsibility, and control is also present. Personality is never a mere play-
ground of mere instincts.*

Here Haldane makes his first mention of animals, and that only
fleetingly.

*An organism which is conscious appears for us no longer a mere organ-
ism, but a person. In the higher animals we seem to perceive personality almost as clearly as in human beings.*

The words 'seem' and 'almost' imply that there is after all a difference, but it is as though Haldane chooses not to go into this. What,
in fact may be considered as an unmistakable difference? Does it
not lie in the fact, as regards consciousness, that while an animal is
certainly conscious in its own degree, it is only the human being
who is conscious of being conscious? Without the latter can we at
all apply the terms 'person' and 'personality'? Is it not just here
that we meet with the gap that Darwin imagined might be
bridged? But the long sought for missing link has yet to be discovered if such a link exists at all.

By person and personality we would normally be thinking of a
self-reflecting being, a being conscious of a self. In all his many
characterizations of personality, this is precisely what he is dealing with. What had he in mind by this mere mention of the animal? He is actually not concerned with building bridges but with

combating the prevalent notion that the living and the conscious have their origin only in 'brute matter.' He has no proof that they do not have such an origin, but this is no reason for believing that they have. The experiences of the shapes and forms of life at the highest level, of conscious individuality, rejects such an idea and so long as men cling to it, it is undermining all essential values. Hence Haldane approaches the nature of conscious human individuality which is the true ground of personality.

> *If we endeavour to read personality into details which we otherwise interpret as mere physico-chemical or biological activity, we can do so only by an act of vain unmeaning imagination. Conscious experience or personality is emphatically not something merely added to details which we otherwise interpret physically or biologically.*

The fact of environment, as we have seen, is to Haldane a matter of utmost importance.

> *. . . our whole universe is a universe of perceived phenomena in which all that is perceived embodies part of what is ourselves.*

> *A person and all his perceived world, thought, motives, and acts, are active manifestations of personality.*

> *. . . personality represents a constant struggle to realise itself. This is why for personality there is always a 'now' entering into the meaning of the past and the nature of the future*

> *History deals essentially with the manifestations of personality, and where, as we pass back in time, we lose sight of the manifestations of personality, we also lose sight of history.*

Haldane touches on the problematical problem of freedom.

> *. . . a man is free in proportion as his perceptions and his actions express his personality in spite of the variety of forms which perceptions and motives take.*

Here we have arrived at a kind of limit. So far all the questions and description have been confined to the single conscious individuality or personality. There now arises the question of what there may be beyond.

Haldane loses no time in making it clear that in using the word 'religion' he is no way concerned with any 'overt forms of religious belief.' He likewise explains his use of the word 'God.' He perceived that all human beings, no matter how they might interpret their ideas in detail, have a common striving for the true, the beautiful, and the good. For 'the good' he sometimes uses the word 'right.' This is a fact of experience which pertains to all mankind. It transcends the single human personality but is an all-human reality. For this he employs the word 'God.'

> *It seems clear that mere individual personality cannot account for our striving after truth, right and beauty; but are we not making a leap in the dark when we interpret them as manifestations in us of what men call God? There would certainly be such a leap if we regarded God as an individual person among other persons and things. But there is no leap in the dark if we regard God as present to and in us. If we did not make use of the word God we should require to use another word with the same impact. We must also attribute personality to God, because truth, right and beauty have no meaning outside the unity of personality. Their authority can be nothing less than that of supreme personality.*
>
> *Thus we must regard what appears to us to be true, good, or beautiful as a manifestation in us, however imperfect, of divine perception, will, and activity. In so far as we are furthering what appears to us as true, good and beautiful, God is present in us.*

Haldane clarifies further his own position.

> *A mere collection of theological beliefs not based on personal experience of truth, right and beauty may have considerable historical or anthropological interest, but is not by itself religion, and may also be associated with entirely baseless or even degrading beliefs and practices. On the other hand, a man's whole experience may be permeated in reality by religion although he disregards or rejects the forms of theological belief under which religion is usually represented.*

What is all important and of greatest significance is that *an ideal of final truth is always before us* and that *the search for truth* is acknowledged by all men as a duty not imposed from outside but born from within. The search for final truth rests with each individual personality *and rendering the partial interpretations of our experience fundamentally consistent with one another.* It is this fact that justifies the use of the word 'God' to *designate the all embracing personality in whose existence ultimate reality exists.* In this sense too, Haldane feels he can state that, *The observations on which the sciences are based embody what is sacred and what, when fully interpreted, appeals to all men.* In the same breath he can turn equally to religion.

> *For religion, and very definitely for Christian religion, God is present in the experiences of all men, and is the source of all higher experience. God is everywhere, was and will be at all times, and our universe is the progressive manifestation of God.*

> *It is in our personal relations with other persons, and with other forms of unity which are independent of ourselves as mere individuals, that we become aware of the personality of God. The fact that man is subject to error does not belie the fact that it is in the search after truth that the presence of God in man is revealed.*

In like manner he affirms that:

> *Right conduct is essentially bound up with truth.*

> *Our experience of the authority of what appears right, like our experience of the authority of what appears true does not, however, depend on mere individual personality and must therefore be regarded as a revelation of the all-embracing personality of God.*

It is as though Haldane is struggling with Kant's concept of duty as a categorical imperative — i.e., duty is something we feel compelled to obey. Haldane, however, is much concerned with establishing a ground of freedom within one. He is in fact saying that to be one with God is to be free.

> *The freedom we experience is divine freedom and no contradiction exits between this and our own freedom. In this way we can reconcile, if we wish, the theological doctrine of divine determination with that of personal freedom.*

Haldane goes next into a considerable consideration of beauty.

Beauty, like goodness and truth, *has the character of appealing to all men,* independent of their individual interests or personalities, *therefore, like goodness and truth it is a manifestation of all-embracing personality.*

> *In our perceptions of beauty, and particularly perhaps of beauty in nature, we are participating directly in divine perception, however imperfectly.*

> *Beauty is thus no mere subjective illusion, but, fleeting as its forms are, something immensely real, though we only see it imperfectly, and it is*

often recalled to us at all, by poets, artists, musical composers and writers who have seen aspects of it and been able to represent them to us.

There follows a challenging statement to the age we live in.

We are living in an epoch in which spiritual reality of every kind is clouded over by materialism, so that we scarcely know what to make of beauty, however much we may feel it. But we can look forward to a time when the clouds of materialism will have passed away, though that time can hardly come until philosophy itself comes into its own.

It is to be remembered that this whole book is offered us in the form of a philosophical survey of the values we live by, quite particularly in and through science. Haldane sees truth, beauty, goodness as a kind of trinity, though he does not use the word, each contained in the other two.

. . . as it appears to the writer, right conduct, truth, and beauty are only different aspects of what is fundamentally the same. Right conduct embodies co-ordinated wholeness, which can be, and often is, called beautiful. It also embodies truth, as standing for a true perception of the relations between different individuals. Similarly, truth as being essentially motivated, involves not only a true realization of co-ordinated relations, but also the furthering of them. In a similar way, beauty involves both truth or right perception and the co-ordinated wholeness which we find also in right conduct.

The theme of wholeness and coordination within a given wholeness was explicitly expressed in describing life, and it meets us again at every point in connection with consciousness, above all the consciousness of man. It is altogether natural, therefore, for the perception of beauty to enter into religion. It should be equally natural for the pursuit of truth in science to enter into religion. The fact that it has not done so is due to the rift that arose in renaissance times, due, in Haldane's view, to *inadequate or antiquated religious and scientific creeds.* It is just this that Haldane is trying to heal.

Coming now to religious interpretation we can see that the conception of God would have no meaning apart from what appears as a world of mere individual personality that the reality of God's existence appears as love in the manifestation of goodness, beauty and truth.

This is the first and only mention of 'love,' which comes here as a consummation of all that went before.

> *Thus in apparent individual personality, with all its defects and limitations, we find the manifestation of God as all-containing personality. The kingdom of God is within us, so that all our experience is transformed, and it no longer appears as that of a universe of mere individual personality and much less as a biological or physical universe, but as a concrete or objectively recognized spiritual universe of active divine personality.*

There follows the thought that truth, beauty, and goodness exist, but still as unfulfilled ideals.

> *Science is a continuous struggle against ignorance, goodness, is a continuous struggle against what is not good, and beauty is a realization of itself in what is otherwise not beautiful, such as paint, or stone, or sounds or the material aspect of nature. Truth, goodness, and beauty are essentially the active, concrete manifestations of personality.*

It is to be noted that in this book Haldane never mentions evolution, nor does he attempt to build an arbitrary bridge from the non-living to the living, or from the merely living to the conscious. He does not attempt to survey the animal world or to determine where animal borders on human. What he does do is to contemplate each of these realms with what he calls common sense perception, remaining steadfast to his own experience and free from speculative theory. His God is not an anthropomorphic phantasy. In the fact that all human beings have the same striving towards the achievement of the true, the good, the beautiful, though each human being has to interpret this in his own individual way, he perceives an all-inclusive higher reality manifesting itself and realizing itself on earth only through man. He does not claim to belong to this or that religion but he inclines toward the Christian image of a God who lives and suffers with and for man — a God he visualizes as a supreme divine Personality. The term 'love' arises almost of itself without further proclamation as the consummation of all that went before. Here coordinated activity is at its highest level within a wholeness that comprises all mankind.

Haldane steers a clear passage between scientific materialism and the type of theological materialism which awaits supernatural manifestations in a world of matter conceived mechanically. From his position he can write:

God's existence cannot be regarded as depending in any way on man's existence, although it is in man's own existence that God's existence is revealed to man. We can imagine a time when no human beings' organisms of comparable development existed, or when beings of greatly superior development will exist, in whom God's existence will appear much more fully. But we know enough at present to be sure that in existence in any form God must be manifested as all-embracing personality, and that the course of evolution must represent a more and more detailed divine manifestation.

Apart from God's existence as living and active, existence has no ultimate meaning. However far we may look backwards in time, we cannot reach a time when the ordered beauty of the heavens — that beauty which seems overwhelming when we contemplate it — was not present. The existence of truth, order and beauty are eternal, since God is eternal.

We meet in Haldane an independent and original thinker and researcher who, as a 'sacred duty' to use his own terms, breaks through the spell of materialism which is still so greatly binding in human thought and action in human affairs today. Our widespread method of education, far from offering a solution, impresses materialism upon the young. He, like Whitehead, stands as a pioneer of an age which is dawning, freed from materialistic doctrines and beliefs, opening up new possibilities of comprehending and evaluating existence on this earth.

· 19 ·

The Word Is Man's

R. A. Wilson was professor of language and literature at the University of Saskatchewan when he wrote, THE MIRACULOUS BIRTH OF LANGUAGE, first published in 1937. The book upholds the unique nature of the human being as revealed through language. He combated the Darwinian idea that language originated with the animal, an idea that has robbed man of his true status. It is language that declares the true gap between animal and man. The way that language has come into being remains a mystery, hence the word miraculous.

Wilson goes right back to Genesis.

> And out of the ground the Lord God formed every beast of the field, and every fowl of the air, and brought them unto Adam to see what he would call them, and whatever Adam called every living creature, that <u>was</u> the name thereof.
>
> R. A. Wilson, THE MIRACULOUS BIRTH OF LANGUAGE

Wilson comments:

> That is the Hebrew writer's brief and naive story of the birth of language; a story which the modern child of ten years will accept at literal face value; which the man of twenty who puts away childish things will reject; and which the philosopher of forty, who has grown in discernment as well as knowledge, will re-accept with some surprise at the amount of factual truth contained in it.

This Biblical story points to a significant difference between name and animal which, since the publication of Darwin's THE DESCENT OF MAN in 1871, has been ignored or even denied. Some of these Semitic

names, writes Wilson, have achieved a permanence which has out-
lasted *countless generations of animals [which] themselves have come into
being and disappeared again in a continuously vanishing stream.*

The next focus is the eighteenth-century contribution of Herder
(1744–1803), which Wilson described as standing between two
main influences; the one, the philosopher–scientist, Kant (1724–1804);
and the other, the poet–scientist, Goethe (1749–1822). Both were
evolutionists but in an opposite sense.

Kant, in his CRITIQUE OF JUDGMENT wrote:

> . . . *the whole technique of Nature, which as perceived in organized
> beings is so incomprehensible to us that we feel ourselves compelled to
> think a different principle for it, seems to have been derived from mat-
> ter and its powers according to mechanical laws.*

Wilson writes:

> *The same idea pervades the contemporary work of Goethe.*

Yet it is not the same for he further wrote:

> *Everywhere in the world he saw development and evolution, not
> mechanical, but organic and vital.*

They are the same only in their idea of progressive development.

Herder was a student of Kant, who was his senior by twenty
years, at Konigsberg from 1762 to 1764. He met and became an
intimate friend of Goethe at Strassburg in 1770. In 1776 he moved
to Weimar to join Goethe with whom he remained in intimate
contact right up to his death in 1803.

Wilson sees Herder's essay, ORIGIN OF LANGUAGE, 1772, not merely
as a milestone but as the starting point for the subsequent development of a science of language.

> *He [Herder] pointed out that when man, in the very first step of his rea-
> soning power, had isolated one object of his environment from all other
> objects, this isolated object 'retained in the mind, was a word in the
> soul.' . . . With the first distinct concept of an object isolated from other
> objects, language was already in his soul, hence it was invented through
> his own resources, and not in a mechanical manner through divine
> instruction. It was not God who invented language for man. Man him-
> self had to invent language in exercising his own powers!*

This setting aside of God cleared the way *for the free scientific investigation of language* pursued since the publication of his essay.

Herder wrote in defense of his view:

> *If it is incomprehensible to others how a human mind could invent language, it is incomprehensible to me how a human mind could be what it is without discovering language for itself.*

Yet the language data of the various peoples was still so meagre that he knew *an exact science of comparative language is not yet possible.*

Wilson also made reference in his book to the biblical story of the Tower of Babel. This states that *the whole earth was of one language and one speech* but then came the aspiration to build a city and a tower *whose top may reach unto heaven.* The story tells how *the Lord came down to see the city and the tower.* When he saw that their vanity and presumption had reached a stage where *nothing will be restrained from them which they have imagined to do,* he decided *to confound their language, that they may not understand one another's speech. So the Lord scattered them upon the face of the earth.*

The legend of an original mother tongue began to acquire greater meaning with the discovery of Sanskrit. It is Sir William Jones (1746–94) who was the first to introduce Sanskrit and comparative linguistics into Europe. It led to the founding of the Asiatic Society in 1784, *for the study of the language and the literature of the East.* Two years later, in his third address to this Society, Sir William Jones made a pronouncement which *became the starting point for the modern science of Comparative Philology in Europe.*

> *The Sanskrit language, whatever be its antiquity, is of a wonderful structure; more perfect than the Greek, more copious than the Latin, and more exquisitely refined than either; yet bearing to both of them a stronger affinity, both in the roots of verbs, and in the forms of grammar, than could possible have been produced by accident; so strong, indeed, that no philologer could examine them all three without beholding them to have sprung from* <u>*some common source,*</u> *which perhaps no longer exists. There is a similar reason, though not quite so forcible, for supposing that both the Gothick and the Celtick, though blended with a very different idiom, had the same origin with the Sanskrit; and the old Persian might be added to the same family.*
>
> WORKS OF SIR WILLIAM JONES

This opened the way to deep study and research and to much insight into the profundities of language growth and development, studies that have continued to this day.

Quotations from two outstanding scholars in this field elucidate Wilson's immediate interest in the subject.

What is the difference between brute and man? What is it that man can do, and of which we find no signs, no rudiments, in the whole brute world? I answer without hesitation; the one great barrier between brute and man is language.

Max Muller, SCIENCE OF THOUGHT: LANGUAGE AND LANGUAGES

But as things are, every community of man has a common language, while none of the lower animals are possessed of such; their means of communication being of so different a character that it has no right to be called by the same name.

W. D. Whitney, LIFE AND GROWTH OF LANGUAGE

These two quotations give quite adequately the view, regarding man and language, which was held by linguistic scientists from 1772, when Herder first clearly formulated it in his essay, until Darwin entered the field in 1871.

Darwin, in his DESCENT OF MAN maintained that:

. . . the difference between the language of man and the cries of animals was not a difference in kind, as had been formerly thought, but a difference in degree only, a difference in definiteness of connotation and distinctness of articulation, (which in turn, followed) upon the different degree of mental development.

Max Muller, on the contrary, maintained that:

articulated language was the evidence of man's 'power of abstraction,' a power which differentiated him completely from the animals.

What concerns Wilson is:

. . . what specifically happened when man emerged from animal nature into a new world, whose new conditions necessitated articulate language. What were the limits of the animal world from which he emerged whose needs were answered by a few animal cries; what were the new horizons, new needs, new potentials opened to him in his new world whose actualization urged him to the making of language?

Wilson, MIRACULOUS BIRTH OF LANGUAGE

In view of Darwin's description of all the ascending steps of animal life toward the life of man, if man does indeed have *a unique and solitary position in the known world*, the character that distinguishes him from the animal needs to be drawn far more distinctly. Whatever that distinction may be, man has to be regarded now as a . . .

> *natural and integral part of the world, and not a mere exotic, or foreigner or temporary sojourner placed by deliberate external design upon the surface of an alien world of mechanical forces which are externally manipulated in his exclusive interests.*

In other words, Darwin's work raised the whole question of man's place in the world to a much more conscious level, and with it the whole question of organic unity from matter to man. And for man it raises the question of dualism within his own consciousness; what must he regard as his higher destiny over and against the world out of which he has emerged?

Wilson cited from Matthew Arnold's Empedocles:

> *No, we are strangers here, the world is of old,*
> *To tunes we did not call, our being must 'keep chime.'*

Also from the poems and novels of Thomas Hardy where *the determining agencies of the world, mechanical for the most part* are not only indifferent to man's destiny but can even be sinister.

The glimpse into man's interior life remains remote from the Darwinian scientific evolution though of primary concern to every thinking human being.

> *Darwin . . . was not the originator of this organic view of the world, but accepting the view from his predecessors and contemporaries, he assembled and organized such a concrete mass of evidences in support of it, and presented it in such a popular, readable and logical form as to give the organic view of the world an almost universal currency among thinking readers. In this respect his was without doubt the most distinct contribution of the last seventy five years to our better understanding of the world.*
>
> Wilson, Miraculous Birth of Language

It is to be recalled that the gaps between inorganic and organic nature and that between organic nature without intelligence and organic nature with intelligence have never been bridged yet.

Darwin wrote in his DESCENT:

> In what manner the mental powers were first developed in the lower
> organisms is as hopeless an inquiry as how life itself originated. These
> are problems for the distant future, if they are ever to be solved by man.

It is only the third gap, that between animal and man, that he
thought he had bridged. In the chapter entitled, 'Comparison of the
Mental Powers of Man and the Lower Animals,' Darwin wrote:

> My object in this chapter, is to show that there is no fundamental dif-
> ference between man and the higher animals in their mental faculties.

> The faculty of language had justly been considered as one of the chief
> distinctions between man and the lower animals. But man, as a highly
> competent judge, Archbishop Whately, remarks, is not the only animal
> that can make use of language to express what is passing in his mind,
> and can understand more or less what is expressed by another. . . . In
> Paraguay the Cebus Azaral when excited utters at least six distinct
> sounds, which excite in other monkeys similar emotions.

> The dog barks in at least four or five distinct sounds. From accumulated
> evidence of this kind, Darwin drew the conclusion at the end of the fourth
> chapter, to use his own words, that the difference in mind between man
> and the higher animals, great as it is, is one of degree and not of kind.
>
> Wilson, MIRACULOUS BIRTH OF LANGUAGE

In 'The Evidence from Language Against Darwin's View,' Wilson
opposes this with all his strength. He emphasized two points in
particular, first that animal sounds *are* _natural_ *sounds, and consequently indefinite in significance* like the interjectory sounds of
human beings which may mean one thing or another, and secondly, *animals do not increase the number of their few natural sounds.*

> These two things bring us to the point of difference between man and the
> animals with respect to languages. At some time, and, as it seems to me,
> from some creative and purposive force at work in the world, there emerged
> into life within the mind of man a new power or faculty for
> _explicitly_ differentiating the objects of the world, both in their distribution
> in Space and their succession in Time; and with this awakened power of
> explicit differentiation, a consequent need and corresponding impulse for
> something far more definite and elaborate than the few nebulous and
> misty-edged natural sounds which satisfied his pre-conscious needs. And
> eventually with this new power of explicit differentiation, and his urge to
> actualize it, man got started upon a free course, first, of shaping these
> vague natural sounds into definite-edged or definitely articulated sounds

— words, as we now call them — that could be clearly distinguished from one another; and second, of investing each definite sound with a definite meaning, a conventional and arbitrary meaning as distinguished from the vague natural significance of natural sounds; and third, of increasing or multiplying without limit the number of these definitely shaped conventionalized sounds. By these three things, the definite shaping of natural sounds, the conventionalization of their meaning, and their multiplication without limit, man has elaborated out of his few original sounds and immense structure of articulate language whose parts are as distinctly differentiated and organized as are the objects of the natural world which this language fabric now reflects. The two conventionalized sounds 'dog' and 'cat,' for example, are as clearly differentiated from one another as are the two natural objects for which they stand. Meantime, the animal world lies unawakened at man's feet without, as we said, showing any need, impulse, or power for transmuting their natural cries into articulate sounds, investing them with conventional meanings, or increasing their number.

This is an enormous difference between man and the animals, a difference in actualized fact not in theory, too obvious to be questioned when attention is called to it, and too significant to be over-looked; and it stands, as I have said, in unequivocal contradiction to the whole tenor of Darwin's arguments.

As to the fact that certain birds can be taught, by a kind of instinctive imitation, a number of sounds beyond their normal compass, nowhere is there any evidence of their breaking *into the realm of free and conscious mind* where articulate language has its birth and growth, and in which man now 'lives, moves, and has his being.'

To debate whether the difference between man and animal be one of degree or kind adds nothing. *Man has broken through some kind of barrier which, up to the present time at least, encloses the minds of the animals,* and the plain scientific question confronting us is, *What is the difference between the two?*

Is the difference of such a kind as can be concretely analysed and described so as to set out the significant characteristics of the human mind in clear and definite differentiation from the background of animal intelligence?

Here he is obliged to come to final reckoning with Darwin which he attempts to do in a statement entitled 'The Fallacy in Darwin's Method.'

Throughout the discussion he [Darwin] makes no inquiry into the nature of the total or central unifying mental faculty of man, nor of the corresponding central unifying mental faculty of the animals; nor does he make any comparison between these two. He proceeds by enumerating the separate sub-faculties, instincts, and emotions, which psychology has differentiated within the total faculty of reason, and taking these one by one he finds by comparison that the animals seem to possess them all in an incipient degree. He finds, for example, that the animals have the same senses as man, the same instincts, the same emotions, such as fear, terror, suspicion, courage, timidity, rage, revenge, as well as the more complex emotions of jealousy, shame, modesty, scorn, humour, that they possess also the more intellectual emotions, such as wonder and curiosity; and that they show the same powers of imitation, attention, memory, imagination and reason. Finding no apparent difference in the operation of these differentiated sub-faculties in these animals and in man, he merely adds up the results instead of unifying them; and comes to the quite illegitimate conclusion that there is no difference in the total faculty of reason in each; no difference between the central unifying mental faculties of man — the nous as Aristotle calls it in his Posterior Analytics — which co-ordinates and uses as its agents the differentiated sub-faculties, and which, in man is conscious both of itself and its sub-faculties, and can examine and carry on a discussion about them as we are doing here. He moves forward in such a plain manner and with such clear matter of fact evidence, that the reader is reduced into the same logical error.

But this method of reasoning and deduction is clearly not sound. We cannot pass at a jump from the apparent identity of these differentiated sub-faculties in man and the lower animals, to the identity of the central faculty of reason itself, which as we have pointed out, includes and uses as its instruments, all these subordinate faculties. And the significant difference between man and the animals, which opened the way for articulate language for man, while restricting animals to natural cries, seems to be a difference in the central unifying faculty, and not in its subordinate agents.

For this reason the new investigation which follows here will consist in a comparison of the unified faculty of man, and the animals respectively, with a view to discovering the difference between the two which led man to articulate language and left the animals without it.

In the second half of his book, "The New Investigation," Wilson set out from the premise arrived at in the first part, that man in his total nature is radically different from the animal and that this difference declares itself in his possession of articulated speech or true language.

Wilson contemplates the sequence which meets us in the world: matter, life, mind, and man in his conscious reason. This represents a continuity which is nevertheless made discontinuous by the gaps which remain unbridged.

Wilson does not attempt in any way to bridge the gaps in the sequence matter, life, animal, man. He characterizes each stage according to its most marked features, leading up to his main theme in regard to the birth and development of the word in man.

For Haldane's statement: *Life manifests itself in two ways — as struc-ture and as activity*, Wilson substitutes the words individuality and freedom. He hastens to explain his particular use of these words:

> A quantity of inorganic matter, a stone, for example has no individuali-ty in the sense of actively related parts, whose special relation to each other depends upon the continuance of a vital unifying principle within the particular body. Break a stone into two parts, and the shape of each part, and the spatial relations of the parts within each half remains the same. Cut a branch from an individual tree, on the other hand, so as to sever it from the unifying and form-sustaining life principle, and thus abandon it to the influence of mechanical laws alone, and in a given time these mechanical laws will destroy the definite formation of its parts and reduce its substance to formless matter.

This reveals, moreover, that the higher stage contains concealed within it the lower stage in metamorphosed form; Wilson does not himself use the latter term.

As for his use of the word 'freedom,' Wilson instances a tree as it organizes and raises its form and matter out of and above the earth's surface. This motion originates and is carried out from within the tree, not from without. This could never have been pre-dicted from a study of non-living matter. By 'freedom' he means this self-motion from within in contrast to mechanical motion acti-vated from without.

Advancing now to animal life, this embodies its life-energies in a more highly organized and self-contained individuality, with a higher degree of freedom. There are added three new faculties, mind, self-motion, and purposive sound or inarticulated language. With *mind* an inner world opens up to be distinguished from the outer perceptual world.

To return to the tree, its self-contained individuality is capable of selecting the sensuous material it needs from its environment, and of synthesizing this into its own physical dimensions and stands confined to its own particular point in space and time.

> The tree . . . has, in other words, no actualized mind.

> In the animal, on the other hand, the new and unique power of mind has actually emerged from the creative and, as I think, purposive energies of the world. The animal has the same power of active assimilation and growth as the tree. Its body has similar limited and defined physical dimensions. But central in its body is the new power which we call mind, which through the avenues of the sense-organs of sight, hearing and smelling radiates or reaches out a certain distance into space and time, beyond the body's limits, so that the animal's individuality, by this new power of mind, extends beyond its own skin, beyond its own material body, and holds in its individual grasp, and actually occupies mentally, a much larger space-and-time environment than the body occupies.

Unlike the plant, *the animal with its double body-and-mind nature lives in a double physical-and-mental world.*

We may regard the *animal's mind as confined within its body and looking out upon the larger world* or, as Wilson prefers to think, *is merely centred or focused within the body, and actually extending to the larger circumference.*

> But however we may choose to describe it, it is clear that in animal existence the creative life-force of the world has produced individualized material organisms though which, as physical space-and-time centres, the mind of the world emerges into some kind of individual consciousness of its outstanding environment of space and time, and takes some kind of mental possession of this.

Along with this comes *the new and unique power of self-motion.* This self-motion is directed toward an object, for example, the squirrel scaling up the oak tree for its acorns, the presence of the acorns in readiness for the squirrel, suggests even further purposiveness in nature, a favorite theme with purposivists but hotly disputed by others. However as Haldane so strongly averred, it is to be remembered, that a creature and its environment make a whole. If we reject the idea of purposiveness, *one can see no other alternative to think out in detailed completeness, the idea of the organic unity of the world.*

Together with mind and locomotion, there arises quite naturally in animal life the cry or call from one animal to another. Here Wilson invents the word 'ruri-language' to distinguish it from true language or speech. It is here Darwin came into error.

> The ruri-language of the animal is the natural accompaniment of mind and locomotion. The three appear as being teleologically related. The plant having no mind nor locomotion has no language.

Wilson is at great pains to establish beyond question the actual difference between his ruri-language and language proper because on this difference rests the final distinction between animal and man.

Animal cries relate to immediate needs, for example, the presence or prospect of food, or the presence or prospect of danger; or they may be expressive of moods, of feelings of joy or pain. Animal needs being limited, the variety of calls is also limited, maybe from one to twelve, and they do not, as in the case of words, increase in number.

It is a matter of utmost significance whether the difference between man and animal is a radical one, and Wilson sees language the key to determining this.

> Man's power of explicit mental differentiation was what brought language into existence.

> There is, however, another interesting and, as I think, legitimate comparison that might help us forward a step towards clearness in conceiving the fact of language. The articulately differentiated sounds of human speech stand to undifferentiated natural sounds in much the same relation as the explicitly differentiated bodies of the various animals stand to the undifferentiated common matter of the earth out of which the various animal bodies have been made. All names of animals have been fashioned by man out of the common element of sound, just as all animals themselves have been fashioned by nature out of the common element of matter.

> The world-force first differentiated common matter into distinguishable individual forms, plants, animals, birds, etc., and in this way added a new story to its life. Similarly, the same world-force (whatever that force may be) working consciously in the mind of man has differentiated natural sounds into distinguishable individual names for these plants, animals, birds, etc., and in this way has again added a new story to world-life. The unconscious organized and multi-form world of matter has now

a duplicate in the conscious organized and multi-form world of mind by means of language symbols. If the world is the veritable unity which we assert it to be, then the fabric of human language which now extends over the world of nature is as distinct a cycle in its evolution as is the cycle of animal life which extends over the surface of insentient nature.

It is interesting to think, under the conception of emergent evolution, of the many steps and long history that lie between the original huge, formless, voiceless matter of the world in the pre-life period and the tiny, individualized, liberated, animated piece of matter that mounts in the skylark's body and gives its portion of the world's life back to the world in song. That would be a typical example of the manner in which the world rises to its actual life and voice.

To those who might regard all this as *outmoded idealism,* Wilson replied that if it is, it has persisted in varying forms from pre-Platonic to post-Hegelian times *and is likely to survive in modified form the present anti-idealistic mode of thought.* And should one complain that it is too much couched in poetic terms rather than in 'sober science' he would equally reply that it is precisely in regard to life and mind that poetry is needed to express what is so *subtle, elusive and fugitive* in experience. He quotes Coleridge in his observation *that poetry has a logic of its own as severe as that of science and more difficult, because more subtle, complex, and dependent upon more fugitive cause.*

Wilson reiterates that for him the organic hypothesis of a 'prime purposive agency' which existed from the beginning, is the only logical one.

In man the purposive activity of the world comes out to complete explicitness. The entire world of art, for example, both of use and beauty, which is now spread over the world of nature on this planet is the product of explicit purpose working through the brain and hand of man, who is nature's chief product. To conceive an unbroken unity in the world one seems forced to carry the purposive activity backward down the scale of existence from the highest form, man, to the lowest form, matter.

At this point, Wilson questioned why he did not immediately use the word 'God' instead of *only vague descriptive words that appear to be evading the issue?*

Because the word 'God' connotes in the minds of most people an anthropomorphic agency, a limited personality who works toward limited, particular ends, in a manner very similar to that in which human beings work.

The scientific thinker cannot fall back on <u>Belief</u>.

We have not reached a stage where we can be more definite than this, therefore we cannot employ the term 'God' — we cannot be more definite than the concept we have reached — we cannot finally name that of which we have no knowledge. We cannot at present reach beyond a hypothesis. This does not reject the possibility of achieving, one day, the knowledge we still lack.

Wilson is not a skeptic; the true scientist is never a skeptic; nor will a true scientist confuse hypothetical truth with the actual truth he is seeking.

Having come so far in his general considerations, Wilson now turns back to what he regards as Darwin's fundamental error in confusing *resemblance* of power with *identity* of power. He illustrates this by offering a graphic picture.

> *If we were to take a six month old Fuegian infant and place him in an educated English speaking home in Canada and its common educational opportunities, what and where would he be in twenty years? He would be first of all in complete working possession of a highly developed language, the instrument by which man has elaborated the world of mind into which he has entered and in which he realises his characteristic destiny.*
>
> *Then, by means of this language, he would have elaborated concretely for himself, the various parts of this mental world, in history, geography, literature, mathematics, science, and would stand in much the same position as any Canadian boy who had a long line of civilized ancestors. The seeming gulf between the savage and the civilized man would be practically bridged in a quarter of a single lifespan.*
>
> *Now put the chimpanzee's six month old offspring in the same home and environment, and at twenty years he would know none of these things. He is excluded by some impassable barrier from man's mental world, the world which man has actualized and elaborated by means of language. Darwin expresses surprise that some men should still think that there is any such barrier between the two. 'Nevertheless,' he writes, 'many authors have insisted that man is divided by an insuperable barrier from the lower animals in his mental faculties.' Well, these authors, as a matter of demonstrable fact, are right and Darwin wrong. The Fuegian is at the outset already across the barrier that stands between nature and free mind, and moves forward in that new world of free mind*

immediately opportunity is given. The chimpanzee is still in the world
of nature, and is blocked, as yet at least, by the barrier that stands
between nature and free mind, whether we can ever explicitly describe
that barrier or not . . . whatever resemblance *there may be in mental fac-*
ulty between the chimpanzee and the savage, it is clearly a resemblance
merely and not an identity of power.

Wilson marvels that scientific minds can fall prey so easily to
unscientific prejudices against old forms of thought and their
mode of expression. He returns to the story of the Fall from innocence as the result of eating the forbidden fruit, the consequent
opening of the eyes to a knowledge of good and evil, truth and
error, etc., and the expulsion from the Garden of Eden which he
sees as the expulsion from the world of nature, in modern colourless phraseology. He sees in that story, one of the most memorable
accounts that will ever be given of the most momentous facts in
the story of emergent evolution of life and mind in the world. He
ventures to suggest that when the novelty of recent discoveries has
worn off a little and modern outlook has settled into a sober perspective again that new and unprejudicial thought will learn to
wonder at an allegory which so vividly images forth a cardinal fact
in world history.

It is remarkable the way that Wilson arrives at this impression out
of his own unprejudiced scientific thinking, enabling him to recognize truth as truth even though presented in forms unfamiliar to
the thought imagery of his time. It is part of his honesty as a
thinker that he does not reach beyond the facts as he sees and
understands them. He does not attempt to explain the transition
from innocence in nature to the discriminating mind. He makes no
reference to the fact that the Fall was consequent on the
Temptation and of the tempter in the shape of a serpent, nor that
the expulsion was commanded by another being, the Lord God,
and carried out by his servants, the cherubim, who were placed at
the portal to prevent re-entry. Maybe that part of the story is still
waiting to be unfolded.

Wilson held to his task, to establish beyond reasonable doubt that
there is, indeed, a gap between animal and man, no less real than
the gap between animal and plant, and below that between living

and the non-living. In doing so he attempts to restore man to his rightful place in the world by virtue of the word, granted to him alone, and the new force of intelligence from which it is born.

> *That is the unique characteristic of the human mind, in each isolated piece of matter of some two and three-quarter cubic feet and one hundred and seventy-five pounds avoir-dupois, which makes up a man's body, there is centred a power which radiates to the furthest boundaries of space and time.*

The next step from this is that for the actual space-time world there is a mental counterpart. In that mental world a journey of thousands of miles which might take years to make can be covered point for point in a matter of moments sitting at one point in space. Thus, from the birth of conscious reason man lives in a double world, a world without and a world within.

This raises the problem:

> *How can man, just come into possession of his new conscious world, actually get started upon the task to which he is called, the task of translating the actualized space-time world of nature into the new-born space-time world of the mind. . . . There is no such problem for the animals in the cycle of nature beneath man.*

Here arises the question of language, clearly, each object in outer nature requires its corresponding symbol in the inner mind world. It was out of this need *that the articulate and cumulative language of man had its birth.* Thus language becomes a new phenomenon in the world *where the reason of the world emerges from its unconscious state to its freed and conscious life.*

To begin with this *new world of conscious mind neither adds to the sum-total of the natural material world,* nor brings changes to it.

> *It is . . . an invisible supra-sensuous world rising above and as a counterpart of the visible sensuous world.*

In the language of St. Paul we might use the terms, 'temporal' and 'eternal.' One is fleeting, the other enduring, and so we arrive at the fact that:

> *. . . language introduced the element of permanence into a vanishing world.*

A self-directing and purposive activity appears everywhere in the plant world, becomes more pronounced and obvious in the animal world, and emerges to explicit activity in man.

The inorganic base out of which it arose (must already have had purposiveness though) not yet apparent to human perception.

The sensuous space-time world of nature is duplicated by the supra-sensuous space-time world of mind, which emerges now, radiating from individualized mind-points, and holds all space and time in its single view; and turning back upon itself is confronted with the endlessly diversified forms of its own pre-conscious evolution.

Men now *required time-symbols lifted above the evanescence of time, and space-symbols released from the fixity of space.* Beginning, presumably, with gesture language in space, man passed on to audible sounds as speech according to the possibilities provided by his vocal organs, namely a given range of vowels and consonants. *Language by conventionalization and by amalgamation of the forms of time and space if freed from both.* Add to this, from a certain time on, the translation of speech into picture forms and then later in to script, and language acquires thereby a durability and a vastness of scope almost beyond measure . . . *since language attains its most precise and perfect expression in poetry,* Wilson most fittingly ends his volume with a sonnet by none other than Shakespeare where this very fact of the lastingness of language is stated not only with the utmost lucidity but with a *beauty imperishable.*

> *Since brass, nor stone, nor earth, nor boundless sea*
> *But sad mortality o'ersways their power,*
> *How with this rage shall beauty hold a plea,*
> *Whose action is no stronger than a flower?*
> *O, how shall summer's honey breath hold out*
> *Against the wreckful siege of battering days,*
> *When rocks impregnable are not so stout,*
> *Nor gates of steel so strong, but Time decays?*
> *O fearful meditation! Where, alack,*
> *Shall Time's best jewel from Time's chest lie hid?*
> *Or what strong hand can hold his swift foot back?*
> *Or who his spoil of beauty can forbid?*
> *Or, none, unless this miracle have might,*
> *That in black ink my love may still shine bright.*

What could express better. . .

> *. . . the unique character of language in its immunity from time and change, its silent and successful resistance to the 'wreckful siege of battering days.' to which all other forms in the world both of nature and the natural arts must sooner or later succumb?*
>
> Wilson, MIRACULOUS BIRTH OF LANGUAGE

In defense of the human word, Wilson concludes with a supreme example of the miraculous power of language, miraculous in its birth and for all time; for through language the status and dignity of man in the created world of nature is upheld.

> *Language, alone . . . has the unique power of transcending time and change, and of becoming thus the adequate instrument for elaborating the inward, supra-sensuous non-vanishing world of mind in which man lives and moves and has his being.*

· 20 ·

New Endeavours

In 1935 MAN THE UNKNOWN, by Nobel Prize winner Alexis Carrell was published. Within a year it went into a popular edition which rapidly ran into several reprintings over the years.

> The ideas and doctrine which Dr. Carrell has enunciated in this book will evoke reverberations in medical and scientific circles for many a year to come.
>
> Sir Arthur Keith, ESSAYS ON HUMAN EVOLUTION

Yet the book was not directed to specialists. As the Preface states it is dedicated:

> . . . to all whose everyday task is the rearing of children, the formation of the guidance of the individual. To school-teachers, hygienists, physicians, clergymen, social workers, professors, judges, army officers, engineers, economists, politicians, industrial leaders, etc., also to those who are interested in the mere knowledge of our body and our mind. In short, to every man and every woman.
>
> Alexis Carrell, MAN THE UNKNOWN

What could be more general? It contains a mass of information culled in the course of many years of research, the thesis being that the essential man remains <u>unknown</u>, and must continue to remain unknown to present theory. Continued ignorance of our nature must lead to our total undoing. Modern civilization has been allowed to ignorantly impose artificial conditions in the workplace, home and school, which effect the food we eat, the air we breathe, and the sounds and impressions we receive all day. These artificial conditions are destroying us by undermining our health, our

morals, and our sanity. Technology has triumphed at the expense
of personality, which is rapidly dissolving and disintegrating. The
book comes like a crusader's call, like the voice of conscience, to
look again, to think again, to rescue man from his ignorance of
himself. Carrell makes use of all the available resources of science
in his search for a more enlightened science, a super-science, which
can include an understanding for the human spirit.

He attributes our failure to know man to the fact that the science
of the lifeless has been made the ground for the science of the living: we begin our study of man by examining his corpse. And so
from the very start, Carrell pleads for modern science to include
the qualitative: *The qualitative is as true as the quantitative.* The
qualitative includes life and consciousness, the quantitative does
not. Personality and purely human dimensions are not confined
to space and time; man is more than meets us by dissection or
analysis. In order to come to a *profounder knowledge of ourselves* —
the only remedy against the evil which besets us — all phenomena concerning man must be considered, inner as well as outer,
mental as well as physiological, clairvoyant and mystical as well
as structural. Specialization has torn man apart into his separate
aspects — the primary need is for a synthesis. Hitherto, the procedure has been to build from the physical to the physiological
and from the physiological to the mental or psychological.
Carrell maintains that this separation in order of precedence is
totally misleading: the physical, the physiological and the mental
work concordantly as one. Beneath all the complexities which
science continues to discover by analysis, the human being
remains single and a whole. His life proceeds in <u>inward time</u>, and
here Carrell points to a clear distinction between physical, physiological, and mental time. Time, as regards organism, is not the
same as physical or chronological time, for an organism carries
its own past along with it:

> *In our infancy we carry within ourselves numerous virtual beings, who
> die one by one. In our old age, we are surrounded by an escort of those we
> could have been, of all our aborted potentialities. Every man is fluid that
> becomes solid, a treasure that grows poorer, a history in the making, a
> personality that is being created. And our progress, or our disintegration,
> depends on physical, chemical, and physiological influences, and, finally*

> on our own will. We are constantly being made by our environment and
> by our self. And duration is the very material of organic and mental life,
> as it means, (here he quotes Bergson) 'invention, creation of forms, con-
> tinual elaboration of the absolutely new.'

Thus time or duration . . .

> is the very material of organic and mental life.

But this does not only apply to the past carried into the present; in
organic process there is all the evidence of 'finality' — of the coordinated striving of multitudinous elements to achieve an end
which is inwardly foreseen; in other words, *to make the future present*. Of the many striking examples illustrative of this, we select
one which is not the less wonderful for being familiar.

Previous to this Carrell had already stated:

> If we attribute to tissues an intelligence of the same kind as ours, as
> mechanists and vitalists do, the physiological processes appear to asso-
> ciate together in view of the end to be attained. The existence of finality
> within the organism is undeniable. Each part seems to know the present
> and future needs of the whole, and acts accordingly. The significance of
> time and space is not the same for our tissues as for our mind. The body
> perceives the remote as well as the near, the future as well as the present.

Body, then is not just what the anatomist, physicist, chemist, phys-
iologist, or psychologist sees; <u>body</u> is a synthesis of all that the separate sciences can tell. Moreover <u>body</u> is not only of the past, nor is
it only in the present: in its activity, in each present moment, it
transmits the past and the previsions the future. Nor can its functions be confined to outer space and inward time, for they include
the mental which is neither space nor time. Yet it comprises a <u>one-
ness</u>, and each organ and each function is a oneness within this
greater oneness. A simple action like the lifting of a hand, whether
in pain, surprise, warning or salute is a single act. In the substratum
of this act there is vast complexity of coordinated bodily functioning down to the cells comprising the separate tissue of the separate
organs; but reality speaks through the <u>singleness</u> of the action, not
through the complex elements underlying it; we can never hope to
reverse the process and seek for the expressiveness of the action
within the complexities. Our minds seem constituted to search into
the parts, but in the process we lose sight of the starting point

which is life itself, manifest in its wholeness, life is ruled by an innate intelligence which our intellectual and abstract thinking may guess at but can never grasp.

Practical instances of the need to re-examine our thinking about phenomena abound in Carrell's book; they challenge the scientist in every field.

This need for a revised outlook springs first and foremost out of the needs of man. Carrell discovers that the root cause of the present trouble lies in the splitting apart of the quantitative and qualitative, and consequently also of mind and matter; this has produced an industrialized civilization which, paying no regard to man as a being of nature, has grown inimical to his welfare. First human nature was set aside by the exclusion of the qualitative, then it was split into mind and matter, and now it is being destroyed.

> We cannot undertake the restoration of ourselves and of our environment before having transformed our habits of thought. Modern society has suffered, ever since its origin, from an intellectual fault — a fault which has been constantly repeated since the Renaissance. Technology has conducted man, not according to erroneous metaphysical conceptions. The time has come to abandon these doctrines. We should break down the fences which have been erected between the properties of concrete objects, and between the different aspects of ourselves.
>
> The error responsible for our suffering come from a wrong interpretation of a genial idea of Galileo. Galileo, as is well known, distinguished the primary qualities of things, dimensions and weight, which are easily measurable, from their secondary qualities, form, colour, odour, which cannot be measured. The quantitative was separated from the qualitative. The quantitative, expressed in mathematical language, brought science to humanity. The qualitative was neglected. The abstraction of the primary qualities of objects was legitimate. But the overlooking of the secondary qualities was not. This mistake had momentous consequences.
>
> In man, the things which are not measurable are more important than those which are measurable. The existence of thought is as fundamental as for instance, the physicochemical equilibria of blood serum. The separation of the qualitative from the quantitative grew still wider when Descartes created the dualism of the body and the soul. Then, the manifestations of the mind became inexplicable. The material was definitely isolated from the spiritual. Organic structures and physiological mechanisms assumed a far greater reality than thought, pleasure, sorrow,

and beauty. This error switched civilization to the road which led science to triumph and man to degradation.

The first step must be to reintegrate the secondary qualities. According to Carrell, this will mean that *Mind will be replaced in matter.* As a result, attention will be paid, in education, in medicine, and in all the other departments of life to the total nature of a human as a single entity, an individual. It would no longer be a case of mind evolving from matter, the view of the materialist, or of matter emanating somehow from mind, the view of the mentalists, but of paying regard to the uniqueness of personality which as a single, indivisible, phenomenon comprises the structural, chemical, physiological and mental all in one, and which so lives in time that past and future are co-active in the present. With this changed outlook, human environment — social, economical, political, and technological — will also change to be more in accordance with human nature and true human needs.

Carrell's statement is obviously inconclusive; he would not have viewed it otherwise. He points to the danger, analyses the causes, seeks the correction and suggests a possible answer. He does not explain the nature of the coordinating forces which establish unity out of multiplicity nor what constitutes the uniqueness of human personality over and above the sum-total of the effects; but he demonstrates beyond a doubt that the dualism on which our present civilization is built is disastrous to man and must be overcome.

In 1947 a book entitled HUMAN DESTINY by Nobel Prize winner Lecomte du Noüy was published. This book, like Carrell's, was greeted with acclaim, this time by churchmen as well as scientists, for it sets out to demonstrate that the true pursuit of science must lead to God. In his introduction du Noüy wrote:

> *Science was used to sap the base of religion. Science must be used to consolidate it.*

He makes his purpose clear from the start.

> *The purpose of this book is to examine critically the scientific capital accumulated by man, and to derive therefrom logical and rational consequences. We shall see that these consequences lead inevitably to the idea of God.*

> *The negation of free will, the negation of moral responsibility; the indi-*
> *vidual considered merely as a physicochemical unit, as a particle of liv-*
> *ing matter, hardly different from the other animals, inevitably brings*
> *about the death of moral man, the suppression of all spirituality, of all*
> *hope, the frightful and discouraging feeling of total uselessness.*
>
> *Now what characterizes man, as Man, is precisely the presence in him*
> *of abstract ideas, of moral ideas, of spiritual ideas, and it is only of these*
> *that he can be proud. They are as real as his body and confer to his body*
> *a value and an importance which it would be far from possessing with-*
> *out them.*
>   Lecomte du Noüy, HUMAN DESTINY

He wishes to revalorize *these higher capacities of man* scientifically
and rationally and to incorporate them into evolution, by considering
them as manifestations of evolution, in the some way as the eyes, the
hands and articulate speech.

Lecomte du Noüy proceeds to launch an exposure of the limitations and fallacies of materialistic theory and doctrine; he battles
his way with energy and ardour, and with unrelenting logic.

Du Noüy's method of assault is unequivocal. Materialism prides
itself on its rationalism; he discloses its irrationalism.
Materialism builds its theory on Chance; he proclaims Anti-
Chance. Materialism works with 'probabilities': he shows that
organic evolution, with which he is mainly concerned, follows
the line of 'improbabilities.' Materialism regards 'fluctuations,'
that is variants of the normal law of averages, as secondary phenomena; he demonstrates that it is just the 'fluctuations' in
organic life, the 'mutants,' which mark out the path of ascending
evolution — they are for him primary phenomena. Materialism
submits the world process to the rule of Determinism, he cham-
pions the idea of Freedom. Materialism assumes a line of 'continuity' running through the whole scheme of nature, despite its
obvious gaps; on the contrary, he underlines the significance of
'discontinuity' as positive evidence of the intervention of a higher source of influence which escapes man's limited 'scale of
observation.' To the materialist declared scientific facts are
absolute; to du Noüy they remain relative. He thus reverses the
assumed truths of the materialist and, by a process of what may
by termed grand negations, arrives at a totally opposite view of

the world and of evolution. Materialism has filled the world with skeptics and agnostics; he pronounces the possibility of the scientific rediscovery of religion. The following are the main links in his chain of reasoning.

First du Noüy examines the nature of 'cause.' To be consistent with itself, materialistic science is obliged to regard all effects as physical in origin; all observable effects must therefore have antecedent physical causes. However, the moment man enters into the picture, the matter changes. Man, through his motives for action, lives by final causes which lie ahead of their effects. With the idea of motives, we are no longer dwelling in physical space alone, . . . *the problem passes imperceptibly from the material realm into the philosophical and religious realms.* If we carry this thought further it totally undermines the naive conception of 'cause.' In the case of man, *it is generally necessary to consider his intention, his will, as the efficient cause.* But for man to be in a position to exercise his will reverts our path through the history of the world to *such extraordinary complex anterior 'causes' that the world loses all significance.* If we imagine immense aeons of time, for example, the geological periods, and then wish to search for a similar *efficient/primitive cause in a will,* we are obliged to move from science to religion. That man can produce outer effects from inner non-spatial, non-physical causes no one can deny; therefore one cannot dismiss with impunity the possibility that the whole of creation may be a outer effect leading back to an inner cause, a motive to the future, a will.

Next du Noüy demonstrates that the conclusions of science can only be <u>relative</u> not <u>absolute</u>. For Man builds his conclusions on his observation of the phenomena; however, his power of observation is limited to his particular <u>scale of observation</u>. A giant or a microbe would, with similar intelligence, observe the same phenomenon differently; they might be guided by their scales of observation to different, or at least, to modified conclusions. *There is no scientific truth in an absolute sense. The phrase <u>Ad veritatem per scientiam</u> is an absurdity.*

For the phenomena on which scientific truth is based are derived from the combination: *Experimenter (man) + objective phenomenon.*

The implication of this statement is considerable. According to this mode of reasoning, (which du Noüy refers back to the Swiss physicist, Professor Charles-Eugene Guye), physically man can never arrive at more than a partial view, or better still, his partial view of the phenomena; to this extent all scientific conclusions would appear to be subjective. Morally considered the matter goes further. Granted that in a man's lifetime the *objective phenomenon* will change but little or not at all, morally, a man, in this case the observer or experimenter, may change considerably. By a process of inner change, by an enhancement of consciousness, be it through art as Sullivan proposed, or through some other form of enlightenment, a man may come to a totally new relation to the phenomenon and arrive at a new level of truth.

Is not this the very essence of progress? The truth we know is the result of our experience related to a given phenomenon; the truth at which the experimenter arrives will depend on the character of his experience and on the power of his perception which he brings to bear upon the phenomenon. What we 'see' of the world depends on what we are capable of seeing; it is common knowledge today that even physically an ancient Greek experienced colour differently from the man of today; morally and spiritually he experienced the world very differently, and his conclusions about the world were accordingly also quite different. Materialism takes for granted the present state of man as a finished product; but man can change. Even materialists have been known to change, when their perceptions and their response to the world has been altered through 'inner causes' which then become undeniably real even if unaccountable by common reason.

Next to be considered and equally far-reaching is the question of the discontinuity in modern science. Briefly, du Noüy's statement goes as follows: An observer wishes to apply himself to a study of the social laws governing society. He reflects that perhaps a good starting point would be to study the behaviour pattern of the factor common to all society, the individual man. Before considering the 'behaviour' of a man, it would be advisable to know something about his physical instrument, and so he turned to a study of the body, to anatomy and physiology. This makes him realise that he should know something about bio-chemistry, which in turn leads back to inorganic chemistry. Still intent on finding the most suitable starting point, he is led successively to molecules, to atoms, and eventually to electrons and protons; he cannot go further back. In following this retrograde course, he has, unbeknown to himself, crossed a number of *irreversible thresholds*, and having now reached the last of these thresholds, namely, electrons, *it is impossible for him by using the inverse method to retrace his steps to any of the original problems*. For each of these domains reveals *properties* which cannot be linked to the *properties* of the previous domain.

> It so happens that the properties of atoms, on our scale of observation (i.e., the result of the reactions of atoms on our nervous system), have not so far been linked to the electronic structure of atoms . . .

nor the properties of atoms to the properties of molecules, and so on.

> He cannot retrace his steps because the properties of life cannot be linked to those of inanimate matter; because thought and psychology of man cannot be deduced from the physio-chemical and biological properties of living matter. But the method here described, the method of science generally, is the true scientific method: analysis.

And it follows from this method that:

> The more deeply man analyses, the further he gets away from the principle problem which he meant to solve. He loses sight of it and is absolutely incapable of rejoining it by means of the phenomena which he studies, although, logically, he feels that there should be a link between them.

In other words, along the path of analysis, reality is seen to crumble away. Whether this is due only to man's scale of observation as the book suggests, or whether it is more properly due to man's mode of observation, will have yet to be considered. It seems strange that the scale of observation should be adequate in each separate field, failing only at the transition to the successive field from the less to the more complex.

Having established this irreversibility, du Noüy next turns to a consideration of the laws of chance and probability and of their attendant phenomenon, dissymmetry. He begins with a familiar example. By the laws of chance, the game of heads and tails must eventually lead to an equal number of heads and tails.

> *However, this is only true of chance <u>alone</u> determines the throw and not*
> *if the coin is lopsided, if there is a dissymmetry, which would favour*
> *either heads or tails.*

According to the laws of probability, the time it would take to
produce a <u>single</u> molecule of a moderate degree of dissymmetry
on a globe the size of the earth would be *about 10^{243} billions of*
years, whereas by the most recent calculations, based on radio-
activity, the earth is estimated to have been in existence for only 2
billion years. Of course, since we are dealing with chance, it
might have happened by a <u>lucky</u> chance, that the appearance of
one such, or at most two or three, actually did take place within
the allotted 2 billion years; were this the case, it would amount to
nothing short of a miracle. But from this relatively simple occurrence to the appearance of life itself is such an immeasurable distance that by the laws of chance it does not even come into question; as for the further advance, from Life to the creation of Man
— by the laws of chance, it is just not thinkable. Du Noüy does
not dismiss the laws of chance; he is concerned only with demon-
strating the all important fact that Life, not to speak of Man, could
not have arisen that way.

> *The laws of chance have rendered, and will continue to render, immense*
> *services to science. It is inconceivable that we could do without them,*
> *but they can only express an admirable, subjective interpretation of cer-*
> *tain inorganic phenomena and of their evolution. What they cannot take*
> *into account or explain is the fact <u>that the properties of a cell are born</u>*
> *<u>out of the co-ordination of complexity</u> and not out of the chaotic com-*
> *plexity of a mixture of gases. This transmissible, hereditary, continuous*
> *co-ordination entirely escapes our laws of chance.*

That being so, there follows the inevitable swing to the opposite:

> *To study the most interesting phenomena, namely Life and eventual-*
> *ly Man, we are, therefore forced to call on an anti-chance as Edding-*
> *ton called it; a 'cheater' who systematically violates the laws of large*
> *numbers, the statistical laws which deny any individuality to the*
> *particles considered.*

The matter does not end there. It appears that the laws of inorganic evolution, based on the laws of chance, not only do not support
but actually contradict the laws of organic evolution. The argument seems simple enough. According to physics, inorganic

nature tends always to develop in one direction only, namely towards an ultimate state of total equilibrium. The second law of thermodynamics makes it clear that every change in state entails a decrease in available energy. Inorganic evolution, therefore, is irreversible in that it inevitably proceeds towards *more and more 'probable' states, characterized by an ever-increasing symmetry, a leveling of energy.* Theoretically, therefore, according to physics, the predicted end of the world can only be one in which . . .

> *all the dissymmetries existing today will by flattened out, where all motion will have stopped, and where total obscurity and absolute cold will reign.*

This accords with Well's picture of a world rapidly running down. But organic evolution shows the very opposite, *A systematic increase in dissymmetries,* both structural and functional *a process which has culminated in the brain of Man.* This immense contradiction in tendency between the path towards ultimate simplification and uniformity in the inorganic world, and that of growing complexity and diversity in organic evolution, du Noüy regards as *an insurmountable obstacle in the path of materialism.*

He is so certain of the clarity of his own exposition that he writes:

> *The old-fashioned materialist who is honestly convinced that human life is without a cause and without a goal, that man is an irresponsible particle of matter engulfed in the maelstrom of purposeless forces, reminds us of the delightful remark made by a brilliant philosopher, Whitehead: 'Scientists who spend their life with the purpose of proving that it is purposeless, constitute an interesting subject of study.'*

Since evolution is a fact which no one today can possibly doubt, and since chance not only fails to explain this fact but by its own logic prohibits its possibility, the only alternative hypothesis, synonymous with anti-chance is finalism. According to du Noüy, the finalistic hypothesis nearly died out because those who advocated it in the past did so from too limited a standpoint. But now finalism must be rejuvenated in a different form. He coins a new term, 'Telefinalism,' to denote the difference, for the finalism which he proposes, in contradistinction to the old, is an emergent one whose goal lies in a very distant future. His view is of something vast and comprehensive, not to be confused with small and incidental instances of perfection which, through the very fact of their isolated perfection, actually contradict the general law.

> We must momentarily forge the details of evolution, its mechanisms, of which we know so little, and try to view the tremendous work of creation as a whole, not statically (that is, by immobilising it), but dynamically (that is, by bearing in mind the fact that it is a succession of constant transformations). We must not allow ourselves to be smothered by particulars, no matter how interesting they are, but must keep our eyes fixed at all times on the fundamental steps of evolution, from the most elementary organism to man and the incredible manifestation of his brain.

Du Noüy has a final tussle with the materialists on the question of free will. Religion is based on the possible choice between good and evil; it presupposes, therefore the capacity to choose, freedom of choice. The materialist, however, intent on finding *a common base for all phenomena (including life and thought)* can never admit free will for it would play havoc *with the magnificently simple concept of a purely mechanical universe.*

The analogy has often been made between a stone in motion and a man in action. The stone, thrown up in the air, may think itself free in falling, not realizing that it is bound by the law of gravitation. So too, a man projected into life, may think himself free, ignorant of the forces which oblige him to act as he does. Du Noüy's retort is that no stone has ever been known to *disobey* the law of gravitation.

> Assuming that it 'thinks' it must have come to the conclusion that it always chooses to fall on the ground eventually. Whether it calls this choice or obedience matters little; what matters is that it never chooses to disobey.

Man, on the contrary, has ever to wrestle with himself; either to yield to his animal instincts for present satisfaction or to deny himself this satisfaction, often with pain, for some higher motive which is *eventually conducive to the greatest joys.* As regards his moral evolution, man is faced with this dilemma perpetually, and no one can deny it. *The real question is as to whether man is free to formulate his choice and to act accordingly, or not.*

A materialist might argue that the entry of the moral factor into the physical universe reflects no more than some fluctuation: that the so-called moral is only a transitory effect of physical law and nothing in itself. Even so,

> . . . *a fluctuation which persists and repeats itself systematically over a period of at least twenty or thirty thousand years can no longer be considered as a fluctuation, but becomes a well-characterised phenomenon.*

To the strictly logical materialist the whole of evolution is nothing but a fluctuation, a temporary departure from the normal, in no way affecting the general and ultimate laws of matter. The hypothesis of evolution based on fluctuations might, on this basis, be admitted even by a materialist. The matter takes on another appearance, however, if we admit the idea of anti-chance in relation to the phenomenon of life. For then the fluctuations from the normal, now called mutants, acquire a particular significance. Du Noüy wrote,

> . . . *the story of evolution shows that its spearhead usually comprises a small number of individuals, the so-called mutant forms.*

This is a most remarkable fact, and the very backbone of the argument for Telefinalism; the fluctuations, or certain fluctuations, are no longer chance but <u>willed</u> variants from the normal, the chosen mutants, which become the stepping stone for an ascending scale of evolution from physical to moral and eventually to spiritual levels of existence. Many a fluctuation or mutant, may fall by the wayside, but the trend of evolution goes on toward a certain goal. The question remains at what point the will of man, or the free will of man, comes into action within this process? Can evolution have an ultimate meaning without man?

Du Noüy is too wise to believe that he can convince materialists by argument, for a faith, even an irrational faith such as he believes materialism to be, *cannot be convinced by mere words and logic.* If he has essayed to refute the materialistic doctrine, to <u>revalorize</u> the data and the theories of science, it is not for the sake of the convinced materialists, not even in the first place for the sake of science itself, but for the sake of mankind in general.

> *Today, when humanity is threatened with complete destruction by the liberation of atomic forces, people begin to realise that the only efficient protection lies in a greater and higher moral development. For the first time in the history of humanity, man is afraid of what he has done with his intelligence and wonders whether he has chosen the right path.*

There are gaps in nature's schemes. Materialism cannot tolerate gaps but has to admit them, hoping one day to establish an absolute continuity. Telefinalism accepts the gaps as significant interventions from a far distant future; these gaps provide for the entry of new properties, new potentials, new laws, by which evolution can advance from stage to stage, from the physical to the organic to the moral to the spiritual. Chance can account for none of this, therefore it is a process that must be willed, it must be motivated. Telefinalism thus resolves itself into a new, a scientific concept of God. Through du Noüy's Telefinalism, God can enter in his own right into the arena of science. The gulf between Faith and Knowledge had not only been bridged — there is no gulf! Science and Religion, like loves long separated, have met and merged again in single harmony. Matter has been led up to the spirit.

What of the long trail left behind; the inorganic deathly dust of this vast universe which mysteriously provides the ground of Life; the multitude of left-overs, living in stagnant, false security, inconsistently awaiting the eternal obscurity and cold that must ultimately enwrap them all? How will Telefinalism dispose of this vast wreckage, or must it remain for ever and ever, an eternal shadow of eternal life, a record of unobliterated failures along the path of man's ascent from body to soul to spirit to ultimate glory? These questions remain unanswered. The only answer which Telefinalism could possibly give would be that whilst we may acknowledge a real future, we may not anticipate its character — we who have ourselves only so recently emerged as conscious beings. A man has work enough in dealing with the present — that is with his own dilemma in the present. If Telefinalism can help him in his immediate task, and if he fulfills his task, then, in the course of his further ascent, he will behold with new powers and capacities as yet undreamed of, what today is still veiled in mystery. Patience, devotion, continued work, faith, will make the way open for what today is still held secret.

Du Noüy says frankly, *With the methods at our disposal we cannot imagine how evolution began.*

> If we accept the idea of evolution, we must recognize the fact that, on an average, since the beginning of the world it has followed an ascending path, always oriented in the same direction.

The direction leading to man and the birth of conscience.

The distinction between the nature of evolution itself and the means and methods it employs as its mechanisms is paramount: the mason is not to be confused with his mallet. Evolution is *a global phenomenon, irreversibly progressive,* and to achieve its ends it makes use of *elementary mechanisms such as adaption (Lamark), natural selection (Darwin), and sudden mutation (Naudinde Vries).*

> *Evolution begins with amorphous living matter or beings such as the Coenophytes, still without cell structure, and ends in thinking Man, endowed with a conscience. It is concerned only with the principle line thus defined. It represents only those living beings which constitute the unique line zig-zagging intelligently through the colossal number of living forms.*

Note the decisive use of the word *intelligently* in this connection. Intelligence is not confined to man. In man world intelligence lights up as individual intelligence. Viewed externally this lighting up of individual intelligence is one of the irreversibles: actually, perceived inwardly, there can be no essential break — for there is one evolution, and what is achieved at the end must have been present as latent possibility from the beginning. Intelligence thus rules the whole process and reveals itself to the mind of man.

> *Adaption, natural selection, mutation have contributed to evolution as its instruments only without being themselves always progressive.*

Du Noüy is untiring in his repetition of this, not to confuse the tools with the one who wields them.

Considering the mechanisms, Du Noüy is particularly concerned with adaptation, for it was 'the marvels of adaptation' which led to the old, discredited conception of finalism. The criterion of adaptation, he says, is *Usefulness,* but . . .

> *It may happen that once the mechanisms are started, they continue blindly and function unintelligently giving birth not only to troublesome but even to harmful monstrosities.*

By contrast, *the criterion of evolution is Liberty.*

> *The evolutive branch — that of Man — successively disengaged itself from all the others, first physiologically and morphologically, up to the appearance of conscious Man, then by widening increasingly, through moral ideas, the gulf which separated this man from the animal.*

Outside of man, all the creatures actually living on our planet are forms which have been left behind.

These abandoned creatures in their multitudes continued to adapt themselves *as best they could . . . but without hope of ever rejoining the evolving line.* Adaptation is a prime phenomenon of living nature. Left to itself, however, it leads to a resultant state of equilibrium which precludes all further progress. *The actual fauna of the world often represent masterpieces of adaptation, but only the 'left-overs' of evolution.* Viewed from the aspect of telefinalism, adaption is only *a means by which an immense number of infinitely varied individuals were developed, thus giving the possibility of effectuating a choice governed by teleological reasons.*

What sort of choice? The answer to this would have astonished the nineteenth-century school: <u>not</u> the creature best adapted; <u>not</u> the most perfect progeny of a given line; <u>not</u> the fittest to survive in the Darwinian sense; but some seemingly unfortunate mutant, relatively unstable and insecure, for . . . <u>*evolution can only continue through unstable systems or organisms.*</u>

Here is the crux and the moral turning point of du Noüy's new interpretation of evolution. A mutant, seemingly weak and ill adapted, externally odd or insignificant beside its lusty compeers, sometimes obliged to struggle insecurely over long periods of time — it is such a one which becomes the chosen vessel — never the other way, the strong, the lusty, the well established! This is the kind of choice by which evolution has mounted from triumph to triumph, always in contradiction to the obvious — always by selecting the fluctuant, the variant, the mutant, the dissymmetrical, the improbable! The ways of Telefinalism — how like the ways of God!

> *Evolution thus strikes us as being a search for a certain kind of utilizable disequilibrium materialised by 'transitory' forms, monstrous at the time of their appearance, less well adapted than the other — as the rareness of their fossils shows — but often richer in future potentialities. We use the word 'often' for it is evident that in certain cases the transitory form led to nothing important. That is why we can say that evolution has all the appearance of being a choice, always made in the same ascending direction towards a greater liberty, amongst hundreds of thousands of individuals, and it is amongst the mutant individuals that the choice takes place.*

Evolution goes on. The animal shape capable of sheltering the spirit, capable of allowing it to develop, is found. . . . Evolution continues in our time, no longer on the physiological or anatomical plane but on the spiritual and moral plane.

Evolution, with the advent of conscious man, ceases to rule by outer law; it becomes the inner law of man's being and can only advance through his volition. The animal fulfills itself in obedience to its natural desires: man has to battle against his inheritance of desires from his animal past. As he stands before us, an accomplished form in nature, he is the embodiment of all the preceding laws and conditions which have brought him to his present stage. The 'vanished past' works on in him as memory, morphologically, physiologically, also in his instincts, passions, impulses — it is against these that *Man must fight to prepare the advent of the spiritual being he is destined to become.*

Du Noüy briefly traces the beginnings of culture, tools, fire, ornamentation and the birth of speech with which he associates the first appearance of true personality, but most trenchant of all in man's further development, the birth of conscience which divides him for all time from his past, unless, by failing to adopt evolution as the law of his being, he should relapse into the animal state of instinct and blind adaptation — always a fearsome possibility.

The moment he asked himself the question whether an act was 'good' or whether another was 'better,' he acquired a liberty denied to the animals.

Henceforth, if he is to evolve . . .

he must no longer obey Nature. He must criticize and control his desires which were previously the only Law. The purely human conflict is born from this permanent, bitter struggle which has lost none of its violence today.

From this all-important moment of the birth of conscience, the last of the irreversibles

. . . a trial on the biological plane (anatomical and physiological) transforms itself into a test on the psychological plane.

And now du Noüy does the most daring thing of all; with a casual apology to the scientists who may not be willing to follow him, he begins to interpret Genesis and the advent of Christ Himself in the light of Telefinalism.

God first breathes in the soul through man's nostrils, and then com-
mands him not to eat of the tree of knowledge of good and evil, knowing
that he will eat it. What does this mysterious language signify?

It signifies that the most important event of evolution has taken place.
It signifies that appearance of a new discontinuity in nature, a discon-
tinuity as deep as that which exists between inert matter and organized
life. It signifies the birth of conscience, and of the last freedom.

Indeed, God could not have forbidden anything to the animals without
contradicting himself. Having built them in a certain way, having sub-
jected them from the very start to the biological laws imposed by their
structure, he could not go back on his orders without a major reason,
namely, the conscience bestowed on this new animal which was required
for his further evolution and which none of the preceding ones possessed.
Now, this is precisely indicated by the fact that God 'breathed into his
nostrils the breath of life; and man became a living soul,' which may be
taken as signifying that He gave him — and him alone — a conscience,
that is to say the liberty of choice. From then on, God can forbid this
creature to obey certain intransgressible orders given to all the others,
the physiological orders, the animal instincts. He can do this because
this new being is free, which signifies that his endocrine bondage can
cease if he wishes. . . . If he chooses to play the part of Man, at the price
of physical suffering and privations, he leaves the animal behind, he pro-
gresses as a man, he continues evolution on the moral plane and is on
the road which will eventually lead him to the spiritual plane.

We think of du Noüy's description of the sad and sorry mutant, of
his 'tenuous and fragile' existence, a stranger to his world, yet
overshadowed by the protective motive concealed in telefinalism,
and we read further:

. . . the fact that, in spite of his disobedience, this guilty man is chosen
as the founder of the human line, proves the henceforth preponderant
importance of the liberty of choice.

But Telefinalism goes much further than that. It dares to include
within its compass none other than Christ Himself as the supreme
of mutants.

Thus Christ can be assimilated to one of the intermediary, transitional
forms, perhaps a million years in advance of evolution, Who came
amongst us to keep us from despair, and to prove to us that our efforts
can and must succeed. He in truth died for us, for had He not been cru-
cified, we would not have been convinced.

Telefinalism has become identified with the God of the Scriptures, and Christ with a mutant form presaging a far future. As for man — *His free choice will act very much as natural selection has done so far.* Here is a new version of the Primary Cause and of the Final End, a new version of the conscious and unceasing approximation of man to God.

Some would say that du Noüy has done more for the theologians than they could possible have done for themselves; others, believe that he has missed the central mystery. Religion speaks of an initial <u>descent</u> from the spirit, and expulsion from Paradise, a Fall; and Christians of a <u>re</u>-ascent in Christ.

Is conscience the last of the irreversibles? What then awaits us in Christ? Does the single, ascendant, zigzagging line really tell the whole tale? Is it science which urged du Noüy to conquer science, is it conscience, it is love of Man? Can science of itself achieve the task, or is there some 'mutant' nearer our time waiting even now to be acknowledged, promising new *properties* which follow closer paths upon the way, in the wake of Christ in this time of threat and danger. Are there new discoveries to be made within the life of present day man? Is Telefinalism a dream or does it carry a true promise?

At the least the book is a noble attempt, provoked by the urgent needs of modern man, to trace a path from matter to spirit, to expand the mind beyond its bondage to the body, to lead from a renewing of science to a renewing of morality. It is a book written with dramatic force by a scientist, intended for the modern Everyman — *in every sense a Moral play* — as the prologue states in the original Everyman. It typifies to a very high degree the hopes and struggles of the twentieth century. It asks for a reassessment of human values: it wants to redeem the values of life and to stir new hope for the future. It demands a review and reassessment of the data on which theories have been built, but it goes further, it opens a way to new paths of exploration.

· 21 ·

Both Mystic and Scientist

The life and work of Pierre Teilhard de Chardin, (1881–1955), demonstrates a most earnest endeavour to wed mystical faith and scientific knowledge into a unity, for in outlook and achievement he was a rare representative of both. He had measureless trust and confidence in the meaning and efficacy of Christ's mission for the whole of humanity. Equally he saw matter as the outermost manifestation of an all-encompassing realm of spirit. The sublime confirmation for him lay in the words of Christ, *This is my body*. From his earliest memories he beheld matter as sacred, the mother substance which made life on earth and evolution possible. At the core of matter he saw a radiant source of creative life and love streaming through the world. No one has conceived of matter nor written of it from this viewpoint. If in his mystical writings he reaches a mood of highest exaltation, in his scientific work, notably in the PHENOMENON OF MAN, he exercizes fully the resources of sound reasoning and clear exposition.

This quote from an intimate sketch THE MAN by Pierre Leroy stands at the beginning of Chardin's LETTERS OF A TRAVELLER and also LE MILEU DIVIN.

Throughout my whole life during every moment I have lived, the world has gradually been taking on light and fire for me, until it has come to envelop me in one mass of luminosity, glowing from within. . . . The purple flush of matter fading imperceptibly into the gold of spirit, to be lost finally in the incandescence of a personal universe . . .

This is what I have learnt from my contact with the earth, the diaphony of the divine at the heart of a glowing universe, the divine radiating from the depths of matter aflame.

His priestly career seemed foreordained. He was born a Catholic with a pious mother to whom he was greatly attached. He referred to her as his *dear saintly maman*. To her he owed *all that was best in his soul.*

On the other hand, his father, M. Teilhard, took pleasure in teaching his children how to understand and appreciate natural history.

During their walks they would all gather mineral, zoological and botanical specimens and it was this interesting collection of local history that first encouraged Pierre's vocation as a scientist.

This latter took a remarkable form. Teilhard described this in the opening pages of his very late work entitled, THE HEART OF THE MATTER. Through his mother he had learned devotion to the Child Jesus, but he described how his *real me* would withdraw, *always in secrecy and alone* in worship of a piece of iron, his *Iron God* he called it. He had his 'idols.' What were they? A ploughspanner hidden in a corner of the courtyard, the top of a little metal rod, or some shell splinters picked up in a neighbouring range.

You should have seen me as, in profound secrecy and silence, I withdrew into the contemplation of my 'God of Iron,' delighting in its possession, gloating over its existence. A God, note, of Iron, and why Iron? Because in all my childish experience there was nothing in the world harder, tougher, more durable than this wonderful substance. There was about it a feeling of full personality, sharply individualized. . . . But I can never forget the pathetic depths of a child's despair, when I realised one day that iron can be scratched and can rust. . . . I had to look elsewhere for substitutes that would console me. Sometimes in the blue flame (at once so material, and yet so pure and intangible) flickering over the logs in the hearth, but more often in a more translucent and more delightfully coloured stone, quartz or amethyst crystals, and most of all glittering pieces of chalcedony such as I could pick up in the neighbourhood.

Long after, in retrospect Teilhard commented:

. . . I cannot but recognize that this distinctive act which made me wor-ship, in a real sense of the word, a fragment of metal contained and concentrated an intensity of resonance and a whole stream of demands of which my entire spiritual life has been no more than this development.

. . . the felicity that I had sought in iron, I can now find only in the
spirit.

So too, the durability, the constancy he imagined and perceived in
iron he now could transfer in devotion to Christ.

Constancy, that has undoubtedly been for me the fundamental attribute
of Being.

At the early age of ten, Pierre Teilhard was sent as a boarder to a
Jesuit school. At that school his interest in iron was replaced by
rocks and minerals. At the age of eighteen he entered the Jesuit
Order. In 1912, aged thirty-one, he was ordained a priest. With the
outbreak of war in 1914, he joined as a stretcher bearer. *With the*
humble rank of corporal he was twice decorated, receiving the Medaille
Militaire and the Legion d'Honneur. In that time of heavy trial he was
both *fearless and selfless.* He emerged with heightened devotion to
the ideal of service, and with his sense of vocation so strengthened,
he took the triple vow of poverty, chastity, and obedience

As the years went on, his studies led him into the fields of geology
and paleontology. He wrote:

The truth is that even at the peak of my trajectory, I was never to feel at
home unless immersed in an Ocean of Matter. So it was that the Sense
of Consistence led to the awakening and expansion of a dominant and
triumphant Sense of the Whole.

This illustrates how the two dominant interests in Teilhard's life,
the religious-mystical and the intellectual-scientific were closely
interwoven almost from the dawn of his childhood consciousness,
and so they continued, separated yet united, the one devoted to
the life within, the other devoted with equal passion to the world
without. At a certain moment in his life there lit up for him the
ideal of a joint fulfillment in the unraveling of the evolution history of earth and man, hence his work, THE PHENOMENON OF MAN
with its ever-repeated pronouncement, *Every without has a within.*
Quite exceptional is his intense regard for the world of matter
without. The following is from an essay, 'The Spiritual Power of
Matter' from his LE MILEU DIVIN.

On the one hand matter is the burden, the fetters, the pain, the sin, and
the threat of our lives. It weighs us down, suffers, wounds, tempts, and

grows old. Matter makes us heavy, paralysed, vulnerable, guilty. Who will deliver us from the body of death?

But at the same time matter is physical exuberance, ennobling contact, virile effort, and the joy of growth. It attracts, renews, unites and flowers. By matter we are nourished, lifted up, linked to everything else, invaded by life. To be deprived of it is intolerable. . . . Who will give us an immortal body?

Asceticism deliberately looks no further than the first aspect, the one which is turned toward death; and it recoils, exclaiming 'Flee!'

There follow lines printed in italics which conclude with a supplication or a prayer:

Teach us, Lord, how to contemplate the sphinx without succumbing to its spell; how it grasps the hidden mystery in the womb of death, not by a refinement of human doctrine, but in the simple concrete act by which you plunged yourself into matter in order to redeem it. By the virtue of your suffering incarnation disclose to us, and then teach us to harness jealousy for you, the spiritual power of matter.

Previously he had written in his priestly vocation of the illusion of

. . . contrasting soul and body, spirit and flesh, as good and evil, in order to prepare the way for our final view of the divine <u>milieu</u>, perhaps we may be allowed to vindicate and exalt that aspect of it which the Lord came.to put on, save, and consecrate: <u>holy matter</u>.

Pierre Teilhard de Cardin, LE MILEU DIVIN

These thoughts from Teilhard should enhance our consideration of THE PHENOMENON OF MAN, a scientific exercise which calls for a fundamental revision of outlook in which man, earth, and cosmos are engaged in one great process of becoming, *an anthropogenesis which is itself the crown of a cosmosgenesis.*

The time has come to realise that an interpretation of the universe even a positivist one — remains unsatisfactory unless it covers the interior as well as the exterior of things, mind as well as matter.

Teilhard's vision was immense. Man was no longer to be regarded as *an isolated unit lost in cosmic solitudes,* because *a universal will to live converges and is harmonized in him.* Man is no longer to be seen *as a static centre of the world . . . but as the axis and the leading shoot of evolution.* Teilhard set about his task with such enthusiasm, providing science with the inwardness it lacked and striving to restore wholeness of vision.

Teilhard seemed to acquiesce with the speculative theories of science regarding the origin of the earth and the constitution of matter, as described by the most modern physics, with its electron, protons, and so on. One way or another, the earth was presumably a fragment detached from the sun and subject to a given force of radiation from it. All this was secondary to the all important consideration that the earth was engendered out of the cosmos and therefore, must have had all the preconditions needed for its further development up to its present state including man.

The problem of continuity in the evolutionary process was present for Teilhard as for others and how to explain its discontinuity. Teilhard's view presumed an active spirituality, a divine working from the very dawn of outer existence. Thus in his view the 'within' was there from the beginning determining and declaring itself stage by stage in the 'without.' Whatever the ultimate nature of the *Stuff of the Universe* as conceived by the physicist, the shining essence of the Divine, concealed as it may be from our seeing, must still be there.

Man possesses a consciousness which can cognize both a Within and a Without which shows that in man

> . . . *the stuff of the universe has a double aspect to its structure. Why then should we confine this double aspect to man alone? Rather does not man by his nature provide a point of departure from which to regard every region of space and time?*

Teilhard explains that

> . . . *'consciousness' is taken in the widest sense to indicate every kind of psychicism, from the most rudimentary form of interior perception imaginable to the human phenomenon of reflective thought.*

This would extend to the minutetest conceivable granules or particles:

> *Atomicity is a common property of the Within and the Without of things.*

If we speak of primordial particles, however remote, should we not be able to equally speak of the *primordial dust of consciousness?*

Once we conclude that the world and all that is in it is divinely conceived and divinely created, where can the reciprocity of inner and outer ever cease?

Now comes the fundamental question raised also by Le Comte du Noüy and dealt with by him in his way. If the physicists are right, then according to the mathematical law of chance and probability based on the Second Law of Thermodynamics, the whole of the physical universe in its energies must eventually equilibrate down to a state of entropy, of immobility and death — the heat death as it has been called. The evolutionary process, however, is always moving in an opposite direction, to ever greater varieties and complexities contrary to the expected probable, rather towards the improbable.

The grand picture of continuity of evolution from matter in its sub-atomic stage up to man, not ending even with man, for man, at his stage, offers a new beginning towards still higher stages of development. But we still do not know how this whole process is brought about, this leap from stage to stage, for these very leaps reveal the discontinuities which underlie the apparent overall continuity.

To appreciate Teilhard's basic and most daring innovation one must first clearly establish his position in regard to the current scientific outlook. This, in his view, has developed itself wholly to the 'without' in total disregard of the 'within.' To the latter it has chosen to remain blind.

> In the eyes of the physicist, nothing exists legitimately, at least up to now, except the without of things. The same intellectual attitude is still permissible in the bacteriologist, whose cultures (apart from some substantial difficulties) are treated as laboratory reagents. But it is still more difficult in the realm of plants. It tends to become a gamble in the case of a biologist studying the behaviour of insects and coelenterates. It seems merely futile in regard to the vertebrates. Finally, it breaks down completely with man, in whom the existence of a within can no longer be evaded, because it is the object of a direct intuition and the substance of all knowledge.

> The apparent restriction of the phenomenon of consciousness to the higher forms of life has long served science as an excuse to eliminate it from its model of the universe. A queer exception, an aberrant function, an epiphenomenon — thought was classed under one or other of these heads in order to get rid of it.

It seems a perverse view on the part of the thinking scientist that because his own type of *consciousness is only recognizable in man*, therefore it is to be regarded as *an isolated instance of no interest to science*. Teilhard's view is the exact reverse.

> *It is impossible to deny that, deep within ourselves, an 'interior' appears at the heart of being, as it were seen through a rent. This is enough to ensure that, in one degree or another, this 'interior' should obtrude itself as existing everywhere in nature from all time. Since the stuff of the universe has an inner aspect of itself at one point of itself, there is necessarily a double aspect to its structure, that is to say, in every region of space and time — in the same way, for instance, that it is granular: <u>coextensive with their without, there is a within to things</u>.*

On this view, consciousness accompanies matter in all its advancing stages of complexity and differentiation, or, looking to origins,

> <u>*Refracted rearwards along the course of evolution, consciousness displays itself qualitatively as a spectrum of shifting hints whose lower terms are lost in the night*</u>.

Conversely, it would follow that the outer scale of advancing evolution is accompanied by a paralleled scale of intensifying degrees of consciousness and that there can never be a state of the absolute absence of consciousness, since it is inherent in the state of matter.

> *The simplest form of protoplasm is already a substance of unheard-of-complexity. This complexity increases in geometric progression as we pass from the protozoan higher and higher up the scale of metazoa. And so it is for the whole of the remainder, always and everywhere.*

> *The degree of a consciousness varies in inverse ratio to the <u>simplicity</u> of the material compound lined by it.*

> *A consciousness is that much more perfected according as it lines a richer and better organized material edifice.*

> <u>*Spiritual perfection (or conscious 'centricity') and the material synthesis (or complexity) are but the two aspects or connected parts of one and the same phenomenon*</u>.

What is the goal of Teilhard's search?

> *We are seeking a qualitative law of development that from sphere to sphere should be capable of explaining, first of all the invisibility, then the appearance, and then the gradual dominance of the <u>within</u> in comparison with the <u>without</u> of things.*

Thus Teilhard pays tribute to the science of physics at the lower and more elementary level, still subject to chance, probability, and entropy, whereas this is countered by the upward trend towards the improbable. What science has so far ignored, the relating of the science of mind to that of matter, the moral to the physical, Teilhard accepted as his very task.

> Without the slightest doubt, <u>there is something</u> through which material and spiritual energy hold together and are complementary. In the last analysis, <u>somehow or other</u>, there must be a single energy operating in the world. And the first idea that occurs to us is that the 'soul' must be as it were a focal point of transformation at which, from all points of nature, the forces of bodies converge, to become interiorized and sublimated in beauty and truth.

In pursuing this further one must ever remember Teilhard's quite exceptional regard for the sacredness of matter. It is endowed with its measure of spirituality from the first. For him what others have termed brute matter simply does not exist. To relate to his hypothesis one has to determine whether what he proposed is still in the realm of science or whether it arises out of a mystical enthusiasm to overcome the dualism which has so disastrously divided life and the soul of man. According to Teilhard,

> The two energies — of mind and matter — spread respectively through the two layers of the world (the <u>within</u> and the <u>without</u>) have, taken as a whole, much the same demeanour. They are constantly associated and in some way pass into each other. But it seems impossible to establish a simple correspondence between their curves. On the one hand, only a minute fraction of 'physical' energy is used up in the highest exercise of spiritual energy; on the other hand, this minute fraction, once absorbed, results on the internal scale in the most extraordinary oscillations.

We move at a leap from quantitative to qualitative considerations. How is the science of today to deal with this?

> A quantitative disproportion of this kind is enough to make us reject the naive notion of 'change of form" (or direct transformation) — and hence all hope of discovering a 'mechanical equivalent' for will or thought. Between the <u>within</u> and the <u>without</u> of things, the interdependence of energy is incontestable.

Our present mode of thought can in no way resolve this dilemma.

> *But it can in all probability only be expressed by a complex symbolism*
> *in which terms of a different order are employed.*

What does Teilhard mean by a *complex symbolism*? How is this to arise other than through a totally different manner of thought? To answer this and to account for the discontinuity within an evolutionary process which by its very nature demands continuity is Teilhard's quest.

> *Some thousands of millions of years ago, not, it would appear by a regular process of astral evolution, but as a result of some unbelievable accident (a brush with another star? an internal upheaval?) a fragment of matter composed of particularly stable atoms was detached from the surface of the sun. Without breaking its bonds attaching it to the rest, and first at the right distance from the sun to receive a moderate radiation, this fragment began to condense, to roll itself up, to take shape. Containing within its globe and orbit, the future of man, another heavenly body — a planet this time — had been born.*

Whatever the manner in which planet earth came into being, most important is the maintained continuity of earth in relation to cosmos, so that man, earth, and cosmos comprise an unbroken unity; geogenesis, anthropogenesis, and cosmogenesis are to be seen as one process inclusive of all three.

And now, turning to *this diminutive, obscure, but fascinating object which had first appeared,*

> *It is the only place in the world in which we are so far able to study the evolution of matter in its ultimate phases, and as far as ourselves.*

The most testing question is still that of the passage from inorganic to organic chemistry, from pre-life to life. Teilhard continues to maintain that everything that revealed itself later must have been present in an incipient state from the beginning — that the inorganic and the organic

> *. . . can only be two inseparable facets of one and the same telluric operation. And that the second, no less than the first, must be regarded as already under way in the infancy of the earth.*
>
> *In the world, nothing could ever burst forth as final across the different thresholds successively traversed by evolution (however critical they be) which has not already existed in an obscure and primordial way.*

The following consideration is also of great importance.

The initial question of consciousness contained in our terrestrial world is not formed merely of an aggregate of particles caught fortuitously in the same net. It represents a correlated mass of infinitesimal centres structurally bound together by the conditions of their origin and development.

This is a law that we can follow right up the scale. The individual elements by their congregated and multiple interactions, give rise to a higher unity which surmounts them but the individual element retains its identity — there is no mere amalgamation of the many into the one. This applies to the highest stages of existence but is present from the earliest beginning.

This that Teilhard calls the 'indivisible' can be applied to the universe in its wholeness; he applies it also to the pre-biosphere.

As we continue peering into the abysses of the past, we can see the colour changing.

From age to age it increases in intensity. Something is going to burst out upon the early earth, and the thing is Life.

We have crossed a tremendous threshold in the passage from the world of physics to that of biology.

The cell is the natural granule of life in the same way as the atom is the natural granule of simple, elemental matter.

Marvelous as it is, marvelous as it seems to us in its isolation among the other constructions of matter, the cell, like everything else in the world, cannot be understood, (i.e., incorporated in a coherent system of the universe) unless we situate it on an evolutionary line between a past and a future.

That evolution is a fact can hardly be disputed, but whether it is directed, whether it is going anywhere are questions to which, quoting Teilhard, *nine biologists out of ten will today say no, even passionately.* He is convinced, however, that he has found a line and a direction to a positive answer which will, eventually, be universally accepted.

He leads us back to his first premises *about the mutual relations between the without and the within of things.* The essence of reality lies in *the interiority contained by the universe at a given moment.* What

determines, or rather reveals this relationship is what he calls the
arrangement, *whose successive advances are inwardly reinforced, as we
can see, by a continual expansion and deepening of consciousness.*

Where are we to find the 'selective mechanism' within organic life
which maintains this play of consciousness? His discovery of the
answer to this all-important question revealed that in which the
continuity of this evolving process is vested.

> *We have merely to look into ourselves to perceive it — the nervous sys-
> tem. We can only really come to grips with one's single 'interiority' in
> the world; our own directly, and at the same time that of other men by
> immediate equivalence, thanks to language.*

> *Not only does the arrangement of animal forms according to their
> degree of cerebralisation correspond exactly to the classification of sys-
> tematic biology, but it also confers on the tree of life a sharpness of fea-
> ture, an impetus, which is incontestably the hall-mark of truth. Such
> coherence — and let me add, such ease, inexhaustible fidelity and
> evocative power in this coherence — could not be the result of chance.*

It is this *differentiation of nervous tissue* which, for Teilhard, is all-
significant.

> *It provides a direction; and by its consequence it proves that evolution
> has a direction. . . . we possess a fundamental variable capable of fol-
> lowing in the past, and perhaps defining in the future, the true course
> of the phenomena.*

And here we have reached a point of heightened interiority, of
maximum convergence, where a new evolutionary advance, a
new arrangement must take place between the tangential and the
radial forces.

> *After thousands of years rising below the horizon, a flame bursts forth
> at a strictly localized point.*

> *Thought is born.*

The crucial point of the theory is how to accord to man his rightful
place in the world of creation. Science, today, still regards him as
an animal and includes him with the hominidae. That he is a
reflective being is looked on as no more than a fortuitous circumstance, a freak of nature. So much attention is focused on the without, so little on the within.

The previous chapter considered a definitive distinction between animal and human intelligence, emphasizing the fact of language proper as distinct from animal nature sounds. Teilhard makes the central and decisive phenomenon that of <u>reflection</u>.

Man can reflect. This is a power . . .

> *acquired by a consciousness to turn in upon itself. to take possession of itself <u>as of an object</u>, endowed with its own particular consistence and value: no longer merely to know, but to know oneself, no longer merely to know but to know that one knows.*

> *The being who is the object of his own reflections, in consequence of that very doubling back upon himself, becomes in a flash able to raise himself into a new sphere. In reality, another world is born. Abstraction, logic, reasoned choice and inventions, mathematics, art, calculation of space and time, anxieties, and dreams of love — all these activities of <u>inner life</u> are nothing else than the effervescence of the newly-formed centre as it explodes upon itself.*

> *Admittedly the animal knows. <u>But it cannot know that it knows</u>: that is quite certain. If it could, it would long ago have multiplied its inventions and developed a system of internal constructions that could not have escaped our observation. In consequence it is denied access to a whole domain of reality in which we can move freely. We are separated by a chasm — or a threshold — which it cannot cross. Because we are reflective we are not only different but quite other. It is not a matter of change of degree, but of a change of nature, resulting from a change of state.*

How are we to envisage the leap that must have taken place from anthropoid to anthropos, from instinct to reason, from animal to man? Teilhard offers the picture of water heated to boiling point, and how at that point — 'without change of temperature' there is *a tumultuous expansion of freed and vaporized molecules.* He also offers the picture of a cone, and how the sections from the base upwards diminish in area constantly, and *then suddenly, with another infinitesimal displacement, the surface vanishes leaving us with a <u>point</u>.* These pictures prepare for understanding the critical threshold with which we are directly concerned. Teilhard's own mode of expression is essential for behind it lives the intensity of his whole endeavour, and introduces his vision of the play of tangential and radial energies. One is dealing in effect with the birth of man as man, giving meaning to the whole existence.

When the anthropoid, so to speak, had been brought 'mentally' to boiling point some further calories were added. Or, when the anthropoid had almost reached the summit of the cone, a final effort took place along the axis. No more was needed for the whole inner equilibrium to be upset. What was previously only a centred surface became a centre. By a tiny 'tangential' increase, the 'radial' was turned back on itself and so to speak took an infinite leap forward. Outwardly, almost nothing in the organs had changed. But in depth, a great revolution had taken place; consciousness was now leaping and boiling in a space of super-sensory relationships and representations; and simultaneously consciousness was capable of perceiving itself in the concentrated simplicity of its faculties. And all this happened for the first time.

The expression 'for the first time' raises many questions. When and where did that 'first time' occur? We are led through a survey of all the main archaeological findings in search of the man proper. Could there have actually been a *first pair* in the scriptural sense? Science would favour the thought of the spontaneous creation of first pairs in a number of places — but this has nowhere been resolved, and Teilhard does not go into it. Rather does he concern himself with the broad question, from geogenesis, to biogenesis, and then to psychogenesis leading to man — which means the engendering and subsequent development of all stages of the mind, in one word — *noogenesis*.

The recognition and isolation of a new era in evolution, the era of noogenesis, obliges us to distinguish correlatively a support proportionate to the operation — that is to say, yet another membrane in the majestic assembly of telluric layers. A glow ripples outward from the first spark of conscious reflection, the point of cognition grows larger. The fire spreads in ever widening circles till finally the whole planet is covered with incandescence. Only one interpretation, only one name can be found worthy of this grand phenomenon. Much more coherent and just as extensive as the preceding layer, it is really a new layer, the 'thinking layer,' which since its germination at the end of the Tertiary period has spread over and above the world of plants and animals. In other words, outside and above the biosphere there is the noosphere.

New words appear: individualisation, personisation, and above all hominization, that is, a process of growing into one's full humanity.

This sudden deluge of cerebralisation, this biological invasion of a new animal type which gradually eliminates or subjects all forms of life that are not human, this irresistible tide of fields and factories — all these signs that we look at day in day out — seem to proclaim that there has been a change on the earth and a change of planetary magnitude.

The greatest revelation open to science today is to perceive that everything precious, active and progressive originally contained in that cosmic fragment from which our world emerged is now concentrated and crowned by the noosphere.

But Teilhard's vision does not stop there. Even as one looked back to origins, so one must *observe what reflection has already provided, and what it announces ahead*. He sees even at this moment that humanity is passing through an age of transition; a critical change of the noosphere. His optimism is immense.

In these confused and restless zones in which present blends with future in a world of upheaval, we stand face to face with all the grandeur, the unprecedented grandeur, of the phenomenon of man. Here if anywhere, now if ever, have we, more legitimately than any of our predecessors, the right to think that we can measure the importance and detect the direction of the process of hominization. And to do so let us probe beneath the surface and try to decipher the particular form of mind which is coming to birth in the womb of the earth today.

Our earth of factory chimneys and offices, seething with work and business, our earth with a hundred new radiations — this great organism lives, in final analysis, because of, and for, the sake of a new soul. Beneath a change of age lies a change of thought.

Teilhard sees working in the man of today,

. . . a new intuition involving a total change in the physiognomy of the universe in which we move.

He sees this present moment with all its multiplying congestions, pressures, growing complexities at the tangential, material level, a rising of a new force of consciousness, of cosmic radial energies, already preparing for a new bursting forth of spiritual energies. His mode of thought retains the same character from stage to stage, level to level. These individual thinking beings, these giants of thought, do not lose their identity in creating a new order of being, a new inclusive wholeness.

In the same beam of light the instinctive gropings of the first cell link up with the learned gropings of our laboratories.

Groping is directed chance.

There opens up a prospect of entry into the superhuman.

> *We are faced with a harmonised collectivity of consciousness equivalent to a sort of super-consciousness. The idea is that of the earth not only becoming covered by myriads of grains of thought, but becoming enclosed in a single thinking envelope so as to form, functionally, no more than a single vast grain of thought on the sidereal scale, the plurality of individual reflections grouping themselves together and reinforcing one another in the act of a single unanimous reflection.*

Teilhard points to <u>a formidable upsurge of unused powers</u>,

> *... a leap forward of the 'radial' — a new step in the genesis of mind — a new domain of psychical expansion — an interior totalisation of the world upon itself, in the unanimous construction of a <u>spirit of the earth</u>.*

Teilhard would carry us still a stage further, to what he calls the Omega point, the point of utmost convergence of all the energies of this world, where the Future-Universal and the Hyper-Personal become one. It is hardly possible to grasp this in its full meaning. We have only pointers to go by.

For instance, we are warned from being led astray

> *... to the cult of a great All in which individuals were supposed to be merged like a drop in the ocean or like a dissolving grain of salt.*

Quite the contrary, following the confluent orbits of their centres, the grains of consciousness do not tend to lose their outlines and blend, but, on the contrary, to accentuate the depth and incommunicability of their *egos*. The more 'other' they become in conjunction, the more they find themselves as 'self.' How could it be otherwise since they are steeped in Omega? Could a centre dissolve? Or rather, would not its particular way of dissolving be to super-centralize itself?

One meets the thought, beyond a noosphere a Christsphere, a universal amortization, an all interpenetrating and uniting power of Love. Humanity is borne into a future, an Omega point which we can no more grasp conceptually than the state of Alpha at the beginning. If one adopts Teilhard's image of the evolutionary process then one may perhaps glimpse a direction in a process which is beyond space and time.

It is none other than Julian Huxley who writes the introduction to THE PHENOMENON OF MAN. He has the highest regard for Teilhard as a human being and as a scientific investigator but, as we learn to know, is unscrupulously honest in regard to his own thinking.

> *The biologist may perhaps consider that in* The Phenomenon of Man *he paid insufficient attention to genetics and the possibilities and limitations of natural selection, the theologian that his treatment of the problems of sin and suffering was inadequate or at least unorthodox, the social scientist that he failed to take sufficient account of the facts of political and social history. But he saw that what was needed at the moment was a broad sweep and a comprehensive treatment. This is what he essayed in* The Phenomenon of Man. *In my view he achieved a remarkable success, and opened up vast territories of thought to further exploration and detailed mapping.*

> *His influence on the world's thinking is bound to be important. Through his combination of wide scientific knowledge with deep religious feeling and a rigorous sense of values, he has forced theologians to view their ideas in the new perspective of evolution, and scientists to see the spiritual implications of their knowledge. He has both clarified and unified our vision of reality.*

> *We, mankind, contain the possibilities of the earth's immense future, and can realise more and more of them on condition that we increase our knowledge and our love. That, it seems to me, is the distillation of* The Phenomenon of Man.

In a brief introduction to Teilhard's LETTERS FROM A TRAVELLER, Julian Huxley writes:

> *We were both biologists by training, but we both had wide interests outside our specialisms. We had the same broad aim in common — that of exploring the vast process of evolution as fully as possible, of attempting to frame some effective picture of its pattern and of man's place within it, of pursuing its implications into the illimitable future*

> *Pere Teilhard's hypothesis as to the increasing convergence of human variety and the resultant increase of psychosocial pressure — which in turn would increasingly direct the course of man's further evolution — were more radical than mine, and I was quite unable to follow him in what he believed was the ultimate goal . . .*

> *However, in spite of wide differences in respect of theology and metaphysics, we found ourselves in agreement and indeed in active co-operation over the subject of the future of mankind, and its transcendent importance for the thought of our times.*

Yet the prime endeavour of THE PHENOMENON OF MAN is precisely to demonstrate that evolution is unthinkable as less than a process of the play of two energies, the one demonstrated in the Without, the 'tangential' and the other, the ever advancing and unfolding power of the radial, the Within, the one to be conceived of as mechanical and terrestrial, the other as psychic and cosmic — a co-operation of an earthly and a heavenly, both having their source and origin in the spirit and their original and final expression in the Being who said, *I am the Alpha and the Omega.*

He tried through his work to establish, in a materialistic age, the true dignity of Man and the sacredness of Matter, but he remained excluded. The world of science has no place for revelation; the Church insists that there is no actual knowledge beyond the material but only revelation, Teilhard lived precariously between.

> *How is it then, that as I look around me, still dazzled by what I have seen, I find that I am almost the only person of my kind, the only one to have seen. . . . How most of all, can it be that 'when I come down from the mountain,' and in spite of the glorious vision I still retain, I find I am so little a better man, so little at peace, so incapable of expressing in my own actions, and thus adequately communicate to others, the wonderful unity that I feel encompassing me?*

> *Is there, in fact, a Universal Christ, a Divine Milieu? Or am I, after all, simply the dupe of a mirage in my own mind?*

> *I often ask myself that question.*

> *Everywhere on Earth, at this moment, in the new spiritual atmosphere created by the appearance of the idea of evolution, there float, in a state of extreme mutual sensitivity, love of God, and faith in the world; the two essential components of the ultra-human.*

> *This is one more proof that Truth has to appear only once, in one single mind, for it to be impossible for anything ever to prevent it from spreading universally and setting everything else ablaze.*

The following moving words about Teilhard close the essay, THE MAN by S. J. Pierre Leroy:

> *He died suddenly, as he had prayed that he might, in the full vigour of life; friend of all men, of all countries, he died in the most cosmopolitan city in the world. It was on Easter Sunday, in the full bloom of Spring, with the city bathed in a flood of sunshine. So it was that in the day of*

the Resurrection, Pere Teilhard was reunited with the Christ whom all his life he had so longed to possess in the blaze of victory.

'Lord, since with every instinct of my being and through all the changing circumstances of my life, it is You whom I have ever sought, You whom I have set at the heart of universal matter, it will be in a resplendence which shines through all things and in which all things are ablaze, that I shall have the felicity of closing my eyes.'

Teilhard de Chardin

· 22 ·

A Physicist Evaluates

Professor Heitler, in his book, MAN AND SCIENCE, offers a striking survey of where science stands today in regard to man. As a physicist he stands firmly within the sciences, yet he writes out of great concern for the well being of mankind and nature as a whole. His questions demand answers, such as *Are we still the overlords, exercising power over our own creation?* His book is a challenging call to grow more truly aware of the incongruities in which we live. For instance, out of fear that our present energy resources may fail, we are erecting more and more nuclear power stations while not yet knowing how to dispose of the radioactive waste products which spell death. Now add to this the threatened possibility of widespread extermination by nuclear or even by bacterial warfare. Or consider the invidious advertising techniques, one of the most immoral being *subliminal suggestion* whereby one is influenced by flashes of light of too short duration for the eye to detect, to buy goods thus surreptitiously advertised. If this method should become common practice, it could serve to eliminate all questions of free choice. Of such practices the term 'the demon of technology' is not inapt, and since technology is 'the offspring solely of science' it might justly be applied to a whole field of sciences. The fact is that 'innumerable' human beings are becoming part of the machines they serve. There is an expansive force in science which is driving it into all fields of life. Heitler instances *statistics in business and civics; industrial psychology; a science of salesmanship;* and the use of *electric brains* for predicting the outcome of planned undertakings, even wars, as though human life is no longer to be ruled by human deliberation but is to be subject to these new, arbitrary laws of chance. These examples indicate some of the dangers that lie ahead. It is as though the aim of science is to produce a type of being in its own image, namely, a thoroughly conditioned robot.

Thus science, with all the material benefits it has conferred on humanity can be wholly inimical to mankind in other respects.

> *Why is it so often that a new invention calls immediately for a counter-invention to protect us from it?*
>
> W. Heitler, MAN AND SCIENCE

In this tendency of science to *expand over all fields of life including the whole dominion of thought,* Heitler sees *the most powerful influence to which our era is subject.* To understand this and to be able to know how to meet it, we need to arrive at a critical analysis of scientific thought as it presents itself today.

> *Whether we speak of 'the origin of the universe' . . . or 'of an act of creation' depends largely on our metaphysical attitude.*

> *The erruption of the causal order of ideas into almost all fields of life is a first step leading away from what is human, and the division between science and man begins.*

> *Any transfer of the deterministic principle to human affairs, including psychology, sociology, history and so on is bound to lead to most serious consequences for humanity. If we really follow the principle of determinism to its logical conclusion and apply it to everything, including man and his psychic and intellectual life, and to human society, the result would be that life would become a huge inescapable and meaningless machine, in which there is no place for the word freedom. For determinism and freedom are simply not compatible. We would also have to expunge from out dictionaries the word ethics and everything associated with it. A machine has no morals.*

> *The entire social organism would collapse, and the final state would probably not be very different from Orwell's* 1984.

> *What we can assert here is that a general world-philosophy based on the principle of determinism is entirely without foundation. Any application to human affairs not only cometh of evil, but is also completely unwarranted.*

Heitler examines the qualitative versus the quantitative. Since Galileo and Newton, science has built on the quantitative, the measurable, to the exclusion of the qualitative. Colour, tone, odour, taste, etc. are denied any real existence in the external world, being confined only to the interior life of sentient being. Heitler takes as an appropriate example, that of the science of colour and life. He draws attention to Goethe's opposition to Newton and his corpuscular theory, equating it with the present-day theory of electromagnetic waves as constituting light.

> To a definite wave-length a definite colour is assigned. . . . The sole object of physical investigation is now no longer the colours but the waves. These electromagnetic waves obey laws just as causal and determinative as mechanics.

To what does this view lead?

> The external reality is the electromagnetic wave; it gives rise in the eye, then in the optic nerve, then in the corresponding brain cell to certain physiological processes. But then comes the mystery — the point at which all these material processes (we count the electromagnetic field in this sense as material) suddenly turn into the colour sensation 'green.' On this point all the sciences concerned, namely physics, physiology and psychology are completely in the dark, because there is no bridge between physiology and psychology, that is, between material and psychical processes.

Newton built his theory of light on the apparent emergence of the scale of prismatic colours from a white beam and concluded that these colours were contained in the beam, so that white is a composite colour. To Goethe, Newton's idea of white was revolting; he spoke of 'Newton's loathsome white.'

What was Goethe's approach? To him *the physics of light is simply the knowledge of our immediate sensation of light.*

> The sensations of light are what we experience of light, and are also the only things on which we can build. Our sensation of light is, so to speak, the definition of light. There is no clear cut boundary separating off our sense impression from an invisible hypothetical external world; the external world is identical with objective perception. Thus human experience is central . . .

Heitler makes the interesting suggestion that Goethe, perhaps, had an intuitive premonition of what would be the consequences of a science that made *unlimited use of the art of measurement* and came to regard this as being alone valid. He adds that *Goethe was a great admirer of the art of measurement in mechanics and geometrical optics.* He was not therefore blindly antagonistic to the science of mathematics or wholly ignorant of it as has sometimes been stated. He adds though that Goethe *did not understand that a purely quantitative science was a logical and practical possibility.*

Goethe held firmly to the ground of concrete experience as opposed to mere theory. He spent ten years exploring the nature of light and colour, including a careful study of optical illusions.

Heitler, the physicist, is concerned with the fundamental question of the relationship between quantitative and qualitative.

> *Physics has sharply delimited the external world with which it deals in accordance with its quantitative point of view. If we also include in this world the physiology of the process of seeing — e.g., eyes, optic nerve, brain cell, which we also investigate by physicochemical means, the final point, the transformation into the sensation of light, remains a complete mystery.*

> *It is at this point . . . that we meet a fundamental limitation of all investigations using the methods of present day science.*

> *Or must we really suppose that the world around us consists solely of measurable data, and that everything that is qualitative is tied up exclusively with sentient living beings? It would be difficult to give a sound reason for this view, although it is the position adopted by our science.*

> *There is one conclusion that we may safely draw from our reflections, namely that our present scientific methods are in principle limited. We have imposed the limitations on ourselves . . .*

> *. . . a causal-quantitative science is certainly not a complete picture, and hence is not 'a picture of the world.' It provides a partial picture, only an aspect of the world, a sort of <u>projection of the world on to a causal-quantitative plane</u>, just as a photograph is a projection of the three dimensional landscape on to the plane of the paper. At least one dimension, we might say, is lacking.*

> *From this causal and quantitative projected image practically every human element has been eliminated.*

> *The world, including living creatures, becomes a senseless machine, running mechanically and quantitatively, which has just to be accepted*

and which cannot be otherwise. But this conception means not only an over-valuation of the quantitative but at the same time an under-valuation of everything that is not quantitative, including man, a devaluation in the extreme case, to absolute zero. Man regarded quantitatively, consists of very interesting chemical substances, possessing even more interesting functions and reactions — but then this is no longer a man.

Our view of the world is scientific, that is materialistic and mechanistic, but our life is the reverse. We cannot hold a mechanistic philosophy and at the same time talk of freedom.

Quantam mechanics introduced us to a world which is not only unfamiliar but incomprehensible: the mechanics of the atom, dating back to 1925, with

. . . the demonstration of the real existence of atoms, and the recognition that the atom itself is a composite structure, consisting of nucleus and electrons.

Heitler attempts to give us a glimpse into the laws and behaviour patterns of that world which though remote has in a short interval of time brought such a drastic influence into our everyday life. The fuller understanding of that world is reserved for the highly trained mathematician.

. . . in quantum mechanics, statements about probability take the place of the definite deterministic predictions of classical physics.

The existence of uncertain quantities is a feature characteristic of quantum mechanics, and is of course basically new.

Since the determinism on which classical physics is built does not hold here, Heitler introduced the law of 'complementarity' which he regarded as *the most important basic principle of quantum physics.*

We call two quantities which cannot simultaneously be sharply defined, complementary.

The laws of quantum mechanics have reference to these two things: the sharply defined values a quantity can take and which are found in a measurement, and the probabilities with which the different values occur when a measurement is taken. The laws do not in any way refer to anything that takes place in space and time, such as for example, motion in an orbit, but to rather abstract things, probabilities, which have meaning and significance and can be understood only in the language of mathematics.

But now comes a further fundamental consideration. We cannot effect a measurement unless someone is there to measure.

In the whole logical structure of quantum mechanics the conscious observer plays an essential part. Man, in so far as he is an observer, can no longer be ignored.

This is a quite radical intrusion of man into nature. In classical physics nature follows its own laws whether it is observed or not.

The moon moves in its orbit whether we are looking at it or not. Physical processes are completely detached from man. In the physics of the smallest systems, the physics of the atom, it is different. In this case, as soon as we observe what happens we also affect what happens; a new state is produced.

The observer has become indispensable; a clear-cut separation of the external world from the observer is not possible as soon as any observations whatsoever are made; for these influence the object in an unpredictable way.

Why the impossibility of separating object and subject should first appear just in the physics of the smallest particles is a question we cannot answer.

And yet it calls for an answer. Are we not on a border land between the substantial and the insubstantial, between the visible and the invisible, between the physical and the metaphysical? Heitler almost inevitably, from the whole tenor of his writing, veers in this direction.

He raises the question as to the nature of mathematics, or human reasoning and intelligence generally.

What can this product of our own intellect have to do with the world around us and its laws, with the external world which is said to be completely detached from and independent of man? If man were indeed so detached, it would be a completely incomprehensible miracle if the world should obey laws expressible only by means of the mathematics we have ourselves invented.

It would follow that there cannot be this degree of separation between human thinking and the external world process.

In one way or another the conclusion is inescapable that there also exists outside of us something of the nature of intelligence — some spiritual *principle (the German word <u>geistige</u> can be employed without religious overtones) — associated both with the laws and events of the material world and with our mental activity.*

In the material world around us there is no such thing as a geometrical point or a geometrical figure, nor is any physical law satisfied with mathematical exactitude.

Heitler turns to Plato who spoke of the *perception of <u>ideas</u> that exist outside ourselves:*

These Platonic 'ideas' are operative in the material world apprehended by the senses, but here they are never realised completely and in perfectly pure form. They give rise to phenomena, forms of motion and so on, which correspond more or less closely, but never quite accurately to the 'original,' i.e., the pure law. But in our intuitive grasp of concepts and laws we can 'apprehend' them in pure form.

Even in classical physics where we are dealing with perceptible objects in space, the fact that these obey complex and abstract mathematical laws raises metaphysical considerations.

The individual atom cannot even be pictured in space and time. Even a bare description of it demands profound mathematical concepts. So it can hardly be thought of as something of a purely material nature; its 'mathematical aspect,' that is, its non-material aspect, is even more strikingly prominent than is the case with an object of classical physics.

Heitler believes that physics in the future will go further in this direction. It is not a question of returning to Plato but

... atomic physics already poses metaphysical questions. These ought to be answered before a philosophy of science can be based on physics.

These metaphysical questions arise in other fields including biology and cosmology. Quantum physics has validity not only for atoms, but also for molecules, large organic molecules, even macro-molecules and thus enters the realm of biochemistry and general biology.

The tendency in the biological field is to interpret life processes in physiochemical terms. Such new sciences as biochemistry and biophysics bear witness to this. Heitler selects three particular themes for consideration, (1) The form and size of a living organism and its separate organs; (2) evolution, the historical development of higher organisms out of lower; (3) the existence of consciousness in animals and in man.

The form and corresponding size of an organism are controlled by heredity and are transmissible. The germ cells, male and female, contain half the number of chromosomes; by their fusion, the total is restored; they are few in the lower organisms and up to around fifty in the higher. Modern theory locates the hereditary principle in the chromosomes and relates individual traits to the genes within the chromosomes.

> A gene is probably scarcely bigger than a single though very large molecule.

> The principle constituent of the chromosomes is the so-called DNA (deoxyribonucleic acid). This has a very long molecule consisting of roughly 10,000 members linked in a chain. It seems that there are only four different kinds of links, which can however be arranged in completely different orders — there is an enormous number of possible arrangements. A single link contains roughly twenty or thirty atoms. The details of the relation of the DNA molecule to the individual genes has not yet been determined with certainty.

The chromosome reproduces itself exactly and exactly once, building itself up from the materials around it, mostly proteins. Nothing similar has been known to occur outside living matter, though *regarded chemically, the DNA molecule is not fundamentally different from any other large molecule.* Clearly, then, some other principle prevails in living nature.

> The reactions of a macro-molecule like DNA can certainly not be treated exactly by quantum mechanics any more than a waterfall can be treated by Newtonian mechanics.

What then brings all this to a final stop?

> It is the fact of the termination of growth at a finite point when the predetermined form is attained that is so incomprehensible physically.

> The cells destined to belong to different organs develop differently and assume different functions.

How could purely physical laws ever bring this about?

> We will never understand the morphology of the living organism if we restrict ourselves to the use of physical and chemical laws only. . . .

Presumably causal and quantitative methods, including quantum mechanics will not suffice.

The idea of <u>wholeness</u> presents itself: *A living cell is already a whole and consists not merely of a number of juxtaposed macro-molecules, and a living organ, and still more a living organism forms a whole and consists not merely of a large number of cells.* There is clearly an 'overall' controlling the situation from the outset. As regards the second theme, that of evolution, or more specifically, how higher organisms evolve from lower ones, Heitler focuses on the biological theory of mutations.

Darwin's theory of evolution is based on the idea of chance variations. He never entered into the nature of chance. They occurred spontaneously without further explanation. Those that were unfavourable to higher development fell by the wayside; those that proved to be favourable were carried forward, and so, by countless chances, evolution advanced. It is just this question of chance that Heitler examines closely.

> *A higher mammal is determined by an enormous number of factors. All the bones, muscles, tendons, nerves and other organs are fairly accurately determined as to position, size and shape.*

Leaving out of account the refinement and complexity of internal structure,

> *. . . If only one of the essential determining factors in the mutation had 'come out wrong' the whole thing would not work. The probability that all this does come out right by chance is so fanatically small that we could not expect to find a squirrel . . . with its incredibly sure-footed climbing feats . . . once in the whole course of the evolution of life.*

> *Consider the DNA molecule . . . the main constituent of the chromosomes, with its 10,000 links, in which four different types occur in various arrangements. If it is the case that hereditary properties are located in the DNA molecule . . . and if we assume that the mutation requisite for an upward step in evolution needs a particular re-arrangement of only 32 links in the DNA molecule . . .*

then

> *Assuming that the 32 links of the chain contain 8 of each type, we get for the odds of a particular arrangement $1:10^{17}$, that is, one to a hundred thousand billion (English, million, million).*

The inevitable conclusion is that whatever evolution may depend on, it most certainly does not depend on chance.

But if not chance, then what are we to look to?

> *Evolution, even more than morphology, forces us to invoke teleological considerations.*

Heitler has already brought forward the thought

> *. . . that there must exist outside man a spiritual principle with which the laws of nature and our own mathematical knowledge of them are bound up.*

> *In a large part of Greek philosophy pure mathematics and particularly geometry was looked on with profound veneration as a reflection of the divine spirit — as in the Pythagorean doctrine of harmonies or the Platonic doctrine of ideas.*

> *For the majority of mankind, and often in particular for its intellectual leaders during the most fertile periods of its history, religion was a living fact.*

Our vague expression, *extra-human spiritual principle* refers to something

> *. . . that has been accepted as a matter of course throughout practically the whole of human history in some concrete sense or other.*

We next turn to the question of consciousness, a term used by Heitler to denote any and every psychic and intellectual activity.

> *If there is one thing of which our knowledge is certain, it is our own consciousness.*

Heitler rejects equally an attempt to compare the brain to an electronic brain. Whatever marvels the latter may achieve in computation, in automatic and accurate book-keeping, even in playing chess against an opponent, it could not exist if a human brain had not invented it.

> *If the nervous system is comparable with an electronic brain, it has certainly not arisen by chance mutation. The chance would be about as likely as that a monkey playing with wires should accidentally 'discover' the circuit diagram for the electronic brain.*

In summation:

Physical laws will certainly be neither sufficient nor appropriate for a complete understanding of typical vital processes. Something is missing, just that fundamental element that constitutes life.

This something, of which so far we have scarcely any conception, will not be 'differential' like physics, i.e., it will not in the first place be operative from point to point; it will involve the wholeness of the living being and its organs, an overall plan, which gives direction not only to the growth of the individual being, but on a much grander scale to evolution.

From direct observation we return to theory.

The smallest place in which it can be effective is presumably that of the aggregates of macro-molecules, such as occur in the chromosomes.

In a footnote Heitler recalls that Teilhard de Chardin ascribes a rudimentary element of consciousness to the macro-molecules:

. . . we are not inclined to go so far, but an element of life, or at least something in which a life force can operate is undoubtedly present here.

On a higher plane there must be scope in this something for consciousness to take a decisive place. So far science knows next to nothing about all this, and these vague indications must suffice.

The question arises as to whether physical laws still have a legitimate place within living organisms. It is clear that Heitler as physicist feels it imperative to explore this further. At the present stage of knowledge it is speculative and inconclusive.

A science which adopts the standpoint that vital processes are defined in a physically determinative way and persists in it can only lead to a complete loss of reverence for life. The consequences for mankind itself would be catastrophic. But we hope that we have indicated reasons enough to show that this standpoint is false.

Heitler points out that Copernicanism was to begin with a revolution in terms of mediaeval theology.

If the universe does not revolve in a physical sense about the earth, why then should it turn in a spiritual sense about man.

It was on this issue that the battle raged. In astronomical terms, the view of the heavens has expanded beyond measure.

The celestial sphere of the fixed stars unfolded itself as a system of countless stars extended over vast spaces, the galactic systems, each star of which resembles our sun, and a very large number of which are certainly surrounded by planets. And this is only our particular 'little galaxy.'

Why should the Creator of all these worlds care specially about this earth of man or even this solar system? Further it followed from Darwin's theory that the origin of life must lead back to a 100 or 1000 million years ago as compared with the traditional period of 6,000 years in which even Newton implicitly believed. The gulf between science and religion widened *to become almost unbridgeable.*

On the one hand *the elimination from science of practically all metaphysical elements* seemed indispensable for the advance of pure science, on the other, it led to the unfortunate result that *henceforth physics was regarded as the sole reality.* As a consequence

> . . . the cosmos and the phenomena of nature were robbed of all spirituality. . . . Ultimately man was reduced to an insignificant being, and the materialistic-mechanistic trend received the impetus we have already described.

> The astronomical picture of the universe with its immense distances and intervals of time, never accessible to man, thus arises by extrapolation of geometry and physics to the universe. It is a picture which is obtained by mental processes on the part of the investigator, but of which man can have no other experience.

> It is after all on the earth that human life is staged, and man is the centre of all mental activity, religious and scientific. The whole grand astronomical picture of the universe, too, originated in terrestrial and human mental activity.

The question as to whether there are living beings in some way comparable to man on other heavenly bodies, Heitler regards as a pseudo-question *not quite as meaningless as 'how many angels can stand on the point of a needle,'* or a modern question as to the colour of an atom.

> We have a feeling of what a year or a thousand years of human history are, and what is meant by a few thousand kilometres of distance. Not much more is needed to extend these conditions to the solar system. But we have no feeling for what millions of years mean, or distances of millions of light-years. They are mathematical and physical extrapolations, based in ordinary well known terrestrial data, to vastly different dimensions. By means of these extrapolations we project our physics into the universe.

The question arises of other possible aspects of the universe which cannot be comprehended through mere sense apprehension. What offers itself can only be something that transcends the senses, namely considerations of the metaphysical. This question meets us again every time we come to the limitations of the purely physical. Heitler reverts here, as he has done before, to earlier times. To the mediaevalists, the metaphysical and the physical, that which was of the heavens and of the earth, were united.

Once again, we look back to Pythagoras and his doctrine of the harmony of the spheres which

> . . . has fascinated thinkers for two millennia, up to and including Kepler. . . . The universe of the Pythagorean and Platonic schools of Greek philosophy was animistic throughout and 'endowed with spirit.'

We think of Indian philosophy and others that go much further back than Pythagoras, even the biblical story of Creation. In these Heitler sees *pictorial representations of metaphysical facts and events also having reference to the cosmos.* He sees in Pythagoras *one of the greatest men humanity has produced.*

> There are recurrent reports throughout the whole of human history of supra-sensuous or mystic experiences and much of this is undoubtedly genuine. The integrity of many outstanding persons is to some extent a guarantee. Much of it is certainly legend or imposture. Modern science does not warrant our simply rejecting all of this or degrading it to the level of hysteria by intense prejudice or arrogance.

> We find metaphysical aspects of the universe hinted at everywhere, aspects in which as yet no connection is recognisable with the picture of the world given by physics and astronomy, but all of which is neverthe-less hardly possible summarily to ignore.

Heitler conceded that there may be aspects of the world of which the physical reveals nothing. If so, they are based on expe-riences of a different kind, which does not necessarily imply conflict; but rather, that we merely lack the concepts that would enable us to see that both the physical and the metaphysical are justified as parts of a higher unity. He is concerned that we *main-tain the freedom from prejudice that befits the scientist,* even in regard to matters that do not enter into the scientific philosophy of Galileo and his successors.

Our route has taken us though several of the most important fields of science.

Through their self-imposed limitations the exact sciences have on the one hand arrived at their triumphant success, and on the other, at a lamentable loss of vital connection with man himself through the exclusion of everything qualitative and therefore also of many domains of wider experience.

The combination of the causal and the quantitative principles led to an almost total estrangement from the realities of living nature including man. The mechanistic superstition, as Heitler calls it, has not only occasioned much misery, but

> ... *leads to a general spiritual and moral drying up which can easily lead to physical destruction. When once we have got to the stage of seeing in man merely a complex machine, what does it matter if we destroy him?*

Is science moral or immoral?

> *The search for truth can surely not be immoral. But we have seen that modern research is conducted mainly along channels leading further and further away from what is human. And then this science puts forward a claim to total validity, setting itself up to be the whole and only truth. But a partial truth that claims to be the whole truth may very well be immoral.*

Heitler reflects that there still is

> ... *a large capital of humanism to preserve man from this, but it must be continually replenished with new life and created anew.*

That the work in various places veered towards the metaphysical was not intended from the first. This intruded itself with the question of the division between subject and object, between the external world quantitatively conceived and man's inner life.

> *Thus the framework of science can hardly be a closed framework; it is opening up and requires to be opened up in various directions, including that of metaphysics.*

> *The sole purpose of this book has been to push open a door, a door in a barrier that surrounds the region of validity of present-day science. For this purpose it was necessary to see the barrier, and that is why we had to concern ourselves so much with the assumptions that are made in science. On the far side of the barrier lies a wide terrain which is, scientifically, practically unknown.*

Our point of view has always been from inside the barrier. The glance, however, was intended to show, at least in vague outline, some of the realities that exist and indeed particularly concern us as human beings but are outside of what science treats nowadays, or even regards as real. They are realities which give us an inkling of scarcely known — perhaps previously surmised and now forgotten — spiritual facts and efficacies which have little in common with the clockwork mechanisms we occupy ourselves with in science today.

Our path can lead only by way of and beyond science. It will be the task of the future to find a way through the door thus opened.

But it is only if even now we clearly recognize, from our scientific standpoint, the existence of such realities, that we can succeed in escaping the barrenness of an extreme materialistic-mechanistic view of the world. In this way only can we overcome the cleavage which the deep gulf existing today between man and his all-powerful science has brought about in ourselves.

Heitler has made explicit the need for the science of today to take stock of itself, and to extend its horizon, in a manner not less scientific, to include the qualitative without which man ceases to be man. He has brought us to an open door but also to an imperative need to grasp reality in its wholeness.

· 23 ·

Goethe: Poet - Scientist

D r. Heitler's questioning brings us to the threshold of modern
enquiry and accentuates the urgency with which seemingly
unanswerable questions are piling up. Whatever triumphs of discovery may yet be in store, so far they have offered little or nothing to illuminate the meaning of human life, or existence in general. Meaning is not part if its vocabulary, yet the questioning is
growing more insistent and demanding. Surely there must be
meaning; the real question is how to arrive at it.

Attention turns increasingly to that inward part of human nature
which science, from Galileo on, has persistently ignored as outside
its domain.

Heitler, contemplating the present state of science, concludes that
something is missing. What is missing and is beginning to be
sought for, is the testimony of just that part of human nature which
has been left out. It is being increasingly admitted that without it
the picture of the world which science offers is not the world as it
really is. Great spirits like Whitehead and Haldane turn to the poets,
to Wordsworth in particular. What have they to offer? What is it that
the intuitive artist has that the experimental scientist has not? What
are the truths, no less valid than scientific truth, which live in art?

> In his scientific work, the scientific man is an artist, and his moral stan-
> dard is superb but the value of his example to the rest of the world is lim-
> ited by the fact that, in his work, the scientific man is not wholly a man.
>
> Sullivan, LIMITATIONS OF SCIENCE

There is part of himself which, as scientist, he has left out. What is to make him whole? What have we actually reached with our present day science?

> *What, for instance, makes us regard a living organism as a whole, and not merely as the sum of its parts? What does this vague notion of 'wholeness' or 'individuality' really amount to? Even if every bodily activity of the animal was explored, in terms of physical and chemical changes, we should still feel that our question was unanswered unless what appears as the <u>purposive order</u> of these changes was also accounted for. But 'purpose' is not yet a scientific notion. It is not employed in the physical and chemical sciences, and the majority of biologists or, at least, physiologists, are reluctant to introduce any ideas which have not been found necessary, in these sciences. This is doubtless an excellent procedure so far as certain limited classes of problems are concerned, but it also seems to lead to the consequences that the most obvious and fundamental problems of biology are not even approached.*

How then is the work of the scientist to be carried further? Sullivan, like Whitehead and Haldane, turns to the intuitive faculties of the poet, but not to the poet alone — rather to the whole of art.

> *Certainly the most significant factor in evolution from the amoeba to man seems to us to have been the increase in consciousness. Also the activities we most value are those that do the most to increase our consciousness of ourselves, of our fellow creatures and of the material universe we live in.*

> *This is obviously the case with art. The great artist, painter, poet, or musician, makes us aware as we have never been aware before. He extends and subtilizes certain elements of our experience and so gives us greater knowledge and mastery of life. It is even possible that he may acquaint us with radically new experiences and if he be a great artist, we feel that these experiences are not freakish, but significant because in the main line of man's development. He voices, 'The prophetic soul of the wide world Dreaming on things to come.'*

This is a remarkable statement coming from a scientific thinker. Why then, we may ask, does not Goethe, who is both a poet and scientist, find no mention here? R. A. Wilson quotes Steinbauer, 'a recent visitor to Weimar.'

> *It is impossible to have an adequate conception of the part played by science in Goethe's life unless one has visited the Goethe house in Weimar.*

The place resembles a museum rather than a private house, and several large rooms of this museum contain nothing but the apparatus and material which Goethe used in his scientific experimentation. Chemicals, rocks and ores of all kinds, and many pieces of intimate instruments occupy table after table. But most surprising of all is Goethe's private library. One would expect to find there a rich collection of belles lettres; instead one finds the shelves lined with journals of chemistry, physics, geology, etc. It is only after such a visit that one appreciates the many sided thoroughness of that great mind.

Wilson, LIMITATIONS OF LANGUAGE

Wilson continues,

Poetry deals primarily with human life. Even in his scientific years Goethe believed that 'the chief study of Mankind is Man,' but he saw that the roots of man's life are in nature, and his scientific research has a purpose in relation to his poetry. It gave a proportioned perspective to his view of life and the world as a whole, and gave depth and unity of design to his representation of life in both his verse and prose. If, as Schiller says of him, 'his spirit works and seeks in every direction, <u>striving to create a whole</u>,' his scientific studies add not a little to that unifying impulse and vision. His work, as Carlyle pointed out, is significantly original and modern, the intellectual faculty as clear as the imaginative faculty is vivid. Everywhere in the world he saw development and evolution, not mechanical, but organic and vital.

An unexpected tribute by the late Philip Toynbee appeared in the SUNDAY OBSERVER some years ago headed 'Back to Goethe.'

I have often thought that Goethe might have become the founder of something very like a new religion. He came at an appropriate apocalyptic moment. He succeeded as nobody did before or has done since, in reconciling the natural world with the yearning world of the human spirit. He was aware of the tragic . . . but transcended the tragic. In our 'times,' in our 'plight,' we have paid more attention to Gide than to Goethe, more attention to Lawrence and Kafka and Flaubert than to the one modern man who still could heal and enlighten us. What a desperate frivolity that has been.

It is interesting that Toynbee referred to Goethe as a <u>modern man</u>. That Goethe's poetry remains a sealed book for the non-German scholar is obvious, but this does not apply to his translated scientific works. That these have also remained more or less a sealed book even to this day, must have some other cause.

Goethe's own views on his science, are expressed in the volume, CONVERSATIONS WITH ECKERMANN.

> *For half a century I have been known as a poet in this country and abroad. No one thinks of refusing me that talent. But it is not generally known, it has not been taken into consideration, that I have also occupied myself seriously through many years with the physical and the physiological phenomena of Nature, observing them with the perseverance which passion alone can give. Thus, when my essay on plants, published nearly forty years before, fixed the attention of botanists in Switzerland and France, there seemed no expression for the astonishment at the fact of a poet thus going out of his route to make a discovery so important. It is to counter this false notion that I have written the history of my studies, to show that a great part of my life has been devoted to Natural History, for which I had a passion. It is by no sudden and unexpected inspiration of genius, but through long prosecuted studies I arrived at my results.*

> *Without my attempts in natural science, I should never have learned to know mankind as it is. In nothing else can we approach pure contemplation of thought, so closely observe the errors of the senses and of the understanding, the weak and the strong points of character. . . . Nature understands no jesting: she is always serious, always severe, always true; she is always right, and the errors and faults are always those of man.*

> *As to what I have done as a poet, he would frequently say to me: I have no pride whatever in it. Excellent poets have lived at the same time as myself, poets more excellent have lived before me, and others will come after me. But that is my century, I am the only person who knows the truth in the difficult science of colours — of that, I say, I am not a little proud, and here I have a consciousness of a superiority to many.*

It was just on this question of colour that Goethe found himself most greatly at variance. He firmly believed his work on colour was more important and would outlive his poetry. He saw art as born from an inner source even as the creations of nature are.

From his TRAVELS IN ITALY:

> *The great works of Art, like the highest creations of Nature, have been brought forth in conformity with true and natural law. All that is arbitrary, fanciful, falls away: here is Necessity, here is God.*

Of man the artist, he wrote:

In that man is placed on Nature's pinnacle, he regards himself as another whole Nature, whose task is to bring forth inwardly yet another pinnacle. For this purpose he heightens his powers, imbues himself with all perfections and virtues, summons discrimination, order, and harmony, and rises finally to the production of a work of Art.

This is the essence of Goethe's outlook: Man is not merely a spectator of nature, but finds himself actively placed within the whole creative process of the world. In the CONVERSATIONS WITH ECKERMANN he elaborates on this:

No productiveness of the highest kind, no great thought that bears fruit and has results, is in the power of anyone, such things are above earthly control. Man must consider them as an unexpected gift from above, as pure children of God which he must receive and venerate with joyful thanks. . . . In such cases, man may often be considered an instrument in a higher government of the world, a vessel worthy to contain a divine influence. I say this when I consider how often a single thought has given a different form to whole centuries, and how individual men have imprinted a stamp upon their age which has remained uneffaced and operated beneficially for generations.

However, there is a productiveness of another kind; one subject to earthly influences, one that man has more in his power — although here also he finds cause to bow before something divine. In this category I place all that appertains to the execution of a plan, all the links of a chain of thought, the ends of which already shine forth: I also place there all that constitutes the visible body of a work of art.

Goethe's view of nature was similar. He lived at one with nature as with a being. In observing nature he sought to free himself from all theory and to make of himself an intensely wakeful and attentive vessel. He immersed himself in the phenomena, whether of plant, animal, man, the world of colour, or whatever else thus, with maximum concentration in the act of pure observation. He waited on nature to awaken the related idea within him; then, it was not an abstract mental notion. The idea, lighting up, maybe after years of devoted observation, was experienced as nature's own relevation within the consciousness of man. The joy of the revealed thought when it came, the intimacy with nature which it brought, could only be likened to the bliss of the mystic in his sense of oneness with God. Out of this, Goethe wrote:

When the healthy nature of man works as one Whole, when he feels
himself to exist in the world as in a great and beautiful Whole, when
the harmonious sense of well-being imparts to him a pure, free delight,
the Universe — if it could be conscious of itself — having attained its
goal, would shout for joy and admire the summit of its own becoming
and being.

At this stage the idea that is born within the soul is a God-given actuality; it becomes a precept for the inward or spiritual eye as surely as an outer object is a precept for the outer physical eye. Here the creative spirit, free from self, achieves for the first time true objectivity. Everything else, all mere theorizing becomes, in the words of James Jeans, *subjective mental constructs*, something imposed on the phenomena by man. Goethe was speaking of experience where others were voicing theories.

Goethe lived at a time when the mathematical-physical conception of the world was dominant amongst scientists *Mathematics is the key to the universe* was the universal slogan. The philosopher Kant declared there was as much truth in a given phenomenon as there was mathematics in it. It was said of Goethe that his failure to understand Newton was due to his lack of mathematics. Goethe had his own view on this.

I receive mathematics as the most sublime and useful science, as long as
they are applied in their proper place, but I cannot commend the misuse
of them in matters which do not belong to their sphere.

I raised the whole school of mathematics against me, and people were
greatly amused that one who had no insight into mathematics could
venture to contradict Newton. For that Physics could exist indepen-
dently of Mathematics, no one seemed to have the slightest suspicion.

By physics is here meant the whole realm of physical phenomena, including light.

It was prejudicial to me that I discovered Newton's theory of light and
colour to be an error, and that I had the courage to contradict the universal
creed. I discovered light in its purity and truth, and I considered it my duty
to fight for it. The opposite party, however, did their utmost to darken the
light; for they maintained that shade was a part of light. It sounds absurd
when I express it; but so it is; for they said that <u>colours</u> which are shadow
and the result of shade, <u>are light itself</u>, or, which amounts to the same thing,
<u>are the beams of light, broken now in one way, now in another</u>.

Goethe felt out of accord not only with the bias towards the mathematical but also with the whole dualistic trend of dividing existence into an outer physical world and an inner moral one. He was
pre-eminently a monist in so far as he saw the world, inner and
outer, as one whole. Within this wholeness there was polarity, day
and night, summer and winter, light and darkness. Never could he
regard darkness merely as the absence of light. Both were equally
real and actual. Every dawn must have its sunset, every sunset its
dawn. Thus all colours, in their infinite variety of shade and tone,
ranged within this polarity, some more towards the light, others
more towards the darkness. Within the soul, too, there is the dramatic play of light and darkness. Therefore it was natural for him
to speak of colours as the deeds and sufferings of light. This to him
was real and objective. To invent a theory which lay beyond the
experienced facts, he could only regard as subjective. Thus he
wrote of such theorists:

> They do not prove the truth, nor is such the intention; the only point
> with those professors is to prove their own opinion.

> The contemplation of the world with all these theorists has lost its
> innocence; the objects no longer appear in their natural purity. If these
> learned men then give an account of their observations, we obtain,
> not-withstanding their love of truth as individuals, no natural truth
> with reference to the object; we always get the taste of a strong sub-
> jective nature.

> My tendencies were opposed to those of my time, which were wholly
> subjective; while, in my objective efforts, I stood alone to my own dis-
> advantage.

Goethe's initial interest in colour came from a contemplation of
works of art. What was it that determined an artist's choice of
colours? He saw colours as constituting a language of their own,
from which the artist could draw at need. He set out their qualities as follows:

> Yellow must possess a bright, gay, mildly stimulating character because
> it is the colour nearer to light. Blue indicates the darkness working in
> it. Therefore it produces a sense of coldness, just as it is reminiscent of
> shadows. Reddish-yellow arises through the intensification of yellow
> towards the side of darkness. Through this intensification its energy
> increases; the gaiety and brightness pass over into rapture. With the

further intensification of reddish-yellow into yellowish-red, the gay,
cheerful feeling is transformed into the impression of power. Violet is the
blue striving towards the light. The repose and coldness of blue hereby
changes into interest. This restless feeling increases in blue-red. Pure
red stands in the centre between yellowish-red and blueish-red. The vio-
lence of the yellow quietens down, the passive repose of the blue is ani-
mated. Red gives the impression of <u>ideal</u> satisfaction, the equalizing of
extremes. A feeling of satisfaction also arises through green which is a
mixture of yellow and blue. The satisfaction here is purer than that pro-
duced by red because the gaiety of the yellow is not intensified and the
repose of the blue is not disturbed through the red shade.

We see how Goethe relates outer sense impression to inner soul experience, what pertains to the science of nature and what to art. For one who is both a scientist and an artist, here truth and beauty meet. By contrast, the spectrum of colours explained in terms of refraction, or more recently, in wave lengths, nowhere touches actual experience; yet, it is the experience that is all-important. For Goethe, the physiological and complementary colours, the after images, colour shadows, colours in the plant and animal kingdoms, colours wherever they occur, are part of a differentiated wholeness, and it is with wholeness that Goethe is ever and again concerned.

Of his scientific work generally, Goethe wrote:

. . . my tendencies have always been confined to such objects as lay ter-
restrially around me and could be immediately observed by the senses.
On this account I have never occupied myself with astronomy, because
there the senses are not sufficient — instruments, calculations, mechan-
ics are added . . . and were not in my line.

If I have done anything with respect to the subjects which lay in my
way, I had this advantage; that my life fell in a time richer than any
other in great natural discoveries. . . . Advances such as I could never
have foreseen are now made even on paths that I opened, and I feel like
one who walks toward the dawn, and when the sun rises, is astonished
at its brightness.

This speaks for Goethe the scientist; but what of the artist?

The artist would speak to the world through an entirety; he does not find
that entirety in Nature . . . it is the fruit of his own mind; or, if you like,
of the aspiration of a fructifying divine spirit.

In this sense, Goethe sees the artist in some degree in everyone.

I am more than convinced that poetry is the universal possession of mankind, revealing itself everywhere and at all times in hundreds and hundreds of men. One makes it a little better than another.

Goethe was forever seeking the totality that holds within it the unity of life. We meet with a striking example of this in connection with his anatomical studies. It concerns a little bone, the intermaxillary, which carries the incisors. He learned that there were authorities claiming that this bone did not exist in man. This to Goethe was untenable: Nature is single, Nature is whole. In her creation of the osteological framework, Nature could not have deviated from the universal practice for the sake of man. If the incisor teeth were there in common with the animals, then the bone must be there even if concealed from the eye. He set out to find the needed evidence, and in the end succeeded.

But that was the way with Goethe. Once he had inwardly grasped a given fact, he would not accept that it could not be otherwise, even if the supporting evidence seemed lacking. This is an example of Goethe's unyielding stand concerning matters that to him were plain. For those who questioned him, his seeming obstinacy could be infuriating once his mind was made up. It was not just obstinacy, rather he could not fail to uphold the truth which he plainly saw. For him it was plain seeing, not opinion or surmise.

In the English-speaking world of the nineteenth century, none could have had so immediate a sympathy and understanding for Goethe as Ralph Waldo Emerson (except perhaps Carlyle). Emerson was himself a master of the word, accurate, richly expressive, intent on penetrating to the heart of things. In his essay on Goethe, the poet, in his REPRESENTATIVE MEN he describes him as follows:

. . . hundred-handed, Argus eyed, able and happy to cope with this rolling miscellany of facts and science, and, by his own versatility, to dispose of them with ease; a manly man, unembarrassed by the variety of coats of convention with which life has got encrusted, easily able by his subtlety to pierce these, and to draw his strength from nature, with which he lived in full communion.

There is a heart-cheering freedom in his speculation. The immense horizon which journeys with us lends its majesty to trifles, and to matters of convenience, and necessity, as to solemn and festive performances. He was the soul of his century.

This is not adulation. Emerson is attempting to describe what in the end is indescribable, the essence of the nature of a phenomenal human being.

> *Eyes are better, on the whole, than telescopes and microscopes. He has contributed a key to many parts of nature, through the rare turn for unity and simplicity in his mind. Thus Goethe suggested the leading idea in modern botany, that a leaf, or the eye of a leaf, is the unit of botany, and that every part of the plant is only a transformed leaf to meet a new conditions; and, by varying the conditions, a leaf may be converted into any other organ, and any other organ into a leaf. In like manner, in osteology, he assumed that one vertebra of the spine might be considered the unit of the skeleton; the head was only the uppermost vertebrae transformed. 'The plant goes from knot to knot, and closes with the flower and seed. So the tapeworm, the caterpillar, goes from knot to knot and closes with the head.' In optics, again, he rejected the artificial theory of seven colours, and considered that every colour was the mixture of light and darkness in new proportions. It is really of very little consequence what topic he wrote upon. He sees at every pore and has a certain gravitation towards truth.*

Emerson deeply appreciated Goethe's total independence as an artist, his freedom from all traditionalism, and his strong sense of realism. In his great world masterpiece there are always the contrasting figures of Faust, the struggling human, and Mephistopheles, the lying devil, ever at his side; two conflicting testimonies to be met at every level in life. Here, Emerson, out of his own unique genius and independence, characterizes Goethe's treatment of Mephistopheles.

> *The Devil had played an important part in mythology at all times. Goethe would have no word that does not carry a thing. The same measure will still serve: 'I have not heard of any crime which I might not have committed.' So he flies at the throat of this imp. He shall be real; he shall be modern; he shall be European; he shall dress as a gentleman, and accept the manners, and walk in the streets, and he will be initiated in the life of Vienna, and of Heidelberg, in 1820 — or he shall not exist. Accordingly, he stripped him of mythological gear, of horns, cloven foot, harpoon tail, brimstone and blue-fire, and, instead of looking into books and pictures, looked for him in his own mind, in every shade of coldness, selfishness, and unbelief that, in crowds, or in*

solitude, darkens over the human thought — and found that the por-
trait gained reality and terror by everything he added, and by every-
thing he took away. He found that the essence of this hobgoblin, which
had hovered in shadows about the habitations of men, ever since there
were men, was pure intellect, applied — as always there is the tenden-
cy — to the service of the senses; and he flung into literature, in his
Mephistopheles, the first organic figure that has been added for some
ages, and which will remain as long as Prometheus.

Emerson was well aware that the Mephistophelian influence was
widespread and gathering force. His own writing is often a call to
man to beware of losing his true identity. Thus in his essay
'History' he wrote:

Ah, brother, stop the ebb of thy soul — ebbing downwards into the
forms into whose habits thou hast now for many years slid. What is our
life but an unending flight of winged facts and events. In splendid vari-
ety these fancies come, all putting question to the human spirit. Those
men who cannot answer by a superior wisdom these facts or questions
of time, serve them. Facts encounter them, tyrannise over them, and
make the men of routine, the men of sense, in whom a literal obedience
to facts has extinguished every spark of that light by which man is truly
man. But if the man is true to his own better instincts or sentiments,
and refuses the dominion of facts, as one that comes of a higher race,
remains fast by the soul and sees the principles, then the facts fall aptly
and supple into their places; they know their master, and the meanest of
them glorifies him.

Emerson saw in Goethe just such a one who answered life's questions out of a *superior wisdom* — a man *of a higher race.*

Genius studies the causal thought, and far back, in the womb of things,
sees the rays parting from one orb, that diverge ere they fall by infinite
diameters. Genius watches the monad through all his masks and he per-
forms the metapsychosis of nature. Genius directs through the fly,
through the caterpillar, through the grub, through the egg, the constant
individual; through countless individuals, the fixed species; through
many species, the genus; through all the genera, the steadfast type;
through all the kingdoms of organic life, the eternal unity. Nature is a
mutable cloud, which is always and never the same. She casts the same
thought into troops of forms, as a poet makes twenty fables into one moral.

This indicates how Emerson empathized with Goethe's approach
to living nature, indeed to life as a whole. Goethe's discovery, for
which he coined the word <u>metamorphosis</u>, was the continuity of

change by inner causes from one outer form to another (for example, from leaf to petal); his novel expression, *anschauende-urteilskraft*
is sometimes translated as <u>perceptual judgment</u> (allowing judgment to form in the course of the observation of phenomena with
live perception but free from theory); his remarkable dual expression, *sinnlich-sittlich,* perceiving the outer form and with it, sensing
or inwardly perceiving the creative element, the living idea (which
causes the formation and delineation of the type, the entity ruling
in all the variations in a given type of species) thus, his <u>archetypal
plant</u>. To stay with the *sinnlich*, the physically perceptible, is only to
fall into matter; to indulge only in the *sittlich* is to drift into dream.
The beholding of the two in their mutual relationship as one, to see
the object and with it the <u>idea</u>, this alone constitutes reality, and
calls for a faculty which Goethe called <u>higher seeing</u> — not just
thinking or imagining but actual seeing with the mind's eye. It was
difficult even for his fellow poet and dramatist, Schiller, to grasp
the difference of what Goethe meant by actually <u>seeing</u> the idea,
and holding an idea as mental image vividly in mind. That Goethe
was somehow differently constituted from others, Schiller knew
very well. Thus, writing to Goethe in 1784, he described in it the
following way:

> For a long time I have, even though from a distance, observed the course
> of your spirit and with ever new wonder noted the path you have traced
> out for yourself. You seek it along the harder path from which all weak-
> er forces would shrink. You take all nature as a whole in order to illu-
> minate a part; and in the totality of their appearance you seek the basis
> of explanation for the individual.

In any given field, Goethe ranges out all the single phenomena in
a series or progression, and then seeks, within the varieties and
changeablilities, for the unifying principle that must be there
underlying and active in them all; that is the invisible element, the
sittlich, accessible to the higher seeing which then illuminates,
shapes, orders and organizes all the individual, outwardly perceived, and single elements, which relate to the *sinnlich*.

This is quite specifically illustrated in Goethe's study of the plant.
He attributed much to Linnaeus as one of his teachers and took
delight in the classifications set before him. But then, what was the

underlying principle that determined them all, in their vast variety, as plants? What was it that lived in the whole kingdom, to make a plant a plant? The moss beside the rose both contain the invisible element, which constant, creative is present in each and all in their degree.

A month later, in May 1787, he wrote to his friend Herder:

> *I must further confide to you that I am very near to the secret of plant generation and organization, and that it is the simplest thing conceivable.*
>
> *The archetypal plant is the most wonderful creation in the world, for which Nature herself should envy me. With this model, and its key, one can invent plants ad infinitum, and consequently, that is to say, plants which could exist even if they do not exist, and are not, as it were, artistic or poetic shadows and fancies, but have an inner truth and necessity. The same law may be applied to all else that lives. Forwards and backwards the plant is ever only leaf, so indissolubly united with the future germ, that one cannot think of one without the other. To grasp such a concept, to sustain it, to discover it in Nature, is a task which places us in a condition that is almost painful, despite its joy.*

What was it that Goethe was seeing? Did his archetypal plant have actual existence?

For Goethe the archetypal plant was unquestionably present, mobile, and alive, while shaping and determining the forms of the plant in all its growing from stage to stage, outwardly most concealed yet most powerfully present in the seed. Goethe's unique way of working was as though Nature herself were working in him and though him.

In an essay *'Anschauende Urteilskraft'* (perceptive judgment or contemplative discernment, literally the power of judgment arising while beholding), Goethe tries to bring us nearer to the nature of his experience.

> *If in the sphere of morality, through belief on God, virtue and immortality we seek to raise ourselves to a higher region and draw near to the First Being, the same should be the case in the sphere of Intellect — that, through the contemplation of an ever-creating Nature, we should make ourselves worthy of spiritual participation in her production. So did I press on untiringly to the Primal Archetype.*

Such a term as *spiritual participation* is wholly foreign to the science of today. With the archetypal plant in consciousness, Goethe felt he could create countless forms of plants which he was certain could take shape, given the right outer conditions.

Goethe stands as a towering figure in the realm of human culture; he has been regarded as the sage of Europe, and the world saw fit to honour the centenary of his death in 1932, and bicentenary of his birth in 1949 on a grand scale. For the latter there was even an international meeting of scientists in Frankfurt with the intention and the hope of coming seriously to terms with what Goethe had offered!

In his book, THE DIGNITY OF MAN, Davenport recounts the content of a lecture given by Heisenberg, the founder of the law of indeterminacy, the law which has radically challenged much of modern thinking. Of this law, James Jeans, in his PHYSICS AND PHILOSOPHY, wrote:

> The classical physics seemed to bolt and bar the door leading to any sort of freedom of the will; the new physics hardly does this; it almost seems to suggest that the door may be unlocked — if only we could find the handle. The old physics showed us a universe which looked more like a prison than a dwelling place. The new physics shows us a universe which looks as though it might conceivably form a suitable dwelling place for free men, and not a mere shelter for brutes — a home in which it might at least be possible for us to mould events to out desires and live lives of endeavour and achievement.

Russell Davenport wrote:

> In 1932, a remarkable address was delivered before the Saxon Academy of Science by one of the greatest modern physicists. The speaker was Professor Werner Heisenberg, formulator of the famous 'principle of indeterminacy,' indispensable to contemporary theorizing in the difficult and highly technical field of quantum mechanics. Having ventured further than all but a few men in the direction of pure quantitative abstraction, Dr. Heisenberg turns, in the address mentioned, to evaluate the results of this manner of enquiry. For this purpose he disregards all the brilliant discoveries with which science is usually credited, and concentrates his attention upon the sacrifices in knowledge that have been made in order to achieve them. 'As facts and knowledge accumulate,' he says, 'the claim of the scientist to an understanding of the world in a certain sense diminishes.' The path of science is a path of renunciation. In

order to view its scientific objectives it has had to renounce 'the aim of bringing the phenomena of nature to our thinking in an immediate and living way.' What does Dr. Heisenberg mean by 'an immediate and living way?' The answer to this question is disclosed in the fact that his address was given on the hundredth anniversary of the death of the great German poet-scientist, Johann Wolfgang von Goethe. Those familiar with the history of science may recall the struggle that Goethe put up against Newtonian optics, and the strange (and in our view inadmissible) theory of colour which he formulated in opposition. The struggle, of course, was won by Newton, even though Newtonian optics have proved quite inadequate to explain the phenomenon of light; and the Goethean theory has ever since been described as a kind of scientific curiosity. But that is really a minor matter. What we can now see, from the perspective of nearly a century and a half, is that an issue was at stake between Goethe and Newton, much more fundamental and far-reaching than any mere theory of light. This issue was precisely the one that we have been attempting to define, and it will serve us well at this point to take brief cognizance of Goethe's view of it.

Sir Isaac Newton, of course, was profoundly instrumental in the development of the scientific spirit of enquiry in quantitative terms. It was the essence of Goethe's argument against Newton that this quantitative approach to Nature could not lead to truth. Goethe insists upon observing nature _in terms of her content_. For him that the colour red could be defined only as a quantitative vibration was intolerable. For Goethe, sensory knowledge, while it may involve illusion, is not _merely_ illusion. It is susceptible of many distortions and contains many subjective variables, but it is not a knowledge of nothing. It is, on the contrary, the 'immediate and living' perception of a qualitative reality, a quality of Nature, which exists and is true. And it can no more be gained by pure quantitative abstraction than a man can quench his thirst by measuring the cubic capacity of a tumbler.

What is true of sensory knowledge is true, for Goethe, of other forms of knowledge. This is because there exists between the _subject_ (the observer) and the _object_ (the observed) an inner unity. The nature of this unity, of which both man and Nature are a part, is a mystery, but with our intuitive faculties and our imagination we can enter this mystery and actually know things — so to speak — from the inside. Hence it is possible for the subject to know the object _by means of contemplating it_. 'My thinking does not separate itself from objects — my contemplation is itself a way of thinking, my thinking a way of contemplating.' As Karl Vietor put it, 'Speculative thinking [for Goethe] can only operate positively when it contributes to the process of heightening feeling and intuition into a clear awareness, so that we are led more deeply into the

phenomenon itself.' Man can know Nature, not by reasoning abstract-
ly, but by discovering himself, in contemplation, as part of her.

That there is such a thing as quantitative truth, all of mathematics and
all of theoretical and applied sciences bear witness. But what led to the
clash between Goethe and Newton was the former's perception that the
scientific spirit of enquiry was proceeding more and more upon the
assumption that the truth about Nature and the universe could be
reached and formulated in exclusively quantitative terms, that the qual-
itative aspect of reality, which is real for the human being, could be
abstracted away and discarded. Against this trend Goethe took an
unequivocal stand.

It is that trend which has led to determinism. James Jean writes:

Practically all modern philosophies of the first rank, Descartes, Spinoza,
Leibnitz, Locke, Hume, Kant, Hegel, Mill, Alexander, as well as many
others, have been determinists in the sense of admitting the cogency of
the arguments for determinism, but many have at the same time been
indeterminists in the sense of hoping to find a loophole of escape from
these arguments.

Davenport, in his book wishes to show that determinism entering
social and political life represents today the greatest threat to
human freedom. He identifies it with the view which underlies the
thinking of Marx and Engels and

. . . has become dominant in our civilization. It is the point of view, root-
ed in the outward-looking consciousness, which insists that external
observation and analysis provide us with our only means of access to
truth. Reality, in other words, is what we can perceive with our senses
and our instruments by looking outward from ourselves, while the
inward-looking consciousness is entangled in endless illusions, so the
argument goes. It is only by examining and analysing things from the
outside that we have any chance of reaching objective truth; it is only in
the external world, indeed that truth is to be found.

Davenport saw in this philosophy the end product of the mecha-
nistic-deterministic thinking which has emerged from the dualism
of the seventeenth and eighteenth centuries and which has now
entered social, political, and economic life as the greatest possible
threat to human moral freedom. He saw this danger exemplified in
the totalitarian states. His appeal is ostensibly from an American to
Americans, but actually to all free democratic societies so far as
these still exist; it is an appeal to the latent forces in humanity to

awaken out of the state of somnolence into which they have fallen. No appeal to the old slogans will serve because these have now been adopted by the advancing negative forces. In the end, he is asking for no less than a re-education of the human race, through a reawakening to spiritual values, and he thinks he has discovered what this may mean.

The two concepts, free will and social freedom — must stand or fall together. The schizophrenic attitude of the Twentieth Century, whereby the concept of free will is accorded little, if any, scientific value, while we continue to make freedom our battle-cry, appears to us, wholly untenable.

A kind of black haze lies over the landscape in which twentieth century man has become lost. Through the haze he cannot see the stars or the heavens, cannot determine his course.

We find that the haze is compounded of fear, which pervades the whole earth in our time, and is just as powerful in the East as in the West. Not a nation — scarcely even an individual —escapes it. And this fear itself constitutes a constant danger to all, because nothing is so unpredictable as the decision of a man who is afraid.

The universal fear may manifest itself as fear of aggression, but its origin is really much more profound . . . today men are in possession of something that was much less in evidence a thousand years ago . . . a sense of self . . . the segregation of the individual from his social context — his emergence as a being in his own right.

He must find his beliefs within himself. He must increasingly do his own thinking . . . but underneath his own consciousness there may exist a kind of malaise, a doubt as to whether he is really right? . . . We know that all we have to do, in order to test the validity of a given fear, is to think. Yet the fact remains that the danger of mass symbolism, in lieu of thinking, is in our time overwhelmingly great . . . thinking for oneself is a fearsome task.

THE CONFUSION OF THE FREE WORLD

The free world treats the human being as if he were a spiritual entity, but when it comes to explaining what this means, or what a spiritual entity is or could be, the free world is confused and inarticulate.

In answering the question of why the Communists have been so successful, therefore, we must on the one hand take into account the clarity and consistency of Marxism, and on the other, the confusion and ambiguity of the doctrines of the free world.

Unless Americans can muster the courage to plunge into the mysteries of man, no possibility remains of escaping the holocaust that everyone feels in his bones.

The kind of evaluation that Western civilizations is unable to make is of man and his relation to the cosmos, his relation to the divine. And it is just this kind of evaluation that America must begin to make. But for one thing, a great many Americans, including their intellectual leaders, are in doubt as to the very existence of anything that could be called divine. And for another (even if this difficulty can be overcome), the techniques of thinking about things do not carry us very far in the direction of discovering anything about the divine. The challenge to hold an open mind toward any different way of thinking is not easily met. One is exposed to murderous cross fire from the academic world, deeply entrenched in the very way of thinking that has led civilization into darkness and disaster. One is even exposed to ridicule.

The achievement of a truly open mind in our time requires courage. . . . Americans have courage; as a people they have always responded to challenges. One of their deep troubles today is that, for all the obvious danger of their predicament, they do not quite know what the challenge is. That challenge of an open mind may be a different kind of challenge from what they have been expecting.

FRAGMENTS ends with a piece entitled 'Special Influences.' Acknowledgment is made to Tom Paine, John Adams, Thomas Jefferson, and Ralph Waldo Emerson *the sage of Concord* ; reflections of Plato and Aristotle; then St. Thomas and the question as to how and why the Thomist meaning of the word Faith has been lost; and the comment that *if Faith could be re-established among men, the apparent disintegration of Western culture could be arrested.* All this turns out to be preparatory to the attention being focused on two teachers *so closely bound in their thinking that they can virtually be viewed as one.* The first is Johaan Wolfgang von Goethe (1749–1832), and the second, his *extraordinary interpreter*, Rudolf Steiner (1861–1925). Davenport knew that this would come as something wholly unexpected to most of his readers. He therefore wrote:

The selection of these two for special acknowledgment may occasion a certain surprise, for Goethe is known chiefly as a poet and novelist, and Steiner as a mystic whose works seem unintelligible and hopelessly out of step with his time. Anyone familiar with the writings of these men, however, will understand our special indebtedness to them.

To begin with, Goethe was not 'just' a poet. He was also a scientist, and according to Karl Vietor he regarded 'the scientific part of his intellectual existence as not less important than his artistic one.' Modern science would disagree with many of Goethe's factual conclusions. But what it cannot escape is his approach to science, his instinctive and stubbornly held view of what science really is. We have shown . . . the contribution Goethe made to our thinking with his emphasis on intuition and contemplation. Goethe was the first empirical scientist to adopt what we have called a living approach to reality. For him, Nature — that is to say, the world and the universe — is not an inanimate void containing inanimate matter, but is alive, and can be understood by the scientist only if he is able and willing to adapt his processes of thought to that supreme fact. Goethe's fundamental position with regard to truth, in other words, is what we have already outlined with regard to freedom. Truth escapes those approaches to reality comprehended under logic, mechanics, mathematics and statistics; to apprehend it, a different approach must be developed. And Goethe's irreplaceable contribution to mankind was that he took the first empirical, experimental steps in that direction.

The man who made all this clear, and carried it further, was Rudolf Steiner. Trained in the natural sciences in Vienna, Steiner edited Goethe's scientific writings, in the Berlin-Stuttgart edition (1892–97). He also participated in the editing of the Weimar edition, which still stands as definitive. He then proceeded to apply and develop the Goethean philosophy of science in numerous fields of learning — in physics, chemistry, medicine, zoology, botany, history, philology, religion, Christology, scriptural interpretation, and so forth. He demonstrated by his enormous works that the Goethean scientific thesis is true; that whenever we can win our way, in scientific spirit, to processes of living thought, it is possible then to enter into and understand mysteries that the natural sciences as hitherto practised, cannot reach. Steiner's life and works constitute a refutation of modern agnosticism. Man's knowledge may not be 'absolute' but it has no observable limits.

That the academic world has managed to dismiss Steiner's work as inconsequential and irrelevant, is one of the intellectual wonders of the twentieth century. Anyone who is willing to study those vast works with an open mind* will find himself faced with one of the greatest thinkers of all times, whose grasp of the modern sciences is equaled only by his profound learning in the ancient ones. Steiner was no more of a mystic than Albert Einstein; he was a scientist, rather — but <u>a scientist who dared to enter into the mysteries of life</u>. If one wishes to disregard the mysteries of life, one can disregard Steiner. It is wholly illegitimate, however, for those who have resolutely shunned the examination of such

* (let us say, a hundred of his titles)

mysteries to declare that his findings are unbelievable. This is precisely the same as if one were to say — not wishing to study the matter — that Planck's theory of quanta (which show that electrons can now be in one place or another place, but never in between) is unbelievable. Steiner's findings are indeed <u>unfamiliar</u>, and for that reason one may feel impelled to reject them. Yet this would be philosophically permissible only if our familiar concepts and modes of thinking had been proven to be absolutely true. And such proof has never been offered — indeed, the very contrary is indicated. Those who are in search of truth, therefore, rather than merely dedicated to the defense of the familiar, must put aside the question of whether Steiner's findings are 'believable or unbelievable' and address themselves to the more rewarding task of finding out, through a sincere study of his works, whether they are true.

Reverting to the question put to St. Thomas:

> *. . . by what means can Faith be re-established in the twentieth century, Rudolf Steiner's answer is that Faith can be re-established <u>only through an advance in knowledge</u>.*

> *We clearly cannot go back to Faith as it was in the thirteenth century, but the new attitude towards science that was pioneered by Goethe and Steiner shows us how we can develop its twentieth century equivalent, <u>an acknowledgment and understanding of the divine</u> — in which all questions pertaining to man are rooted, which is constantly at work in human affairs, and which is, in fact accessible to a science that employs living processes of thought.*

These are the closing words of Davenport's book — his parting message and pointer to the future. It was Davenport's earnest hope and prayer for the future that led him, in a last flash of vision, to point to Goethe and Steiner as having the gifts we desperately need to cope with our problems today — to Goethe as a forerunner and to Steiner as truly contemporary and leading on.

· 24 ·

The Enigma of
the Thinking Mind

What is mankind? Our sciences have assembled a vast amount of information yet we know only that we do not know. Without that knowledge life remains meaningless. We have no ground to stand on, nothing to build on, hence the chaos in which we live.

It has not always been so, Davenport recalls that St. Thomas Aquinas, in his time, could confidently meet *the enigma of human life — Nature, Man, and God* on the grounds of Reason and Faith. He believed man could find an answer to every question that concerned him with the aid of Reason and Faith which were *not mutually antagonistic but mutually consonant*.

But Reason and Faith as then understood have died for us. In fact, what we have called Reason, as employed in the sciences has led to the undermining of Faith.

What is left for the future? Without faith how can we live? Is there no means of arriving at a new faith to carry life forward into the future just as in the past the old faith was able to sustain life? Davenport sought his answers from Rudolf Steiner, and quoted him as saying that it is indeed possible to arrive at such a new faith, *but only through an advance in knowledge*.

What could such an advance in knowledge signify? It surely could not mean the mere extension of knowledge in its present form.

Was this what Steiner was indicating in describing Goethe as the Galileo of the organic? And yet, a hundred and fifty years after Goethe's death, despite all of Steiner's endeavours, his view of the world is still seldom recognized and often rejected.

The fact is that we are so accustomed to our present mode of thinking, so impressed with its practical results, that it has become scarcely possible to imagine anything different that could still deserve the name of science. We are apt to forget how relatively recent this science is, that it takes us back no further than to Galileo, and that it then came as a great innovation which drastically changed the whole of human outlook. To remember this is to be open to the thought that there may also be other great changes to come. It is only in the twentieth century that serious questioning in this direction began.

Consider that until the present scientific age began, and as far back as history can see, man was viewed as a microcosm within the great world as macrocosm. Every aspect of a person's being had its counterpart in the heavenly spheres above. Man's life on earth was in continuous correlation with the sun, moon, and stars. No detail could be left out. Every hair of one's head was accounted for, a universe devoid of spirit was not to be imagined.

With the advent of science, all this was swept away or relegated to the world of legend or dreams. And what has arrived in its place? Today mankind finds itself in a spiritless world of no conceivable origin or predictable end. As to humanity, there are inconclusive theories as to how it arose and what it is, but to ask why it is, is considered a foolish and fruitless question. Life is thought to be no more than a transient moment in an endless meaninglessness. Yet something is stirring in our minds to oppose this empty outlook and to re-examine the premises on which it has been built.

> The nineteenth-century view seems to have been that we were within reasonable distance of obtaining a complete understanding of man and the universe. It is only now that we are beginning to realise our comparative ignorance of both.
>
> The nineteenth century regarded European civilization as mature and late, the final expression of the human spirit; we are only now beginning to realise that it is young and childish. The race, it seems, is still in its

infancy, and whatever has hitherto been achieved is little more than the advance from crawling to the first few hesitant steps that prelude rather than are walking.

The sense of new beginnings is characteristic not only of contemporary science but of contemporary art. In art, as in science, there is a tendency to break with past traditions and experiment with new methods.

The nineteenth century was the end of an epoch; we, it is increasingly evident, are at the beginning of another.

Joad, GUIDE TO MODERN THOUGHT

This coupling of science with art in the same connection calls up quite another picture of the centuries of science. The result of the division into primary and secondary qualities, first voiced by Galileo, regarded only what was in the strictest sense impersonal as being objective, and all else, insofar as it touched the person directly, as being subjective. Therefore the subject came to be identified with the subjective, even though the subject in man is, in truth, the very guarantor of his free and independent being. Thus art and science, like religion and science, took their separate ways, each offering its own distinct testimony to life.

As noted, 1564 saw the birth of both Galileo and Shakespeare. They could not have been closer contemporaries, yet they represented totally opposite aspects of life as a whole. Galileo, the scientist, set the course for an exploration of the outer world, while Shakespeare, the poet, was a master explorer of man's inner world.

Shakespeare's influence, no less than Galileo's, reaches right into the present time. He leads us from innocent laughter, through sobering moods and gathering glooms into the greater tragedies; but then, by a kind of miracle, he brings us, through the later comedies, to scenes of forgiveness, reconciliation, and renewing love. He carries us from the bournes of death to the restoration of hope, vision, and faith in a future still distant but yet to come.

Conversely science, with all the knowledge and practical benefits it has brought to humanity, has nevertheless estranged us from our innermost being; thereby we suffer a kind of inner death, not to speak of the recent holocausts of outer death. While science was dissecting and vivisecting life in search of its secrets, Shakespeare, through the art of the poet, called on he deeper intuitive faculties to lift Nature to a new grandeur, wonder, and gathering might. Thus does Shakespeare's testimony stand in opposition to that of Galileo, Bacon, Descartes, and those who followed in their wake.

This contrasting picture has progressed through the years. Over against Newton with his law of universal gravitation stood Milton with his PARADISE LOST and PARADISE REGAINED. While Dalton was pronouncing his theory of atoms which has dominated science ever since, came Blake with his four-fold vision, his SONGS OF INNOCENCE and SONGS OF EXPERIENCE, and his PROPHETIC BOOKS. During the early decades of the nineteenth century with technology on the way, Goethe completed FAUST with its final victory over Mephistopheles, the father of lies and minister of darkness and death. In those same decades with materialism gathering force, lived the great romantic poets: young Keats, a worshipper of the sun, Apollo; Shelly with his PROMETHEUS UNBOUND and its final message of Love as the universal liberator of man; Wordsworth living with his 'Immanent Presence' of all things from the daisy up to man; and Coleridge, through whose many often broken utterances there shines the brightest light of all. It is in this same matter-bound nineteenth century that the towering genius of Beethoven created the choral song ending of his Ninth Symphony with its message of love for all mankind which still sings throughout the world. And at the time when materialism was reaching its peak, Wagner produced his PARSIFAL, dispelling doubt and uncertainty, and bringing affirmation of life from an undying source. Nor may we forget Bruckner, with his sacred measures swinging between exhalation and whispering tenderness, while holding increasing numbers spellbound with unspoken hope. Think of Turner, considered among painters as the father of the moderns. Inspired by Goethe, he released colour, in his own work, from its earthboundedness to realms ethereal.

Thus in the nineteenth century with its claims to objectivity, while science was reducing mankind to the status of a mere object in nature, art was revealing man in his moral-aesthetic greatness with unlimited potentials. We have named but a few outstanding figures out of many in the many lands. In the twentieth century prominent scientists wrestle with past and established scientific values, and seek a way from abstract theory to live awareness. On the other hand, art was given to mankind to keep the spirit alive.

The scientists of the nineteenth century were a close knit band, the discoveries and conclusions of the one supplementing and confirming those of the others; this is not so in the twentieth century. It is mainly the biologists, and closely allied with them, the behaviourists, who seem intent on interpreting all life processes in terms of the non-living. By contrast, it is mainly among physicists who have carried the investigation of matter to its furthest limits that the greatest readiness for the institutional evidences of art and religion come closest to reality. There are divided views on almost every issue. Interpretations of what Davenport called the 'essential enigmas — Nature, Man, and God' are in considerable state of flux. The most crucial questions concern the nature and the origin of human consciousness and whether or not mankind has a meaningful participation and contribution in the world existence.

> *Copernicus abolished the primacy of man's planet in the universe, Darwin abolished the primacy of man within his planet, and materialist psychology has abolished the primacy of mind within man.*

> *Thus, in the vast immensities of astronomical space and geological time life seemed like a tiny glow, a feeble and uncertain flicker, destined one day, when the heat of the sun had cooled to such an extent that the earth was no longer able to support life, to be ignominiously snuffed out in the one corner of the universe which had known it.*

> *In every direction the material and the brutal underlies and conditions the vital and spiritual; matter everywhere determines mind, mind nowhere determines matter.*

There follows along this line of thought, the remorseless prognostication:

> *One day, the last man, callous alike to hate and love, will exhale to the unfriendly sky the last human breath, and the globe will go rolling on, bearing with it through the silent fields of space the ashes of humanity, the pictures of Michaelangelo, and the remnants of the Greek marbles frozen to its surface.*

Materialism can hardly come to any other conclusion: In contrast, come the following quotations from the WORLD OF MODERN PHYSICS.

> . . . *we have seen reason to suppose that the world that science studies is not the real world, but a selected or abstracted aspect of something other that underlies it. This 'something other' is not and cannot be known by the methods of science.*
>
> *If we ask, then, how the reality is to be conceived, it is probable that we shall get a number of different answers, varying with the personality of the answerer. It is a mathematician's mind according to Sir James Jeans, a universal mindstuff according to Professor Eddington, an organic unity rather like a person according to Professor Whitehead, a stream of force of life according to Bergson.*
>
> *To this reality, the approach is not through science but through art, through the appreciation of nature, and above all through religion.*

It is worth noting the words *the appreciation of nature*, a term we would never expect to find in any standard textbook.

> . . . *there are avenues for the exploration of the universe other than that of science, notably through the aesthetic, the moral, and the religious consciousness. These avenues are not only as valid as the approach through science, they may even be more important since while, as we have seen, science does not give us information about the reality of things, or rather about the reality behind them, art and religion may do so.*

Joad quotes Schroedinger as saying:

> *In the new universe, it appears, our religious insight is granted as great validity as our scientific insight.*
>
> Joad, GUIDE TO MODERN THOUGHT

Such statements point to a remarkable change of attitude in regard to knowledge and life as a whole. They indicate a dawning sense of something new entering human consciousness which would alter not only the nature of knowledge as hitherto understood but the very art of knowing — a change, in fact, in man himself. They do not pre-suppose a return to past values of a mystical and religious character but rather the rediscovery, in modern forms acceptable to the scientific spirit, of basic realities which underlay them. Goethe comes so close to this that one may again wonder why he is still so little understood. The fact is that Goethe felt himself to be standing within nature, whereas the scientist up to now has held to the attitude of standing as though separate from nature and viewing it from outside. He has constantly forgotten, in his role as onlooker, that he is himself most intimately interwoven with nature and is part of it. Thus he has come to analyse himself, as though he were no more than a complicated piece of matter. Rudolf Steiner emphasized this, for on it depends an important step to be undertaken before we can arrive at an advance in knowledge. That step we need to discover. We cannot become Goethean by imitation or emulation of him, yet we need to study him in order to recognize in him faculties that others need yet to cultivate and acquire.

Therefore, Steiner strives to show how in Goethe the observational and intuitive faculties met directly in his *sinnlich-sittlich* mode of perception. It is this that made Goethe the Galileo of the organic. To apprehend the nature of an organism requires more than the outer sense can tell. This 'more' calls for an act of intuition. For example, the idea of wholeness which to Goethe was so obvious is in itself an intuitive concept: for Goethe this was an immediate part of his knowledge. With the perception and idea of wholeness, we stand within the phenomena: there is then no room for theory. Goethe did not have to labour for this; it was his native born gift. Therefore, Steiner could write of Goethe's view of nature that it *emanated from his personality, none else could have achieved it.*

It is just this particular ability which causes difficulty in his being accepted. The scientist is accustomed to moving between fact and theory as two separate components of knowledge which he then seeks to knit together; Goethe's claim to an integral, intuitive, and immediate knowledge must seem subjective, unsubstantiated, and unproven just because it appears to be inseparable from his personality. For Goethe, to stand not within but outside the phenomenon, and theorize about it eliminates the actual experience of it, this he regarded as subjective and unreal. We are reminded in this of Jean's *subjective mental constructs*. To reach Goethe, the poet-scientist, and consider what he represents seriously, calls for a definite step to be taken, a re-education of what we are, by awakening something of the intuitive artist which is latent in everyone. Goethe stands before us as a phenomena which engages us and which we may not pass by.

The uniqueness of Goethe's personality was evidenced very early in his life. At the age of six he heard from Old Testament stories of altars being raised to God. He resolved that he, too, would raise an altar to God. He rose very early one morning and set about assembling what he needed. His father had a music stand with a pyramidal top for part playing. On the sides of this Goethe arranged various natural objects from his own collection. This he surmounted with a small enamel dish into which he placed some fumigating pastilles. The sun had by then risen but was obscured by some buildings to the east. As soon as it rose above them, with the aid of a burning glass, he focused its light on to the pastilles with the desired effect. The act of devotion was now complete and perfect. Unknown to the child in this act, scientist, artist, and priest had met. In total simplicity he had mediated between God and Nature. We have here a first glimpse of Goethe's undivided, or better said, his unified nature which remained with him all his life.

It is not surprising to learn of his distress on meeting the phrase, *Nature conceals God* in a treatise written by someone whom he had greatly respected. His immediate response was :

> *My pure, profound, and practical mode of conception had taught me to see God within Nature and Nature within God inviolably; it had constituted the basis of my whole existence.*

The following are Steiner's comments:

> *Goethe's mode of perception afforded him the certainty that he experienced Eternal Law in the penetration of Nature with Ideas, and Eternal Law for him is identical with the Divine.*

> *Goethe felt himself at one with Nature and creating as part of her being.*

> *He did not want to connect one thought with another in a merely logical sense. Such an activity of thought seemed to him rather to depart from reality. He felt he must sink his spirit in the experience in order to reach the ideas. The mutual interplay of idea and perception was for Goethe a spiritual breathing.*

Such an expression as sinking the spirit in the experience in order to reach the ideas is to be taken quite literally. Thus, Goethe himself writes:

> *Nature proceeds according to ideas in the same way that man follows an idea in all that he undertakes.*

What then are ideas, whence do they arise, and how are we related to them? Without ideas we remain unenlightened, we remain in the dark. In contemplating an outer phenomenon, do the ideas that light up for us derive from the phenomenon of which they are intrinsically a part, activating, shaping, determining what we outwardly see or do they merely arise within the mind in what is otherwise a mind-less nature? Is intelligence, a thinking consciousness, a life in ideas, confined to man alone, and all else proceeds merely by causal law? This, for Steiner, touches the very core of the mystery of man's being and his life on earth. Man, by exercising his ideas, can alter the con-ditions of nature, but he cannot transcend them. Whence come those ideas which are in no way connected with outer phenomena? Do they derive from a creative source within man himself? Whence do the ideas arise which lead to the art, aesthetics, and religion which some scientists begin to regard as realities lying beyond the scope of science? Steiner is greatly occupied with this question of the life of ideas, a question which hardly concerned Goethe for he took his thought life, like his perceptual life, for granted; but it must concern the man of today who is obliged to question the validity of his ideas.

> When man really succeeds in rising to the idea and in comprehending from out of the idea the details of perception, he accomplishes the same thing as Nature accomplishes by allowing the creations to come forth from the mysterious Whole.

According to this, far from being a mere onlooker, man, through his life in ideas, is an integral part of Nature, fulfilling his own role according to her laws. The following passage enlarges further on man's role as part of Nature.

> So long as one has no sense of the working and of the creative activity of the idea, his thinking is divorced from living Nature. But directly he senses the way in which the idea lives and is active in his inner being, he regards himself and Nature as one Whole, and what makes its appearance in his inner being as a subjective element is for him at the same time objective; he knows that he no longer confronts Nature as a stranger. but he feels that he has grown together with the whole of her. The subjective has become the objective; the objective is wholly perme-ated with the spirit.

> The cognitive faculty appears to man as subjective only as long as he does not notice that it is Nature herself who appears through this faculty.

> Subjective and objective meet when the objective world of ideas lives in the subject, and when all that is active in Nature herself lives in the

spirit of man. When this happens all antithesis between subject and object ceases.

The significance of this statement can hardly be overestimated. It leads to the surmounting of the rift between subject and object, mind and body, faith and science, created by Galileo, Descartes, and Bacon respectively; the abyss between self and world that has dominated thinking since their time. It becomes clear that it is not nature that cut man off but that it is a man who cut himself off from nature thereby becoming a stranger not only to nature but to himself. It is man himself who created the unreal fable of the thinking mind in a mindless world.

In the old microcosmic-macrocosmic teaching, man felt himself central in the world process, therefore directly related from within himself to everything that met him both from inner and from outer sources; and life had meaning.

For St. Thomas Aquinas, Reason ascending from below and Revelation descending from above met in man. He thus stood central in all respects between God and Nature and all things had their meaning. Then man in his inwardness was set aside, was decentred, to become both the master and the slave of matter divorced from himself. Life then lost all its intrinsic meaning. Yet, by the law of contrasts, it is in the dark hour that we discover a new groping for an abiding and meaningful reality.

Into this world Goethe appeared as one before his time, transcending all sense of isolation and separateness from the world, confident in thought and deed of being central in the world creative process. His archetypal plant is not something he added to nature. In his apprehension of it, it was nature declaring herself not merely to him but in him.

But the twentieth-century man, in his mental isolation from all that transpires within and around him, is trying to piece his world together with abstract theories which he cannot immediately grasp and understand. With a science built on the inert and lifeless, on physical causation and deterministic principles, he remains remote from the world and from himself. This remoteness from which he

suffers, and which robs him of all meaningful goals, he must overcome. He has to take a step in freedom beyond that which Goethe
had to offer. Joad's three dethronements, the earth in the heavens,
man on the earth, and mind in man, were not problems for Goethe;
he was secure in his grasp of unity and wholeness, but for the scientist of today, they offer the greatest problems.

The following statement by Goethe reveals his position:

I have been clever, but I have never thought about thought.

Steiner comments on this :

*For the very reason that Goethe's thinking was entirely filled with
objects he perceived, because his thinking was filled with objects he perceived, because his thinking was a perception, his perception a thinking,
he could not come to the point of perceiving thought itself as a thought.*

The term Steiner uses is not <u>did not</u> but <u>could not</u>, and he adds the
very decisive words:

*But the idea of freedom is only obtained through the perception of
thought.*

From this point on, Davenport's statement that Goethe and Steiner
are *so closely bound together in their thinking that they can virtually be
viewed as one* cannot be taken as wholly true. Steiner has particularly to do with the art of thinking, and with thinking as a path to
inner freedom. For Steiner, the crucial problem of today is that of
freedom, whereas we are caught and surrounded unceasingly by
conditions of un-freedom.

Is it possible that Goethe, with all his greatness, in some way fell
short of the modern idea of freedom and that this is left to the
twentieth century man to discover?

Goethe lived with an abundance of riches. His writings contain
countless truths which others treasure and to which Steiner made
reference all his life. It is as though all this was given Goethe. By
comparison, modern man, with all his triumphs in the technological field, stands in a state of inner poverty, as though bereft and
shackled. Science has set its seal on every aspect of practical life
today, yet all the while releasing powers which result in growing
un-freedom for humanity.

Goethe, the Galileo of the organic, has opened up for us a world of new possibilities but he cannot directly help us, though humanity has never been in more desperate need of help in this respect than we are today.

> *If I know my relationship to myself and to the external world, I call it truth. And so, each one can have his open truth, and it is nevertheless always the same.*

But what if one is quite uncertain in regard to the relationship of oneself and to the external world?

> *For Goethe truth is not a rigid system of concepts that is only capable of assuming one rigid form. . . . He wants living concepts by means of which the spirit of the single man can connect the perceptions together in accordance with his individual nature. To know the truth, means for Goethe to live in the truth. And to live in the truth means nothing else than that in the consideration of each single object man perceives what particular inner experience comes into play when he confronts the object.*

This holds true for someone who can confront an object or a phenomenon with a mind totally free from preconceived notions or theories, that is to say, with a childlike open-mindedness. It is only then that new discoveries can be made, but so often it is theory that blinds the free seeing. That is why Goethe was opposed to theoretical dissertations.

> *Let no man seek behind the phenomena for they themselves are all the doctrine.*

And Steiner adds:

> *Goethe is convinced that in this world of ideas man has direct experience of the mode of action or the creative being Nature.*

But what if one lacks this conviction which for Goethe is part of his nature? For example, in his ITALIAN JOURNEY, he wrote:

> *The conception that a living being is produced from outside for certain extraneous ends, and that its form is determined by a purposeful, primeval force, has already delayed us many centuries in the philosophical consideration of Nature, and still holds us back. It is, if one may so express it, a paltry way of thinking, which, like all paltry things, is paltry just because it is convenient and sufficient for human nature in general.*

What Lamarck and Darwin had to say later would for Goethe have been mere theories, external to and by no means born from within the phenomena; both were alike blind to the actual truth, the direct perception of the creative idea, the ideal image actively shaping and determining what meets the outer eye. That, for him, was not living in the truth.

But what if one is constituted so that one knows 'the idea' only as a notion in one's own mind which one then tries to corroborate by reference to the outer phenomena? Is that not the way that the whole of our science has been built up, the theories shifting with each new observation?

For Goethe the idea was the prime, the Ur-phenomena, for example, the archetypal, the Ur-plant, a living idea, a formative force, at the heart and centre of the plant kingdom, and that each single plant from the most perfect to the most simple, had a direct relationship to it. The modern scientist would never claim that his idea is more than a theory, a hypothesis, whereas with Goethe the idea grew to an inner certainty which, once perceived, could never be refuted. It is Goethe's claim to irrefutability that makes the scientist of today hold him at bay.

> But nor does Goethe in his contemplation of form call upon a purposive Creative Being who determined from the outset what the form should be in order to fulfill certain pre-ordained conditions.

Goethe was first and foremost a morphologist.

> Goethe's aim is not to explain Nature by the intention of some supernatural being, but out of the internal formative law. An individual organic form arises because the archetypal plant or animal assumes a definite form in a special case. This form must be of such a kind that it is able to live in the conditions surrounding it.

Heredity and environment are clearly part of the conditions but, for Goethe, they could never be the final determining factors, least of all in connection with the human being in whom Nature transcends her outer limitations for new works of inner creation. Faust is subject to outer conditions but these alone could never determine Faust. Here one sees at once how for Goethe art and nature follow similar laws so that he could very well say with equal certainty of both *This is Necessity; this is God*. In the idea, ruling in the one and in the other, a universal law reveals itself. This universal law will best reveal itself in that which is most perfect in nature as also in man. Hence Goethe took the most perfect in any given sphere as the measure for the less perfect in that sphere, the highest plant, as best revealing where the lesser plant stopped short — a method of approach which is the very opposite to what is customary today. Goethe's method is to proceed from the whole to the part, where the accepted method today is to begin with the smallest possible element or component and then to seek to construct the whole. This mechanistic method may serve for the machine but breaks down completely before the wholeness of an organism.

Only now is the fallacy of applying mechanistic thinking to organic life being increasingly recognized. In Goethe's view the ideal form is fully present though invisibly or ideally in the seed; it then grows to visibility in the process of developing the final form of the plant. The inwardly perceived idea *(sittlich)* and the outwardly observed object *(sinnlich)* meet in the human act of consciousness and this meeting can only occur in man. This uniting of the idea with the precept to arrive at the whole is left to each individual to achieve for himself and thus in freedom. It is here, with this act of cognition, that human freedom begins. This train of thought brings us to this central point, at which, in a manner that is appropriate for the present time, man may once again feel himself centred in himself and therefore also in life as a whole — the point where the distinction between the subjective and the objective falls away. This provides the starting point for arriving by conscious effort at the experience of unity and wholeness which Goethe already possessed but which he did not fully penetrate with his thinking. Just because it came to him as a gift, it fell short of the final experience of freedom.

The period between the time of Goethe who died in 1832, and entry into the twentieth century was one of most rapid development both in the outer conditions of life and in terms of human outlook. Goethe lived to see the release of steam power and with it the commencement of the age of technology, which from then on was spread throughout the world. With the arrival of electric power came an immense expansion of industrial and economic enterprises. All the means of communication across the earth speeded up and at the same time broadened greatly the gap between the wealthy and the poor. Here was the incentive for Marx's DAS KAPITAL, with its far-reaching revolutionary consequences reaching right through to the era of twentieth century dictatorship. Concurrently the no less revolutionary Darwinian doctrine of evolution, based on chance variations and the struggle for existence was supported by the findings of the new contemporary sciences of geology and embryology. This view of animal ancestry, with the discovery of hypnosis, gave rise to the exploration into the subconscious and the birth of psychoanalysis. Pavlov followed with his experiments on dogs leading to the behaviourist theory of the conditioned reflex. Thus, stage by stage, every vestige of human moral independence was eroded away.

To all this was added the discovery of the spectroscope and the projection of terrestrial materialist conceptions into the heavens. Then came the discovery of the electron and radio-activity leading in the direction of the theoretical dissolution of matter. While the concept of the atom changed, the atomistic mode of thinking continued. With the establishment of the electromagnetic field and the wave theory of light, the ground was prepared for Einstein to launch his theory of relativity with the consequent abolition of the securely grounded norms of space, time, and gravity. And out of all this came the startling new quantum physics giving rise to a newly conceived non-Newtonian universe, referred to as 'the new universe.'

How immeasurably removed all this is from the mind of Goethe with its complete certainty of Nature in God and God in Nature and Man at one with both! Steiner, living from 1861 to 1925, had confronted all the above changes. While he was elucidating the work of Goethe and the creative character of his thinking and his discoveries, Steiner was having to address a type of mind totally divorced from any such considerations. He saw that human freedom, inner and outer, was completely at stake and that, if humanity failed to discover the true sources of inner freedom, life could only deteriorate into social, political, economic, and moral disaster.

Inner freedom requires first and foremost the ability to grow free from oneself. Goethe with his unified nature never had that problem. Living as he did in nature and in his own creative work, he felt at one with nature and with God. He never experienced separateness from Aquinas' NATURE, MAN, AND GOD. Reason and Faith held an inborn meaning for him without which he could never have achieved his FAUST who was destined to succeed from the start. Therefore, feeling centred in his life in ideas and in his life of observation or perception, he had no need to separate his thinking as an object of perception in itself.

For the twentieth-century man, the situation was quite different. For him it was not even sufficient just to think about thought, which Goethe actually did not do. He needed to <u>perceive</u> the process of his thinking and how his life in ideas entered into consciousness. He as subject had to become objective to his own so-called subjective life of ideas. He had to adopt a position where the idea that arose in him itself became an object of perception. This he could achieve only in an act of freedom where no outer cause could prevail. All that was left man when all else was taken from him was his capacity for thinking. Thus Steiner focuses on the activity of thought as offering the only way to freedom. In his discovery of himself in inner freedom man restores meaning to life. The rediscovery of meaning becomes also the rediscovery of man.

Steiner leads us to this central point of experience — the idea as object of perception.

> *Man has no participation into the coming into existence of all other perceptions. The idea of these perceptions come to light within him. The ideas, however, would not be there if the productive power to bring them to manifestation did not exist within us. The ideas may be in truth the content of what is working in the objects, but they come to evident existence as a result of the activity of man. <u>Therefore, man can only cognize the essential nature of the world when he perceives his own activity.</u>*

This is the cardinal point on which all else depends. It might also by described as the eye of the needle through which we pass from mere outer speculation to inner certainty.

> *In every other perception he does nothing more than penetrate the idea in operation; the object in which it is operating remains as perception outside his mind.*

In the perception of the idea, the operating activity and what it has brought about are contained in his inner being. He has the whole process completely within him. The perception no longer seems to have been generated by the idea; the perception is the idea.

The man who perceives this self production activity has the feeling of freedom.

This is the inception of an activity which can only arise within humanity. Mankind stands in the world and is part of the world. In this life in ideas one manifests ones own unique contribution within the world process. From this point, one can relate oneself to every single object, fact, and event that meets us. In this experience, one is beholden to no one but oneself. Here, in mankind, subject and object meet. Steiner calls this the highest metamorphosis that can take place for humanity.

As soon as man attains to the highest metamorphosis he moves with certainty in the realm of things. At the central point of his personality he has attained the true point of departure for all observation of the world. He will no longer seek for unknown principles, for causes that lie outside himself, he knows that the highest experience of which he is capable consists in the self-contemplation of his own being.

This is not to be confused with any kind of introspection which is merely becoming engrossed in oneself. That would be becoming lost to the world. Here is meant the very opposite, the contemplation of what man is as man, a wholly objective contemplation which reaches out equally to every human being and to all humanity.

Those who are wholly permeated by the feeling which this evokes, will attain the truest relationship to things. Where this is not the case man must seek for the higher form of existence elsewhere, and since it is not to be discovered in experience, they will conjecture that it lies in an unknown region of reality. An element of uncertainty will make its appearance in their observation; in answering the question which nature puts to them they will perpetually plead the unfathomable.

Consider again Goethe's statement:

I have never thought about thought.

Now Steiner's answering statement:

But the idea of freedom is only obtained through the perception of thought.

Are we then to infer that Goethe was not in the full sense free?

Because, however, the direct perception of the most inward experience eluded him, he groped insecurely around these limits. For this reason he says that man is not born 'to solve the problems of the universe, but to seek where the problem commences and then to keep the boundary of the comprehensible.' Instead of penetrating right through experience in the consciousness that the true has only meaning to the extent to which it is demanded by the nature of man, he came to the conclusion that 'a higher influence favours the constant, the active, the rational, the ordered and the ordering, the human and the pious' and that 'the moral world order' manifests in the greatest beauty where it 'comes indirectly to the assistance of the good, the valiant sufferer.'

Because Goethe did not know the most inward human experience, it was impossible for him to attain to the ultimate thoughts concerning the moral World order which essentially belongs to the contemplation of Nature. The ideas of things are the content of the active creative elements in them. Man experiences moral ideas directly in the form of ideas. A man who is able to experience how in perception of the world of ideas, the ideal itself becomes self-contained, filled with itself, is also able to experience how the moral element is produced within the nature of man.

In the idea of things man stands centrally in the world of nature and that of which he is part declares itself in him as the idea; so, the moral idea also arises within him. Thus he may know himself centrally in the realm of morality, at one with it, therefore the moral idea is equally a manifestation of himself, and of his own moral being. He does not need to ascribe the moral to a world order that exists apart from himself. In so far as the moral idea arises within him, he _is_ that moral world order. To use other terms, it is not God declaring himself as an outer being but God declaring himself from within man, being part of that being. That mankind has moral ideas reveals that we are a part of a moral world order.

A man who knows the ideas of Nature only in relationship to the world of perceptions will want to relate moral concepts also to something external to them. He will seek a reality for these concepts similar to the reality that exists for concepts that have been acquired from experience. A man, however, who is able to perceive ideas in their own proper essence will be aware that in the case of moral ideas nothing external corresponds to them, that they are produced directly in spiritual experience as ideas.

They work on man as moral powers by virtue of their own content only. . . . Man himself has brought them forth and he loves them as he loves his children. Love is the motive power of action. Spiritual delight in one's own production is the source of the moral.

The implication of this is of great importance. In the case of the outer phenomenon, we do not need to seek behind the phenomenon to explain it. The phenomenon is the bearer of its own doctrine revealed in the operative idea. The moral idea arising within man carries its own substance and reality and does not need a *deus ex machina* to explain it. If the moral idea is not truly self-born in its total character as man perceives it, if he has to derive it from some other source outside himself, then he is subject to an authority outside him, and therefore he is not free.

There are men who are incapable of giving birth to moral ideas. They assimilate those of other men through tradition. And if they have no perceptual feeling for ideas per se, they do not recognize the source of the moral that can be experienced within the mind. They seek that source in a superhuman will that lives outside them. Or they believe that outside that physical world which is experienced by man there exists an objective Moral World Order whence the moral ideas are derived.

In other words, we forsake the realm of self-born knowledge for one of assimilated belief. In the following passage by Goethe one sees that because he did not confront the innermost fact of human experience, where the idea is born as a wholly free creation, he addressed himself to a world or a being transcending the independence of experience.

However strongly the earth with its thousands upon thousands of phenomena attracts man, he will raise his gaze with longing to the heavens because he feels deeply and vividly within himself that he is a citizen of the spiritual realm the belief in which we can neither reject nor surrender.

There is a thus a note of resignation that we cannot achieve the highest.

That which defies solution we leave with God as the All-determinant, All-liberating being.

The difference between Goethe and Steiner is aptly expressed in the following.

Goethe:

> *Man knows himself only to the extent that he knows the world. Every fresh object, contemplated with deliberation, opens up a new faculty within us.*

Steiner:

> *The truth is exactly the reverse, man knows the world to the extent to which he knows himself.*

Our quest is to interpret Steiner's phrase <u>an advance in knowledge</u>, one that can restore meaning to life and foster a new faith for the future.

> *The will to know is a demand of human nature and not of the objects. They can impart no more of their being than he demands from them. . . . Man only knows that there exists something more in the things than perception gives because this other element lives in his inner being.*

Thus world knowledge and self-knowledge are inseparable. Today mankind has accepted a world knowledge divorced from man and a human knowledge without the human. Our task must be to reinstate mind in man, man in his true stature, and the earth in her rightful place in the heavens.

With the rise of scientific materialism, the divine world order withdrew from human consciousness, so if one begins within human consciousness, by penetrating to the <u>reality of the idea</u>, the way opens via man himself for the rediscovery of what in truth sustains him and his world.

> *That which man can otherwise only speak of as unfathomable, impenetrable, divine, appears before him in its true form in self-perception. Because in self-perception he sees the ideal in direct form, he acquires the power and faculty to seek for and recognize this ideal element in all outer phenomena also, in the whole of nature.*

> *A man who has experienced the flash of self-perception does not any longer set out in quest of a 'hidden' God behind the phenomena; he apprehends the divine in its different metamorphoses <u>within Nature</u>.*

> *The spirit of man knows that in its inner being there works, as in its own will, the motive power that brings forth all things, and that the highest moral decisions lie within itself.*

> *Man may be conscious of limitations in regard to a particular thing,*

may be dependent on a thousand others, but on the whole he sets his own moral goal and moral direction.

The operative element of all other things is manifested in man as idea; the operative element in man is the idea which he himself brings forth. The process that takes place in Nature as a whole is accomplished in each single human individuality; it is the creation of an actuality from out of the idea, man himself being the creator. For at the basis of his personality, there lives the idea which imparts content to itself.

Goethe:

Nature in her creation is so bounteous that after multifarious plant forms she makes one wherein all others are contained, after multifarious animals one being who contains them all — Man.

Here Goethe's intuitions are at their noblest and best, but, in terms of knowledge and the idea as the veritable spiritual seed throughout creation, Steiner takes us one step further.

Nature is so mighty in her creation that she repeats in each individual human being the process by means of which she brings forth all creatures directly out of the idea, inasmuch as moral acts spring from the <u>ideal</u>* *basis of personality.*

Elsewhere Rudolf Steiner has expressed this differently: the universe is the riddle that confronts man, and man himself is the key.

---

* N.B. the word 'ideal' as used here is not meant as idealistic, but simply as idea.

· 25 ·

A Philosophy of Freedom

THE BASIS FOR A MODERN WORLD CONCEPTION

Rudolf Steiner has been introduced mainly as Goethe's interpreter. Of Goethe, he wrote:

When he observed Nature, the ideas lay before him.

Consider Goethe's own words:

I have never thought about thought,

This evoked the comment:

*But the idea of freedom can only be attained through the perception of
thought.*

Steiner relates how, at the age of nine or ten, he saw in his teacher's
office at the elementary school, a book entitled GEOMETRY which he
was allowed to borrow. He describes how, for weeks on end, his
mind was . . .

*filled with the coincidence, the similarity of triangles, squares, poly-
gons. I racked my brain over the question: where do parallel lines actually meet? The theorem of Pythagoras fascinated me.*

Much later in life he recalled his reflections:

*That one can live within the mind in the shaping of forms perceived only
in oneself, entirely without impression upon the external senses, became*

for me the deepest satisfaction, I found in this a solace for the unhappiness which my unanswered questions had caused me. To be able to lay hold on something in the spirit alone brought me an inner joy. I am sure that I learned though geometry to know happiness for the first time.

In my relation to geometry I must perceive the first budding form of a conception which later gradually evolved within me. This lived within me more or less unconsciously during my childhood, and about my twentieth year took a definite and fully conscious form.

I said to myself: The objects and occurrences which the senses perceive are in space. But just as this space is outside man, so there exists within man, a sort of soul-space which is the scene of action of spiritual beings and occurrences.

I could not look upon thoughts as something like images which the human being forms of things: on the contrary, I saw in them revelations of a spiritual world on the field of action of the soul. Geometry seemed to me to be a knowledge which appears to be produced by man, but with nevertheless has a significance quite independent of him. Naturally, I did not as a child say this to myself distinctly, but I felt that one must carry knowledge of the spiritual world within oneself in the manner of geometry. For the reality of the spiritual world was to me as certain as the physical.

He had to confirm for himself that this inner world was as real as was the outer world.

I wished to say to myself that the experience of the spiritual world is just as little an illusion as is that of the physical world.

Steiner next tells of a priest, whom he learned to love, when he came to the school twice a week for religious instruction. One day he gathered some of the children round him and launched onto an account of the Copernican system:

... the revolution of the earth around the sun its rotation round its axis, the inclination of the axis, about summer and winter, as well as the zones of the earth. In all of this I was completely absorbed; I made similar drawings for days together, and then received from the priest special instruction about eclipse of sun and moon. Thenceforth, I directed my craving for knowledge towards this subject.

He had still another connection with this priest.

We school boys had to perform the duties of ministrants an choristers during Mass, rites for the dead, and funerals. The solemnity of the Latin language and the liturgy were things in which my boyish soul found a vital happiness. . . . The instruction in the Bible and the catechism imparted by the priest had far less effect upon my inner world than what he accomplished as celebrant of the cultus in mediating between the sensible and the supersensible world. From the first all this was for me no mere form, but a profound experience.

There is a kind of riddle which recurs at different stages in Rudolf Steiner's growing years. Imagine it this way. One is standing within the spiritual world. One's experiences in that world are self evident to oneself. This inner spiritual world and the outer world of nature both present realities which must be most intimately connected. What is there in the outer world to confirm the validity of the experiences of this inner world? The attention focuses on thinking. If one can develop a thinking which penetrates to the inner reality that lives in outer nature that same thinking should be capable of grasping the nature of the experience in the spiritual world. Time and again one is brought back to the essential nature of pure thinking — a thinking that is stripped of all externals, as in the pure thinking of geometry. This is how the problem presented itself to Steiner as a lad of fourteen.

I said it myself that it is possible after all to come to an understanding of the experience of the spiritual world through one's own soul only if one's process of thinking itself has reached such a form that it can attain to the reality of being which is in the phenomena of nature.

Once one has realised that thinking is itself a spiritual activity and therefore should be able to take hold of spiritual reality, the problem begins to resolve itself. He seeks the outer to confirm the inner, what he perceives in nature to confirm what he beholds in the spirit.

It was just at this point that, passing by a book shop, Steiner saw in the window a copy of Kant's CRITIQUE OF PURE REASON. He gathered up his very few pennies to procure it. *Many a page I read more than twenty times.* It was an exercise for him onto the nature of thinking.

I wished to build up thought within myself in such a way that every thought should be completely subject to survey, that no vague feeling should incline the thought in any direction whatever.

I wished to establish within myself a harmony between such thinking and the teaching of religion. For this also at that time had the strongest hold upon me. In this field we had excellent textbooks. From these books I took with the utmost devotion the system of dogmas and symbols, the description of the Church liturgy, the history of the Church, These teachings were to me a <u>vital matter</u>. But my relation to them was determined by the fact that for me the spiritual world counted among the contents of human perception. The very reason why these teachings penetrated so deeply into my mind was that in them I realised how the human spirit can find its way knowingly into the supersensible.

He pursued his study of Kant and added Fichte.

I now worked more consciously to the end that I might mould into forms of <u>thought</u> the immediate <u>perception</u> of the spiritual world which I possessed.

During his first year at college Karl Julius Schroer who became a great influence in his life was lecturing on Goethe and Schiller. *From the very first lecture he captivated me.* He had to deliver a discourse under Schroer and selected as his theme, *To what extent in his actions is man a free being.* When not tutoring or attending classes he spent time in the library.

There for the first time I then read Goethe's <u>Faust</u>. In fact, until my nineteenth year, when I was inspired by Schroer, I had never gone as far as this work.

His college studies continued congruent to his private explorations in philosophy.

I had to study mathematics and natural science. I was convinced that I should find no relation with them unless I could place their findings upon a solid foundation of philosophy. But I beheld a spiritual world <u>as reality</u>. In perfectly clear vision the spiritual individuality of everyone was manifest to me. This had in the physical world its expression. It united itself with that what came as a physical germ from the parents. The dead human being I followed in his way into the spiritual world.

After the death of a schoolmate, I wrote about this phase of my spiritual life to one of my former teachers who had continued to be a close friend after my Realschule days. He wrote back to me with unusual affection, but he did not deign to say one word about what I had written regarding the dead schoolmate. And this is what happened to me always in this matter of my perspective of the spiritual world. No one would pay any attention to it.

It was at this time, as though in compensation, that Steiner became acquainted with . . .

> *a simple man of the people. Every week he went to Vienna by the same train that I took. He gathered medicinal plants in the country and sold them to apothecaries in Vienna. We became fast friends. With him it was possible to look deeply into the mysteries of nature. He carried on his back his bundle of medicinal plants, but in his heart he bore the findings which he had won from the spirituality of nature in the gathering of these herbs.*

Steiner's studies and researches went on.

> *The life of thought came gradually to seem to me the reflection radiated into the physical human being of what the soul experiences in the spiritual world. Thought-experience was for me existence in a reality which — as something actually experienced through and through — doubt dared not approach.*

> *Is this world, then, a reality complete in itself? When the human being weaves thought in connection with it which brings light into the world of the senses, is he actually bringing into this world of the senses, something which is foreign to it? This certainly does not at all accord with the experience that we have when we confront the world of the senses and break into it by means of thoughts. Thought then surely appears to be that by means of which the world of the senses expresses <u>its own nature</u>.*

In this connection there ever and again recurs the question of the special place which mathematics has in human thinking.

> *Mathematics retained its importance for me as the foundation also under my whole striving for knowledge. For mathematics provides a system of precepts and concepts which have been arrived at independently of any external sense impression. . . . Through mathematics one learns to know the world, and yet, in order to do this, it is necessary first to evoke mathematics out of the human mind.*

Precisely out of the sphere of mathematics, there came to him a totally new experience.

> *Through the more recent synthetic lectures and by private study, there came into my mind the perception that a line prolonged infinitely toward the right hand would return again from the left to its starting point. The infinitely distant point on the right is the same as the point infinitely distant on the left.*

It occurred to me that by means of such conceptions of the more recent geometry it might be possible to form a conception of space, which otherwise remained fixed in a void. The straight line returning on itself like a circle seemed to me to be a revelation. I left the lecture at which this had first passed before my mind as if a great load had fallen from me. A feeling of liberation came over me. Again, as in my early boyhood, something joy-bestowing had come to me out of geometry.

This raised the problem of time. This was to find its answer later in Steiner's new approach to the question of reincarnation:

The receding past meets once again, transformed into the approaching future. Thereby past and future, like space, are raised out of fixity to appear as an evolving life reality.

He makes the following important comment in regard to his studies:

I may state that I never permitted my insights into the spiritual to become a disturbing factor while engaged in the endeavour to learn the sciences as they were then developed. I applied myself to what was taught, and only in the background of my mind did I have the hope that some day the blending of natural science with the science of the spirit would result for me.

The crucial question in all Steiner's early studies and researches was contingent upon what he could find in the world of outer culture to give support to his life of inner experience. He found this rested in the relationship of a man to his thinking.

I was deeply stirred by the reading of Schiller's letters concerning the aesthetic education of man. The reference to the fact that human consciousness oscillates between different states afforded me a connection with the pictures I had formed of the inner working and weaving of the human soul.

. . . not only in thoughts which reproduce external things and occurrences, but thoughts that he experiences as thoughts in themselves. This living in thoughts revealed itself to me as quite different from that in which the human being ordinarily exists and also carries on ordinary scientific research. If one penetrates deeper and deeper into thought experience one finds that spiritual reality comes to meet this thought experience.

In ordinary consciousness we have . . .

on the one hand, the living quality of sense-perception, on the other, the abstractness of thought-perceiving. Spiritual vision perceives spirit as the senses perceive nature; but it does not stand apart in the thinking from the spiritual percept as the ordinary consciousness stands in its thinking apart from the sense-percept. On the contrary, spiritual vision thinks while it experiences spirit, and experiences while it sets to thinking the awakened spirituality in man.

This outlines Steiner's progress in his own words through childhood, youth, and into early adult life. One may see it as a continuous process of penetration down into the physical sense-perception as this lies in others. He had reached a point in his own experiences where there needed to be no contradiction between the spiritual and the physical; yet how was he to bring this to others?

Of his intimate friendships, there was no one with whom he could share what really lived for him. He met a great variety of people, but ever in inner loneliness. Within the thinking life as this met him, the great exception lay in the geometry. Here was thinking crystal clear, self-sustained, free of the physical senses, and also of everything personal and subjective. This was to be the pattern on which to frame his thoughts about the spiritual in a way that others might freely apprehend.

Steiner's work was far removed from the merely visionary; it was instead a matter of long and arduous spiritual research. Like all research it called for reticence until such time as it reached a certain degree of completion and there was a suitable public to which to communicate it.

At the beginning it became clear to me that in the portion of the human organization in which the formation is directed chiefly to the nerves and the senses, the sensible-supersensible form stamps itself most strongly upon the sense-perceptible. The head organization appeared to me as that in which the sensible-supersensible also becomes most strongly manifest in the sensible form. On the other hand, I was forced to look upon the organization consisting of the limbs as that in which the sensible supersensible, most completely conceals itself, so that in this organization the forces acting in nature external to man continue their work in the shaping of the human body. Between there two poles of the human organization everything seemed to me to exist which expresses itself in a rhythmic way, the processes of breathing, circulation, and the like.

At the time I found no one to whom I could have spoken of these perceptions. If I intimated here or there something about them, they were looked upon at once as the result of a philosophical idea, whereas I was

certain that they were disclosed to me out of anatomical and physiolog-
ical empirical knowledge free of pre-conceptions.

It is difficult to imagine the degree of suffering in being perpetually incomprehensible or misunderstood.

> *For the soul-depressing mood which grew out of the isolation in the*
> *matter of my perceptions, I found inner release only when I read again*
> *and again the conversation that Goethe had with Schiller as the two*
> *went away from a meeting of the Society of Scientific Research in Jena.*

This conversation Steiner often quoted. They had heard a lecture
on botany and were both in disagreement with it. Goethe drew a
sketch of what was intended to represent the archetypal plant, an
entity seen in leaf, in blossom, in the separate details but 'not seen'
to the outer eye in its wholeness — a sensible-supersensible,
sinnlich-sittlich form. Schiller, still under the influence of Kantian
dualism could only see Goethe's 'whole' as an 'idea' arrived at by
the reasoning mind but not an actuality.

> *Goethe would not allow this to pass. He 'saw' the whole spiritually as*
> *he saw the group of details with his senses, and he admitted no differ-*
> *ence in principle between the spiritual and the sensible perception, but*
> *only a transition from one to the other. To him it was clear that both had*
> *a right to a place in empirical reality. Schiller, however, did not cease to*
> *maintain that the archetypal plant was no experience but an idea.*
> *Goethe then replied on the basis of his thinking, that in case he saw the*
> *idea before him with this eyes.*

> *I derived comfort after a long struggle of the mind from what came to*
> *me out of the understanding of these words of Goethe, to which I felt*
> *that I had penetrated. Goethe's way of viewing nature appeared to me as*
> *in keeping with spirit.*

> *Impelled now by the inner necessity, I had to study in detail, all of*
> *Goethe's scientific writings.*

In 1884, on the recommendation of Schroer, Steiner received an
invitation from Joseph Kurchner *to edit Goethe's scientific writings*
with introductions and running explanatory comments. This was to be
part of an edition of German National Literature, a standard edition in five volumes.

For a brief time he was editor of a weekly newspaper, and this
brought him *into rather close relations with persons whose activities had*

to do with the most various phases of public life. This caused him to study Karl Marx, Friedrich Engels, Robertus, and other writers on social economics.

> *To none of these could I gain inner relation. It was a matter of personal distress to me to hear that the material economic forces in human history carry forward man's real evolution, and that the spiritual world is only a superstructure in ideas over this substructure of the 'truly real.' I knew the reality of the spiritual. The assertions of the theorizing Socialists meant for me the closing of men's eyes to genuine reality.*

> *In this connection, however, it became clear to me that the 'social question' itself was of immense importance. But it seemed to me the tragedy of the times that this question was dealt with by persons wholly possessed by the materialism of contemporary civilization. It was my conviction that just this question could be rightly put only from the standpoint of a spiritual world view.*

His editorship of this paper ended through a financial controversy between its owner and its founder.

> *Thus as a young man of twenty-seven I was filled with 'questions' and 'riddles' regarding the outer life of humanity, whereas the nature of the soul and its relation with the spiritual world had presented itself before my inner being in a perception completes in itself, taking on more and more definite forms. And this work took increasingly the direction which some years later led to the composition of* The Philosophy of Freedom.

In 1888 he was invited to contribute to an Weimar edition of Goethe's other scientific writings which lay in the archives there. This led to his first visit to Germany and particularly to Weimar.

> *My sojourn for some weeks in Goethe's city was a festival time in my life. For years I had lived in the thoughts of Goethe; now I was permitted to be in the places where these thoughts had arisen. I passed these weeks in the inspiring impression arising from this feeling. . . . With the utmost intensity I worked my way into this portion of his legacy.*

And now he makes a clear distinction between Goethe's art of knowing and his own.

Moreover, it was my destiny to link my own views with those of Goethe. In this linking there were, of course, many opportunities to show that nature is spiritual, because Goethe himself strove towards a spiritual view of nature; but one does not in the same way have the opportunity to speak of the world of pure spirit as such, since Goethe did not carry his spiritual view of nature all the way to the direct view of the spirit.

The physical world was seen as an effect on the mind made through the senses. Reality lay elsewhere beyond the grasp of consciousness.

> I had sought to make clear in my book that no unknown lies <u>behind</u> the sense world, but that <u>within</u> it lies the spiritual. And as to the domain of human ideas, I sought to show that these have their existence in that spiritual world. . . . In truth therefore, the sense world is spiritual world, and the mind is in living union with this recognized spiritual world as it extends its consciousness over it. . . . Thus my endeavour to reach the spirit through the expansion of human consciousness was set over against the view that 'spirit' exists only in the mental representations within the human being, and apart from this can only be conceived. This was fundamentally the view of the age to which I had to introduce my Philosophy of Freedom.

This points to the unreality of our present seeing of the world: It carries a kind of blindness in it, a half-seeing.

> Whoever recognizes as an attribute of thinking its capacity of perception extending beyond apprehension through the senses must necessarily also attribute to thinking objects existing beyond the limits of mere sense-perceptible reality. But these objects of thinking are ideas. As thinking takes possession of the Idea, it merges with the primordial foundation of the world; that which works without, enters into the spirit of man; he becomes one with objective reality at its highest potency. Becoming aware of the idea within reality is the true communion of man.

> Thinking has the same significance in relationship to Ideas as the eye has for light, the ear for sound: it is the organ for perception.

But this is incomprehensible for the man attuned to the present notion which regards thinking as something separate from and therefore quite outside the phenomena.

At the time of the publication of this book in 1894, when Steiner was in his thirty third year, there was no one who understood what he meant by thinking as <u>experiencing in the spirit</u>.

> Through my experience of the spiritual world in direct perception, nature was revealed to me as spirit; I wished to create a natural science in keeping with the spirit.

And now the question comes again: whence does the moral ethical arise in consciousness since it is nowhere to be perceived in nature?

> *What impels man to moral action is a revelation of the spiritual world in the experiencing of this world by the mind. If man perceives himself in moral action as in reciprocal relation with the spiritual world, he is then experiencing his <u>freedom</u>, For the spiritual world acts within the mind, not by way of compulsion, but in such a way that man must develop freely the activity which causes him to embrace the spiritual.*

In other words, the moral can only arise in freedom in the mind of man as his contribution to life as a whole.

> *In pointing out that the sense world is spiritual in its essential being and that man, as a soul-being, by means of true knowledge of the sense-world is moving and living in a world of spirit — herein lies one objective of my <u>Philosophy of Freedom</u>.*

One might say, that from the time of Galileo, man has found himself increasingly severed from the spirit; so THE PHILOSOPHY OF FREEDOM OR SPIRITUAL ACTIVITY in terms of pure thought, opens a way for him to reunite himself with the spirit.

> *Is man in his thinking and acting a spiritually free being or is he compelled by the iron necessity of purely natural law?*

This leads to the further question:

> *What does it mean to have knowledge of the reasons for one's action?*

Here we meet a fundamental fact.

> *We may consider man as a knower and also as a doer, but to this must be added the thought that man is <u>a conscious doer</u>. This he can only be by virtue of his thinking.*

It is *thinking that gives to man his characteristic stamp.*

> *The way to the heart is through the head. Love is no exception. Whenever it is not merely the expression of bare sexual instincts, it depends on the mental picture we have of the loved one. And the more idealistic these mental pictures are, the greater is our love.*

One of the main tasks of the book is to overcome the prevailing dualism.

> *The universe appears to us in two opposite parts, I and World. We erect this barrier between ourselves and the world as soon as consciousness*

first dawns on us. But we never cease to feel that, in spite of all, we belong to the world . . . we are beings within and not without the universe. . . . This feeling makes us strive to bridge over this antithesis, and in this bridging lives ultimately the whole spiritual striving of mankind. . . . Only when we have made the world-content into our thought-content do we begin again to find the unity out of which we have separated ourselves.

Observation and thinking are the two points of departure for all the spiritual striving of man, in so far as he is conscious of such striving. . . . But thinking as an object of observation differs essentially from all other objects . . . for he observes something of which he is the creator . . . . this observation is the most important one he can make . . . in thinking we have got hold of one corner of the world process which requires our presence of anything is to happen. Hence for the study of all else that happens in the world, there can be no more fundamental starting point than thinking itself.

In so far as we observe a thing it appears to us as given; in so far as we think we appear to ourselves as being active. We regard the thing as object and ourselves as subject. . . . Thinking lies beyond subject and object. It produces these two concepts just as it does all others. Thinking is thus an element which leads me out beyond myself and connects me with the objects. It is just this which constitutes the double nature of man. He thinks and thus embraces himself and the world. But at the same time, it is by means of thinking that he determines himself as an individual confronting the things.

The illusory view that denies reality to sense perceptions, would classify these as being merely subjective. This illustrates that the idea or concept is every bit as real as the percept; only where they meet does one touch reality.

The percept is not something finished and self contained but only one side of the total reality. The other side is the concept. The act of knowing is the synthesis of percept and concept. Only the percept and concept together constitute the whole thing.

In contrast to the content of the percept which is given from without, the content of thinning appears inwardly. The form in which this first makes its appearance we call intuition. Intuition is for thinking what observation is for the precept.

Thinking and feeling correspond to the two-fold nature of our being. . . . Thinking is the element through which we have part in the universal cosmic process; feeling is that through which we can withdraw into ourselves, into the narrow confines of our being. Our thinking links us to the world; our feeling leads us back into ourselves and thus makes us individuals.

Are there limits to knowledge?

In our knowledge we are concerned with questions which arise for us thorough the fact that a sphere of percepts conditioned by space, time, and our subjective organization is confronted by a sphere of concepts pointing to the totality of the universe. My task consists in reconciling these two spheres, with both of which I am well acquainted. Here one cannot speak of a limit of knowledge. . . . It may be that at any particular moment, this or that remains unexplained because, through our place in life, we are prevented from perceiving the things involved. What is not found today, however, may be found tomorrow. The limits to these causes are only temporary, and can be overcome by the process of perception and thinking.

Since every percept has its corresponding concept, each act of uniting these two points to an all-inclusive world-totality with no definable limits either to knowledge or to the human being as the active agent in the process is a liberating thought.

'The Reality of Freedom' begins with a consideration of the three factors of human life: thinking, feeling, and willing. It demonstrates how thinking is universal in character, whereas the philosophy of feeling (mysticism) and that of willing (thelism) inevitably begin as experiences of an individual or personal nature which are then expanded to appear as universals.

'The Idea of Freedom' contains the very crucial essence of the question of freedom. It begins with a reassessment of the nature of thinking:

. . . if we would grasp the essential nature of spirit in the form in which it presents itself most immediately to man, we need only look at the self-sustaining activity of thinking. . . . And of this we shall be able to say, that it is brought into consciousness for us through intuition. Intuition is the conscious experience — in pure spirit — of a purely spiritual content. Only through intuition can the essence of thinking be grasped.

If an act is to take place, it must have both a motive or aim and the ability to carry it out. Here the term characterological disposition is introduced.

*The immediately present mental picture or concept, which becomes the
motive, determines the aim or purpose of my will; my characterological
disposition determines me to direct my activity towards the aim.*

A moral idea, born of intuition without compulsion, inner or outer,
would be at one and the same time the highest motive and the
highest driving force a man could have.

*To live in love towards our actions, and to <u>let live</u> in the understanding
of the other person's will, is the fundamental maxim of free <u>men</u>.*

There comes a challenging question and with it the answer:

*Which of us can sat that he is really free in all his action? Yet in each of
us there dwells a deeper being in which the free man finds expression.*

*Or life is made up of free and unfree action. We cannot, however, think
out the concept of man completely, without coming upon the <u>free spirit</u>
as the purest expression of human nature. Indeed, we are men in the
true sense only in so far as we are free.*

*Nature makes of man merely a natural being; society makes of him a
law-abiding being; only he himself can make of himself a <u>free man</u>.*

*The free man acts morally because he has a moral idea. He does not act
in order that morality may come into being. Human individuals, with
the moral ideas belonging to their nature, are the prerequisites of a
moral world order. The human individual is the source of all morality
and the centre of earthly life. State and society exist only because they
have arisen as a necessary consequence of the life of individuals.*

This reads like a crowning statement of ethical individualism is
essentially the crowning conclusion of this book. The chapters that
follow give extended expression to this in one direction or another.

The philosophy of Monism steers a clear way between mystical,
transcendental, and metaphysical tendencies on the one hand, and
the mundane, prosaic, and materialistically conceived utopianism
on the other.

*Monism knows that Nature does not send man forth from her arms
ready made as a free spirit, but that she leads him up to a certain stage
from which he continues to develop until he comes to the point where he
finds his own self.*

*The centre and source of progress towards becoming a free spirit is with-
in man, 'just as every rosebud has within it a rose.'*

Monism rejects the concept of purpose in every sphere with the sole exception of human action. Nothing is purposeful except what man has first made so, for purposefulness arises only through the realization of an idea. In a realistic sense, an idea can only become effective in man. Therefore human life can only have the purpose and the ordering of destiny which man gives it. To the question — what is man's task in life? There can be for monism but one answer; the task he sets himself. My mission in the world is not pre-determined but is at every moment the one I choose for myself.

Moral laws, however are first created by us. We cannot apply them until we have created them . . . they apply to individuals and not . . . as natural laws do, to specimens of a general type. Considered as an organism. I am such and such a generic specimen and I shall live on accordance with nature, if I apply the laws of my general type to my particular case; as a moral being, I am an individual and have laws of my very own.

This view appears to contradict the fundamental doctrine of the theory of evolution. But it only appears to do so.

In view of the fact that in the world in general the natural and the moral are views as worlds apart, the following statement is all the more surprising.

Ethical individualism, then, is not in opposition to a rightly understood theory of evolution, but follows directly from it. Heackel's genealogical tree for the protozoa up to man as an organic being, ought to be capable of being continued without an interruption of natural law and without a break in the uniformity of evolution, up to the individual that is moral in a definitive sense. But on no account could the nature of a descendant species be deduced from the nature of an ancestral one. However true it is that the moral ideas of the individual have perceptibly developed out of these of his ancestors. It is equally true that the individual is morally barren unless he has moral ideas of his own.

The appearance of completely new moral ideas through moral imagination is for the theory of evolution no more miraculous than the development of a new animal species out of an old one.

First, must be born the idea (moral intuition), then this takes shape as a mental picture (moral imagination) and subsequently applied in life (moral technique). To this process there can be no prescribed limit. It represents the transition from natural evolution to moral-spiritual evolution from natural to human creativity. And here the monistic philosophy finds special expression.

*. . . For monism — moral processes are products of the world like every-
thing else that exists, and the causes must be sought in the world, that
is, in man, since he is the bearer of morality. What happens to man and
in man through all this, becomes a moral element only when — in
human experience — it becomes his own.*

Then follows an amazing and — for our time — challenging
conclusion:

*Ethical individualism, then, is the crowning feature of the edifice that
Darwin and Haeckel have striven to build for natural science. It is spir-
itualized theory of evolution carried over into moral life.*

*Moral ideas spring from the moral imagination of man. Their realization
depends on this desire for them being intense enough to overcome pain and
misery. They are <u>his</u> intuitions, the driving forces which his spirit har-
nesses; he <u>wants</u> them, because their realization is his greatest pleasure.*

*The view which I have here developed refers man back to himself. . . . It
no more acknowledges a value of life that is not recognized by the individual than it does a purpose of life that has not originated in him. It
sees in the individual who knows himself through and through, his own
master and his own assessor.*

*. . . the moral life of mankind is the sum-total of the products of the
moral imagination of free human individuals. This is the conclusion
reached by monism.*

*The grounds for the actual translation of an idea into reality by man,
monism can find only in man himself. If an idea is to become action,
man must first <u>want</u> it before it can happen. Such an act of will, therefore, has its grounds only in man. Man is then the ultimate determinant
of his action. He is free.*

Recall the opening question, *Is man in his thinking and acting a spiritually free being?* This is the most poignant question of our time.
The whole social future depends on it. Steiner has set before us
many different aspects of this question, leading to the last three
cryptic words, <u>he is free</u>. At the time of the book's publication,
there was no one who accompanied him that far. But the book has
been published, and remains waiting to be recognized.

As one reads on, one become aware not only of a great clarification
but also of an intensification of experience.

*Already before his time, I had lived a life of meditation, but the
impulse to this had come from knowing through ideas its value for a*

spiritual world view. Now, however, something came about within me which required meditation as a necessity of existence for the life of soul. The soul-life at the stage then attained needed meditation just as an organism at a certain stage in its evolution needs to breathe by means of lungs.

Rudolf Steiner reviews many aspects of the faculty of cognition as though placing before himself ever and again the question what is it that constitutes cognition?

Beyond his work in meditation, there is a third form of knowledge of which he wrote:

. . . it can come into existence through the spiritual man only when he can make himself as free from the physical organism as if it did not exist at all.

As meditation leads, on the one hand, to a knowledge of the spiritual, there follows, on the other hand, as a result of the findings from such self observation, the inner strengthening of the spiritual man, independent of the organism, and the consolidation of his being in the spiritual world, just as the physical man has his consolidation in the physical world. Only, one becomes aware that the consolidation of the spiritual man in the spiritual world increases immeasurably when the physical organism does not limit this process of consolidation; whereas the consolidation of the physical organism in the physical world yields to destruction — at death — when the spiritual man no longer sustains its consolidation out of himself.

What I wished to do was to speak of knowledge in such a way that the spiritual should be, not merely recognized, but recognized as being of such a nature that man may reach it with his perception.

He held that the potential for this lies *inside what is attainable by man within his totality of experience,* and he ever resisted the view of *an* unknown *spiritual in some kind of 'beyond' region.*

All that was designated in physics and physiology as 'existing behind subjective sensation, caused me, if I may use such an expression, cognitional discomfort.

On the other hand, I saw in the thinking of Lyell, Darwin, Haeckel something which, although incomplete as it issued from them, is nevertheless capable of becoming sound in the course of evolution.

Lyell's basic principle — to explain by means of ideas resulting from the present observation of the earth-process those phenomena which elude sense-observation because they belong to past ages — seemed to me fruitful in the direction indicated. To seek for understanding of the physical structure of man by training his forms from the animal forms as Haeckel does in comprehensive fashion in his Anthropogenie (The Evolution of Man) appeared to me a good foundation for the further development of knowledge.

This is very different from the customary denial of the reality of sense-experience, declaring it to be due merely to the play of particles in motion upon the nervous system — a form of thinking derived from the arbitrary separation of the primary and secondary qualities, so that, in the Kantian view, one experiences effects but can never reach the *thing-in-itself* which is the source of the effects. Such a view bars man

from any access to the spiritual world. If he relates himself to the sense world in such a way that one thing explains another within that world (the present stage of the earth's development explaining past geological ages; animal forms explaining those of man), he may be ready to extend this intelligibility of beings and events also to the spiritual.

It is remarkable the difficulties that many still encounter in making the distinction that Steiner presents here.

As to my experiences also in this area, I can say: 'This is something which just at that time became confirmed in me in vision, although it had long before been living present in my conceptual world.'

One gains the impression as one follows the pages of his biography that, following the experience he described as the revolution in his mind, Steiner was re-examining all he had experienced hitherto, always with the question of how to reach his fellow human beings.

What is the character of the path in the life of the soul which leads from the unfree natural will to that which is free — that is, to that which is truly moral? And, in order to find an answer to this question, it was necessary to observe how the divine-spiritual lives in each individual human soul.

In all his later teachings this is never lost sight of; the recognition of individual inner moral freedom is ever maintained.

It is from the individual human soul what the moral proceeds; in the wholly individual being of the soul, therefore, must the moral impulse come to life.

Moral laws — as commands — which come from an external relation in which man finds himself, even though these laws had their primal origin in the spiritual world, do not become moral impulses within man by reason of the fact that he directs his will in accord with them, but only by reason of the fact that he himself, purely as an individual, experiences the spiritual and essential nature of their thought-content. Freedom has its life in human thinking, and it is not the will which is of itself free, but thinking which empowers the will.

In my Philosophy of Freedom, *therefore, I had already found it necessary to lay all possible emphasis upon the freedom of thought in relation to the moral nature of the will,*

This idea also was confirmed in very special degree through the life of meditation. The moral world-order stood out before me in ever clearer light as the only clearly realised imprint on earth of such ordered ranks of action as are to be found in the spiritual regions raged above. It showed itself as that which only he lays hold upon in his conceptual world who is able to acknowledge the spiritual.

In regard to what prevailed in general in the cultural life around him, steeped as it was in materialistic thinking, he wrote:

Not that I rejected everything produced by this cultural life, but I had a sense of profound distress in the presence of much that was good which I could cherish, for I believed that I saw the forces of destruction ranging themselves against what was good as the evolutional germ of the cultural life.

Thus, from all directions I experienced the question: How can a way be found whereby that which is inwardly beheld as true may be set forth in such forms of expression as can be understood by this age?

Whichever way one attempted to meet this question, one was *forced to feel that all the struggles put forth have been in vain.*

Must one become silent?

He thought of the possibility of a periodical with the resolve, *I would not 'become silent' but would say as much as it was possible to say. . . . The periodical bore the name,* Magazine of German and Foreign Literature. *It served as an organ for a Free Literary Society, founded by younger writers in Berlin, with branches in many other German cities.* He was called on to give lectures in this Society.

It was now a necessity, inherent in the fact that I stood within the spiritual world, that I should share truly in a wholly inner manner in these relations into which I had entered. I made every effort to imagine myself in the position of my circle of readers and of the membership of the Society, in order to discover from the type of mind of these persons the forms into which I should have to mould what I wished spiritually to present.

He had no way to reach them:

The interest of these men were only in a few instances deeply rooted. Even in the case of these few, there existed no strong underlying forces of the spirit, but rather a general desire seeking for expression in all kinds of artistic and other cultural forms.

Thus the question soon arose for me whether I was justified inwardly and before the spiritual world in working within this circle . . . those persons caused me to ask myself with regard to my inner living experience: Must one become silent?

Steiner quotes from an article he wrote in November, 1897.

Our conception of Nature is clearly striving towards the goal of explaining the life of the organism according to the same laws by which also the phenomena of inanimate nature must be explained. . . . The mechanistic conception of the phenomena of life steadily gains ground. But it will never satisfy one who has the capacity to cast a deeper glance into nature's processes . . .

Contemporary researchers in nature are too cowardly in their thinking. Where the wisdom of their mechanistic explanation fails, they say the thing is to us inexplicable. . . . A bold thinking lifts itself to a higher mode of perceiving. It seeks to explain by higher laws that which is not of a mechanical character. All our natural-scientific thinking remains behind our natural-scientific empirical knowledge. At present the natural scientific form of thinking is much praised. It is said that we live in a natural-scientific age. But at the bottom this natural-scientific age is the poorest that history has to show. Its characteristic is to remain caught by the mere facts and the mechanical forms of explanation. Life will never be grasped by this form of thinking, because such a grasp requires a higher manner of conceiving than that which belongs to the explanation of the machine.

I believe that natural science can give back to us the consciousness of freedom in a form more beautiful than that in which men have ever possessed this consciousness. In our soul-life laws are operative just as natural as those which send the heavenly bodies round the sun. But these represent something higher than all the rest of nature. This Something is present nowhere save in man alone. Whatever flows from this — in

*that is man free. He lifts himself above the rigid necessity of laws of the
inorganic and organic; he heeds and follows himself alone.*

Steiner adds that these words were not italicized in the magazine.
They were written clearly to stir the mind to a new questioning.
While outwardly greatly engaged in public activities, arising form
his editorship of the magazine, Rudolf Steiner recorded in Chapter
XXVI, profound experiences in his inner life; an indication of what
they meant to him follows.

In regard to his relation to Christianity, he described how he first
met it as

> *the doctrine of the Beyond which was in force in the Christian creeds. . . .
> What religion has to say, what it has to give as moral precepts, was sup-
> posed to be derived from revelations which came to man from without.
> Against this idea, my view of the spirit was opposed.*

> *For him the moral life proceeds, not from without in the form of com-
> mandments obeyed, but from the unfolding of the human soul and spir-
> it, wherein lives the divine.*

In other words, Christianity cannot be acquired from without; it
has to be perceived and lived from within. Then it declares itself in
its own character to each one.

> *What occurred at the time in my mind in viewing Christianity was a
> severe test for me.*

Christianity entered the stage of human history in fulfillment of
the great mystery teaching that preceded its coming. He emphasized the fact that such tests are in inevitable part of inner development and are to be surmounted in order to gather the force and
insight to proceed further. It is a test to hold to the spirit within the
realm of perceptual experience rather than in some world apart.
Then came a test in regard to outer nature. Steiner saw in the science of nature *the basis upon which man might attain to insight into the
world of the spirit.* what has prevented this so far? In the mind we
encounter errors. In the spirit one encounters Beings who inculcate
these errors into human thinking. Thus, in regard to the mechanistic view of the world, there are Beings who are the inspirers of this.

> *For anyone who does not stand in living reality within the world of
> the spirit, as I do, such a submergence into a certain trend of thinking*

signifies a mere activity of thought, For one who experiences the world of the spirit it signifies something essentially different. He is brought into contact with Beings in the world of the spirit who desire to make such a trend of thinking the sole prevailing one . . . spoke later of Ahrimanic Beings . . . for these, it is absolute truth that the world must be a machine. They live in a world that borders directly upon the sense world.

In my own ideas I never for one moment became a victim of this world, not even in the unconscious. For I took the utmost pains to insure that all my knowledge should be reached in a state of discriminating consciousness. So much the more conscious was also my inner struggle against these demonic powers who wanted to cause the knowledge of nature to become, not perception of the spirit, but a mechanistic-materialistic way of thinking.

He who seeks for knowledge of spirit must <u>experience</u> these worlds; for him a mere theoretical thinking about them does not suffice. At that time I had to save my spiritual perception by inner battles. These battles were the background of my outer experience.

In this time of testing I succeeded in progressing further only when in spiritual vision I brought before my mind the evolution of Christianity.

The unfolding of my soul rested upon the fact that I had stood in spirit before the Mystery of Golgoltha in most inward, most earnest solemnity of soul.

The thought then hovered before me that the turn of the century must bring a new spiritual light to humanity. It seems to me that the exclusion of the spiritual from human thinking and willing had reached a climax. A change of direction in the process of human evolution seemed to me a matter of necessity.

Many were speaking in this way. But they did not see that man will seek to direct his attention to a real world of spirit as he directs it through his senses to nature. They supposed only that the subjective spiritual temper of the mind would undergo a change. That a real, new objective world could be revealed — such a thought lay beyond the range of vision of that time.

That Steiner spoke as openly about spiritual matters as he apparently did on this occasion brought a strong reaction from some who thought themselves guardians of the *ancient knowledge*. One in particular *represented vigorously the conviction that esoteric spiritual knowledge should not be publicly propagated like ordinary knowledge.*

If I was to develop a public activity on behalf of spiritual knowledge, I had to decide to break with this tradition. I found myself confronted by the requirements of the contemporary spiritual life. In the presence of these, the practice of keeping things secret, which was a matter of course in ancient times, was an impossibility. We live in the age which demands publicity whenever any kind of knowledge appears.

But then comes an additional statement of great importance.

Moreover, I was under no obligation to any one to guard mysteries for I accepted nothing out of 'ancient wisdom.' What I possess of spiritual knowledge is entirely the result of my own research. Only, when an item of knowledge has come to me, I then introduce whatever of the 'ancient knowledge' has already been made public from some direction or other, in order to point out to the harmony between the two and, at the same time, the advance which is possible to contemporary research.

Thus, after a certain time it was quite clear to me in the public presentation of spiritual knowledge I should be doing the right thing.

To this conclusion he held unswervingly in all the years that followed. Steiner was invited to lecture regularly to the members of the Theosophical Society associated with them.

I explained, however, that I could speak only about what I vitally experienced within myself as spiritual science.

One might say that the long protracted 'silence' was now ended.

Within this section I was then able to develop my Anthroposophical activity before a constantly increasing audience.

No one was left in uncertainty of the fact that I would bring forward in the Theosophical Society only the results of my own research through direct vision.

While attending a Theosophical Congress in London, Steiner was told by a *leading personality . . . that the true Theosophy was to be found in his book Mysticism. . . .*

There was now no longer any reason why I should not bring forward this spiritual knowledge in my own way before the Theosophic public, which was then the only audience that responded without restriction to a knowledge of the spirit. I subscribed to no sectarian dogmatics; I remained a person who uttered what he believed he was able to utter entirely according to what he himself experienced as the world of the spirit.

. . . I never advanced into the spiritual realm in a mystical-emotional way, but chose always to go by way of crystal-clear concepts. Experiencing of concepts, of ideas, led me out of the realm of ideas into the spiritual realm.

The true evolution of the organic from primeval times to the present confronted my imagination for the first time after the composition of Conceptions of the World and of Life.

During the writing of this book, I still had in mind the natural-scientific view derived from the Darwinian mode of thinking. But this I considered only as a succession of sense-perceptible facts present in nature. Within this succession of facts were active for me spiritual impulses, as these were conceived by Goethe in his idea of metamorphosis.

Thus, the natural-scientific evolutionary succession, as represented by Haeckel, never constituted for me something wherein mechanical or merely organic laws hold sway, but something wherein the living spirit leads the living beings from the simple through the complex up to man. I saw in Darwinism a mode of thinking which is on the way to Goethe but remains behind this.

All this was still thought by me in idea-content; only later did I work through to imaginative perception. This perception first brought me the knowledge that something of the nature of real being, different for the simplest organisms, was present within spiritual reality in primeval times — that man, as a spiritual being is older than all other beings, and that in order to assume his present physical form, he had to cease to be a member of the World Being which comprised him and all other organisms. Hence, these latter are waste elements in human evolution; not something that he has left behind, which he severed from himself in order to take on his physical form as the image of the spiritual form. That man is a macrocosmic being who bore within him all the rest of the terrestrial world, and who has become a microcosm by eliminating all the rest — this was for me a knowledge to which I first attained in the earlier years of the new century.

Of course, this was a total reversal of the commonly held view. Rudolf Steiner, in this description gives us a glimpse of how the evolutionary process within his own consciousness advanced form one phase to another. We can then understand better what he writes in the 1918 edition of his philosophy.

Once experienced, the world of spiritual perception cannot appear to man as something foreign to him, because in his intuitive thinking he already has an experience which is purely spiritual in character.

The Philosophy of Freedom forms the philosophical foundation for these later writings. For it tries to show that the experience of thinking, when rightly understood, is in fact an experience of the spirit.

. . . a living comprehension of what is meant in this book by intuitive thinking will lead quite naturally to a living entry into the world of spiritual perception.

It is a remarkable fact that when Rudolf Steiner could at last openly and freely develop his teachings. The way lay open for launching the teaching of Anthroposophy or Modern Spiritual Science. Schooled in the methods and disciplines of Natural Science it advances to a newly awakened knowledge and insight into the spiritual grounds of human and world existence.

What Rudolf Steiner brought to the twentieth century comes to meet the deeper seated questions and needs of humanity seeking to find expression in the unfolding life of today.

· 26 ·

Quest for Meaning

The two outstanding achievements of Rudolph Steiner in the nineteenth century were the editing and elucidating of Goethe's scientific writings and the publication of his PHILOSOPHY OF FREEDOM in 1894. Ten years elapsed before the time was appropriate for the first issue of LUCIFER. The long years of waiting were ended for he had by then turned forty-two. With the LUCIFER journal his life task of Anthroposophy, or Modern Spiritual Science, began.

Since man came into being, there has always been a spiritual science and initiate teachers to lead humanity forward. These initiates all drew their wisdom and authority from the same high source so that there could be no disagreements between them, but the teachings had to undergo a change to concur with the times and particular needs of the peoples they were serving. So it was with Anthroposophy in meeting the scientific challenge of the twentieth century. It marked a turning point in the whole of history that had been long previsaged, as the following ancient legend of the East confirms.

The legend tells of four successive epochs leading into the present time. There was once a Golden Age of long duration when humanity was very young and lived a blissful existence in the presence of the gods. Next came a Silver Age of long but lesser duration, with humanity growing up and with the gods still near but more withdrawn. There followed a Bronze Age lasting ten thousand years, with humanity well grown and the gods now only remembered in myth and legend. After the Bronze Age came Kali-Yuga, the dark age to last through five thousand years, with humanity full grown, but the gods forgotten.

The dates for the dark age, by our mode of reckoning, were from 3101 B.C. to A.D. 1899, that is from the dawn of Egypt to the end of the nineteenth century.

It is hard to think of the lofty spiritual culture of Egypt, the wealth and beauty of Greek art and philosophy, the great schools of learning and the cathedral cities of the Middle Ages, the advent and spread of Christianity and the brilliant advances in the sciences, as all contained within the age of darkness, an age of dwindling light. Yet if we ask, how is it with man of today; how does he stand in the world and in his own eyes; by what does he live; what answers do we meet?

It is interesting to note that the OXFORD ENGLISH DICTIONARY dates the word 'atheist' back to 1571, well within this modern age, and describes atheist as *one who denies or disbelieves the existence of a God.* It dates the word 'agnostic' to 1870, and defined as *one who holds that anything beyond material phenomena cannot be known.* As for the state of Christianity, we quote from Ralph Waldo Emerson's urgent address of 1838 to the senior class of the Harvard Divinity School.

> *And it is my duty to say to you that the need was never greater of new revelation than now. From the views I have already expressed, you will infer the sad conviction I share, I believe, with numbers, of the universal decay and now the almost death of faith in society. The soul is not preached. The Church seems to totter to its fall, almost all life extinct. On this occasion, any complaisance would be criminal which told you, whose hope and commission it is to preach the faith of Christ, that the faith of Christ is preached.*

From 1838 to 1899 seems a long time, but what has not happened in that time to diminish faith further, all in the closing decades of Kali-Yuga! Here are cited some of the main events contributing to that decline.

- Darwin's DESCENT OF MAN to confirming man's animal origin.

- Pavlov's experiments with dogs, confirming the nature of the conditioned reflex as the basis for the behaviourist psychology, and the autonomous Self a s a mere illusion.

- The release of steam and electric power boosting material prosperity has led to Marxist Socialism translating this into a doctrine for the masses that possession means power and the road to freedom. As well as Engel's companion view that man is matter and society is subject to determinism.

Beyond that, in the physics laboratories, the discovery of the electromagnetic field has provided ground for a relativistic philosophy, and the discovery of the electron and radioactive substances has paved the way for atomic fission and nuclear power.

Here then is a trend of developments crowding the last decades of Kali-Yuga in order to deepen and perpetuate the darkness further. These were the circumstances that confronted Rudolf Steiner at the turn of the century and beyond. There were some among the more enlightened who came to think of the nineteenth century as the end of an epoch, with a new one to follow, but what that new epoch was to be and how it was to come about there was no knowing.

To Rudolf Steiner it was fully clear that life had reached a stage where there had to be a change of direction — from the dominant hold of materialism to an awakening to the spirit, a transition from the age of darkness, to a new age of light — if civilization was not to plunge into an abyss of even greater darkness to its own destruction. Thus the launching of LUCIFER, THE JOURNAL OF THE LIGHT-BEARER, came at a determining point in history. That was when Rudolf Steiner came forward for the first time as an initiate teacher. In an age of science built on the pursuit of outer knowledge, he had to open a disciplined way to a science of the spirit. He had been thoroughly grounded in the former as a basis for the latter. It was a question of carrying the same scientific impulse of the times further to a Modern Spiritual Science, or Western Initiation Science. Steiner could be described as a Seer-Spiritualist of the West, the founder of a science built on conscious seership or spiritual perception.

To give the reader an over-all impression of what Rudolph Steiner accomplished between 1904 and the time of his death in 1925, we quote from a book compiled and edited by the late John Davy. As the SUNDAY OBSERVER science correspondent for many years, he had traveled widely and met notable scientists and researchers from varied fields. Then, while retaining his close connection with

the OBSERVER, he became a leading figure and teacher at Emerson
College in Sussex, England, an adult school for training and
research based on the work of Rudolf Steiner.

This quote is from Davy's forward:

> Rudolf Steiner died on March 30th, 1925, in his studio workshop at
> Dornach, Switzerland. He lay before a thirty foot carving in wood, 'The
> Representative of Humanity' on which he had continued to work as long
> as he could. The circumstances of his death show the central aim of his
> life, to open a way to a deeper understanding of man, and to translate
> this understanding into a renewal of human life and culture.
>
> The collection of essays which appears half a century later is, therefore,
> not a memorial to the past, but a report on work in progress. Steiner
> died surrounded by new beginnings in many fields of work which he
> had helped to initiate. These have now developed and spread all over the
> world.

The following excerpts are from John Davy's opening essay entitled RUDOLF STEINER, INITIATE OF THE WILL.

> Moving round the world today, one may come upon a school, a farm, a
> village community of mentally handicapped adults, a group of doctors
> running a hospital, a group of architects, a scientific laboratory, artists,
> drama groups, a substantial pharmaceutical firm, a toy factory, an
> industrial consultancy, a bank and other enterprises, all of them
> acknowledging a fundamental debt to Rudolf Steiner.
>
> The debt is centred in a view of the human being and the significance of
> his life on earth to which Steiner gave the name of 'Anthroposophy.' But
> it is a view which has led right into the details of work in many differ-
> ent professions. It is easy to recognise that one man may inspire many
> others with some kind of common philosophical or moral outlook. It is
> harder to accept that he could have sufficient enterprise in so many dif-
> ferent fields that he could offer detailed practical help in all of them. Yet
> this was the actual experience of those who asked Steiner during his life-
> time, for help in renewing many kinds of work, and it continues to be
> the experience of those who have followed on.
>
> But the most formidable obstacle for modern man is to comprehend
> Steiner as an 'initiate' — as a human being possessing capacities of spir-
> itual perception developed to a high degree.

Davy wishes to free his use of the word 'initiate' from lingering
associations with earlier times when whole cultures were guided

by priests or 'priest-kings,' and likewise from Eastern sources exercising spiritual authority on their pupils.

> *We are not prepared nowadays to leave creative initiative to a few gurus or leaders but claim, at the very least, the right of everybody to formulate his own thoughts, coloured by his own feelings, and to translate these, in so far as they can be absorbed by the community, into actions. Steiner belongs explicitly within the essentially western tradition of individual spiritual freedom in judgment and in striving.*

> *He was concerned, therefore, to show a 'path of knowledge' whereby, in the words which open his book Knowledge of the Higher Worlds, faculties which slumber in every human being may be gradually discovered and developed. His position is democratic rather than autocratic, showing a way to his fellows rather than a revelation to his followers. He may be described as an initiate of Will, in contrast to the Initiates of Wisdom of former times.*

The activities and enterprises originating from Steiner's teachings continue to grow and multiply in number and variety, spreading through the world and engaging the lives of increasing numbers of people.

It is my aim to survey in broad outline the main stages by which Rudolf Steiner brought Anthroposophy into the world.

The journal LUCIFER, by amalgamation with another existing journal, became LUCIFER-GNOSIS. Consider Steiner's opening words.

> *In the monthly magazine Lucifer-Gnosis I was able to bring to publication for the first time what became the foundation of Anthroposophical work. In this periodical first appeared what I had to say about the efforts that the human mind must make in order to achieve its own comprehension of knowledge and spirit. How to Attain Knowledge of the Higher Worlds came out in serial form from number to number.*

These numbered serials were later compiled into a book which will comprise our beginning. The English edition has reversed the wording to KNOWLEDGE OF THE HIGHER WORLDS AND ITS ATTAINMENT.

There were two such series, THE WAY OF INITIATION and INITIATION AND ITS RESULTS, very different in their presentations and yet each outlining a continuous path towards actual initiation. An image which Steiner often used was the of the same tree

seen from different sides — so that the differences actually sup-
plement one another to lead to a total view.

> *There slumber in every human being faculties by means of which he can*
> *acquire for himself a knowledge of higher worlds.*

Note the words <u>every human being</u>, and <u>can acquire for himself</u>.
Because Steiner addresses himself to <u>every</u> human being without
exception, and he places the responsibility as to how far one is
willing to go on each individual. The pre-condition is one of
unquestionable freedom. The <u>conditions</u> will be seen to be neither
arbitrary nor imposed, but arise from life itself and follow from
one another quite naturally. They call on qualities that are innate
and call to be carried further.

The first basic quality, says Steiner, is devotion, in this case to *truth*
and the pursuit of higher knowledge. This higher knowledge stands
as a goal. Devotion brings forward other qualities, *The heights of*
the spirit can only be climbed by passing through the gates of humility.
This speaks for itself, but it has to be practiced. Any kind of development means coming to terms with oneself, and this is never
easy. Thus, one is advised to set aside some moments in the day
and in those moments *to discover what remains in us of adverse, dis-*
paraging and negative judgments of the world and life and instead *to*
develop thoughts which evoke admiration, respect and veneration.
Again, there is all the difference between knowing that negativity
of soul is undermining and turning this into an exercise as a condition for progress. According to Steiner, *Such practices, can bring*
magical results.

One must also set apart moments of retreat, even if only for five
minutes a day

> *. . . in which to let the experiences and the messages of the outer world*
> *echo in one's own completely silent self. Every flower, every animal,*
> *every action will unveil in such moments secrets undreamed of.*

Such exercises bring about tranquillity of soul and so prepare us
for the greater inner tranquillity needed for the further step.

> *The student must set aside a small part of his daily life — at such times*
> *he must rest himself free from is work-a-day life . . . he must seek the*
> *power of confronting himself with the tranquillity of a judge . . . sorrow*

and joy, every thought, every resolve appears different when we con-
front ourselves.

Out of this quiet mode of procedure there grows the certainty that

> *. . . every human being bears within himself, beside what we may call*
> *an every day man, a higher being, and each individual can only himself*
> *awaken this higher being within him.*

> *This higher man becomes the inner ruler who directs the outer man with*
> *sure guidance.*

> *In spiritual science everything depends upon the energy, inward truth-*
> *fulness and uncompromising sincerity with which we confront our own*
> *selves as a complete stranger.*

The whole endeavour is how by degrees, to outgrow ourselves.
This leads on to the all-important question of meditation. This is
something everyone can practice, but for it to be effective the previous exercises are needed, providing for the inner peace and concentration needed. What this can lead to is beautifully described
by Steiner. It is well to begin with a thought which is itself born of
the meditative life of a great teacher.

> *Calm, inward contemplation and converse with the purely spiritual*
> *world filling his soul. Such inward contemplation must become a natur-*
> *al necessity in the life of the student. He is newly plunged into a world*
> *of thought. He must develop a living feeling for this life of thought activ-*
> *ity. He must learn to love what the spirit pours into him. . . . he sees that*
> *his thoughts do not merely harbour shadowy pictures, but that through*
> *them hidden beings speak to him. Formerly sound reached him through*
> *his ears — now it resounds through his soul. An inner language, an*
> *inner world is revealed to him. When by means of meditation man rises*
> *to be united with the spirit, he brings to life the eternal within him,*
> *which is limited by neither birth nor death.*

To achieve this is to have gained a great enrichment in life which
benefits oneself and others and can be of great importance in itself.
Yet it is only a preliminary to setting out seriously on a path of esoteric development directed to the acquisition of higher stages of
consciousness. That Rudolf Steiner can offer this openly and in
book form is a recognition of the deepest need of our time, for the
human being to find the spirit again, and to do so individually. The
path unfolds in three stages as indicated, Probation, Illumination,

Initiation. Steiner makes it clear that the whole book and its method of presentation is still to be considered as essentially elementary in character, though if pursued faithfully, it can lead to fulfillment. But the way is open, each step leading to another, and each to a betterment of life.

In the book, the exercises follow one another, clearly described and in familiar words and images. Therefore at this stage it would seem best to leave the reader who is interested to pursue his own quest. That is why the book was placed, by Rudolf Steiner, into our hands. However, there is one particular overall question which the present author will present, and that is how has spiritual science in its practice complemented the science of today?

Remember that the primary concern is how to reintegrate man into his universe, from which, since the time of Galileo, with the qualitative values denied, he has been excluded. Quantitative science has reduced him to a shell.

Spiritual Science on the other hand, proceeds by focusing on certain experiences which can only be apprehended inwardly, and by enhancing them, raises what would be otherwise classed as the merely subjective to a new objectivity.

An example of this is the first exercise which comes under Probation. It is based on pure observation, free from theory, but includes the observer as well as the observed. The exercise is simple in nature, but it calls for maximum and ever-renewing effort.

Observe a plant that is growing, budding and blossoming, and in doing so note the feeling that rises up to meet it; then in similar fashion observe a plant that is fading, wilting, withering, and the response this calls forth. Let these not be mere fleeting impressions. Repeat this time and again, with maximum concentration, excluding all other impressions and feelings. There is nothing obscure about this practice. It is not easily done, because feeling is generally regarded as merely subjective and therefore, as matter of knowledge, insignificant. Rudolf Steiner explained that:

> *The student must at such times banish everything else from his soul and entirely surrender himself to the impression. He will soon convince*

himself that a feeling which hitherto would merely have flitted through his soul, now swells out and assumes a powerful and energetic form — the more the attention is fixed in this way in something growing, blossoming, and flourishing, then on something fading and decaying, the more vivid do these feelings become. . . . Just as the natural forms are built out of living nature to become the eyes and ears of the living body, so will the organs of clairvoyance build themselves from the feelings and thought thus evoked. But this is only the case if the effort is made to cultivate these feelings in the way described. . . . Both these feelings are forces which when cultivated, lead to the most significant results. The soul world, the so-called astral plane, begins to dawn for the student . . . to broaden out slowly before him.

This is one example only to show that for the spiritual scientist what transpires within the soul in response to outer phenomena can be observed, checked, compared with the findings of others, and thus lifted to a level of objectivity, so that man himself becomes the gateway to higher knowledge. He stands centrally in the world process as the mediator between the spiritual and the physical world.

Steiner has stated that the world is the riddle and man is the key to it, but only to the extent that he comes to know himself. Probation opens up the kingdom of life; Illumination, the kingdom of soul; and Initiation, the kingdom of the all-ruling conscious spirit.

The importance of the above and similar exercises is that it enables us to distinguish between what is merely personal and subjective and what is an all-important law of human nature and therefore objective. The contrast of the two conditions of the plant presents itself externally and independent of the human being. The corresponding contrast in the responses within the soul are in exact accordance with the outer phenomena and in this there is nothing personal or subjective. As phenomena, the inner is as objective as the outer. Only the two together make for the true and whole experience. The outer relates to an outer, physical law made accessible in the course of evolution through to the life of the senses. The inner relates to man's physical being and, if cultivated to a sufficient degree, makes visible an inner psychic world. The subject man thus comes to acquire an additional, higher faculty of perception.

Galileo's decision to deny objective validity to sense perception because it engages responses that lie outside the calculable is now beginning to be seen as a subjective mental conception which has lead to a world construction indifferent to mankind. The world construction is itself beginning to be viewed as unreal leading to the new question of how to bring man back to restore the sense of reality. The psychic is as much a part of man as the physical and opens up equally objective realities. Once one proceeds in this direction one can begin to see it as an essential extension of the present state of knowledge.

From the section on Enlightenment:

> The thoughts here mentioned should pass through the student's soul accompanied by vivid feelings, and no other thought, no other feeling, must mingle with them and disturb what should be an intensely attentive observation. The student says to himself, the stone has a form; the animal also has a form. The stone remains motionless in its place. The animal changes its place. It is instinct (desire) which causes the animal to change. Instincts, too, are served by the form of the animal. Its organs and limbs are fashioned in accordance with these instincts. The form of the stone is not fashioned in accordance with desires, but in accordance with desireless force. By sinking deeply into such thoughts, and while doing so, observing the stone and the animal with rapt attention, there arise in the soul two quite separate kinds of feelings.

Steiner speaks of genuine and patient practice. . . . over and over again.

> At first the feelings are present as long as the observation lasts. Later . . . something living remains in the soul. The student has then only to reflect, and both the feelings will always arise, even without the contemplation of an outer object. Out of these feelings and the thoughts that are bound up with them, the organs of clairvoyance are formed. If the plant should then be included, it will be noticed that the feeling flowing from it lies midway between the feelings derived from the stone and the animal both in quality and degree. The organs thus formed are spiritual eyes.
>
> How Enlightenment proceeds, of the student then, in the sense of the foregoing exercises, from the stone, the plant and the animal up to man, and how, after Enlightenment, under all circumstances, the union of the soul with the spiritual world is effected, leading to Initiation

The section 'Some Results of Initiation' is built on ancient teachings which tell of certain higher organs of perception, chakras or lotus flowers located in the soul-body or astral body and also certain parts of the physical body. In early times these organs were active so that all people possessed a degree of natural clairvoyance. It was chiefly in a state of sleeping-waking, when the light of day was darkened, that in a dim kind of way, they knew themselves membered in a spiritual world. The astral organs were then in motion but this ended with Kali-Yuga.

Today the time has come when, by consciously directed effort, these organs can be set in motion again so that a new kind of clairvoyance can be born, but this time in full self-awareness by virtue of the incarnated ego. Once humanity was guided from above; the law came from without, as with the Ten Commandments or under strict guidance along a given path or dharma. Since the time of Christ the law speaks from within, and the responsibility for fulfillment of the path or quest must rest with each individual.

With KNOWLEDGE OF HIGHER WORLDS, Rudolf Steiner opened a path for all to take who have the will. It is not an easy path for it calls for no less than the will to overcome oneself in order to arrive at one's true self. Yet, even if we reach but a small way on that path, to have a path at all is very different from not having a path, and every step is a gain.

Here our own individual quest for meaning begins . . . a quest for the rediscovery of man.

> The thought then hovered before me that the turn of the century must bring a new spiritual life to humanity. It seemed to me that the exclusion of the spiritual from human thinking and willing had reached its climax. A change of direction in the process of human evolution seemed to me a matter of necessity.

Select Bibliography

The following list has been compiled to represent as nearly as possible the editions used by Mr. Edmunds in writing this text. At times it was impossible to locate the exact edition he used, so other available editions (some British, some American) are cited here. Some volumes are out of print and could not be given their full publication data. Occasionally original publication dates are appended in parentheses for clarity.

A.E. [George William Russell] *The Interpreters*. London: Macmillan & Co., 1922.

Blake, William. *The Complete Poems*. Penguin, 1977.

Cannon, H. Graham. *Lamarck and Modern Genetics*. Springfield, Ill: Charles C. Thomas, 1959.

Carrell, Alexis. *Man the Unknown*. London: Hamish Hamilton, 1935.

Chardin, Pierre Teilhard. *The Heart of the Matter*, New York: Harcourt, Brace & Co., 1991.

———. *Letters From a Traveller, 1923–55*. London: William Collins Sons, 1956; New York: Harper and Row, 1957.

———. *Le Mileu Divin*. London: William Collins Sons, 1960.

———. *Phenomenon of Man*. London: William Collins Sons; New York: Harper and Row, 1959.

Darwin, Charles. *Autobiography*. London: Watts, 1929..

———. *The Descent of Man and Selection in Relation to Sex*. London: John Murray, 1888.

———. *The Origin of the Species by Means of Natural Selection; or, Preservation of Favored Races in the Struggle for Life*. London: John Murray, 1906.

Davenport, Russell W. *The Dignity of Man*. New York: Harper and Brothers, 1955.

Descartes, René. *The Discourse on Method and Metaphysical Meditations of Descartes*. trans. G.B. Rawlings. London: Walter Scott.

Drake, Stillman. *Discoveries and Opinions of Galileo*. Doubleday & Co., 1957.

Du Noüy, Lecomte. *Human Destiny*. New York: David McKay & Co., 1947.

Eddington, Sir Arthur. *The Expanding Universe*. Cambridge University Press, 1933.

———. *The Nature of the Physical World*. Cambridge University Press, 1929.

———. *The Philosophy of Physical Science*. Cambridge University Press, 1958.

————. *Stars and Atoms*. London: Oxford Clarendon Press, 1929.

Einstein, Albert. *Cosmic Religion*. New York: Covici, Friede, 1931.

————. *Mein Weltbild*. 1934.

————. *Out of My Later Years*. New York: Philosophical Library, 1950.

————. *Theory of Relativity (and Other Essays)*. New York: Citadel Press, 1996.

————. *The World As I See It*. New York: Covici, Friede, 1934.

Emerson, Ralph Waldo. *Essays: First Series*. Vol. II of *Complete Works*. New York: Boston Houghton, Mifflin and Co. Cambridge: Riverside Press, 1887.

————. *Representative Men*. Vol. IV of *Complete Works*. New York: Boston Houghton, Mifflin and Co. Cambridge: Riverside Press, 1887.

Engels, Frederick. "The Introduction to the Dialectics of Nature." *Collected Works of Mark and Engels*. New York: International Publishers, 1971.

Fairley, Carker. *A Study of Goethe*. London: Oxford University Press, 1961. (1947)

Galileo. *Philosophy of Science*. "The Assayer" trans. A.C. Dento and S. Morgan Besser. New York: Meridian, 1960.

Gillespie, Charles C. *The Edge of Objectivity*. Princeton University Press, 1960.

Godwin, William. *The Enquiry Concerning Political Justice, and Its Influence on General Virtue and Happiness*. 1793.

Gosse, Edmund. *Father and Son: A Study of Two Temperaments*. Penguin Books in association with William Heinemann Ltd., 1949. (1907)

Haldane, J. S. *The Sciences and Philosophy*. London: Hodder Stroughton, 1929.

Harvey, William. *Anatomical Exercises on the Generation of Animals*. 1653.

————. *Motion of the Heart and Blood in Animals*. 1628.

————. *The Generation of Animals*. 1627.

Heitler, W. *Man and Science*. Edinburgh: Oliver and Boyd, 1963.

Huxley, Julian. Religion without Revelation. New York, Lodnon: Harper & Brothers, 1927.

Loyle, Fred. "Nature of the Universe." Broadcast lecture series on the BBC, April 1, 1950 to May 10, 1951.

Jeans, Sir James. *Physics and Philosophy*. New York: Dover, 1981. (1943)

Joad, C. E. M. *Guide to Modern Thought*. London: Faber and Faber, 1933.

Kant, Immanuel, *Critique of Judgment*. Oxford University Press, 1978. (1790)

————. *Critique of Practical Reason*. Prometheus, 1996. (1788).

————. *Critique of Pure Reason*. Everyman Library, 1994. (1781)

Keith, Sir Arthur. *Essays on Human Evolution*. London: Watts, 1946.

Koestler, Arthur. *The Act of Creation*. London: Pan Books, 1975.

————. *The Sleepwalkers: A History of Man's Changing Vision of the Univese*. London: Hutchinson, 1959.

Kropotkin, Prince Piotr. *Mutual Aid: A Factor of Evolution*. Consortium, 1988.

Langdon-Davies, John. *Man and His Universe*. New York, London: Harper & Brothers, 1930.

Lewes, George Henry. *The Life and Works of Goethe*. 2 vol. London: D. Nutt, 1855.

Lewis, C. S. *The Abolition of Man*. Oxford University Press, 1943.

————. *That Hideous Strength*. London: Pan Books, 1955. (1945)

Lindbergh, Charles. *On Flight and Life*. New Yokr: Charles Scribner's Sons, 1948.

Lodge, Sir Oliver. *Ether and Reality*. London: Hodden & Stoughton, Ltd. 1925.

———. *Pioneers of Science*. London: Macmillan, 1898.

Lodge, Rupert. *The Grerat Thinkers*. Associated Faculty Press, 1968.

Malthus, Thomas. *An Essay on the Principle of Population*. London: Pelican, 1970. (1798)

Muller, Max. *Science of Thought*. Vol 2: *Language & Languages*. New York: Scribner's , 1887.

Newton, Isaac. *Optiks*. London: W & J Innys, 1721.

Polanyi, Michael. *Personal Knowledge*. Chicago: University of Chicago Press, 1958.

———. *Study of Man*. Chicago: Univeristy of Chicago Press, 1962.

Pouchet, F. A. *The Universe: or The Infinitely Great and the Infinitely Little*. London: Blackie and Sons, 1871.

Russell, Bertrand. *Mysticism and Logic*. London: George Allen & Unwin, 1976. (1917)

Salisbury, Trane. *Dialogues*. University of Chicago Press, 1953. (1632)

Schiller and Goethe. *Schiller and Goethe: From 1794–1805*. Vol. I: 1794–1797. trans. L. Dora Schmitz. Covent Garden: George Bell and Sons, 1877.

Sherrington, Sir Charles. *Goethe on Nature and on Science*. Cambridge University Press, 1942.

Skinner, B. F. *Beyond Freedom and Dignity*. New York: Alfred A. Knopf, 1971.

Solovyov, Vladimir. *War Progress and the End of History*. Lindisfarne Press, 1990.

Spender, Stephen. *Great Writings of Goethe*. New York: New American Library, 1958.

Steiner, Rudolf. *The Course of My Life: An Autobiography*. Hudson, N.Y.: Anthroposophic Press, 1951.

———. *Goethe the Scientist*. Hudson, N.Y.: Anthroposophic Press, 1950.

———. *Goethe's Conception of the World*. London: Anthro Publishing Co., 1928.

Teignmouth, Lord [John Shore]. *The Works of William Jones*. London: Classic Press, 1804; Philadelphia: W Poyntell & Co., 1805

Wallace, Alfred Russel. *Darwinism: An Exposition of the Theory of Natural Selection with Some of Its Applications*. London, New York: Macmillan & Co., 1891.

———. *Miracles and Modern Spiritualism*. New York: Arno Press, 1975.

———. *My Life*. London: Chapman & Hall, 1905.

———. *The World of Life*. London: Chapman and Hall, 1914.

Wells, H. G. *Mind at the End of Its Tether*. New York: Didier, 1946.

Whitehead, Alfred. *Science and the Modern World*. New York: The Macmillan Co., 1948. (1925)

Whitney, W .D. *Life and Growth of Language*. New York: D. Appleton & Co., 1898. (1875)

Wilson, R. A. *The Miraculous Birth of Language*. London: J.M. Dent & Sons, 1946. (1937).